Dan S. Mills

The
Revelations
of the
Prophet
Joseph Smith

The Revelations of the Prophet Joseph Smith

A Historical and Biographical Commentary
of the Doctrine and Covenants

Lyndon W. Cook

Deseret Book

Salt Lake City, Utah

First Deseret Book printing April 1985

Library of Congress Catalog Card Number 85-70650

ISBN 0-87747-947-X

Printed in the United States of America

10   9   8   7   6   5   4   3   2

For my parents
Adrian and Martha Cook

Contents

Foreword

Like all scripture, the Doctrine and Covenants contains doctrine in a personal setting. To better know the setting is to better appreciate the message. These revelations show people struggling to know the Lord, and the Lord struggling with people. A hundred people important to church history are here, and many obscure individuals who drifted out of the mainstream. These lives are subtle counterpoints to the main themes of the revelations.

Lyndon Cook, a talented researcher, has spent untold hours gathering data on the revelations and the people mentioned in them. In addition to competently using public documents, such as marriage records, deeds, and censuses, he has searched early journals and Church minute books that even few historians see. The result is a rich supplement for a careful reading of the Doctrine and Covenants and, at the same time, a quick reference tool for reviewing a single section. Most of the material here comes from primary sources. Thus the reader has, not another rehash of published material, but a new tool that efficiently rewards any time spent with it.

—Richard L. Anderson
Brigham Young University

Preface

While it is true that the revelations contained in the Doctrine and Covenants are best understood within the context of their history, it is equally true that the history of Joseph Smith and his fellow disciples is a reflection of their conscious effort to fulfill the instructions of the revelations. This treatise carefully analyzes and succinctly presents essential historical facts of each section in the Doctrine and Covenants. The intent is to bring into sharper focus the reasons for which the revelations were received. Without that awareness, we have a set of answers but are ignorant of the questions. The importance of understanding the contextual background of the revelations was pointed out by Brigham Young, the Prophet's successor: "When revelations are given through an individual appointed to receive them, they are given to the understandings of the people . . . . After a lapse of years, [these revelations] become mystified to those who were not personally acquainted with the circumstances at the time they were given." Referring to section 58 of the Doctrine and Covenants, President Young continued:

> The revelation which I have read was perfectly plain, and could readily be understood by all the brethren then in Jackson County, Missouri, and in Kirtland, Ohio, as easily as you can understand me when I talk about digging canals, buildings dwellings, tabernacles,

temples, and storehouses, or when I talk about drawing sand and clay, burning lime, &c....When Joseph received this revelation, it was as plain to the understanding of the Saints, as are my instructions when telling you what to do.

It is important to understand that most of the revelations in the Doctrine and Covenants are administrative in nature; fewer than one-fifth of these canonized sections of scripture has a purely doctrinal message. In the beginning stages of the Restoration divine confirmation (in the form of a written revelation) was needed to solve many procedural problems. "Most of the revelations he [Joseph] received in the early part of his ministry," emphasized Brigham Young, "pertained to what the few around him should do in this or in that case—when and how they should perform their duties." The written revelation was thus to be the Prophet's vehicle for establishing the temporal kingdom during its first decade. However, as Joseph Smith matured in his calling and gained the support of his followers a letter or a verbal instruction was sufficient to bind his word. The 1840s, as well as bringing increased interest among the Saints, brought a sense of urgency to the Prophet for expounding doctrine. But the written revelation largely gave way to public preaching and official newspaper editorials.

Because the revelations witnessed that God had again established his covenant with man, the early Saints affectionately referred to this body of scripture as the "Book of Covenants." While the inclusion of seven Lectures on Faith in 1835 served as the basis for calling the sacred volume a book of "doctrine" as well as covenants, the revelations consistently remained segregated from the uncanonized theological lectures under the title "Covenants and Commandments of the Lord." Yet for all its importance as a canon of latter-day laws and promises, this unique book of revelation also contains many items of doctrinal import. Especially has this been true since 1876 when several new doctrinal sections were added. It was not, however, until 1921 (when the lectures were excluded) that the revelations were officially referred to as both doctrine and covenants. Confident that the modern scripture would assume a prominent role in Restoration literature, the original committee of publication declared this book to be the very "foundation of the Church" and the "salvation of all the world." In it, they boldly proclaimed, was found the "keys of the mysteries of the Kingdom" and the "riches of eternity."

Careful research has preceded the writing of this work. Behind every statement is a document. It is hoped that the serious student of the Doctrine and Covenants will benefit from the close attention given to detail and the extensive use of new source documentation.

In several instances exact dates of reception have been found for the revelations. Dates and places of reception as well as dates and sources of first LDS publication are now conveniently accessible. Inasmuch as some revelations have been revised by those committees appointed to arrange them for publication, significant textual additions and deletions have been noted. However, for an exhaustive textual study of manuscript and printed versions of the revelations one should consult Robert J. Woodford's dissertation (Brigham Young University, 1974).

A major contribution of this book is the presentation and documentation of an abundance of biographical data never before printed. The names of 133 persons (131 men and 2 women) are mentioned in either the headnote or the text of revelations in the Doctrine and Covenants. Each of these personalities is given individual attention. Through the use of vital statistics, census records, probate and land records, church records, journals and diaries, letters, and other memorabilia, the writer has created biographical profiles for numerous Doctrine and Covenants personalities heretofore virtually unknown among Church members today. Included in the biographies are dates and places of birth and death; dates of baptism and priesthood ordination; and (where applicable) names of wives and children and dates of marriage, sealing, endowment, disfellowshipment, and excommunication. Much of this data is here printed for the first time.

Special care has also been given to the dating of Joseph Smith's activities and those of his associates—mission appointments and other assignments, departure and arrival dates, and other important historical data hitherto unidentified. The maps accompanying this work complement the history and biography.

The Doctrine and Covenants represents communication from God to man. "The plea of many in this day," said the latter-day seer, after years of persecution and harassment, "is that we have no right to receive revelations." However, he warned, "If we do not get revelations, we do not have the oracles of God." Again pointing to the need for divine communication Joseph Smith declared: "Salvation cannot come without revelation." If God does not reveal himself to man, man cannot know God. Without such divine communication, therefore, man remains ignorant of the process of salvation.

Most sections in the Doctrine and Covenants represent revelation to Joseph Smith through the Holy Ghost—"impressions to the mind and the heart." However, this sacred record also contains prayers, answers to questions, visions, items of instruction, declarations of belief, letters, minutes, instructions from heavenly messengers, and statements of fact. Some sections included in our present edition of the Doctrine and Covenants (e.g., 2, 13, 85, 121, and 130) were not initially considered scripture. But because of their worth and contribution to Mormon doctrine and thought, they have been accepted by the Church membership as scripture.

Acknowledgments

I am indebted to many individuals who have assisted either directly or indirectly in the preparation of this work. In addition to public records, materials used in this study have been gathered primarily from three libraries: Church Archives, Historical Department of The Church of Jesus Christ of Latter-day Saints, Salt Lake City, Utah; Harold B. Lee Library, Brigham Young University, Provo, Utah; and Library-Archives, the Reorganized Church of Jesus Christ of Latter Day Saints, Independence, Missouri. Thanks are given to the kind, talented staffs at these institutions.

I am particularly grateful to LaMar C. Berrett, a director of the Religious Studies Center at Brigham Young University, for extending the financial assistance that enabled me to spend research time in Ohio, Iowa, Missouri, Illinois, and Wisconsin, where many important materials were uncovered.

Special thanks are given to Richard L. Anderson, professor of history and scripture at Brigham Young University for his friendship, encouragement, and good judgment as a historian. His intense interest in early Mormonism was contagious as I worked under his direction more than a decade ago. I appreciate the painstaking efforts of Robert J. Matthews, Dean of Religious Instruction at Brigham Young University, who has carefully read the manuscript and offered many helpful suggestions.

Donald J. Barney, manager of Seventy's Mission Bookstore, first recognized the importance of this study and has gone well beyond the extra mile in bringing it to publication. John N. Drayton, assistant director of the University of Oklahoma Press, has contributed significantly to the style and readability of this work.

I especially remember the exceptional cooperation of James L. Kimball, Jr., at Church Archives. Chad Flake, Dennis Rowley, and Hyrum Andrus at Brigham Young University Library, and Madelon Brunson and Patricia Roberts at RLDS Library-Archives have greatly assisted me in this work. Others who have contributed significantly are Donald Q. Cannon, Andrew F. Ehat, A. Dean Larsen, Haybron Adams, Dean C. Jessee, Larry C. Porter, and Ronald Watt.

Finally, I am greatly indebted to my wife, Lynette, for her encouragement and patience during the writing and preparation of this volume.

Although others have read the manuscript and offered valuable suggestions, I alone am responsible for any errors in fact or judgment contained in this work.

Explanation of Procedure

Although the names of many persons mentioned in the Doctrine and Covenants appear in several different revelations, a "Biographical Note" for such an individual will be presented only once: where his or her name first appears in either the headnote or the text of a revelation. For subsequent references, one should refer to the index.

The "Publication Note" found in each section of this book refers to first LDS publication only. A few revelations were first printed and published by non-Mormons.

All revelations now found in the Doctrine and Covenants have remained since their first inclusion. The "Publication Note" identifies the edition in which the revelation first became part of the Doctrine and Covenants. Editions of the Doctrine and Covenants in which revelations were first included are: 1833 (entitled Book of Commandments), 1835, 1844, 1876, 1908, and 1981. For purposes of this study, the Book of Commandments will be considered the first edition of the Doctrine and Covenants.

The following abbreviations are used throughout the text and in the notes.

History of the Church   Joseph Smith, Jr. *History of The Church of Jesus Christ of Latter-day Saints*, ed. B.H. Roberts, 2nd ed. rev., 7 vols. (Salt Lake City: Deseret News, 1932-51).

Millennial Star	*The Latter-day Saints' Millennial Star*, 1840-1970. Manchester and Liverpool, England.
Times and Seasons	*Times and Seasons*, 1839-1846. Nauvoo, Illinois.
Journal of Discourses	*Journal of Discourses*, 26 vols. (1855-1886) Liverpool, England.
"Journal History"	Journal History of The Church of Jesus Christ of Latter-day Saints, Church Archives, Salt Lake City, Utah.
Jenson's *Biographical Encyclopedia*	Andrew Jenson, *Latter-Day Saint Biographical Encyclopedia*, 4 vols. (Salt Lake City: Andrew Jenson Memorial Association, 1936).
Elders' Journal	*Elders' Journal of The Church of Latter Day Saints*, October-November 1837. Kirtland, Ohio. *Elders' Journal of The Church of Jesus Christ of Latter Day Saints*, July-August 1838. Far West, Missouri.
History of Joseph Smith by His Mother	*History of Joseph Smith By His Mother*, Lucy Mack Smith (Salt Lake City: Bookcraft, 1958).
Evening and Morning Star	*The Evening and the Morning Star*, June 1832-July 1833. Independence, Missouri. December 1833-September 1834, Kirtland, Ohio. *Evening and Morning Star*, June 1832-September 1834, Independence, Missouri, and Kirtland, Ohio [Kirtland, Ohio, January 1835-October 1836].
Messenger and Advocate	*Latter Day Saints' Messenger and Advocate*, October 1834-September 1837, Kirtland, Ohio.
Autobiography of Parley P. Pratt	*Autobiography of Parley Parker Pratt*, ed., Parley P. Pratt (Salt Lake City: Deseret Book Co., 1938).

"Far West Record"	The Conference Minutes, and Record Book, of Christ's Church of Latter Day Saints, Belonging to the High Council of Said Church, or their Successors in office, of Caldwell County Missouri, Far West: April 6, 1838 (1830-39), Church Archives.
"The Scriptory Book of Joseph Smith"	The Scriptory Book of Joseph Smith Jr—President of the Church of Jesus Christ of Latterday Saints in All the World, Far West April 12th 1838 (1838), Church Archives.
"Kirtland Council Minute Book"	The Kirtland Council Minute Book (1832-37), Church Archives.
"Kirtland Revelation Book"	The Kirtland Revelation Book (1831-34), Church Archives.
"Nauvoo High Council Minutes"	Nauvoo High Council Minutes (1839-45), Church Archives
"Pottawatamie High Council Minutes"	A Record of the appointment and transactions of the Twelve presiding High Council appointed to preside over the affairs of the Church of Jesus Christ of Latter day Saints remain[in]g East of the Missouri River (1846-49), Church Archives.

Commentary

Sections 1-72

Section 1

Date. 1 November 1831.

Place. Hiram, Portage County, Ohio.

Hiram, the city of highest elevation in the Western Reserve, is thirty miles southeast of Kirtland, Ohio. When Joseph Smith received this revelation, he and his family were living in the home of John and Elsa Johnson, members of the Church.

Historical Note. Known as the "Lord's Preface," this revelation was received by Joseph Smith between the first two sessions of a special conference held 1-12 November in Hiram, Ohio. According to the "Far West Record" (1 November 1831), the "Preface [was] received by inspiration." In attendance at the conference were Joseph Smith, Oliver Cowdery, David Whitmer, John Whitmer, Peter Whitmer, Jr., Sidney Rigdon, William E. McLellan, Orson Hyde, Luke S. Johnson, and Lyman E. Johnson. The conference had been convened to make necessary decisions and arrangements for the printing of the revelations received by Joseph Smith.

In the first of five sessions, "[Oliver Cowdery] made a request desiring the mind of the Lord through this conference of Elders to know how many copies of the Book of Commandments, it was the will of the Lord should be published in the first edition of that work.

Voted that there be ten thousand copies struck."[1]

The first printing was halted on 20 July 1833 when a mob in Independence, Missouri, destroyed the printing press along with all but a few unbound sheets of the Book of Commandments.

This powerful revelation clearly points out that: Joseph Smith is God's prophet, the Book of Mormon is true, and the church organized by Joseph Smith is the only true and living church on the earth.

Publication Note.   Section 1, first published in the *Evening and Morning Star* (March 1833), was included in the Book of Commandments in 1833.

Biographical Note.   Joseph Smith, Jr.

Son of Joseph Smith and Lucy Mack. Born 23 December 1805 at Sharon, Windsor County, Vermont. Married Emma Hale at South Bainbridge, Chenango County, New York, 18 January 1827. Nine children: Alvin[2], Thaddeus, Louisa, Joseph, Frederick Granger Williams, Alexander Hale, Don Carlos, male child[3], David Hyrum. Adopted twins: Joseph and Julia Murdock. Moved to Harmony, Pennsylvania, 1827. Purchased about 13 acres in Harmony from Isaac Hale. Translated Book of Mormon 1829. Received Aaronic Priesthood 15 May 1829 from John the Baptist. Received Melchizedek Priesthood from Peter, James, and John shortly after 15 May 1829. Published Book of Mormon 26 March 1830. Organized Church 6 April 1830. Moved from Harmony to Fayette, New York, September 1830. Began work on inspired translation of Bible June 1830. Moved to Kirtland, Ohio, January 1831. Ordained to High Priesthood 3 June 1831. Traveled to Independence, Missouri, in summer of 1831; there identified future site of New Jerusalem. Moved to Hiram, Ohio, 12 September 1831. Tarred and feathered 24 March 1832 at Hiram, Ohio. Ordained and sustained President of High Priesthood 25 January 1832. Traveled to Independence, Missouri, in summer of 1832 to regulate Church affairs. Moved back to Kirtland, Ohio, September 1832. Traveled to Albany, New York City, and Boston in fall of 1832 on Church business. Traveled to Upper Canada on preaching mission in fall of 1833. Traveled to New York state in spring of 1834 to borrow money and recruit for Zion's Camp. Traveled to Clay County, Missouri, in summer of 1834 to assist Missouri Mormons in obtaining possession of their lands. Traveled to Michigan in fall of 1834 to visit members of Church. Again visited members of Church in Michigan in summer of 1835. Received important priesthood keys from Elias, Elijah, and Moses 3 April 1836. Traveled to Salem, Massachusetts, on Church business in summer of 1836. Traveled to Palmyra and other places in New York state in spring of 1837 to escape persecutions of enemies in Ohio. Traveled to Upper Canada to visit

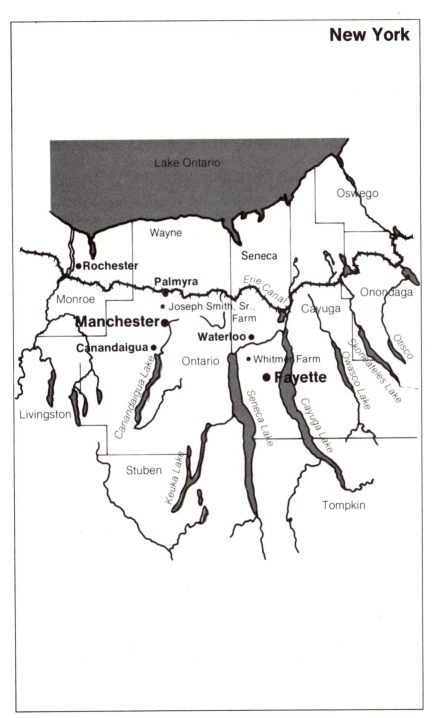

New York

Lake Ontario

Oswego

Wayne

Seneca

●Rochester

Palmyra

Erie Canal

Onondaga

Monroe

● Joseph Smith, Sr., Farm

Cayuga

Otisco

Manchester●

Waterloo●

Canandaigua ●

Ontario

● Whitmer Farm

●**Fayette**

Skeneateles Lake

Owasco Lake

Canandaigua Lake

Seneca Lake

Cayuga Lake

Livingston

Stuben

Keuka Lake

Tompkin

Saints July-August 1837. Traveled to Far West, Missouri, October-November 1837 to regulate Church affairs. Moved to Far West, Missouri, arriving 14 March 1838. Arrested and incarcerated in Liberty Jail November 1838 for treason and murder. No conviction. Escaped from Missouri law-enforcement officers April 1839. Located in Commerce, Illinois, in summer of 1839. Left Nauvoo for Washington, D.C., 29 October 1839 to seek redress for wrongs committed against Saints in Missouri. Arrived 28 November. Met with President Martin Van Buren 29 November 1839. Returned to Nauvoo 4 March 1840. Elected lieutenant-general of Nauvoo Legion February 1841. Sealed to additional wives 1841-44.[4] Arrested 5 June 1841 on Missouri treason charge. Discharged 10 June 1841. No conviction. Organized Female Relief Society March 1842. Elected mayor of City of Nauvoo May 1842. Began administering temple endowment May 1842. Arrested 8 August 1842 as accessory in attempted murder of Lilburn W. Boggs. Released same day on *habeas corpus*. Remained in hiding at or near Nauvoo until December 1842. Discharged from 1842 arrest 5 January 1843. Sealed to wife, Emma, 28 May 1843. Arrested 23 June 1843 on Missouri treason charge. Discharged 2 July 1843. No conviction. Candidate for presidency of United States 1844. Arrested and incarcerated in Carthage Jail June 1844. Killed by mob at Carthage, Hancock County, Illinois, 27 June 1844.[5]

Section 2

Date.   21-22 September 1823.

Place.   Manchester, Ontario County, New York.

At the time he received this revelation, Joseph Smith was living at his father's home in Manchester, New York, The Smiths had moved from Palmyra to Manchester in 1818.

Historical Note.   During the evening of 21 September 1823 and the early morning of the following day, Moroni, an ancient Nephite prophet, made three appearances to Joseph Smith in his bedroom, instructing him that the Lord had a work for him to do. Moroni told the Prophet that hidden in a nearby hill were gold plates that contained an account of former inhabitants of America. Quoting Old and New Testament prophecies, including the third and fourth chapters of Malachi, Moroni told Joseph Smith of the Lord's desire that the gold plates be translated.[1]

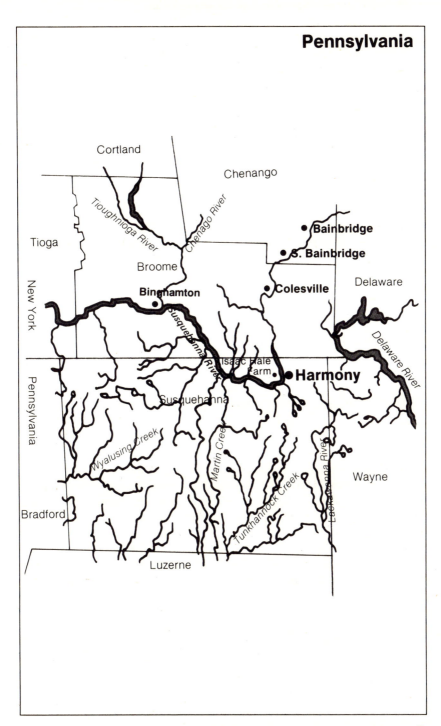

Pennsylvania

Cortland

Chenango

Tioughnioga River

Chenago River

Tioga

Bainbridge

S. Bainbridge

Broome

Delaware

New York

Binghamton

Susquehanna River

Colesville

Delaware River

Isaac Hale Farm

Harmony

Susquehanna

Pennsylvania

Wyalusing Creek

Martin Creek

Tunkhannock Creek

Lackawanna River

Wayne

Bradford

Luzerne

Publication Note.   Section 2 was first published in the *Times and Seasons* (15 April 1842) and was first included in the Doctrine and Covenants in the 1876 edition.

Section 3

Date.   July 1828.

Place.   Harmony, Susquehanna County, Pennsylvania.

Located approximately 150 miles from Palmyra, New York, Harmony was the home of Isaac Hale, Emma Smith's father. Because of persecution in Manchester, New York, Joseph and Emma Smith moved to Harmony about December 1827.

Historical Note.   Martin Harris, a Palmyra farmer who became interested in the Prophet's religious pursuits, served as Joseph Smith's scribe in the translation of the Book of Mormon from 12 April to 14 June 1828. During these two months, the men translated and wrote 116 pages of manuscript. Not long after Martin Harris began writing, he began soliciting permission to take the manuscript pages home to show his wife and others. The Prophet inquired of the Lord and, after much importuning, obtained permission on condition that the translation be shown to five persons only: his wife (Lucy), his brother (Preserved), his father and mother (Nathan and Rhoda), and his wife's sister (Mrs. Cobb).[1]
    After Martin Harris's departure, Emma Smith gave birth to a son, on 15 June 1828. The infant died the same day. When Emma had recovered sufficiently, the Prophet left for Manchester to visit his family and check on Martin Harris. It was not long until he found that Martin Harris had not strictly adhered to the specified conditions and through carelessness had lost the manuscript. Upon learning that the manuscript was missing, Joseph Smith exclaimed as he wept and walked the floor,

> Oh, my God! All is lost! all is lost! What shall I do? I have sinned—it is I who tempted the wrath of God. I should have been satisfied with the first answer which I received from the Lord; for he told me that it was not safe to let the

writing go out of my possession . . . .How shall I appear
before the Lord? Of what rebuke am I not worthy from
the angel of the Most High?[2]

Immediately after the Prophet had returned to Harmony from
Manchester, a heavenly messenger, presumably Moroni, appeared
to him and returned the Urim and Thummim (which had been
taken in consequence of his wearying the Lord regarding Martin
Harris's request). The Prophet received section 3 at this time.[3]

Publication Note.   Section 3 was first published as chapter 2 in the
Book of Commandments in 1833.

Biographical Note.   Martin Harris.

Son of Nathan Harris and Rhoda Lapham. Born 18 May 1783 in Easttown,
Saratoga County, New York. Married first cousin Lucy Harris. Three
children: Duty L., George W., and Lucy. Owned 240 acres of land in
Palmyra. Served as scribe to Joseph Smith during translation of Book of
Mormon. One of Three Witnesses of Book of Mormon June 1829. Assisted
financially in publication of Book of Mormon. Baptized 6 April 1830.
Ordained priest by June 1830. Ordained high priest 3 June 1831. Member of
Literary and United firms. Member of Kirtland high council 1834. Member
of Zion's Camp. Assisted in choosing twelve apostles in 1835. Married
Caroline Young in 1837 after death of first wife. Five children: Martin Jr.,
John, Julia, Solomon, and Ida Mae. Excommunicated December 1837.
Rebaptized 6 November 1842. Did not gather with Saints in Nauvoo. Did
not follow Brigham Young after Prophet's death. Joined James Strang
movement and served a mission for Strangites in England 1846. Joined
William E. McLellan in organizing new church January 1847. Wife,
Caroline, left him 1856 to gather with the Saints in Utah. Joined William
Smith in organizing new church about 1858 in Kirtland. Served as custodian
of Kirtland Temple. Arrived in Salt Lake City, Utah, August 1870.
Rebaptized and received endowment September 1870. Died 9 July 1875 in
Clarkston, Cache County, Utah.[4]

Section 4

Date.   February 1829.

Place.   Harmony, Susquehanna County, Pennsylvania.

Historical Note.   After Joseph Smith had received section 3, (in July 1828), the plates and Urim and Thummim were again taken from him. Desiring to obtain them again, the Prophet continued his "supplication to God, without cessation," and on 22 September 1828 he had the "joy and satisfaction" of again receiving the Urim and Thummim and the plates.[1]

Joseph Smith did not immediately proceed to translate the plates, however, but "went to laboring with [his] hands upon a small farm" that he had purchased from Isaac Hale to provide for his family. The farm, consisting of about thirteen acres, was deeded to Joseph Smith on 25 August 1830 for $200.[2]

Speaking of the Prophet's dire circumstances during the winter of 1828, Joseph Knight, Sr., wrote,

> Now he Could not translate But little Being poor and nobody to write for him But his wife and she Could not do much and take Care of her house and he Being poor and no means to But work. His wifes father and familey ware all against him and would not h[e]lp him. He and his wife Came up [to Colesville] to see me the first of the winter 1828 and told me his Case. But I was not in easy Circumstances and I did not know what it mite amount to and my wife and familey all against me about helping him. But I let him have a pair of shoes and three Dollars in money to help him a little.[3]

In early 1829,[4] Joseph and Emma received a visit from the Prophet's father, and possibly other members of the Smith family.[5] The call provided an opportunity for the Manchester Smiths to meet the Hales (Joseph's in-laws), to learn of the progress of the Book of Mormon translation, and to give moral support to their son. During the visit, section 4 was received for Joseph Smith, Sr., the Prophet's father.[6]

Publication Note.   Section 4 was first published as chapter 3 in the Book of Commandments in 1833.

Biographical Note.   Joseph Smith, Sr.

Son of Asael Smith and Mary Duty. Born 12 July 1771 at Topsfield, Essex County, Massachusetts. Married Lucy Mack 24 January 1796 at Tunbridge, Vermont, there began farming. Eleven children: male child, Alvin, Hyrum, Sophronia, Joseph, Samuel Harrison, Ephraim, William, Catherine, Don Carlos, and Lucy. Moved to Palmyra, New York, 1816. One of Eight Witnesses to Book of Mormon. Baptized 6 April 1830. Moved to Kirtland, Ohio, 1831. Ordained to High Priesthood 3 June 1831. Ordained Patriarch of Church 18 December 1833. Member of Kirtland high council. Worked on Kirtland Temple. Served mission to eastern states 1836. Appointed assistant counselor to First Presidency 3 September 1837. Moved to Far West, Missouri, in summer of 1838. Located in Nauvoo 1839. Died 14 September 1840, in Nauvoo, Hancock County, Illinois.[7]

Section 5

Date.   March 1829.

Place.   Harmony, Susquehanna County, Pennsylvania.

Historical Note.   Shortly after the visit of the Prophet's parents in February 1829 (see section 4), Martin Harris came to Harmony, Pennsylvania, to see Joseph Smith. Apparently humbled and repentant for having lost the 116 pages of manuscript, yet desiring to ascertain if Joseph Smith was in possession of the gold plates, Martin Harris sought out the Prophet.[1] The revelation instructed Joseph Smith to stop translating the Book of Mormon for a time.

Textual Note.   Much of two verses that appeared in the Book of Commandments in 1833 were deleted in 1835 and from subsequent editions of the Doctrine and Covenants. They are included below.

Book of Commandments

1981 Edition

5   And thus, if the people of this generation harden not their hearts, I will work a reformation among them, and I will put down all lyings, and deceivings, and priestcrafts, and envyings, and strifes, and idolatries, and sorceries, and all manner of iniquities, and I will establish my church, like unto the church which was taught by my disciples in the days of old.
6   And now if this generation do harden their hearts against my word, behold I will deliver them up unto satan, for he reigneth and hath much power at this time, for he hath got great hold upon the hearts of the people of this generation: and not far from the iniquities of Sodom and Gomorrah, do they come at this time: and behold the sword of justice hangeth over their heads, and if they persist in the hardness of their hearts, the time cometh that it must fall upon them. Behold I tell you these things even as I also told the people of the destruction of Jerusalem, and my word shall be verified at this time as it hath hitherto been verified.

18   And their testimony shall also go forth unto the condemnation of this generation if they harden their hearts against them;
19   For a desolating scourge shall go forth among the inhabitants of the earth, and shall continue to be poured out from time to time, if they repent not, until the earth is empty, and the inhabitants thereof are consumed away and utterly destroyed by the brightness of my coming.
20   Behold, I tell you these things, even as I also told the people of the destruction of Jerusalem; and my word shall be verified at this time as it hath hitherto been verified.

Publication Note.   Section 5 was first published as chapter 4 in the Book of Commandments in 1833.

Section 6

Date.   April 1829 (on or after 7 April; see Historical Note below).

Place.   Harmony, Susquehanna County, Pennsylvania.

Historical Note. While Joseph Smith was still residing in Harmony, Pennsylvania, Oliver Cowdery was teaching school in Palmyra. Because it was customary for school teachers to board with the families of their pupils, Oliver Cowdery came to live with the Smith family, where he first learned about Moroni's appearances to Joseph Smith and the translation of the plates. When school closed in the spring, Oliver Cowdery traveled to Harmony to meet the Prophet. Arriving on 5 April 1829, he received a first-hand account of the glorious work of the Restoration, and on 7 April he began serving as Joseph Smith's scribe.

Concerning Cowdery's involvement in the translation, Joseph Knight, Sr., wrote,

> In the spring of 1829 Oliver Cowdery a young man from Palmry went to see old Mr. Smith about the Book that Joseph had found. And he told him about it and advised him to go Down to Pensylvany and see for him self and to write for Joseph. He went Down and Received a Revelation Concerning the work and he was Convinced of the truth of the work and he agreed to write for him till it was Done. Now Joseph and Oliver Came up to see me if I Could help him to some provisions, [they] having no way to Buy any . . . .I Bought a Barral of Mackrel and some lined paper for writing . . . .some nine or ten Bushels of grain and five or six Bushels taters and a pound of tea, and I went Down to see him and they ware in want. Joseph and Oliver ware gone to see if they Could find a place to work for provisions, and found none. They returned home and found me there with provisions, and they ware glad for they ware out.[1]

Of his experience with Joseph Smith during the translation of the Book of Mormon, Oliver Cowdery wrote,

> These were days never to be forgotten—to sit under the sound of a voice dictated by the *inspiration* of heaven, awakened the utmost gratitude of this bosom! Day after day I continued, uninterrupted, to write from his mouth, as he translated, with the *Urim* and *Thummim*, or as the Nephites would have said, "Interpreters," the history, or record, called "The Book of Mormon."[2]

Publication Note. Section 6 was first published as chapter 5 in the Book of Commandments in 1833.

Biographical Note. Oliver Cowdery.

Son of William Cowdery and Rebecca Fuller. Born 3 October 1806 at Wells, Rutland County, Vermont. Became acquainted with and began writing for Joseph Smith as scribe on translation of gold plates April 1829. With Joseph Smith received Aaronic and Melchizedek priesthoods in spring of 1829. One of Three Witnesses to Book of Mormon June 1829. Charter member of Church 6 April 1830. First scribe to assist Joseph Smith in translating Bible. Led Lamanite mission to Missouri in winter of 1830. Returned to Ohio August 1831. Ordained to High Priesthood 28 August 1831 by Sidney Rigdon. Accompanied by John Whitmer to Missouri November-December 1831 with manuscript revelations for printing. Member of Literary and United firms. Married Elizabeth Ann Whitmer 18 December 1832. Six children: Maria Louise, Elizabeth Ann, Josephine Rebecca, Oliver Peter, Adeline Fuller, and Julia Olive. No grandchildren. Left Missouri for Ohio in July 1833 to confer with Joseph Smith concerning persecution in Jackson County. Arrived in Kirtland before 18 August 1833. Traveled to New York October 1833 to purchase printing materials. Member of Kirtland high council. Assisted in administering Church affairs during summer of 1834 while Joseph Smith was in Missouri. Ordained Assistant President of Church 5 December 1834. Assisted in choosing twelve apostles 1835. Appointed Church recorder 1835. Participated in dedication of Kirtland Temple 1836. With Joseph Smith received priesthood keys from Elijah, Elias, and Moses 3 April 1836. Returned to Missouri 1837. Arrived in Far West 20 October 1837. Excommunicated from Church for apostasy 12 April 1838 at Far West, Missouri. Practiced law in Tiffin, Ohio, and Elkhorn, Wisconsin. Ran unsuccessfully for state legislature in Wisconsin 1848. Rebaptized by Orson Hyde 12 November 1848 at Kanesville, Iowa. Died 3 March 1850 in Richmond, Ray County Missouri.[3]

Section 7

Date. April 1829 (after 7 April).

Place. Harmony, Susquehanna County, Pennsylvania.

Historical Note. In April 1829, while Joseph Smith and Oliver Cowdery worked on the translation of the Book of Mormon, they received several revelations. The basis for section 7 was their difference of opinion concerning whether John the Apostle had died or been translated. Agreeing to settle the matter by the Urim and Thummim, they inquired of the Lord and received section 7.[1] The headnote to this section in the Book of Commandments indicates that it is a translation of an ancient parchment "written and hid up" by John the Revelator. The parchment would not have been in the Prophet's possession, rather, it would have been seen and translated by means of the Urim and Thummim.

Textual Note.   The text of section 7, as published in the Book of Commandments, was much shorter than that contained in our present edition. The additional verses were first placed in the 1835 edition of the Doctrine and Covenants. Following is the text as found in the 1833 Book of Commandments:

> And the Lord said unto me, John my beloved, what desirest thou? and I said Lord, give unto me power that I may bring souls unto thee.—And the Lord said unto me: Verily, verily I say unto thee, because thou desiredst this, thou shalt tarry till I come in my glory: And for this cause, the Lord said unto Peter:—If I will that he tarry till I come, what is that to thee? for he desiredst of me that he might bring souls unto me: but thou desiredst that thou might speedily come unto me in my kingdom: I say unto thee, Peter, this was a good desire, but my beloved has undertaken a greater work. Verily I say unto you, ye shall both have according to your desires, for ye both joy in that which ye have desired.

Publication Note.   Section 7 was first published as chapter 6 in the Book of Commandments in 1833.

Section 8

Date.   April 1829 (after 7 April).

Place.   Harmony, Susquehanna County, Pennsylvania.

Historical Note.   Anxious to exercise the gift of translation that the Lord had bestowed upon Oliver Cowdery (see D&C 6:25), Joseph

Smith and Oliver Cowdery inquired of the Lord and received the revelation now identified as section 8.[1]

Textual Note.   In the Book of Commandments verses 6 and 7 read differently. Compare the following:

Book of Commandments	1981 Edition
Now this is not all, for you have another gift, which is the gift of working with the rod: behold, it has told you things; behold there is no other power save God, that can cause this rod of nature, to work in your hands.	6. Now this is not all they gift; for you have another gift, which is the gift of Aaron; behold, it has told you many things; 7. Behold, there is no other power, save the power of God, that can cause this gift of Aaron to be with you. 8. Therefore, doubt not, for it is the gift of God; and you shall hold it in your hands, and do marvelous works; and no power shall be able to take it away out of your hands, for it is the work of God.

The original text suggests that Joseph Smith and Oliver Cowdery may have had a tangible instrument other than the Urim and Thummim with which to translate. This idea is further substantiated in verse 8 of the 1981 edition, wherein the Lord said, "You shall hold it in your hands."

Publication Note.   Section 8 was first published as chapter 7 in the Book of Commandments in 1833.

Section 9

Date.   April 1829 (after 7 April).

Place.   Harmony, Susquehanna County, Pennsylvania.

Historical Note.   According to his desire on the one hand and the Lord's permission and blessing on the other, Oliver Cowdery proceeded to translate the Book of Mormon, even as Joseph Smith. But upon doing so, Oliver began to fear and failed to exercise sufficient faith to receive the necessary inspiration. Pursuant to this failure, Joseph Smith inquired of the Lord and received section 9. Therein the Lord instructed Oliver Cowdery to resume his role as scribe and promised that Oliver would assist in future translations.[1]

Publication Note.   Section 9 was first published as chapter 8 in the Book of Commandments in 1833.

Section 10

Date.   Summer 1828.

In all editions of the Doctrine and Covenants before 1921, the date of section 10 was given as May 1829. However, Elder Brigham H. Roberts, who edited the *History of the Church* for publication in 1902, gave as his opinion that the date May 1829 was "clearly in error," that the revelation was received in the summer of 1828.[1] Roberts's interpretation undoubtedly influenced the committee that prepared the 1921 edition. But even though the date in the headnote was changed to "the summer of 1828," the revelation has not been moved from where it was placed in the earlier editions.

The "Manuscript History of the Church" for the years 1828-29 was written by James Mulholland, the Prophet's scribe, in the summer of 1839. An insert in that section of the history places section 10 immediately after section 3. Although the May 1829 date of reception for section 10 (contained in both the 1833 and 1835 editions of the Doctrine and Covenants) was not altered by Mulholland, his work clearly attests to the 1828 reception of section 10. The "wicked man" reference to Martin Harris certainly suggests an 1828 setting, as do the instructions on the manner of proceeding with the translation of the Book of Mormon after the loss of the 116 pages of manuscript and the temporary withdrawal of the Urim and Thummim and the gold plates in 1828.[2]

Place.   Harmony, Susquehanna County, Pennsylvania.

Historical Note.   After Joseph Smith had received section 3, both the gold plates and the Urim and Thummim were taken from him.

But "in a few days they were returned to me," declared the Prophet, "when I inquired of the Lord, and the Lord said thus unto me [section 10 follows]."[3]

Verses 10, 11, 14, 41, 42, and 43, which speak of the loss of the 116 pages of manuscript, were quoted almost verbatim in Joseph Smith's preface to the first edition of the Book of Mormon. Since the preface is no longer part of the Book of Mormon and sheds light on the historical background of section 10, it here included in its entirety.

As many false reports have been circulated respecting the following work, and also many unlawful measures taken by evil designing persons to destroy me, and also the work, I would inform you that I translated, by the gift and power of God, and caused to be written, one hundred and sixteen pages, the which I took from the Book of Lehi, which was an account abridged from the plates of Lehi, by the hand of Mormon; which said account, some person or persons have stolen and kept from me, notwithstanding my utmost exertions to recover it again— and being commanded of the Lord that I should not translate the same over again, for Satan had put it into their hearts to tempt the Lord their God, by altering the words, that they did read contrary from that which I translated and caused to be written; and if I should bring forth the same words again, or, in other words, if I should translate the same over again, they would publish that which they had stolen, and Satan would stir up the hearts of this generation, that they might not receive this work: but behold, the Lord said unto me, I will not suffer that Satan shall accomplish his evil design in this thing: therefore thou shalt translate from the plates of Nephi, until ye come to that which ye have translated, which ye have retained; and behold ye shall publish it as the record of Nephi; and thus I will confound those who have altered my words. I will not suffer that they shall destroy my work; yea, I will shew unto them that my wisdom is greater than the cunning of the Devil. Wherefore, to be obedient unto the commandments of God, I have, through his grace and mercy, accomplished that which he hath commanded me respecting this thing. I would also inform you that the plates of which hath been spoken, were found in the township of Manchester, Ontario county, New-York.

Publication Note. Section 10 was first published as chapter 9 in the Book of Commandments in 1833.

Section 11

Date.   May 1829 (after 25 May).

Hyrum Smith arrived in Harmony, Pennsylvania, after Samuel H. Smith's baptism on 25 May 1829. Thus, section 11 was of necessity received after that date.[1]

Place.   Harmony, Susquehanna County, Pennsylvania.

Historical Note. Shortly after Samuel H. Smith returned to Manchester, New York, Hyrum Smith became interested in the Prophet's activities and traveled to Harmony to visit him. At Hyrum Smith's request, Joseph inquired of the Lord through the Urim and Thummim and received section 11. The Prophet later wrote the following concerning his brother Hyrum:

> Brother Hyrum, what a faithful heart you have got! Oh may the Eternal Jehovah crown eternal blessings upon your head, as a reward for the care you have had for my soul! O how many are the sorrows we have shared together; and again we find ourselves shackled with the unrelenting hand of oppression. Hyrum, thy name shall be written in the book of the law of the Lord.[2]

Publication Note.   Section 11 was first published as chapter 10 in the Book of Commandments in 1833.

Biographical Note.   Hyrum Smith.

Son of Joseph Smith and Lucy Mack. Born 9 February 1800 at Tunbridge, Orange County, Vermont. Married Jerusha Barden 2 November 1826 in Manchester, New York. Six children: Lovina, Mary, John, Hyrum, Jerusha, and Sarah. One of Eight Witnesses to Book of Mormon 1829. Ordained priest 9 June 1830. Ordained elder before June 1831. Ordained to High Priesthood 3 June 1831. One of committee of three to superintend construction of sacred edifices in Kirtland, Ohio. Member of Zion's Camp 1834. Member of Kirtland high council. Worked on Kirtland Temple. Participated in Kirtland Temple dedication 1836. Appointed assistant counselor to First Presidency 3 September 1837. Appointed second counselor in First Presidency in Far West, Missouri, 7 November 1837. After death of first wife, married Mary Fielding December 1837. Two children: Joseph Fielding and Martha Ann. Arrested and incarcerated in Liberty Jail November 1838-April 1839 for treason. No conviction. Located in Nauvoo, Illinois, 1839. Ordained Patriarch and Assistant President of Church 24 January 1841. Received endowment 4 May 1842. Sealed to wife, Mary, 29 May 1843. Sealed to Mercy R. Thompson for time 11 August 1843. Member of Nauvoo City Council. Arrested and incarcerated in Carthage Jail June 1844. Killed by mob 27 June 1844 at Carthage, Hancock County, Illinois. Nauvoo Temple proxy sealings to Jerusha Barden and Mary Fielding 15 January 1846, to Susan Ivers (born 1789 in Massachusetts) 29 January 1846, and to Lydia Dibble and Polly Miller (born 1795 in New York) 30 January 1846.[3]

Section 12

Date.   May 1829.

Place.   Harmony, Susquehanna County, Pennsylvania.

Historical Note.   Joseph Knight, Sr., a resident of Colesville, New York, in 1829, was one of the first individuals to step forward and assist the Prophet during the translation of the Book of Mormon by supplying money, food, and writing materials. He also paid attorney's fees for Joseph Smith. The Prophet, who always maintained a great love and high esteem for Joseph Knight, Sr., said,

> For fifteen years he has been faithful and true, and even-handed and exemplary, and virtuous and kind, never deviating to the right hand or to the left. Behold he is a righteous man, may God Almighty lengthen out the old man's days; and may his trembling, tortured, and broken body be renewed, and in the vigor of health turn upon

him if it be Thy will, consistently, O God; and it shall be said of him, by the sons of Zion, while there is one of them remaining, that this was a faithful man in Israel; therefore his name shall never be forgotten.[1]

Of his early acquaintance with the Prophet, Joseph Knight, Sr., wrote,

> He came to me perhaps in November [1826] and worked for me until about the time that he was Married, which I think was in February [January 1827]. And I paid him the money and I furnished him with a horse and Cutter to go and see his girl Down to Mr. Hails. And soon after this he was Married . . . .
> He had talked with me and told me the Conversation he had with the personage which told him if he would Do right according to the will of God he mite obtain [the plates].
> Old Mr Smith and Martin Harris Come forrod to Be Baptize for the first. They found a place in a lot a small Stream ran thro and they were Baptized in the Evening because of persecution . . . .I had some thots to go forrod, But I had not red the Book of Morman and I wanted to exeman a little more I Being a Restorationar and had not examined so much as I wanted to. But I should a felt Better if I had gone forward. But I went home and was Baptised in June with my wife and familey.[2]

Publication Note.   Section 12 was first published as chapter 11 in the Book of Commandments in 1833.

Biographical Note.   Joseph Knight, Sr.

Son of Benjamin and Hannah Knight. Born 26 November 1772 at Oakham, Worcester County, Massachusetts. Married Polly Peck by 1796. Seven children: Nahum, Esther, Newel, Anna, Joseph, Polly, and Elizabeth. Moved to Bainbridge, New York, 1809. Two years later moved to Colesville, Broome County, New York; remained for nineteen years. Owned farm, gristmill, and carding machine. Baptized 29 June 1830. Family formed nucleus of small branch of Church in Colesville. Moved to Kirtland, Ohio, 1831. Left Ohio for Jackson County, Missouri, June 1831. Resided in Jackson, Clay, and Caldwell counties in Missouri. Located in Nauvoo 1839. Received house and lot donated by high council of Nauvoo. Ordained priest

18 March 1841. Received endowment in Nauvoo Temple 13 December 1845; sealed to dead wife, Polly, 2 February 1846. Sealed to Phebe Crosby (born 1800 in New York) 2 February 1846. Died 3 February 1847 at Mt. Pisgah, Harrison County, Iowa, during Mormon exodus from Illinois.[3]

Section 13

Date.   15 May 1829.

Place.   Harmony, Susquehanna County, Pennsylvania.

Historical Note.   Section 13 contains part of the instructions and prayer of ordination given by John the Baptist on 15 May 1829. This heavenly messenger informed Joseph Smith and Oliver Cowdery that he was ministering under the direction of Peter, James, and John, three of the Lord's ancient apostles. Within a few days of John the Baptist's visit, these three apostles also appeared to the Prophet and Oliver Cowdery and conferred upon them the Melchizedek Priesthood.[1] Several accounts of the restoration of the Aaronic and Melchizedek priesthoods were written and published fewer than six years after the events. (See, for example, *Messenger and Advocate* [October 1834].) Consider the following 1835 account in the handwriting of Oliver Cowdery:

> [Joseph Smith] was ordained by the angel John, unto the lesser or Aaronic priesthood, in company with myself, in the town of Harmony, Susquehannah county, Pennsylvania, on Friday the 15th day of May, 1829: after which we repaired to the water, even to the Susquehannah river, and were baptized: he first ministering unto me, and after, I do him. But before baptism our souls were drawn out in mighty prayer, to know how we might obtain the blessings of baptism and of the Holy Spirit according to the order of God, and we diligently sought for the right of the fathers and the authority of the holy Priesthood, and the power to administer in the same; for we desired to be, followers of righteousness and the possessors of greater knowledge, even the knowledge of the mysteries of the kingdom of God. Therefore we repaired to the woods, even as our father Joseph said we

should, that is, to the bush, and called upon the name of the Lord, and he answered us out of the heavens: and while we were in the heavenly vision the angel came down and bestowed upon us this priesthood: and then, as I have said, we repaired to the water and were baptized. After this we received the high and holy priesthood: but an account of this will be given elsewhere, or in another place.[2]

In 1848, when Cowdery returned to the Church, he gave a similar testimony concerning the restoration of the Priesthood:

I was present with Joseph when an holy angle from god came down from heaven and confered, or restored the Aronic priesthood. And Said at the Same time that it Should remain upon the earth while the earth Stands. I was also present with Joseph when the Melchesideck priesthood was confered by the holy angles of god.—which we then confirmed on each other by the will and commandment of god. This priesthood is also to remain upon the earth untill the Last remnant of time. This holy priesthood we confered upon many. And is just as good and valid as if god had confered it in person.[3]

Publication Note. Section 13 was first published in the *Times and Seasons* (1 August 1842) and was later included in the 1876 edition of the Doctrine and Covenants.

Section 14

Date. June 1829.

Place. Fayette, Seneca County, New York.

Historical Note. Most of the Book of Mormon was translated between April and June 1829 in Harmony, Pennsylvania. As the work of translation continued, meager financial conditions and local animosity prompted Joseph Smith and Oliver Cowdery to find assistance in finishing the work. The Prophet and Oliver, both of whom had become acquainted with the Whitmer family in Fayette, New York, decided to ask the Whitmers for help. (The Whitmers knew of the translation: before going to Pennsylvania, Oliver had conversed with David Whitmer about the ancient record and, after arriving in Harmony, had sent the Whitmers a small transcript of the translation.) Oliver Cowdery wrote, explaining the situation in Harmony and asking if they could live with the Whitmer family while completing the translation. In response David Whitmer traveled the 135 miles to Harmony to help with the move. The party left for Fayette about 1 June. Section 14 was received in Fayette shortly after their arrival.[1]

David Whitmer later said of Joseph Smith and the translation:

> He was a religious and straight forward man. He had to be, for he was illiterate and he could do nothing himself. He had to trust in God. He could not translate unless he was humble and possessed the right feelings toward everyone. To illustrate so you can see: One morning when he was getting ready to continue the translation, something went wrong about the house and he was put out about it. Something that Emma his wife, had done. Oliver and I went up stairs and Joseph came up soon after to continue the translation, but he could not do anything. He could not translate a single syllable. He went down stairs, out into the orchard, and made supplication to the Lord; was gone about an hour—came back to the house, and asked Emma's forgiveness and then came up stairs where we were, and then the translation went on all right. He could do nothing save he was humble and faithful.[2]

Publication Note.   Section 14 was first published as chapter 12 in the Book of Commandments in 1833.

Biographical Note.   David Whitmer.

Son of Peter Whitmer and Mary Musselman. Born 7 January 1805 near Harrisburg, Dauphin County, Pennsylvania. One of Three Witnesses of Book of Mormon 1829. Baptized, and possibly ordained apostle, June 1829. Married Julia Ann Jolly, daughter of William Jolly, 9 January 1831 at Seneca County, New York. Two Children: David J. (born in Missouri), and Julia A.E. (born in Ohio). Ordained elder 6 April 1830. Moved to Kirtland, Ohio, by June 1831. Ordained high priest 25 October 1831. Moved to Jackson County, Missouri, by October 1832. Chosen and ordained successor to Joseph Smith and President of the Church in Missouri 7 July 1834. Chosen to receive "endowment" in Kirtland Temple 23 June 1834. Left Missouri for Kirtland by September 1834. Assisted in choosing twelve apostles 1835. Appointed as general agent for Literary Firm September 1835. Participated in Kirtland Temple dedication 1836. Paid personal property tax on one horse and one cow in Kirtland 1836. Expressed sympathy to apostate sentiments in Kirtland 1837. Returned to Missouri before 29 July 1837. Rejected by Missouri Saints as president of Church in Missouri 5 February 1838. Excommunicated from Church 13 April 1838 at Far West, Missouri, for apostasy. After leaving Church, located in Richmond, Ray County, Missouri; operated a livery stable. For fifty years maintained strict separation from Church. Recognized by peers as prominent citizen and businessman. Elected to fill unexpired term of mayor in Richmond 1867-68. Died 25 January 1888 at Richmond, Ray County, Missouri.[3]

Section 15

Date. June 1829.

Place. Fayette, Seneca County, New York.

Historical Note. See Historical Note for section 14.[1]

Publication Note. Section 15 was first published as chapter 13 in the Book of Commandments in 1833.

Biographical Note. John Whitmer.

Son of Peter Whitmer and Mary Musselman. Born 27 August 1802 in Pennsylvania. Baptized June 1829 by Oliver Cowdery. One of Eight Witnesses of Book of Mormon June 1829. Assisted Joseph Smith in arranging and copying revelations July 1830. Ordained elder 9 June 1830. Served as scribe to Joseph Smith in translation of Bible. Called by revelation as Church historian 8 March 1831; ordained contrary to his wishes 9 April 1831 in Kirtland. Ordained high priest 3 June 1831 by Lyman Wight. Began history of Church, called "The Book of John Whitmer," which spanned years 1831-38. Appointed to accompany Oliver Cowdery to Jackson County, Missouri, with revelations for printing November 1831. Left Ohio 20 November 1831, stopped in Winchester, Indiana, for week, and arrived in

Jackson County, Missouri, 5 January 1832. Member of Literary and United firms. Married Sarah Jackson 10 February 1833 in Jackson County, Missouri. Five children: Nancy Jane, John Oliver, Sarah Elizabeth, Jacob David Jackson, and Alexander Peter Jefferson. Ordained counselor to David Whitmer as one of presidents of Church in Missouri 8 July 1834. Chosen to receive "endowment" in Kirtland Temple 23 June 1834. Left Clay County, Missouri, for Kirtland 28 April 1835; arrived 17 May 1835. Appointed editor of *Messenger and Advocate* in Kirtland 18 May 1835, contrary to his wishes. Edited publication June 1835-March 1836. Participated in dedication of Kirtland Temple 1836. Paid personal property tax on one horse and one cow in 1836 in Kirtland. Returned to Clay County, Missouri, by 25 July 1836. In 1836-37, together with W.W. Phelps, began to administer affairs of Church in Missouri independent of high council. With W.W. Phelps, located gathering place at Far West, Missouri; identified temple site; and purchased property in own names with Church funds—all without approval of Church high council or membership. (These actions created much confusion and difficulty for Church in Missouri and finally resulted in Whitmer's excommunication.) Held title to hundreds of acres in Caldwell County, Missouri. Despite difficulties, upheld as counselor to David Whitmer November 1837. Rejected 5 February 1838. Excommunicated 10 March 1838 at Far West, Missouri. Left Far West 19 June 1838 and resided in Richmond until after Saints were forced out of Missouri 1839. Recognized as excellent farmer and stock raiser. Resided in Far West, Missouri, until death, 11 July 1878.[2]

Section 16

Date.   June 1829.

Place.   Fayette, Seneca County, New York.

Historical Note.   See Historical Note for section 14.[1]

Publication Note.   Section 16 was first published as chapter 14 in the Book of Commandments in 1833.

Biographical Note.   Peter Whitmer, Jr.

Son of Peter Whitmer and Mary Musselman. Born 27 September 1809 at Fayette, Seneca County, New York. One of Eight Witnesses of Book of Mormon June 1829. Baptized by Oliver Cowdery and ordained elder by 9 June 1830. Called by revelation with others September 1830 to preach gospel to Lamanites. Party of four left New York latter part of October 1830. Arrived in Kirtland, Ohio, area by 1 November 1830; there made numerous converts. Arrived in Independence, Jackson County, Missouri, 13 December 1830; there employed as tailor. Left Missouri for Ohio after 4 August 1831. Arrived in Ohio 1 September 1831; there suffered few weeks of illness. Attended conferences of Church in Hiram and Portage, Ohio, 11 and 21 October 1831. Ordained high priest 25 October 1831. At conference said, "My beloved brethren ever since I have had an acquaintance with the writing of God, I have eternity with perfect confidence." Attended conferences in Hiram, Ohio, November 1831; there appointed to have inheritance in Zion for assisting Joseph Smith in bringing forth sacred writings, particularly revelations. Returned to Independence, Missouri, by 24 August 1832. Married Vashti Higley 14 October 1832 in Jackson County, Missouri. Ceremony performed by Oliver Cowdery. Three children: Emma, Kate, and Vashti P.; last child born 20 May 1837, after Whitmer's death. Appointed to receive "endowment" in Kirtland Temple 23 June 1834. Arrived in Kirtland before 6 January 1836; appointed and set apart as high councilor for Missouri (to fill vacancy occasioned by death of brother Christian). Returned to Clay County, Missouri, by September 1836. Died of tuberculosis near Liberty, Clay County, Missouri, 22 September 1836.[2]

Section 17

Date.   June 1829.

Place.   Fayette, Seneca County, New York.

Historical Note.   In March 1829, before Joseph Smith became acquainted with Oliver Cowdery, the Lord revealed the following promise: "And the testimony of three witnesses will I send forth of my word" (D&C 5:15). During the translation the Prophet and his scribe discovered Moroni's instruction to the modern translator that he would be privileged to "show the plates unto three."[1] The Prophet noted, "Almost immediately after we had made this discovery, it occurred to Oliver Cowdery, David Whitmer, and the aforesaid Martin Harris . . . that they would have me inquire of the Lord to know if they might not obtain of him the privilege to be these three special witnesses."[2] Accordingly the Prophet inquired of the Lord and received section 17.[3] David Whitmer stated that the viewing of the plates occurred about the end of June 1829.[4]

Of this significant event, Oliver Cowdery later said,

I beheld with my eyes. And handled with my hands the gold plates from which it was translated. I also beheld the Interpreters. That book is true. Sidney Rigdon did not write it. Mr Spaulding did not write it. I wrote it myself as it fell from the Lips of the prophet. It contains the everlasting gosple, and came in fulfillment of the revelations of of John where he Says he seen an angle come with the everlasting gosple to preach to every nation tunge and people. It contains principles of Salvation. And if you will walk by its light and obey it[s] precepts you will be Saved in the everlasting Kingdom of God.[5]

David Whitmer made the following statement concerning the viewing of the plates:

I was plowing in the field one morning and Joseph and Oliver came along with a revelation stating that I was to be one of the witnesses to the Book of Mormon. I got over the fence and we went out into the woods near by, and sat down on a log and talked awhile. We then kneeled down and Joseph prayed. We then got up and sat on a log and were talking, when all at once a light came down from above us and encircled us for quite a little distance around; and the angel stood before us. He was dressed in white, and spoke and called me by name and said "Blessed is he that keepeth His commandments." This is all that I heard the angel say. A table was set before us and on it the records were placed. The Records of the Nephites, from which the Book of Mormon was translated, the breast plates, the Ball or Directors, the Sword of Laban and other plates. While we were viewing them the voice of God spoke out of heaven saying that the Book was true and the translation correct.[6]

Martin Harris is recorded as saying, "as many of the plates as Joseph Smith translated I handled with my hands, plate after plate."[7] He also affirmed, "The angel did show to me the plates containing the Book of Mormon."[8]

Publication Note. Section 17 was first published in the *Messenger and Advocate* (September 1835), and was included as section 42 in the 1835 edition of the Doctrine and Covenants. The 1835 edition was available for purchase about mid-September 1835.

Section 18

Date.   June 1829 (before 14 June).

On 14 June 1829 Oliver Cowdery addressed a letter to Hyrum Smith from Fayette, New York, which contained portions of section 18. (Note particularly verses 10-13 and 42.) The letter, included below, verifies that Section 18 was received before the date of the letter:

> Fayette June the 14 1829
> Dear Brother Hyrum
> These few lines I write unto you feeling anxious for your steadfastness in the great cause of which you have been called to advocate and also feeling it a duty to write you at every opportunity remember the worth of souls is great in the sight of God behold the Lord your God suffered death upon the cross after the manner of the flesh wherefore he suffered the pains of all men that all men might repent and come unto him and he hath risen again from the dead that he might bring all men unto him upon conditions of repentance and how great is his joy in the soul that repents and behold he commandeth all men everywhere to repent and baptized and not only men but women children which have arrived to the years of accountibility Stir up the minds of our friends against the time we come unto you that then they may be willing to take upon them the name of Christ for that is the name by which they shall be called at the Last day and if we know not the name by which we are called I fear we shall be found on the hand I have many things to write but if the Lord will I shall shortly come unto Zion Please tell Mrs. Rockwell that those shoes fit well and I received them as from the Lord tell him that whatever he does in the cause of Zion he will in no way loose his reward. Now may the grace of God the Father and of our Lord Jesus Christ be and abide with you all Amen this from your Bro. Oliver A fellow labourer in the cause of Zion
>
> Oliver Cowdery
>
> PS give my love to all those who anxiously inquire after my property &c[1]

Place.   Fayette, Seneca County, New York.

Historical Note. This revelation, received for Oliver Cowdery and David Whitmer, explains the eternal worth of the human soul, the importance of the Atonement, and the obligation of the Saints to preach the gospel. It also states that twelve apostles will be called and that Oliver Cowdery and David Whitmer will choose them. In fulfillment of this revelation, the twelve apostles were chosen in February 1835 by the Three Witnesses of the Book of Mormon.[2]

Note verse 9 which designates Oliver Cowdery and David Whitmer apostles.[3]

Publication Note. Section 18 was first published as chapter 15 of the Book of Commandments in 1833.

Section 19

Date.   March 1830.

Place.   Manchester, Ontario County, New York.

Historical Note. When the translation of the Book of Mormon was nearly completed, Joseph Smith, Oliver Cowdery, and Martin Harris solicited Egbert B. Grandin, manager and principal owner of the *Wayne Sentinel*, a newspaper printed in Palmyra, to print the manuscript. Grandin declined the request as did Thurlow Weed of Rochester when confronted with the proposition. The Prophet and his associates finally prevailed upon E.B. Grandin, and Martin Harris later signed a mortgage (25 August 1829) that bound Harris to pay Grandin $3,000 within eighteen months for the printing of 5,000 copies of the Book of Mormon or forfeit sufficient of his 240-acre Palmyra farm to pay the $3,000.[1] In March 1830, prior to the completion of the printing of the Book of Mormon, a group of townspeople near Palmyra voted not to purchase the book if it were published. Fearful that he might lose his farm if the book did not sell, Harris approached the Prophet Joseph Smith regarding the matter, and requested a revelation. Joseph Knight, Sr., remembering the occasion, made the following remarks:

> [Martin Harris] Came to us and after Compliments he says, "The Books will not sell for no Body wants them.

Joseph says, "I think they will sell well." Says he, "I want a Commandment [revelation]." "Why," says Joseph, "fulfill what you have got." "But," says he, "I must have a Commandment." Joseph put him off. But he insisted three or four times he must have a Commandment. [The following day] he got up and said he must have a Commandment to Joseph and went home. And along in the after part of the Day Joseph and Oliver Received a Commandment which is in Book of Covenants [section 19].[2]

Publication Note.   Section 19 was first published as chapter 16 in the Book of Commandments in 1833.

Section 20

Date.   April 1830 (June, as per Book of Commandments).

Place.   (Fayette, Seneca County, New York, as per Book of Commandments).

Historical Note.   Known as the "Articles and Covenants of the Church of Christ," section 20 served as a constitution for the restored Church.[1] The revelation was at once a formal declaration of belief as well as a written *modus operandi* for administering the affairs of the divine organization.[2] Authored by Joseph Smith and Oliver Cowdery, section 20 soon became a standard against which proper conduct and procedure were measured. The writing of this revelation was begun sometime in 1829 but apparently not completed until *after* 6 April 1830.[3] Section 20 was first presented to the Church membership for sustaining vote on 9 June 1830 at the first conference of the Church in Fayette, New York.[4]

The "Articles and Covenants" were read aloud to the congregation almost as a routine requirement at the early Church conferences. But as Church leaders became more conversant with the revelation, an entire reading became less frequent. The continual reference to the revelation, evidenced throughout Church records during the lifetime of Joseph Smith, served to teach proper Church policy and procedure to leader and layman alike.[5]

Publication Note.   Section 20 was first published in the *Evening and Morning Star* (June 1832) and was included as chapter 24 in the Book of Commandments in 1833.[6]

Section 21

Date.   6 April 1830.

Place.   Fayette, Seneca County, New York (Manchester, New York, as per Book of Commandments).

Historical Note.   The Church was officially organized on Tuesday, 6 April 1830, at Fayette, New York. The six charter members were Joseph Smith, Oliver Cowdery, Hyrum Smith, David Whitmer, Samuel H. Smith, and Peter Whitmer, Jr.[1] The name of the new church was "The Church of Christ."

The state law under which the "Church of Christ" was incorporated was entitled "An Act to provide for the Incorporation of Religious Societies," passed 5 April 1813. The law, which stipulated that a certificate of incorporation be recorded with the county clerk, designated that "any number of discreet persons of their church . . . not less than three, nor exceeding nine" could "transact all affairs relative to the temporalities thereof."[2]

On 3 May 1834 the name of the Church was changed to "The Church of the Latter Day Saints";[3] and on 26 April 1838, eight years after the Church's organization, the final designation of the Church was given by revelation: "The Church of Jesus Christ of Latter-day Saints."[4] Concerning the organization of the Church, Joseph Knight, Sr., wrote,

> Now in the Spring of 1830 I went with my Team and took Joseph out to Manchester to his Father. When we was on our way he told me that there must be a Church formed But did not tell when . . . . I stayed a few Days wating for some Books to Be Bound. Joseph said there must Be a Church Biltup . . . . On the sixth Day of April 1830 he Begun the Church with six members and received the following Revelation Book of Covenants Page 177 [section 21]. They all kneeled down and prayed and

Joseph gave them instructions how to Bild up the Church and exorted them to Be faithfull in all things for this is the work of God.[5]

Publication Note.   Section 21 was first published as chapter 22 in the Book of Commandments in 1833.

Section 22

Date.   April 1830.

Place.   Manchester, Ontario County, New York.

Historical Note.   Initially considered part of the "Articles and Covenants" of the Church, section 22 was given to Joseph Smith in answer to the question of whether believers who had received baptism in other churches, should again be baptized. In 1873 Orson Pratt recalled the historical setting of this revelation,

> In the early days of this Church there were certain persons, belonging to the Baptist denomination, very moral and no doubt as good people as you could find anywhere, who came, saying they believed in the Book of Mormon, and that they had been baptized into the Baptist Church, and they wished to come into our Church. The Prophet Joseph had not, at that time, particularly inquired in relation to this matter, but he did inquire, and received a revelation from the Lord [section 22] .... These Baptists had to be re-baptized: there was no other way to get into this Church.[2]

Publication Note.   Section 22 was first published as chapter 23 in the Book of Commandments in 1833.[3]

Section 23

Date. April 1830 (6 April, according to the Book of Commandments).

Place. Manchester, Ontario County, New York.

Historical Note. In the Book of Commandments section 23 was printed as five separate revelations (i.e., chapters 17, 18, 19, 20, and 21).

Publication Note. Section 23 was first published in the Book of Commandments in 1833.

Biographical Note. Samuel Harrison Smith.

Son of Joseph Smith and Lucy Mack. Born 13 March 1808 at Tunbridge, Orange County, Vermont. Baptized 25 May 1829. One of Eight Witnesses to Book of Mormon June 1829. Ordained elder 9 June 1830. Traditionally recognized as first missionary of Church. Sent with Orson Pratt to preach in Kirtland, Ohio; arrived 27 February 1831. Ordained high priest 3 June 1831. Returned to Ohio September 1831. Appointed to serve mission to "eastern lands" with William E. McLellan 25 October 1831. This mission was short-lived because of McLellan's "murmuring." Called with Orson Hyde to preach in "eastern countries" 25 January 1832. On this eleven-month mission baptized sixty converts. Attended School of Prophets in Kirtland. Assisted in laying foundation stones for Kirtland Temple July 1833. Worked on Kirtland Temple. Member of Kirtland high council 1834-38. Married Mary Bailey 13 August 1834. Four Children: Susanna Bailey, Mary Bailey, Samuel Harrison Bailey, and Lucy Bailey. Owned land in Kirtland and paid personal property tax on two cows 1834-35. Participated in Kirtland Temple dedication 1836. Served mission to New York in summer of 1836. Member of and owned stock in Kirtland Safety Society. Moved to Far West, Missouri, March 1838. Later settled at Marrowbone in Daviess County. Participated in Battle of Crooked River October 1838. Located in Quincy, Illinois, 1839. Later moved onto George Miller's farm at Macomb, McDonough County, Illinois. Moved to Nauvoo about 1840. Called to Presiding Bishopric of Church January 1841. Called as bishop of Nauvoo Ward. Elected alderman in City of Nauvoo February 1841. Member of Nauvoo Legion. Served mission in Scott County, Illinois, 1841. Married Levira Clark of Geneva, Scott County, Illinois, 1841. Three children: Levira Annette Clark, Louisa Clark, and Lucy Jane Clark. Initiated into Masonry 9 April 1942. Moved to Plymouth, Illinois, in fall of 1842. Received endowment 17 December 1843. Died 30 July 1844 at Nauvoo, Hancock County, Illinois.[1]

Section 24

Date.   July 1830.

Place.   Harmony, Susquehanna County, Pennsylvania.

Historical Note.   On 9 June 1830 the first conference of the Church was convened in the home of Peter Whitmer, Sr., in Fayette, New York. Immediately after the conference the Prophet and others left for Harmony, Pennsylvania. Shortly after arriving home in Harmony, Joseph Smith, Emma, and a few others went to visit the Knights in Colesville, New York, where many believers were baptized. During this visit the Prophet was twice arrested for being "disorderly" in preaching but both times was acquitted.[1] Escaping his enemies in Broome and Chenango counties, the Prophet managed to arrive home in Harmony only to leave to visit the Knights again and confirm some who had been baptized earlier. Upon returning once more to his small farm in Harmony, the Prophet received section 24.

   During this period there were only three branches of the Church: Manchester, consisting primarily of the Smith family; Fayette, consisting primarily of the Whitmer family; and Colesville, consisting primarily of the Knight family. (See map.)

Publication Note.   Section 24 was first published as chapter 25 in the Book of Commandments in 1833.

Section 25

Date.   July 1830.

Place.   Harmony, Susquehanna County, Pennsylvania.

Historical Note.   Section 25 is a revelation given through Joseph Smith for his wife, Emma. Just prior to Joseph's receiving this revelation, both Joseph and Emma suffered much humiliation and harassment from non-Mormons in Chenango and Broome counties in New York. Herein Emma Smith is counseled not to "murmur," designated an "elect lady," and requested to make a selection of "sacred hymns."

Writing of his affection for Emma twelve years later, the Prophet said,

> What unspeakable delight, and what transports of joy swelled my bosom, when I took by the hand, on that night, my beloved Emma—she that was my wife, even the wife of my youth, and the choice of my heart. Many were the reverberations of my mind when I contemplated for a moment the many scenes we had been called to pass through, the fatigues and the toils, the sorrows and sufferings, and the joys and consolations, from time to time, which had strewed our paths and crowned our board. Oh what a commingling of thought filled my mind for the moment, again she is here, even in the seventh trouble—undaunted, firm, and unwavering—unchangeable, affectionate Emma![1]

On 30 April 1832, members of the Literary Firm (the organization responsible for Church publications) met in Independence, Missouri, and directed William W. Phelps "to correct and print the hymns which had been selected by Emma Smith in fulfilment of the revelation."[2] But the destruction of the Church printing press in Independence delayed the printing of the hymns, and Church leaders in Kirtland renewed efforts to print the work in September 1835. On 14 September 1835 it was "decided that Sister Emma proceed to make a [more complete] selection of sacred hymns according to revelation, and that President W. W. Phelps be appointed to revise and arrange them for printing."[3] The Church hymnal, which appeared about February 1836,[4] contained a preface, apparently written by Phelps, and ninety hymns. Only the words were printed; no music was included. Forty-two of the hymns had appeared earlier in Church periodicals. Thirty-four were authored by Mormons: twenty-six by W. W. Phelps, three by Parley P. Pratt, one by Thomas B. Marsh and Parley P. Pratt, and one each by Eliza R. Snow, Edward Partridge, Philo Dibble, and William C. Gregg.[5] On 7 October 1839 a conference of the Church voted to reject a small collection of hymns published by David W. Rogers in New York in 1838. Twenty days later the same conference authorized Emma Smith to prepare a second edition of the 1835 hymnal. Although Brigham Young, Parley P. Pratt, and John Taylor published a hymn book for the Saints in England in 1840, the second official Church hymnal, selected by Emma Smith, was published in Nauvoo in 1841 under the direction of Ebenezer Robinson. Plans were under way for a third edition of Emma's hymn book in early 1843. She advertised in the *Times and Seasons* that "persons having Hymns adapted to the worship of the Church of Jesus Christ of Latter Day Saints, [were] requested to hand them, or send them to Emma Smith, immediately."[6] There is no evidence, however, that this third edition was ever printed.

Publication Note.   Section 25 was first published as chapter 26 in the Book of Commandments in 1833.

Biographical Note.   Emma Hale Smith Bidamon.

Daughter of Isaac Hale and Elizabeth Lewis. Born 10 July 1804 at Harmony, Susquehanna County, Pennsylvania. Married Joseph Smith, Jr., 18 January 1827 at South Bainbridge, Chenango County, New York. Nine Children: Alvin, Thaddeus, Louisa, Joseph, Frederick Granger Williams, Alexander Hale, Don Carlos, male child, and David Hyrum. Adopted twins: Joseph and Julia Murdock. Assisted as scribe in translation of Book of Mormon. Baptized 28 June 1830 by Oliver Cowdery. Given revelation July 1830; instructed to prepare hymn book for Church. Confirmed member of Church about 1 August 1830. Moved from Harmony to Fayette, New York, September 1830. Moved with husband to Kirtland, Ohio, January 1831. Resided in Hiram, Ohio, September 1831-September 1832. Moved back to Kirtland, Ohio, September 1832; resided there until 1838. Moved to Far West, Missouri, 1838, arriving in March. Located temporarily near Quincy, Illinois, 1839 after Mormon expulsion from Missouri. Moved to Nauvoo, Illinois, in summer of 1839. Appointed first president of Female Relief Society 17 March 1842. Sealed to Joseph Smith 28 May 1843 and endowed before 28 September 1843. Did not migrate west with main body of Saints 1847. Married Major Lewis C. Bidamon 23 December 1847. No children. Died at Nauvoo, Hancock County, Illinois, 30 April 1879.[7]

Section 26

Date.   July 1830.

Place.   Harmony, Susquehanna County, Pennsylvania.

Historical Note.   During the month of July 1830, Joseph Smith began to arrange and copy the revelations that he had received thus far. This he did with the assistance of John Whitmer, who was residing with Joseph and Emma in Harmony.[1] Reference is made in section 26 to the "next conference," which was held 26 September 1830 in Fayette, New York.

Publication Note.   Section 26 was first published as chapter 27 in the Book of Commandments in 1833.

Section 27

Date.   August 1830.

According to Newel Knight, verses 1-4 were received about 1 August 1830, but the Book of Commandments indicates that they were received 4 September. Both Newel Knight and the 1835 edition of the Doctrine and Covenants record that verses 5-18 were received in September 1830.

Place.   Harmony, Susquehanna County, Pennsylvania.

Historical Note.   During the first week of August 1830, Newel Knight and his wife went to Harmony to visit Joseph and Emma Smith. Because neither Emma nor Sally Knight had been confirmed members of the Church, the two couples decided to attend to that ordinance and partake of the sacrament.[1] Remembering this occasion, Newel Knight recorded,

> Brother Joseph set out to procure some wine for the occasion, but he had gone only a short distance, when he was met by a heavenly messenger, and received the first four verses of the revelation. . . .
> In obedience to this revelation we prepared some wine of our own make, and held our meeting, consisting of only five persons namely, Joseph Smith and wife, John Whitmer, and myself and wife. We partook of the sacrament, after which we confirmed the two sisters into the Church, and spent the evening in a glorious manner. The Spirit of the Lord was poured out upon us. We praised the God of Israel and rejoiced exceedingly.[2]

Newel Knight further stated that section 27 was originally two separate revelations: the first four verses were received in Harmony, Pennsylvania, and the remaining verses were received in Fayette, New York.[3]

Publication Note.   Verses 1-4 of section 27 were first published in the *Evening and Morning Star* (March 1833) and, later in the same year, were included in the Book of Commandments.[4] The entire revelation was published in the 1835 edition of the Doctrine and Covenants.

Section 28

Date.   September 1830.

Place.   Fayette, Seneca County, New York.

Historical Note.   No longer enjoying the protection of Isaac Hale, and concerned about their personal safety, the Prophet and his family determined to leave Harmony, Pennsylvania permanently. Having learned of the persecution against Joseph Smith in Harmony, Peter Whitmer, Sr., invited the Prophet and Emma to come and live with his family in Fayette. About the last of August 1830 Newel Knight took his team and wagon to Harmony to move Joseph, Emma, and their family to Fayette. They arrived about 1 September 1830.[1]

Shortly after arriving in Fayette, the Prophet became greatly distressed over Hiram Page's claim to certain revelations, which he allegedly had received by means of a seerstone. Newel Knight described the incident in his journal:

> [Page] had managed to get up some discussions of feeling among the brethren by giving revelations concerning the government of the Church and other matters, which he claimed to have received through the medium of a stone he possessed. . . . Even Oliver Cowdery and the Whitmer family had given heed to them . . . . Joseph was perplexed and scarcely knew how to meet this new

exigency. That night I occupied the same room that he did and the greater part of the night was spent in prayer and supplication. After much labor with these brethren they were convinced of their error, and confessed the same, renouncing [Page's] revelations as not being of God.[2]

Section 28, received prior to the second conference of the Church (26 September 1830), came in response to the Hiram Page difficulty. Among other matters, this revelation called Oliver Cowdery to take a mission to the American Indians, and clearly implied that the New Jerusalem would be located "on the borders by the Lamanites" (i.e., Missouri).[3]

Publication Note.   Section 28 was first published as chapter 30 in the Book of Commandments in 1833.

Biographical Note.   Hiram Page.

Born in Vermont 1800. Studied medicine at young age. Traveled considerably in state of New York and Canada as physician. Located in Seneca county, New York; there became acquainted with Whitmer family. Married Catherine Whitmer 10 November 1825. Nine Children: John, Elizabeth, Philander, Mary, Peter, Nancy, Hiram, Oliver, and Kate. One of Eight Witnesses to Book of Mormon 1829. Baptized 11 April 1830 by Oliver Cowdery. Ordained teacher by 9 June 1830. Received false revelations through use of seerstone in fall of 1830, deceiving many of Whitmer family. Moved to Kirtland, Ohio, 1831. On 3 June 1831 listed as teacher. Later ordained high priest, probably in Missouri. Moved to Jackson County, Missouri, 1832. With others attempted to settle difficulties between Mormon and non-Mormons in Jackson County, Missouri, 1833. Moved with family to Clay County, Missouri; resided there until 1836. Located in Far West, Missouri; there owned 120 acres. Severed connection with Church in 1838 when members of Whitmer family were excommunicated. Settled in Ray County, Missouri, after leaving Church. Located on farm near Excelsior Springs. Died 12 August 1852 near Excelsior Springs, Ray County, Missouri.[4]

Section 29

Date.   September 1830 (on or about 26 September, according to Newel Knight Journal).

Place.   Fayette, Seneca County, New York.

Historical Note.   The headnote in the Book of Commandments states that section 29 is, "a Revelation to the church of Christ, given in the presence of six elders, in Fayette, New York 1830." The minutes of the second conference of the Church (26 September 1830), found in the "Far West Record," list six elders present in addition to Joseph Smith: Oliver Cowdery, David Whitmer, John Whitmer, Peter Whitmer, Samuel H. Smith, and Thomas B. Marsh. These six men are undoubtedly the same six referred to in the headnote. The second conference of the Church was held in the home of Peter Whitmer, Sr.[1]

Drawing on biblical and Book of Mormon passages, the message of this revelation is doctrinal and eschatological.

Publication Note.   Section 29 was first published in the *Evening and Morning Star* (September 1832) and was included as chapter 29 in the Book of Commandments in 1833.

Section 30

Date.   September 1830 (before 26 September, according to "Far West Record," p. 2).

Place.   Fayette, Seneca County, New York.

Historical Note.   Section 30, given to David, Peter, Jr., and John Whitmer at Fayette, New York, was originally three separate revelations in the Book of Commandments. Among other matters, section 30 called Peter Whitmer, Jr., to accompany Oliver Cowdery on his mission to the Lamanites.

Publication Note.   Section 30 was first published as chapters 31, 32, and 33 in the Book of Commandments in 1833.

Biographical Note.   Philip Burroughs.

Son of Jonathan Burroughs. Born in New Hampshire about 1795. Elected "overseer of the highways and fence viewer" for Junius, Seneca County, New York, April 1819. Residing in Seneca Falls, Seneca County, New York, 1830. Church meeting held in home September 1830. Apparently, with his wife, member of Church.[1]

Section 31

Date.   September 1830.

Place.   (Fayette, Seneca County, New York, according to Manuscript History of the Church).

Historical Note.   Thomas B. Marsh became acquainted with Oliver Cowdery in fall of 1829, while the Book of Mormon was being printed. Upon learning that a new church had been organized, Marsh moved his family to Palmyra, New York, in September 1830. During the month of September, Marsh was baptized by David Whitmer in Cayuga Lake and ordained an elder at Whitmer's home in Fayette.[1]

Section 31 instructs Thomas Marsh to preach the gospel and is named a spiritual "physician unto the church."

Publication Note.   Section 31 was first published as chapter 34 in the Book of Commandments in 1833.

Biographical Note.   Thomas Baldwin Marsh.

Son of James Marsh and Molly Law. Born 1 November 1799 or 1800,[2] in Acton, Middlesex County, Massachusetts. Married Elizabeth Godkin 1 November 1820. One known child: James G. Marsh. Baptized by David Whitmer 3 September 1830 in New York. Ordained elder September 1830. Revelation received for Marsh September 1830 names him "physician to the Church." Ordained high priest by Lyman Wight 6 June 1831. Appointed to travel to Missouri with Ezra Thayer. Thayer slow preparing to leave; Marsh left with Selah J. Griffin. Returned to Kirtland January 1832. Appointed to preach in East with Ezra Thayer 25 January 1832. Led small group of Saints to Jackson County, Missouri, in fall of 1832, arriving November 1832. Appointed inheritance of thirty acres on Big Blue River in Jackson County.

Taught school in Lafayette County, Missouri. Chosen to receive "endowment" in Kirtland 23 June 1834. Appointed member of Clay County, Missouri, high council 8 July 1834. Returned to Kirtland, Ohio, January 1835 in company with Edward Partridge. Ordained one of twelve apostles 26 April 1835. Participated in dedication of Kirtland Temple 1836. Appointed with Elisha Groves to collect money for poor Saints in Missouri 1836; successful in obtaining $1,450. Appointed, with David W. Patten, as president *pro tem* of Church in Missouri 5 February 1838. Owned 320 acres of land in Caldwell County, Misouri. Appointed sole proprietor of Church printing establishment in Far West, Missouri, 23 June 1838. Became disaffected in fall of 1838. Signed affidavit against Joseph Smith October 1838. Excommunicated for apostasy 17 March 1839. Remained in Missouri eighteen years; taught biblical geography. After death of wife, traveled to Florence, Nebraska, and sought out Church leaders. Rebaptized 16 July 1857 in Florence, Nebraska. Arrived in Utah September 1857. Return to Church approved by Church leaders in Utah 6 September 1857. Married to Hannah Adams 4 October 1857. Settled in Spanish Fork, Utah, 1859; there listed as high priest. Taught school in Spanish Fork. Reordained elder 11 March 1859. Ordained high priest by November 1861. Received endowment and sealed to Hannah Adams in Endowment House 1 November 1862. Moved to Ogden, Utah. Died January 1866.[3]

Section 32

Date. October 1830 (before 17 October, see Historical Note below).

Place. (Probably Manchester, Ontario County, New York).[1]

Historical Note. Section 28 mentioned that Oliver Cowdery was to "go unto the Lamanites and preach my gospel." In section 30 Peter Whitmer, Jr., was told to take his "journey with your brother Oliver...[and] build up my church among the Lamanites." As these two brethren were preparing to leave for the West, it was asked if others could accompany them on this mission. In response to this request, Joseph Smith inquired of the Lord and received section 32. As indicated in the revelation, Parley P. Pratt and Ziba Peterson were to accompany Oliver Cowdery and Peter Whitmer, Jr.[2] These fearless missionaries, who departed after 17 October 1830, signed their names to the following statements:

Manchester, New York, Oct. 17, 1830

I Oliver, being commanded by the Lord God, to go forth unto the Lamanites, to proclaim glad tidings of great joy unto them, by presenting unto them the fullness of the Gospel, of the only begotten Son of God; and also, to rear up a pillar as a witness where the temple of God shall be built, in the glorious new Jerusalem; and having certain brothers with me, who are called of GOD TO ASSIST ME, whose names are Parley, and Peter and Ziba, do therefore most solumnly covenant with God that I will walk humbly before him, and do this business, and this glorious work according as he shall direct me by the Holy Ghost; ever praying for mine and their prosperity, and deliverance from bonds, and from imprisonment, and whatsoever may befall us, with all patience and faith. Amen

Oliver Cowdery

We, the undersigned, being called and commanded by the Lord God, to accompany our brother Oliver Cowdery to go to the Lamanites and to assist in the above mentioned glorious work and business, we do, therefore, most solumnly covenant before God, that we will assist him faithfully in this thing, by giving heed to all his words and advise, which is, or shall be given him by the spirit of truth, ever praying with all prayer and supplication, for our and his prosperity, and our deliverance from bonds, and imprisonments and whatsoever may come upon us, with all patience and faith. Amen.

Signed in the presence of Joseph Smith jun.,

David Whitmer

Parley P. Pratt
Ziba Peterson
Peter Whitmer[3]

This preaching effort, known as the "Lamanite mission," significantly extended the western boundaries of Mormonism. Although the purpose of the mission was to take the Book of

Mormon message to the American Indians situated west of Missouri, ironically, its success was in the Western Reserve among whites.[4]

Publication Note.   Section 32 was first published as section 54 in the 1835 edition of the Doctrine and Covenants.

Biographical Note.   Ziba Peterson.[5]

Baptized 18 April 1830 by Oliver Cowdery. Ordained elder before 9 June 1830. Appointed to accompany Oliver Cowdery, Peter Whitmer, Jr., and Parley P. Pratt on the Lamanite Mission to Missouri in October 1830; left New York late October 1830. Stopped in Kirtland, Ohio, area two to three weeks; baptized several converts. Arrived in Independence, Missouri, 13 December 1830; immediately found employment. Accompanied by Peter Whitmer to preach to Indians across Missouri River 8 April 1831. Accompanied Oliver Cowdery in preaching to whites residing in Lafayette County, Missouri, April 1831. Reprimanded for impropriety 1 August 1831. Made confession for inappropriate actions 4 August 1831. On 11 August 1831 married Rebecca Hooper (born 1809 in Indiana), who was converted in Lafayette County, Missouri. Known children: Emily, Charles, Cynthia, Cornelius, Mary, Thomas, A. S. (female child), and George Washington. Children all born in Missouri. Reordained elder 2 October 1832 by Lyman Wight. Became disaffected before May 1833. Delivered over to buffetings of Satan 25 June 1833. Left Lafayette County, Missouri, for California 3 May 1848. Arrived in mining town later known as Hangtown November 1848. Sheriff of Hangtown (later known as Placerville) 1848-49. Died in Placerville, Eldorado County, California, after January and before June 1849. Wife and children moved to Sonoma, Sonoma County, California, by 1850. Widow, Rebecca, died 21 April 1896 in Yountville, Napa County, California.[6]

Biographical Note.   Parley Parker Pratt.

Son of Jared Pratt and Charity Dickinson. Born 12 April 1807 in Burlington, Otsego County, New York. Married Thankful Halsey 9 September 1827. One child: Parley Parker. Baptized and ordained elder September 1830. Appointed to travel with Oliver Cowdery, Peter Whitmer, Jr., and Ziba Peterson on Lamanite Mission to Missouri October 1830; left New York late October 1830 and stopped in Mentor, Ohio, about 1 November 1830. At Mentor presented Sidney Rigdon copy of Book of Mormon. After Rigdon's baptism, 14 November 1830, continued with Lamanite missionaries to Missouri, arriving in Independence 13 December 1830. Returned to Kirtland, Ohio, before 1 March 1831. Called with others to preach to Shakers

March 1831. Ordained high priest 3 June 1831. Called to travel with brother, Orson, to Missouri June 1831. Resided in Jackson County, Missouri, 1831-33. Presided over School of Elders in Jackson County, Missouri, 1833. Appointed President of Branch Number Eight in Jackson County 11 September 1833. Sent to Kirtland with Lyman Wight 1 January 1834 to counsel with Church leaders in Ohio concerning Saints' regaining Jackson County properties. Arrived in Kirtland before 24 February 1834. Traveled with Joseph Smith and others to New York state February-March 1834 to recruit for Zion's Camp. Member of Zion's Camp 1834. Appointed to receive endowment in Kirtland 23 June 1834. Appointed member of Clay County high council 8 July 1834. Ordained apostle 21 February 1835. Mission to Pennsylvania, New York, and New England 1835. Participated in dedication of Kirtland Temple 1836. Served mission to Toronto, Canada, 1836. Wife, Thankful, died 25 March 1837. Married Mary Ann Frost 9 May 1837. Four children: Nathan, Olivia, Susan, and Moroni. Mission to New York City 1837-38; there published *Voice of Warning* 1837. Moved to Far West, Missouri, arriving 7 May 1838. Arrested for murder and treason November 1838. Incarcerated in Richmond and Columbia, Missouri, November 1838-July 1839. No conviction. Published pamphlet on Missouri persecutions 1839. Left for mission to England with others of twelve apostles 29 August 1839. Arrived in England 6 April 1840. First editor of *The Latter-day Saints' Millennial Star* (Manchester, England). Returned to America for family July 1840. Arrived England 17 October 1840; resumed editorship of *Millennial Star*. Returned to Nauvoo from England 7 February 1843. Sealed to Elizabeth Brotherton 24 July 1843. No children. Mission to East in fall of 1843. Returned to Nauvoo by November 1843. Received endowment 2 December 1843. Member of Council of Fifty 11 March 1844. Campaigned for Joseph Smith's candidacy for president of United States in spring of 1844. Arrived in Nauvoo 10 July 1844, after Prophet's death. Sealed to Mary Wood 9 September 1844. Four children: Helaman, Cornelia, Mary, and Mathoni. Sealed to Hannahette Snively 2 November 1844. Three children: Alma, Lucy, and Henriette. Sealed to Belinda Marden 20 November 1844. Five children: Nephi, Belinda, Abinadi, Lehi, Isabella. On 1 December 1844 appointed to go to New York City, edit *The Prophet*, supervise immigration, and assume presidency of all eastern branches of church. Returned to Nauvoo 26 August 1845. Sealed to Sarah Huston 15 October 1845. Four children: Julia, Mormon, Teancum, and Sarah. Sealed to Phoebe Sopher 8 February 1846. Three children: Mosiah, Omner, and Phoebe. Moved from Nauvoo February 1846, and located family in Council Bluffs. Named Mount Pisgah, Iowa, 1846. Sealed to Martha Monks 28 April 1847. One child: Ether. Sealed to Ann Agatha Walker 28 April 1847. Five children: Agatha, Malona, Marion, Moroni, and Eveline. Called again to England 1847. Moved to Great Salt Lake Valley in fall of 1847. Remained in Utah until 1851. Assisted in forming Constitution of Provisional Government of Deseret 1849. Received commission from governor and legislative assembly to explore southern Utah 1850. Headed company of fifty men. Called to preside over Pacific

Islands and South America 1851. Left Salt Lake City 16 March 1851, arrived in San Francisco July 1851. Sailed for Valparaiso, Chile, 5 September 1851 to preach gospel. Arrived 8 November 1851. Returned to San Francisco 21 May 1852. Returned to Salt Lake City 18 October 1852. Sealed to Keziah Downes 27 December 1853. No children. Appointed to second mission to California 6 April 1854. Left Salt Lake City 5 May 1854. Arrived in San Francisco 2 July 1854. Returned to Salt Lake City 18 August 1855. Sealed to Eleanor J. Macomb 14 November 1855. No children. Visited eastern branches of Church December 1856-March 1857. Murdered 13 May 1857 in Van Buren, Crawford County, Arkansas.[7]

Section 33

Date.   October 1830.

Place.   Fayette, Seneca County, New York.

Historical Note.   Section 33 is a revelation to Ezra Thayer and Northrop Sweet, both of New York. Through Joseph Smith they had sought the will of the Lord concerning them.

Publication Note.   Section 33 was first published as chapter 35 in the Book of Commandments in 1833.

Biographical Note.   Ezra Thayer.

Son of Ezra Thayer and Charlotte French. Born 14 October 1791 at Randolph, Windsor County, Vermont. Married Polly Wales 1810. Except for son, Andrew, names of children unknown. Builder of bridges, dams, and mills in Palmyra, New York, area. Acquainted with, and provided employment for Joseph Smith, Sr., family in New York. Lived in Ontario County, New York, 1820-30. Baptized October 1830 by Parley P. Pratt. Stated concerning conversion:

> When Hyrum began to speak, every word touched me to the inmost soul. I thought every word was pointed to me. God punished me and riveted me to the spot. I could not help myself. The tears rolled down my cheeks, I was very proud and stubborn. There were many there who knew me, I dare not look up. I sat until I recovered myself before I dare look up. They sung some hymns and that filled me with the Spirit. When Hyrum got through, he picked up a book and said, "here is the Book of Mormon." I said, let me see it. I then opened the book, and I received a shock with such exquisite joy that no pen can write and no tongue can express. I shut the book and said, what is the price of it?

"Fourteen shillings" was the reply. I said, I'll take the book. I opened it again, and I felt a double portion of the Spirit, that I did not know whether I was in the world or not. I felt as though I was truly in heaven.

Martin Harris rushed to me to tell me that the book was true. I told him that he need not tell me that, for I knew that it is true as well as he.[1]

Ordained elder by June 1831. In (unpublished) revelation, given May 1831 in Kirtland, Ohio, instructed to board with Joseph Smith, Sr. Revelation continued,

> Let my servant Ezra humble himself and at the [June 1831] conference meeting he shall be ordained unto power from on high and he shall go from thence (if he be obedient unto my commandments) and proclaim my gospel unto the western regions with my servants that must go forth even unto the borders of the Lamanites.[2]

Ordained high priest 3 June 1831 by Lyman Wight. In Section 52 directed to accompany Thomas B. Marsh to Missouri; unable to prepare in time and did not go. In 10 October 1831 conference of church instructed to remain with family in Kirtland until spring 1832. William W. Phelps instructed by conference to rebuke Thayer for giving disrespect to Church. On 25 January 1832 again called to accompany Thomas B. Marsh on mission. Appointed to purchase tannery from Arnold Mason for Church 2 April 1833. Member of Zion's Camp 1834. Membership suspended 1835 for impropriety. Later restored to full fellowship. Moved to Missouri 1838. Settled in Nauvoo after being expelled from Missouri. Mission to New York 1843. Member of Council of Fifty before 18 April 1844. Left Nauvoo on mission to campaign for Joseph Smith as President of United States 9 May 1844. Did not support leadership of Twelve Apostles after Prophet's death. Dropped from Council of Fifty 4 February 1845. Residing in Michigan 1860; there baptized into Reorganized LDS Church by W. W. Blair.[3]

Biographical Note.   Northrop Sweet.

Born 1802 in New York. Married before 1828 to Elathan Harris (born 1805), daughter of Emer Harris. Eight children: Benjamin, Salina, Sarah, Roxann, Garrin, Susan, Hezekiah, and Hiram. Baptized October 1830 by Parley P. Pratt. Living in Palmyra 1830. Ordained elder by 3 June 1831. Shortly after moving to Ohio, 1831, was influenced by false spirits and received revelation instructing him to be prophet. Left Church 1831. With Wycom Clark and others, organized short-lived church called "The Pure Church of Christ." Paid tax on two cows in Kirtland 1834. Living in Lake County, Ohio, 1840. Moved to Batavia, Branch County, Michigan, about 1845. Moved to Bethel, Branch County, Michigan, by 1870. Farmer; 1860 assets of $1,500. Married Eunice Hanmer 14 April 1861. Living in Bethel with son Hezekiah 1880. No death recorded in Branch County, Michigan.[4]

Section 34

Date. 4 November 1830.

Place. Fayette, Seneca County, New York.

Historical Note. Section 34 was received for Orson Pratt, a talented, well-known Mormon personality. Orson was converted to the Church in September 1830 by his brother, Parley P. Pratt. Remembering the occasion, Parley wrote that members of his immediate family only partially believed his message of the Restoration, but, said he, "my brother Orson, a youth of nineteen years, received it with all his heart."[1]

In October 1830 Orson traveled over two hundred miles to see the Prophet Joseph Smith who was residing at Fayette.[2] He reported that he left a "farming occupation in the eastern part of the State of New York"[3] to visit the place where the Church was organized. Orson recalled that it was in Father Peter Whitmer's chamber where section 34 was received: "Written from the mouth of the Prophet by John Whitmer, one of the witnesses of the Book of Mormon."[4]

Publication Note. Section 34 was first published as chapter 34 in the Book of Commandments in 1833.

Biographical Note. Orson Pratt.

Son of Jared Pratt and Charity Dickinson. Born 19 September 1811 in Hartford, Washington County, New York. In youth studied arithmetic, bookkeeping, geography, grammar, and surveying. Baptized 19 September 1830 by Parley P. Pratt in Canaan, Columbia County, New York. Ordained elder 1 December 1830 by Joseph Smith. Served first mission to Colesville, New York, late 1830. Preached with Lyman Wight to Lorain County, Ohio, early 1831. Appointed to travel to Missouri with brother, Parley P. Pratt, June 1831. Returned to Ohio late 1831. Preached with Lyman E. Johnson in Lorain County, Ohio, January 1832. Appointed to preach in eastern states with Lyman E. Johnson 25 January 1832. Ordained to High Priesthood 2 February 1832 by Sidney Rigdon. Left with Lyman E. Johnson for East 3 February 1832. Preached in Pennsylvania, New York, New Jersey, Vermont, New Hampshire, Connecticut, and Massachusetts. Joined with William Snow 10 November 1832. Returned to Kirtland 17 February 1833, having baptized 102 persons. Attended School of Prophets in spring of 1833. Left Kirtland with Lyman E. Johnson 26 March 1833 to preach again in East. Returned to Kirtland 28 September 1833, having baptized 50 persons. Worked on Kirtland Temple. Left Kirtland again for East with Lyman E.

Johnson 27 November 1833. Returned to Kirtland 13 February 1834. Appointed to assist in gathering volunteers for Zion's Camp 24 February 1834. Member of Zion's Camp. Appointed member of Clay County, Missouri, high council 8 July 1834. Ordained one of twelve apostles 26 April 1835. Left 4 May 1835 on mission to East with members of twelve apostles. Returned to Kirtland 25 September 1835. Took short mission along Ohio River with William Pratt 14 October to 16 November 1835. Served mission to Upper Canada and Jefferson County, New York, 6 April to 12 October 1836. Married Sarah Marinda Bates 4 July 1836. Twelve children: Orson, Lydia, Celestia, Larissa Sarah Marinda, Vanson, Laron, Marlon, Marintha Althera, Harmel, Arthur, Herma Ethna, and Loila Menella. Charter member of Kirtland Safety Society 1837. Mission to Jefferson County, New York, October 1837. Appointed to preside over branch of Church in New York City in spring of 1838. Pursuant to request to return to Missouri, with family left New York City and arrived in St. Louis mid-November 1838; spent winter there. In fulfillment of D&C section 118, met with others of twelve apostles in Far West, Missouri, 26 April 1839. Helped brother, Parley P., escape from Boone County Jail, Missouri, 4 July 1839. Left Illinois on mission to England 29 August 1839. Arrived in Liverpool 6 April 1840. Preached several months in Edinburgh, Scotland. Returned to Nauvoo mid-July 1841. Given responsibility for English literature and mathematics at University of Nauvoo August 1841. Rebelled against Joseph Smith August 1842. Excommunicated 20 August 1842. Rebaptized and reordained to apostleship 20 January 1843. Elected to Nauvoo city council 6 February 1843. Left on mission to East with others of twelve apostles 1 July 1843. Returned October 1843. Received endowment 23 December 1843. Member of Council of Fifty 11 March 1844. Left on mission to Washington, D.C., April 1844. Returned to Nauvoo 7 August 1844, after Prophet's death. Sealed to Charlotte Bishop in fall of 1844. No children. Sealed to Adelia Ann Bishop 13 December 1844. Six children: Lucy Adelia, Elzina, Lorum, Lorus, Eltha, and Orthena. Sealed to Mary Ann Merrill 27 March 1845. Five children: Milando, Vianna, Oradine, Lathilla, and Valton. Mission to New York City August 1845 to preside over eastern churches. Returned to Nauvoo 11 December 1845. Sealed to Sarah Louis Chandler 17 January 1846. No children. Exodus from Nauvoo February 1846. First to enter Great Salt Lake Valley, July 1847. Appointed to preside over all branches of Church in England, Scotland, Wales, and Ireland 1848. While in England, authored fifteen pamphlets and edited *Millennial Star*. Several times elected speaker of house of Territorial Legislature of Utah. In 1852 appointed president of all branches of church in United States and Canada. Sealed to Marion Ross 19 February 1852. Six children: Marian Agnes, Larinda Marissa, Milson, Irintha, Ray, and Ruby. Sealed to Sarah Louisa Lewis 20 June 1853. One child: Willow. Sealed to Juliett Ann Phelps 14 December 1855. Seven children: Alva, Clomenia, Ortherus, Margaret, Rella, Neva, and Julius. Sealed to Eliza Crooks 24 July 1857. Five children: Lerius, Dora, Jared,

Onthew, and Samuel. Appointed to open up gospel in Austria April 1864; unsuccessful. Sealed to Margaret Graham 28 December 1868. Published Book of Mormon in Deseret Alphabet in New York 1869. Appointed "Historian and General Church Recorder" 1874. Under direction of Brigham Young, prepared 1876 edition of Doctrine and Covenants. Edited and rearranged 1878 edition of Pearl of Great Price. Died 3 October 1881 in Salt Lake City, Utah.[5]

Section 35

Date.   December 1830 (7 December 1830, as per the *Ohio Star* [5 January 1832]).

Section 35, as published in the *Ohio Star* on 5 January 1832 and in the *Painsville Telegraph* on 17 January 1832, carried the date 7 December 1830. The *Star* received a copy of this revelation from Simonds Ryder, who had received his copy from David Whitmer.

Place.   (Fayette, Seneca County, New York, as per Book of Commandments).

Historical Note.   In October 1830 Oliver Cowdery, Peter Whitmer, Jr., Ziba Peterson, and Parley P. Pratt started on a mission to Missouri to preach to the Lamanites. About 1 November 1830 the party arrived in Mentor, Ohio, at the residence of Sidney Rigdon. Pratt, who previously had associated with Sidney Rigdon in the Campbellite religion, was anxious to present Rigdon with a copy of the Book of Mormon. After two weeks' examination of the book and the message of these four missionaries, Rigdon was baptized, on 14 November 1830. Shortly thereafter Sidney Rigdon, accompanied by Edward Partridge, set out for Fayette, New York, to see Joseph Smith. They arrived on or before 7 December 1830.[1]

Verse 20 instructed Sidney Rigdon to write for Joseph Smith. Manuscripts used in the inspired translation of the Bible affirm that Rigdon did begin serving as Joseph Smith's scribe in December 1830.[2]

Publication Note.   Section 35 was first published as chapter 37 in the Book of Commandments in 1833.

Biographical Note.   Sidney S. Rigdon.

Son of William Rigdon and Nancy Gallaher. Born 19 February 1793 at St. Clair Township, Alleghany County, Pennsylvania. Remained on father's farm in Pennsylvania until about 1819. Joined Regular Baptists and received license to preach in March 1819. Moved to Warren, Trumball County, Ohio, May 1819. Married Phoebe Brook 12 June 1820. Eleven children: Athalia, Nancy, Sarah, Eliza, Sidney Algernon, John W., Lucy, Phoebe, Hortencia, Ephraim, and Samuel Carver. Baptists of Pittsburgh, Pennsylvania, selected Rigdon as minister 1822. In August 1824 informed congregation he no longer upheld doctrines they endorsed. Labored as tanner two years, 1824-26. Invited to become minister of Regular Baptist church in Bainbridge, Geauga County, Ohio, 1826. Accepted call to be leader of Regular Baptist Church in Mentor, Geauga County, Ohio, 1827. Formally departed Baptist fold at Mentor. Like Walter Scott, Alexander Campbell, and Adamson Bently, believed remission of sins and reception of Holy Ghost followed baptism by immersion. Fellowship withdrawn September 1828 for embracing "novel notions." Joined Campbell and others in founding new denomination, "The Disciples of Christ," about 1830. Received gospel from Parley P. Pratt, Oliver Cowdery, Ziba Peterson, and Peter Whitmer, Jr., November 1830. Baptized 14 November 1830, in Mentor, Ohio. Traveled to Fayette, New York, December 1830 to see Joseph Smith. Served as Prophet's scribe during major part of inspired translation of Bible. Returned to Ohio February 1831. Ordained high priest 3 June 1831. Accompanied Prophet to Independence, Missouri, June-August 1831. Dedicated land of Zion for gathering of Saints 2 August 1831. Ordained one of Presidency of High Priesthood 8 March 1832. Member of United and Literary firms. Traveled with Joseph Smith and others to Jackson County, Missouri, April 1832 to regulate Church affairs. Returned to Kirtland, Ohio, 26 May 1832. Relinquished position in High Priesthood in summer of 1832 after preaching that kingdom had been taken from Saints. Restored to former office. On 18 March 1833 appointed counselor to Joseph Smith in Presidency of High Priesthood. Traveled with Joseph Smith to Upper Canada in fall of 1833. Appointed spokesman for Joseph Smith by revelation 12 October 1833. Participated in dedication of Kirtland Temple 1836. Traveled to Massachusetts with Prophet and others in summer of 1836 on Church business. Charter member of, and owned stock in, Kirtland Safety Society 1837. Traveled to Far West, Missouri, in fall of 1837 to regulate Church affairs. Moved to Far West, Missouri, 1838, arriving 4 April 1838. Arrested 31 October 1838 for treason. Incarcerated in Liberty Jail November 1838 to February 1839. No conviction. Assisted in founding Nauvoo, Illinois, 1839. Accompanied Joseph Smith and others to Washington, D.C., 1839-40 to present Saints' grievances to Congress. Member of Nauvoo city council. Postmaster of Nauvoo. Entered Masonic order 15 March 1842. Cut off from Church 13 August 1843 for plotting with apostates to have Prophet arrested and taken to Missouri. Subsequently reinstated. In October 1843 Joseph Smith requested Rigdon be dropped from the First Presidency, but Rigdon upheld by Church membership. Chosen as Prophet's running mate as vice-presidential candidate for United States after James Arlington Bennet and Solomon Copeland had declined offer. Member of Council of Fifty 19 March 1844. Received endowment 11 May 1844. Left Nauvoo 18 June 1844 for Pittsburgh, Pennsylvania; arrived 27 June 1844. Returned to Nauvoo 3 August 1844. Claimed right as guardian of Church 8 August 1844. Excommunicated and delivered over to buffetings of Satan 8 September 1844; left Nauvoo for Pittsburgh. Organized church by April 1845. Published newspaper at Pittsburgh. Moved to Franklin County, Pennsylvania in May 1846. Located in Cuba, Alleghany County, New York, by 1850. Subsequently settled in Friendship, New York; died there 14 July 1876.[3]

Section 36

Date.   December 1830 (after 7 December).[1]

Place.   (Fayette, Seneca County, New York, as per Book of Commandments).

Historical Note.   As mentioned in the Historical Note for section 35, Sidney Rigdon and Edward Partridge traveled to Fayette, New York, in December 1830 to see Joseph Smith. The Prophet later referred to Edward Partridge as "a pattern of piety, and one of the Lord's great men."[2] This revelation called Edward Partridge to the ministry.

Publication Note.   Section 36 was first published as chapter 38 in the Book of Commandments in 1833.

Biographical Note.   Edward Partridge.

Son of William Partridge and Jemima Bidwell. Born 27 August 1793 at Pittsfield, Berkshire County, Massachusetts. After completing four years as apprentice, became journeyman hatter in Clinton, New York, 1813. Moved to Painesville, Ohio; there owned hatting business and married Lydia Clisbee 22 August 1819. Seven children: Eliza Maria, Harriet Pamelia, Emily Dow, Caroline Ely, Clisbee, Lydia, and Edward. United with Campbellites in 1828. After hearing message of Lamanite missionaries November 1830, traveled with Sidney Rigdon to Fayette, New York, December 1830 to see Joseph Smith. Baptized 11 December 1830. Ordained elder 15 December 1830. Traveled to share gospel with relatives in Massachusetts December

1830-January 1831. Returned to Ohio by 4 February 1831. Called as first bishop of Church 4 February 1831. Ordained high priest 3 June 1831. Appointed to travel to Missouri with Prophet June 1831. Directed to move family to Missouri August 1831. Responsible for allocating inheritances to Saints in Jackson County, Missouri. Member of United Firm. Dedicated office of *Evening and Morning Star* 29 May 1832. Tarred and feathered 20 July 1833. Acknowledged as presiding officer of Church in Missouri 11 September 1833. Appointed to receive "endowment" in Kirtland 23 June 1834. Traveled to Kirtland 27 January-29 April 1835 with Thomas B. Marsh. Received patriarchal blessing 4 May 1835. Mission to eastern states 2 June-3 November 1835. Participated in dedication of Kirtland Temple 1836. Returned to Missouri in summer of 1836. Moved from Clay County, Missouri, to Far West in fall of 1836. Arrested and incarcerated November 1838 for treason. No conviction. Joined family in Quincy, Illinois, January 1839. Settled in Nauvoo in summer of 1839. Appointed bishop of upper ward in Nauvoo 5 October 1839. Died 27 May 1840 in Nauvoo, Hancock County, Illinois. Nauvoo Temple proxy sealing to Lydia Clisbee 14 January 1846.[3]

Section 37

Date.   December 1830 (after 7 December).[1]

Place.   (Canadaigua, Ontario County, New York, as per Book of Commandments).

Historical Note.   Section 37 is the first revelation which addressed the need of the Church membership to move to Ohio.[2] The revelation also instructed Joseph Smith and Sidney Rigdon to stop the work of translating the Bible until they moved to "the Ohio."

Having learned from the Book of Mormon that many plain and precious things had been taken out of the Bible, and having divine direction, the Prophet commenced an inspired translation of the Bible (which was intended to be published). Although the translation may have begun as early as June 1830, the earliest established date is 21 October 1830 (in Fayette, New York).[3] Despite many interruptions, the major work of translation continued from 21 October 1830 to 2 July 1833. In this work of revision Joseph Smith was assisted by at least three scribes: Oliver Cowdery, John Whitmer, and Sidney Rigdon (the last having done most of the scribal work). Although Joseph Smith placed much importance on this project of translation, many duties and pressures precluded its completion or publication during the Prophet's lifetime.[4]

Numerous sections in the Doctrine and Covenants have a direct or indirect association with the inspired translation of the Bible. Consider the following: appointing of scribes: sections 25, 35, and 47; ceasing and beginning translation: sections 37, 45, 73, 91, and 93; printing the translation: sections 94, 104, and 124; doctrinal revelations received as a direct result of the translation: sections 76, 77, and 86; doctrinal revelations apparently received in conjunction with the translation: sections 74, 84, 88, 93, 102, 107, 113, and 132; and other related revelations: sections 26, 41, 42, and 90.[5]

Publication Note.   Section 37 was first published as chapter 39 in the Book of Commandments in 1833.

Section 38

Date.   2 January 1831.

Place.   Fayette, Seneca County, New York.

Historical Note.   Section 38 was received at the third conference of the Church (Sunday, 2 January 1831) at the home of Peter Whitmer, Sr., in Fayette, New York. No minutes of this conference were kept, except a note in the "Far West Record," which explains that a conference was held and a revelation received.

Inasmuch as section 37 had commanded the Church to assemble together "at the Ohio," the congregation sought to know more concerning the matter. In response to their request, the Prophet inquired of the Lord and received section 38. Orson Pratt, remembering the occasion, stated:

> This brings to my mind a revelation which was given in a general conference on the 2d day of January 1831; the church then having been organized about nine months. All the Saints were gathered together from various little branches that had been established, in the house of old Father Whitmer . . . whose house became conspicuous as the place where the Prophet Joseph Smith received many

revelations and communications from heaven. In one
small room of a log house nearly all the Latter Day Saints
east of Ohio were collected together. They desired the
Prophet of the Lord to inquire of God and receive a
revelation to guide and instruct the church that were
present. Br. Joseph seated himself by the table; br.
Sidney Rigdon...was requested to act as scribe in
writing the revelation from the mouth of the Prophet
Joseph.[1]

Not all the New York Saints were willing to sell their farms and
move to Ohio. John Whitmer, aware of the concerns of those
present, stated that the idea of the Church membership moving
west caused "divisions among the congregation" some of whom
asserted that the revelation had been invented by Joseph Smith
himself.[2] Newel Knight recalled that the instructions to gather to
Ohio required much preparation and obliged the Saints to make
"great sacrifices of our property."[3]

Around 23 January 1831 Joseph Smith and Sidney Rigdon, among
others, left New York for Ohio; they arrived about 30 January 1831.[4]
Most New York Saints had arrived in the Kirtland, Ohio, area by
mid-May 1831.[5]

Publication Note.   Section 38 was first published in the *Evening and
Morning Star* (April 1833) and was included as chapter 40 in the Book
of Commandments in 1833.

Section 39

Date.   5 January 1831.

Place.   Fayette, Seneca County, New York.

Historical Note.   Shortly after the close of the third conference of
the Church (2 January 1831), James Covell came to see Joseph Smith.
A Baptist minister for some forty years, Covell covenanted that he
would obey any command the Lord gave through Joseph Smith.
Section 39 was received following the establishment of this
covenant.[1]

Publication Note.   Section 39 was first published as chapter 41 in the Book of Commandments in 1833.

Biographical Note.   James Covell.

Son of James Covell and Sarah Grover. Born 1 March 1756 at Dover, New York. Married Lydia Black. Longtime Baptist minister. Settled in Queensbury, Washington County, New York, by 1790. Moved to Cazenovia, Madison County, New York, by 1800; resided there until 1806. Removed to Marcellus, Onondaga County, New York, 1806. Living in Chautauqua County, New York, by 1830. Learned of restoration of gospel by January 1831. Rejected Joseph Smith's counsel to be baptized and move to Ohio. Died 1 December 1844 in Mayville, Chautaugua County, New York.[2]

Section 40

Date.   January 1831 (after 5 January 1831).

Place.   Fayette, Seneca County, New York.

Historical Note.   Upon Covell's rejection of the Lord's counsel (see section 39), section 40 was received by Joseph Smith. Section 40 is the last of the revelations in the Doctrine and Covenants that were received in New York before the Church membership moved west to Ohio.[1]

Publication Note.   Section 40 was first published as chapter 42 in the Book of Commandments in 1833.

Section 41

Date.   4 February 1831.

Place.   Kirtland, Geauga County, Ohio.

Although Kirtland, Ohio, became part of Lake County in 1840, the town was within the boundaries of Geauga County during the 1830s,

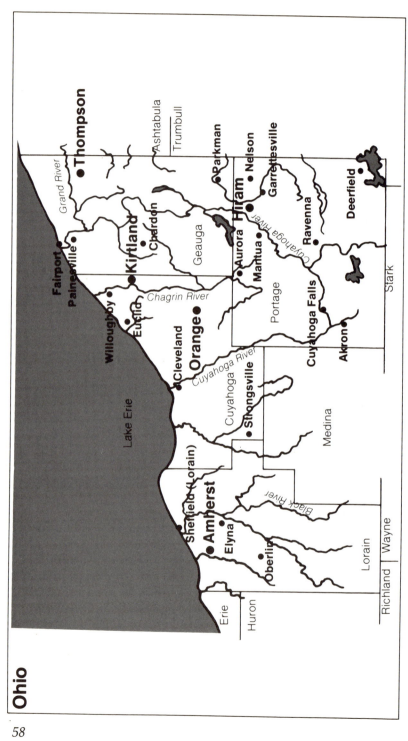

Ohio

58

when Joseph Smith received the revelations now found in the Doctrine and Covenants. For this reason Geauga County will be used in this study.

Historical Note. Joseph Smith arrived in Kirtland, Ohio, about 30 January 1831.[1] Section 41, the first of the Doctrine and Covenants revelations received in Ohio, spoke of "my law"[2] soon to be revealed to the Saints and called Edward Partridge to discontinue his life as a merchant and be ordained a bishop.

Accordingly, Partridge, who owned a hatting business in Painesville, Ohio, was ordained a bishop by Sidney Rigdon.[3]

Section 41 also commanded that a house be built for Joseph Smith, in which he was to live and translate the Bible. In later years a house may have been constructed for the Prophet, but by the fall of 1832, only the upper level of the Newel K. Whitney store had been prepared as a residence for the Prophet and his family.

Publication Note. Section 41 was first published as chapter 43 in the Book of Commandments in 1833.

Section 42

Date. 9 February 1831 (9 February and 23 February. The Book of John Whitmer records that verses 1-73 were received 9 February 1831. According to the "Kirtland Revelations Book," verses 74-77 were received 23 February 1831. Verses 78-93 were received 23 February 1831, as per the *Evening and Morning Star* [October 1832].).

Place. Kirtland, Geauga County, Ohio.

Historical Note. Sections 38 and 41 both promised that the Lord would shortly give "his law" unto the Church. In accordance with the instructions of D&C 41:2-3, the elders "united in mighty prayer," and by their faith section 42 was received. On 9 February 1831, when part of section 42 was received, twelve elders joined in prayer; and on 23 February 1831, when the final portions of section 42 were received, seven elders met together to inquire of the Lord.[1]

Comparison of extant manuscript copies of section 42 reveals variations in the text, suggesting that portions, if not all, of what is now section 42 were responses to specific questions. Because this revelation was received in portions on two different days, it appears that specific inquiries were made on both days. Consider the following questions and answers:

1. Verses 70-73 appear to be a response to the question, "How [are the Elders] to dispose of their families while they are proclaiming repentance or are otherwise engaged in the service of the Church?"[2]

2. Part of section 42, as found in the Book of Commandments, appears to be a response to the question: "What preparation shall we make for our Brethren from the East & where & how?"[3] The answer: "There shall be as many appointed as must needs be necessary to assist the bishop in obtaining places for the brethren from New York, that they may be together as much as can be, and as they are directed by the Holy Spirit."[4]

3. Question: "Shall the Church come together into one place or remain as they are in separate bodies?"[5] Answer: "And every Church shall be organized in as close bodies as they can be [because of the enemy] and this for a wise purpose—even so. Amen."[6]

4. Question: "How far is it the will of the Lord that we should have dealings with the world & how we should conduct our dealings with them?"[7] Answer: "Thou shalt contract no debts with them & again the Elders & Bishop shall council together & they shall do by the direction of the Spirit as it must be necessary."[8]

5. Question: "[What is the] law regulating the church in her present situation till the time of her gathering[?]"[9] Answer: "The first commandment in the law teaches that all the Elders shall go into the regions westward and labour to build up Churches unto Christ wheresoever they shall find any to [teach] them [to] obey the gospel of Jesus Christ except Joseph & Sidney and Edward and such as the Bishop shall appoint to assist him in his duties according to the Law which we have received this commandment as far as it respects these Elders to be sent to the west is a special one for the time being incumbent on the present Elders who shall return when directed by the Holy Spirit."[10]

6. The preface to verses 74-77 was "How to act in Cases of Adultery,"[11] and

7. Verses 78-93 were entitled "Points of the Law."[12]

Known simply as "The Law,"[13] or "The Law of the Church," section 42 contains instructions relative to the law of consecration and stewardship, the Decalogue, and the law of discipline with regard to members who violate Church rules.

Although the Prophet wrote to Martin Harris on 22 February 1831 that the Saints had "received the laws of the Kingdom since we came here and the Disciples in these parts have received them gladly,"[14] John Whitmer indicated that there were "some that would not receive the Law." Whitmer explained:

> The time has not yet come that the law can be fully established, for the disciples live scattered and are not organized, our numbers are small, and the disciples untaught, consequently they understand not the things of the Kingdom.[15]

Publication Note.   Verses 12-77, or variations thereof, were first published in the *Evening and Morning Star* (July 1832).[16] Verses 78-93, or variations thereof, were first published in the *Evening and Morning Star* (October 1832). Verses 1-77, or variations thereof, were included as chapter 44 in the Book of Commandments. Verses 78-93, or variations thereof, were included as chapter 47 of the Book of Commandments.

Section 43

Date.   February 1831.

Place.   Kirtland, Geauga County, Ohio.

Historical Note.   In early 1831 a self-styled prophetess by the name of Hubble (possibly a convert) came to Kirtland, Ohio. This lady declared the Book of Mormon to be true and affirmed that she would become a "teacher in the Church of Christ."[1] Inasmuch as some new converts in the Kirtland area believed the "revelations and commandments" of the Hubble woman, the Prophet inquired of the Lord concerning the matter.

Ezra Booth, an early apostate, wrote the following with respect to this woman named Hubble:

> A female, professing to be a prophetess, made her appearance in Kirtland, an so ingratiated herself into the

esteem and favor of some of the Elders that they received her as a person commissioned to act a conspicious part in Mormonizing the world. Rigdon, and some others, gave her the right hand of fellowship, and literally saluted her with what they called the "kiss" of charity. But [Joseph] Smith . . . declared her an imposter, and she returned to the place from whence she came. Her visit, however, made a deep impression on the minds of many, and the barbed arrow which she left in the hearts of some, is not as yet eradicated.[2]

Publication Note.   Section 43 was first published in the *Evening and Morning Star* (October 1832) and was included as chapter 45 in the Book of Commandments in 1833.

Section 44

Date.   February 1831.

Place.   Kirtland, Geauga County, Ohio.

Historical Note.   Section 44 calls for a conference of the Church to be held in Ohio. This gathering, which occurred in Kirtland and is known as the fourth conference of the Church, was the first of its kind to be held in Ohio. The minutes of the first day of this conference, dated 3 June 1831, are found in the "Far West Record." At this conference Joseph Smith and others were ordained to the High Priesthood.

The revelation also mentions the law of consecration and the responsibility of caring for the poor.[1]

Publication Note.   Section 44 was first published as chapter 46 in the Book of Commandments in 1833.

Section 45

Date. 7 March 1831.

Place. Kirtland, Geauga County, Ohio.

Historical Note. On 4 March 1831 a special conference was held in Kirtland, Ohio, and several elders were sent forth to preach the gospel. Concerning section 45 John Whitmer wrote, "In these days the Lord blessed his disciples greatly, and he gave revelation after revelation, which contained doctrine, instructions, and prophecies. The word of the Lord came to the Seer as follows [section 45]."[1]

Section 45, which focuses on events having to do with the second coming of Christ, instructed Joseph Smith to begin translating the New Testament (compare Matthew 24 and Joseph Smith-Matthew). Until this time work on the inspired translation had been limited to the book of Genesis. With Sidney Rigdon as scribe, the Prophet began translating the New Testament March 8. The manuscript bears the following notation: "A Translation of the New Testament translated by the power of God."[2]

Publication Note. Section 45 was first published in the *Evening and Morning Star* (June 1832) and was included as chapter 48 in the Book of Commandments in 1833. Verses 72-75 were not published as part of this revelation until 1844.[3]

Section 46

Date. 8 March 1831.

Place. Kirtland, Geauga County, Ohio.

Historical Note. On 8 March 1831 Joseph Smith and Sidney Rigdon began translating the New Testament. John Whitmer, who also assisted in the work of revision at this time, recorded that discussion relative to admitting non-members to sacrament and confirmation meetings served as the basis for receiving section 46.[1] Barring the unbaptized from Church meetings, said Whitmer, had "caused some to marvel, and converse about this matter."[2] Verses 3-6 clarified that "earnest seekers" should be permitted to attend.

The revelation also instructed the Saints to seek the best spiritual gifts, and warned of being deceived by false spirits.[3]

Publication Note.   Section 46 was first published in the *Evening and Morning Star* (August 1832) and was included as chapter 49 in the Book of Commandments in 1833.

Section 47

Date.   8 March 1831.[1]

Place.   Kirtland, Geauga County, Ohio.[2]

Historical Note.   According to John Whitmer, Joseph Smith informed him that it was his responsibility to "keep the church history." Whitmer replied that he would prefer not to have that assignment but would do it if it was the will of the Lord.[3] In response to Whitmer's desire for a revelation on the matter, the Prophet inquired of the Lord and received section 47. Although the directive for Whitmer to be the custodian of the Church history was given on 8 March 1831, he was not ordained to this position until 9 April 1831.[4]

The history that John Whitmer wrote as Church Historian began on 12 June 1831 and continued until he left the Church. He called this history, "The Book of John Whitmer." Prior to this appointment, John Whitmer had served as scribe to Joseph Smith in the work of translating the Bible and in copying revelations received by Joseph Smith. Inasmuch as section 47 instructed Whitmer to transcribe "all things" given to the Prophet, it is significant to note that this revelation was given one day after Joseph Smith had received a directive to begin translation of the New Testament.

On 31 July 1832 Joseph Smith reminded John Whitmer of "the commandment to him to keep a history of the church & the gathering and beware [to keep] himself approved whereunto he hath been called."[5] A year later, expressing concern over his calling as Church historian, Whitmer wrote to Oliver Cowdery, "I want you to remember me to Joseph in a special manner, and enquire of

him respecting my clerkship [;] you very well know what I mean &
also my great desire of doing all things according to the mind of the
Lord."[6]

After his excommunication in 1838, John Whitmer refused to turn
over his history to the Church.[7] The record eventually became the
property of the Reorganized LDS Church.

The "other office" to which Oliver Cowdery had been appointed
(verse 5) was undoubtedly that of "second elder," and missionary to
the Lamanites (D&C 20:3; 28:8).

Publication Note.   Section 47 was first published as chapter 50 in
the Book of Commandments in 1833.

Section 48

Date.   March 1831.

Place.   Kirtland, Geauga County, Ohio.

Historical Note.   Section 42 (1833 edition) had directed the
membership of the Church in Ohio to "assist the Bishop in
obtaining places for the brethren from New York." Because the New
York Saints, in Fayette, Manchester, and Colesville, were making
preparations to move to Ohio, Church leaders were naturally
concerned as to "how they should act in regard to purchasing lands"
on which the New York Saints could settle.[1] Upon inquiry Joseph
Smith received section 48.[2] The revelation directed the Ohio Saints
to share their surplus properties with the New Yorkers, and if more
was needed, it would have to be purchased by the newcomers.

Publication Note.   Section 48 was first published as chapter 51 in
the Book of Commandments in 1833.

Section 49

Date. March 1831.[1]

Place. Kirtland, Geauga County, Ohio.

Historical Note. Near present-day Cleveland, Ohio, is a suburb known as Shaker Heights. In 1831 this area was the site of a Shaker settlement called North Union or Union Village. Because the settlement was only fifteen miles from Kirtland, it was inevitable that the Latter-day Saint elders would contact the Shakers.

The principles and practices of Shakerism were very austere. Believing in the purity of the body, many lived as vegetarians and celibates. Shakers did not believe in a physical resurrection. They taught that God was a dual being who manifested himself in the form of a man—Jesus—and in the form of a woman—Ann Lee. In addition, the Shakers accepted modern revelation and consecrated their property.

One early convert to Mormonism in Ohio was Leman Copley. A Shaker before his baptism into the LDS church, Copley was eager to share his newly found faith with his friends in North Union. Copley, it is said, "teased to be ordained to preach" and desired that the Lord should speak on some particulars of his former religion.[2] Pursuant to Copley's request, section 49 was received by Joseph Smith.

The revelation commanded Sidney Rigdon and Parley P. Pratt to accompany Leman Copley to North Union and preach the gospel to this group, officially called the United Society of Believers in Christ's Second Appearing.

With the revelation in hand, these three missionaries made their way to the Shaker village. (This was not the first time, however, that elders had contacted this religious group: In the fall of 1830 Oliver Cowdery had related to them the story of Moroni's appearance and the translation of the gold plates.) Sidney Rigdon and Leman Copley arrived in the village on a Saturday evening and discussed religion with Ashbell Kitchel, apparently a Shaker of some prominence. Kitchel berated Copley for renouncing Shakerism in favor of Mormonism, declaring the latter "an easier plan." The next morning Parley P. Pratt arrived and the three attended the Shaker service. At the close of the meeting, Sidney Rigdon asked if he could deliver a message from the Lord. With their permission Rigdon stood and read section 49 to the congregation. After delivering his message Elder Rigdon asked if any would receive baptism, where-upon those present indicated that they were perfectly satisfied with Shakerism and would not accept the revelation as being from God.[3]

Publication Note.   Section 49 was first published in the *Evening and Morning Star* (November 1832) and was included as chapter 52 in the Book of Commandments in 1833.

Biographical Note.   Leman Copley.

Son of Samuel Copley. Born 1781 in Connecticut. By 1800 Copleys had moved to Pitsford, Rutland County, Vermont; there united with Shakers. Leman moved to Cleveland area (site of Shaker community) as early as 1820. Married Salley (born 1779 in Massachusetts). One known child: Reuben. By 1830 held title to large tracts of land in Thompson, Ohio. Baptized and ordained elder by March 1831. Appointed with Sidney Rigdon and Parley P. Pratt to preach gospel to Shaker community in Union Village, near Cleveland. (Shakers rejected gospel message March 1831.) Agreed to permit members of Church from New York to settle on his property; broke promise by June 1831. (This prompted Colesville Branch to move to Missouri.) Fellowship withdrawn in summer of 1831; reextended by October 1832. Testified against Joseph Smith in Philastus Hurlburt trial 1834; disfellow-shipped. Made satisfaction 1 April 1836. Did not gather with Saints. A successful farmer, had real estate valued at $3500 in 1850. Probably died in Madison Township, Lake County, Ohio, after 1860.[4]

Section 50

Date.   May 1831 (9 May, as per *Evening and Morning Star* [August 1832]).

Place.   Kirtland, Geauga County, Ohio.

Historical Note.   After the departure of the Lamanite Missionaries to Missouri and before the arrival of Joseph Smith in Kirtland, Ohio (February 1831), extreme spiritual abnormalities were manifested among new converts in the Kirtland area. Several new members of the church were influenced by spiritual gifts and powers that led them to behave contrary to the will of God.

Parley P. Pratt, an eyewitness to these events, recorded the following:

As I went forth among the different branches, some very strange spiritual operations were manifested, which were disgusting, rather than edifying. Some persons would seem to swoon away, and make unseemly gestures, and be drawn or disfigured in their countenances. Others would fall into ecstacies, and be drawn into contortions, cramps, fits, etc. Others would seem to have visions and revelations, which were not edifying, and which were not congenial to the doctrine and spirit of the gospel. In short, a false and lying spirit seemed to be creeping into the Church.[1]

To determine the nature of the spiritual workings among new converts of the Church, Elder Pratt, among others, went to Joseph Smith and asked him to inquire of the Lord concerning the matter.[2] "After we had joined in prayer in his translating room," said Pratt, Joseph Smith "dictated in our presence" section 50.[3]

Section 50 gave instructions on the procedure of discerning "the spirits which have gone abroad in the earth."[4]

Publication Note.   Section 50 was first published in the *Evening and Morning Star* (August 1832) and was included as chapter 53 in the Book of Commandments in 1833.

Biographical Note.   John Corrill.

Born 17 September 1794 at Worcester County, Massachusetts. Residing in Ashtabula, Ohio, 1830. Married Margaret. Five known children: Betsy, Nancy, Whitney, Foster, and Mary. Baptized 10 January 1831. Ordained elder before June 1831. Ordained high priest and set apart as assistant to Bishop Edward Partridge 3 June 1831. Served mission to New London, Ohio, early 1831. Appointed to travel with Lyman Wight to Jackson County, Missouri, June 1831. Moved family to Missouri 1831. Presided over Branch Number Four in Independence. Prominent Church leader 1831-38. Imprisoned for short time in Independence 1833. Settled in Clay County, Missouri, after expulsion from Jackson County. Owned property in Clay County. Appointed to receive "endowment" in Kirtland 23 June 1834. Participated in dedication of Kirtland Temple 1836. Returned to Clay County, Missouri, by November 1836. Assisted in settling Far West, Missouri. Owned property in Caldwell County. Appointed "Keeper of the Lord's Storehouse" 7 November 1837. Appointed to assist as Church historian 8 April 1838. Elected state representative for Caldwell County, Missouri, 1838. Voiced opposition to Joseph Smith August 1838. Filed affidavit for loss of property in Missouri 1840. Excommunicated 17 March 1839. Published work against Church: *A Brief History of the Church of Christ of Latter Day Saints (Commonly Called Mormons)* (St. Louis, 1839). Residing in Quincy, Illinois, in 1840.[5]

Biographical Note.   Joseph H. Wakefield.

Born about 1792. Lived in Watertown, Jefferson County, New York, 1820-30. Baptized and ordained elder before May 1831. Appointed to preach with Parley P. Pratt in Western Reserve May 1831. Ordained high priest 3 June 1831. Appointed to preach gospel with Solomon Humphrey in "eastern lands" June 1831. Preached in St. Lawrence County, New York; there baptized George A. Smith September 1832. Owned property in Watertown 1833. Moved to Kirtland in summer of 1833. Influenced by dissident Mormons in Kirtland 1833-34. Claimed that because Joseph Smith came out from translating room and immediately engaged in playing with children, he was not true prophet. One of committee of Kirtland citizens who attempted to defame Joseph Smith and prove Book of Mormon written by Solomon Spaulding. Excommunicated by January 1834.[6]

Section 51

Date.   May 1831 (20 May).[1]

Place.   Thompson, Geauga County, Ohio.

Historical Note.   As the New York Saints began to arrive in Ohio in May 1831, Church leaders sought further direction in organizing them according to the law of consecration. In response to the request of Bishop Edward Partridge, Joseph Smith inquired of the Lord and received section 51.[2]

Orson Pratt, in 1874, stated that he was present when this revelation was received. He said "no great noise or physical manifestation was made; Joseph was as calm as the morning sun." However, Pratt noticed a change in the Prophet's countenance, "His face was exceedingly white, and seemed to shine."[3]

Textual Note.   Verse 5 of section 51, as we now have it, was not originally part of the revelation, but subsequently added. The following passages, relating to the law of consecration, were initially part of the revelation but subsequently deleted. These verses, as well as other instructions on the subject of obtaining deeds, seem to form the basis for Bishop Edward Partridge's actions in retaining title to all consecrated properties in Jackson County, Missouri:

> Wherefore let my servant Edward receive the properties of this people which have covenanted with me to obey the laws which I have given and let my servant Edward receive the money as it shall be laid before him according to the covenant and go and obtain a deed or article of this land unto himself of him who holdeth it if he harden not his heart for I have appointed him to receive these things and thus through him the properties of the church shall be consecrated unto me.[4]

When members of the Church arrived in Missouri they were to convey to the bishop legal title to their assets. While surplus consecrations were to be used for the benefit of the poor (and therefore retained by the bishop), the bishop was to provide "inheritances" for the Saints. Normally this would be achieved by turning back to each member his personal property as well as a parcel of land. What is interesting, however, is that initially this distribution did not secure to the member private ownership of his stewardship. Early contracts used by Bishop Partridge in Jackson County stipulated that real estate was "leased" to the individual member, that personal property was "loaned," and that in cases of transgression or unworthiness, members forfeited any or all of their stewardship properties.[5] These early arrangements were defective for obvious reasons and, when challenged by some dissenters, were not upheld by the courts. These procedures were subsequently modified so as "to give a deed, securing to him who receives . . . his inheritance . . . to be his individual property, his private steward-ship."[6] It was also agreed that if a member was determined not worthy to belong to the Church, he could claim that to which he held title but could not claim gifts or donations he had made to the bishop.[7]

Publication Note.   Section 51 was first published as section 23 in the 1835 edition of the Doctrine and Covenants.

Section 52

Date.   7 June 1831 (6 June).

The Manuscript History of the Church notes that in 1831 the June priesthood conference was convened on 6 June. However, B. H. Roberts points out that the conference minutes (recorded in the "Far West Record") affirm that it commenced on Friday, 3 June.[1] In his history John Whitmer states that the meeting convened on 3 June and continued until Sunday, 5 June, and that section 52 was received the following day (Monday, 6 June).[2] Levi Hancock recorded that the revelation was received in the evening of 6 June 1831.[3] Another source pointing to 6 June 1831 as the date of reception is the journal of John Smith (not the Prophet's uncle). He recorded the following:

> firday June 3th went to Kirtland to attend conference but did not reatch there till sat 4th & conference was over & I continued there untill 6th & after the commandments had come forth for the Elders to go to the Missura I returned & reached my home in Northampton on tus 7th & went to labour.[4]

Place.   Kirtland, Geauga County, Ohio.

Historical Note.   In accord with the instructions of section 44, a three-day priesthood conference was convened in Kirtland, Ohio, 3-5 June 1831. Section 52 was received at the close of these meetings. The minutes of the first day of conference (recorded in the "Far West Record") list sixty-two present and reveal that the time was spent in ordaining and "giving exhortation."[5]

Joseph Smith and twenty-two other elders were ordained to the High Priesthood on the first day of the conference, marking the first occasion on which any were ordained to that office in this dispensation.[6]

The revelation directed fourteen pairs of elders, including Joseph Smith and Sidney Rigdon, to travel to Independence, Missouri. The missionaries were to "preach by the way" and to hold a conference upon their arrival.[7] There was great interest in the Missouri mission since the New Jerusalem was to be identified. Joseph Smith and those traveling with him left Kirtland on 19 June 1831 and arrived in Independence in mid-July.[8]

Whereas twenty-eight elders were to travel west, Joseph H. Wakefield and Solomon Humphrey were to travel to the "eastern countries;" and Jared Carter and George James were to be ordained priests.

The mission calls in verses 22 and 32 were later revoked.[9]

Publication Note. Section 52 was first published as chapter 54 in the Book of Commandments in 1833.

Biographical Note.   Wheeler Baldwin.

Born 1 or 7 March 1793 at Albany County, New York. Living in Strongsville, Cuyahoga County, Ohio, in 1830. Married Mary (born 20 July 1793). Baptized 8 January 1831. Ordained elder before 3 June 1831. Ordained high priest 3 June 1831 by Lyman Wight. Appointed to travel to Missouri June 1831; apparently did not go. Attended Orange, Ohio, conference 25-26 October 1831; there stated he rejoiced to hear testimonies of those who had been "up to the land of Zion." Moved to Jackson County, Missouri, by 5 October 1832. Settled in Caldwell County, Missouri, by 1836; owned property. Located in Lee County, Iowa, after Mormon expulsion from Missouri 1839. On 6 March 1840, Iowa high council appointed Wheeler Baldwin, Lyman Wight, and Abraham O. Smoot to obtain affidavits and other documents to be forwarded to Washington, D.C. Received endowment 7 January 1846 in Nauvoo Temple. Did not move to Utah. Joined Alpheus Cutler's group in Mills County, Iowa, about 1852. Moved with Cutlerites to Manti, Fremont County, Iowa, in 1854. Joined Reorganized Church in March 1863. Presided over Reorganized Church branches in the counties of Mills, Fremont, Taylor, and Page (Iowa). Died 11 May 1887, near Stewartsville, Missouri.[10]

Biographical Note.   Heman Bassett.

Born 1814. Baptized and ordained elder by spring of 1831. One of first to withdraw from Church in Ohio. Active participant in abnormal spiritual activities in Kirtland, Ohio, early 1831. Living in unauthorized communal order in Kirtland area prior to Prophet's arrival from Fayette, New York, February 1831. By May 1831 had declared Mormonism hoax. Revelation received 6 June 1831 instructed Joseph Smith, "In consequence of transgression, let that which was bestowed upon Heman Bassett be taken from him." Died 1876 in Philadelphia, Pennsylvania.[11]

Biographical Note.   Ezra Booth.

Born in Connecticut 1792. Removed to Nelson, Ohio, by 1819; there married Dorcas Taylor 10 March 1819. Methodist minister. Converted to Church through miraculous healing of Elsa Johnson's arm about May 1831. Ordained elder before June 1831. Ordained high priest 3 June 1831 by Lyman Wight. Appointed to travel to Missouri with Isaac Morley June 1831. Attended Church conference in Jackson County, Missouri 4 August 1831. Directed to purchase canoes for Ohio elders returning to East. Arrived in Ohio by 1 September 1831. Mission to Missouri; there became disillusioned and lost faith in Joseph Smith's divine calling. Fellowship withdrawn 6 September 1831. Chastised 11 September 1831, for evil actions. Officially denounced Mormonism 12 September 1831. Considered first Mormon apostate to publish anti-Mormon literature. Authored nine letters against Church; published them in *Ohio Star* (October-December 1831). Residing in Mantua, Portage County, Ohio, 1860; owned farm.[12]

Biographical Note.   Reynolds Cahoon.

Son of William Cahoon and Mehitabel Hodge. Born 30 April 1790 in Cambridge, Washington County, New York. Married Thirza Stiles 11 December 1810. Seven children: William F., Leroni Eliza, Pulaski, Daniel, Andrew, Julia, and Mahonri Moriancumer. Moved to Western Reserve 1811; began farming. Soldier in War of 1812. Located near Kirtland, Ohio, 1825. Baptized 11 October 1830 by Parley P. Pratt. Shortly after baptism, ordained elder by Sidney Rigdon. Ordained high priest 3 June 1831 by Joseph Smith. Appointed to travel to Jackson County, Missouri, with Samuel H. Smith June 1831. Returned to Kirtland by September 1831. On 11 October 1831 appointed to obtain money and/or property to assist Prophet in finishing inspired translation of Bible. Ordained counselor to Bishop Newel K. Whitney 10 February 1832. Appointed to obtain money to build sacred edifices in Kirtland 4 May 1833. Worked on Kirtland Temple. Revelation dated 1 November 1835 reproved Cahoon for "iniquities." Charter member of, and owned stock in, Kirtland Safety Society 1837. Moved to Missouri; arrived 7 June 1838. Appointed counselor in stake at Adam-Ondi-Ahman 28 June 1838. Located in Iowa after Mormon explusion from Missouri. Appointed counselor in Iowa Stake 19 October 1839. Received endowment 12 October 1843. Member of Council of Fifty 11 March 1844. Received patriarchal blessing 24 January 1845 from John Smith. Sealed to Lucina Roberts Johnson (born 1806 in Vermont) 16 January 1846. Three children: Lucina, Rais, and Truman. Sealed to Mary Hildrath 16 January 1846. No known children. Located in Winter Quarters 1846. Arrived in Salt Lake City, Utah, 23 September 1848. Died in South Cottonwood Ward, Salt Lake County, Utah, 29 April 1861.[13]

Biographical Note.   Jared Carter.

Son of Gideon Carter and Johanah Sims. Born 14 June 1801 in Benson, Rutland County, Vermont. Married Lydia Ames 20 September 1825. Nine known children: Evaline, Ellen, Orlando, Clark, Lydia, Jared, David, Rosabella, and Joseph. Residing in Chenango, Broome County, New York, 1830. Baptized February 1831 by Hyrum Smith. Moved to Amherst, Ohio, 1831. Revelation in June 1831 instructed Carter to be ordained priest. Ordained elder by September 1831. Left for mission to East 22 September 1831 with Ebenezer Page. Preached in New York and Vermont. Returned to Amherst 29 February 1832. Appointed by revelation to preach in eastern states March 1832. Left for New York with Calvin Stoddard 25 April 1832. Left Stoddard in New York and continued on to Vermont with Sylvester Smith and Gideon Carter. Baptized seventy-nine converts on this mission. Returned to Kirtland 19 October 1832, and then to Amherst. Left on mission to Michigan with Moses Daley 1 December 1832. Returned May 1833. Appointed member of committee to obtain subscriptions for construction of school for elders 4 May 1833. Committee later became responsible for construction of several sacred buildings in Kirtland. Assisted in laying foundation stones of Kirtland Temple 23 July 1833. Appointed to preach in Upper Canada with Phineas Young 20 February 1834. Worked on Kirtland Temple. On 7 March 1835 received blessing for working on Kirtland Temple. Tried before Church court 16 September 1835 for "rebelling against the advice and counsel" of First Presidency as well as for "erring in judgment." Acquitted upon humble confession. Participated in dedication of Kirtland Temple March 1836. Charter member of, and owned stock in, Kirtland Safety Society January 1837. Appointed member of Kirtland high council 4 September 1837. Ordained high councilor 9 September 1837. Left for Far West, Missouri, late September 1837. Appointed member of Far West high council 3 March 1838. Expelled from Missouri 1839; located in Nauvoo, Illinois. Accused of being in league with George W. Robinson, Sidney Rigdon, and John C. Bennett March 1843. Became disaffected in 1843. Subsequently became reconciled. Disfellowshipped 8 September 1844. On 16 September 1844, made confession for errors and promised to return to Church. Member of Yoree Branch of Church in Chicago, Illinois January 1847. Died in Illinois by 1850. Wife, Lydia, and children residing in DeKalb County, Illinois, 1850.[14]

Biographical Note.   Simeon Carter.

Son of Gideon Carter and Johanah Sims. Born 7 July 1794 at Killingworth, Middlesex County, Connecticut. Family resided in Massachusetts 1810-20. Married Lydia Kenyon 2 December 1818. Three children. Moved to Amherst, Ohio, by 1830. Baptized 22 February 1831. Ordained elder by June 1831. Ordained high priest 3 June 1831 by Lyman Wight. Appointed by revelation to travel to Jackson County, Missouri, with Solomon Hancock June 1831. Returned to Ohio by September 1831. Appointed to collect funds to assist Prophet in inspired translation of Bible at Orange, Ohio, 25 October 1831. Moved family to Jackson County, Missouri, before February 1833.

Appointed to preside over Branch Number Nine in Jackson County 11 September 1833. Located in Clay County, Missouri, 1833. On 23 June 1834 appointed to receive "endowment" in Kirtland Temple. Appointed member of Clay County high council 7 July 1834. Participated in dedication of Kirtland Temple 1836. Located in Far West, Missouri, 1836; there purchased several parcels of land. Member of Far West high council. Expelled from Missouri 1839; located in Lee County, Iowa. Called on mission to Germany 1841; apparently did not go. Received endowment 15 December 1845 in Nauvoo Temple. Sealed in Nauvoo Temple to Hannah Dunham (born 1800 in Vermont) 19 January 1846. Mission to England 1846-49. Married Louisa Holland Gibbons 14 November 1849. Three children: Simeon, Louisa, and Samuel. Arrived in Salt Lake Valley 15 August 1850. Located in Brigham City, Box Elder County, Utah. Died there 3 February 1869.[15]

Biographical Note. William Carter.

Baptized and ordained elder before 3 June 1831. Appointed by revelation to travel to Missouri with Wheeler Baldwin 6 June 1831; apparently did not go. Stripped of priesthood 1 September 1831. Positive identification cannot be made, but was *not* "one of the Utah pioneers who put the first ploughs into the ground and planted the first potatoes in Salt Lake Valley."[16]

Biographical Note. Zebedee Coltrin.

Son of John Coltrin and Sarah Graham. Born 7 September 1804 in Ovid, Seneca County, New York. Moved with family to Geauga County, Ohio, 1814; settled in Strongsville, Cuyahoga County, Ohio, shortly thereafter. Married Julia Ann Jennings (born 1813 in Pennsylvania) before April 1828. Apparently had five children, all of whom died in infancy. Baptized 9 January 1831 by Solomon Hancock. Confirmed 19 January 1831 by Lyman Wight. Ordained elder 21 January 1831 by John Whitmer. Appointed to travel to Missouri with Levi W. Hancock 6 June 1831; baptized many and established large branch of church in Winchester, Indiana, 1831. Returned to Ohio 15 June 1832. Ordained high priest by Reynolds Cahoon 17 July 1832. Attended School of Prophets 1833. On 20 February 1834 appointed to preach in Upper Canada. Member of Zion's Camp 1834. Temporary member of Clay County high council 1834. Ordained seventy 28 February 1835. Ordained president of First Quorum of Seventy 1 March 1835. Attended School of Elders in Kirtland 1836. Attended dedication of Kirtland Temple 1836. Released as president of First Quorum of Seventy 6 April 1837. Charter member of, and owned stock in, Kirtland Society 1837. Settled in Nauvoo 1839. Later moved to Kirtland; there chosen counselor in Kirtland Stake presidency 22 May 1841. Returned to Nauvoo by 1842. Assisted in rescuing Joseph Smith from Dixon arrest 1843. Appointed to travel to Michigan to campaign for Joseph Smith as President of United States April 1844. Received endowment 22 December 1845. Left Illinois with Saints 1846. Located in Winter Quarters. Arrived in Salt Lake Valley 24 July 1847. Returned to Winter Quarters November 1847. Took family to Utah 1851. Directed to locate in Spanish Fork, Utah, 1852. Ordained patriarch 31 May 1873 by John Taylor. Married Mary Mlott. Eight known children: John Graham, Mary Mlott, Zebedee, Haman, Electa, Sarah, Elizabeth, and Hugh. Died in Spanish Fork, Utah County, Utah, 21 July 1887.[17]

Biographical Note.   Edson Fuller.

Born 1809 in New York. Carpenter by trade. Married Celira (born 1811 in Ohio) about 1830. Six known children: Coryeden, Ceylor, Ellen, Elma, William, and Orrin. Fuller resided in Chardon, Ohio, from at least 1830 to 1843; there joined Church early 1831. Ordained elder before 3 June 1831. Appointed by revelation to travel to Jackson County, Missouri, with Jacob Scott 6 June 1831. Apparently did not go to Missouri but did preach gospel and baptize converts in Western Reserve. (Baptized David Johnson, brother to Benjamin F. Johnson.) Troubled with false spirits soon after baptism. Stripped of priesthood 1 September 1831. shortly thereafter denied faith. Moved to Grand Rapids, Kent County, Michigan, by 1850.[18]

Biographical Note.   Selah J. Griffin.

Born about 1792. Blacksmith by trade. One known child: Loyal C.R. Residing in Morgan, Ashtabula County, Ohio, 1820. Moved to Kirtland before 1827. Elected supervisor of highways for Kirtland 2 April 1827. Joined Church in Kirtland before June 1831. Ordained elder 6 June 1831 by Joseph Smith. Appointed by revelation to travel to Jackson County, Missouri, with Newel Knight June 1831. Subsequently directed to travel with Thomas B. Marsh. After completing mission, moved family to Jackson County, Missouri; resided in Independence Branch. Located in Clay County, Missouri, November 1833. Visited Kirtland area 1835-36. Ordained seventy 1836. Resided in Caldwell County, Missouri. Expelled from Missouri 1839. Filed affidavit 6 January 1840 for loss of personal property in Missouri. Residing in Knox County, Illinois, 1840. Did not migrate West with Saints.[19]

Biographical Note.   Levi Ward Hancock.

Son of Thomas Hancock and Amy Ward. Born 7 April 1803 in Old Springfield, Hampden County, Massachusetts. Moved with family to Ontario County, New York, 1805. Moved to Chagrin, Ohio, about 1820. Cabinetmaker by trade and good musician. Baptized by Parley P. Pratt 16 November 1830. Ordained elder soon thereafter by Oliver Cowdery. Appointed by revelation to travel to Jackson County, Missouri, June 1831 with Zebedee Coltrin; had much success, establishing large branch of Church in Winchester, Indiana. Married Clarissa Reed 1833. Eight children: Mosiah, Sariah, Elizabeth Amy, Francis Marion, John Reed, Levison, Levi W., and Joseph Smith. Member of Zion's Camp 1834. Ordained seventy 28 February 1835. Ordained president of First Quorum of Seventy shortly thereafter; served in position until death. Moved to Missouri 1838. Located in Nauvoo 1839. Member of Nauvoo Legion. Probable member of Council of Fifty 18 April 1844. Received endowment 12 December 1845. Left Illinois for West 1846. Member of Mormon Battalion July 1846-July 1847. Arrived in Salt Lake City October 1847. Married Emily Melissa Richey before 1849. Three known children: Emily Melissa, Temperance, and Levi W. Residing in Salt Lake City 1850. Located in Payson, Utah, 1850-51. Elected representative to territorial government from Utah County September 1851. Assisted in settling Manti, Sanpete County; there elected territorial representative 1852. Appointed to preach gospel along Wasatch Front October 1852. Back to Payson by 1855. Married Anne Tew 19 July 1857. Seven children: Levison, Zenis, Zenil, Ether Thomas, Cyrus, Solomon, and Samuel. Located in Salt Lake Tenth Ward by 1862. Appointed to go on cotton mission November 1862. Returned to Salt Lake City by 1863. About 1866 moved to Southern Utah and assisted in settling Harrisburg, Leeds, and Washington. Ordained patriarch 1872. Married Elizabeth Woodville Hovey and Mary Mogen. No known children. Died in Washington, Washington County, Utah, 10 June 1882.[20]

Biographical Note.   Solomon Hancock.

Son of Thomas Hancock and Amy Ward. Born 14 August 1793 at Springfield, Hampden County, Massachusetts. Moved with family to Ontario County, New York, about 1805. Joined Methodist Church 1814. Well known for excellent singing ability. Married Alta Adams 12 March 1815. Ten known children: Leucina, Rufus, Eliza, Joseph, Charles, George Washington, Asael, Agnus, Nephi, and Ammaron. Residing in Wolcott, Ontario County, New York, 1820. Moved to Columbia, Ohio, by 1823. Settled in Chagrin, Ohio, by 1830. Baptized by December 1830. Ordained elder before June 1831. Appointed by revelation to travel to Jackson County, Missouri, with Simeon Carter 6 June 1831. Returned to Chagrin late 1831. Moved family to Missouri 1832. Located temporarily in Van Buren County, Missouri, after Mormon expulsion from Jackson County 1833. On 23 June 1834, chosen to receive "endowment" in Kirtland. Appointed member of Clay County high council 7 July 1834. Mission to eastern states in fall of 1834. Wife Alta, died 18 January 1835. Participated in dedication of Kirtland Temple 1836. Married Phebe Adams 28 June 1836. Five known children: Isaac, Alta, Solomon, Elijah, and Jacob. Located in Caldwell County, Missouri, by December 1836; there owned property. Member of Far West high council. Sung hymn at dedication of Far West temple site 4 July 1838. Settled in Adams County,

Illinois, in spring of 1839. Moved to Lima, Hancock County, Illinois, 1841. Appointed member of high council in Lima 11 June 1843. Instructed to settle in Yelrome 8 October 1844; presided over Yelrome Branch. Received endowment 17 January 1846. Left Illinois April 1846. Located in Pottawattamie County, Iowa. Died 2 December 1847.[21]

Biographical Note.   Solomon Humphrey.

Son of Solomon Humphrey and Lucy Case. Born 23 September 1775 in Canton, Hartford County, Connecticut. Married Ursula Andrews. One known child: Luther. Residing in St. Lawrence County, New York, 1830. Converted to Church by Don Carlos Smith 1831. Ordained elder before June 1831. In June 1831 appointed by revelation to accompany Joseph H. Wakefield on mission to "eastern lands"; preached in St. Lawrence County, New York, and surrounding areas; there baptized George A. Smith 10 September 1832. Assisted in laying foundation stones of Kirtland Temple 23 July 1833. Member of Zion's Camp 1834. Volunteered to preach gospel in Missouri August 1834. Died in Clay County, Missouri, September 1834.[22]

Biographical Note.   George Fitch James.

Son of Stephen James. Born 1797 in Massachusetts. Married Caroline C. (born and previously married in Connecticut). Moved to Ohio by 1820. Located in Brownhelm, Lorain County, Ohio, by 1830. Three known children: Stephen, William, and Frederick. Stepdaughter, Jane A. Baptized by June 1831. Appointed to be ordained priest June 1831. Ordained elder by Hyrum Smith 18 November 1831. Disfellowshipped. On 4 April 1834 council of high priests reconsidered complaint against James and extended hand of fellowship. Additional charges brought November 1834. Did not gather with Saints in Missouri or Illinois. In 1844 contacted by Simeon Carter and encouraged to move to Nauvoo. Despite promise to do so, remained in Ohio. Listed in 1850 census as farmer with assets of $1,000. Died in Brownhelm, Lorain County, Ohio, November 1864. Widow died in Nebraska.[23]

Biographical Note.   Newel Knight.

Son of Joseph Knight and Polly Peck. Born 13 September 1800 at Marlborough, Windham County, Vermont. Moved with family to Bainbridge, New York, about 1809. Located with family in Colesville, New York, 1811. Married Sally Coburn (born 1804 in New York) 7 June 1825. Three known children: infant, Samuel, and Eli. Baptized May 1830 by David Whitmer. Ordained priest 26 September 1830. Located in Thompson, Ohio, May 1831. Ordained elder before June 1831. Led Colesville Branch to Jackson

County, Missouri, June-July 1831. Ordained high priest before 3 July 1832. Settled in Clay County, Missouri, after Saints expelled from Jackson County 1833. On 23 June 1834 appointed to receive "endowment" in Kirtland. Appointed member of Clay County high council 7 July 1834. Wife, Sally, died 15 September 1834. Arrived in Kirtland in spring of 1835. Married Lydia Goldthwaite (born 1812 in Massachusetts) 24 November 1835. Seven children: Sally, James, Joseph, Newel, Lydia, Jesse, and Hyrum. Participated in dedication of Kirtland Temple March 1836. Left Kirtland for Clay County, Missouri, 7 April 1836; arrived 6 May. Appointed member of high council in Far West, Missouri. Moved to Nauvoo 1839. Member of Nauvoo high council 1839-45. Received endowment 13 December 1845 in Nauvoo Temple. Left Nauvoo with Saints 1846. Died 11 January 1847 in Knox County, Nebraska.[24]

Biographical Note.   Isaac Morley.

Son of Thomas Morley and Edith Marsh. Born 11 March 1786 at Montague, Hampshire County, Massachusetts. Served in War of 1812. Married Lucy Gunn in Massachusetts 20 June 1812. Seven known children: Philena, Lucy Diantha, Editha Ann, Calista, Cordelia, Theresa A., and Isaac, Jr. Moved to Western Reserve before 1830. Assisted in introducing agriculture to Western Reserve. Baptized 15 November 1830. Ordained elder shortly thereafter. Ordained high priest 3 June 1831 and set apart as counselor to Bishop Edward Partridge. Appointed by revelation to travel to Missouri with Ezra Booth June 1831. Arrived in Jackson County July 1831. On 11 September 1831 chastised for unbelief and directed to sell farm in Kirtland and locate in Missouri. Member of Independence Branch in Jackson County. Suffered persecution in Jackson County, Missouri, 1833. Located in Clay County, Missouri, 1833. Appointed 23 June 1834 to receive "endowment" in Kirtland Temple. Left Missouri for Kirtland in early 1835. Arrived in Kirtland by May 1835. Appointed to accompany Edward Partridge on mission to eastern states May 1835. Left Kirtland 2 June 1835. Returned to Kirtland in late October having traveled, baptized three, and preached eighteen times. Revelation dated 7 November 1835 commended Morley for "integrity of his heart" and instructed him to attend Hebrew School as well as solemn assembly. Participated in dedication of Kirtland Temple March 1836. Returned to Missouri by May 1836. Located in Far West, Missouri, in fall of 1836. Ordained patriarch 7 November 1837. Arrested and temporarily incarcerated for treason, arson, murder, etc., November 1838. No conviction. Expelled from Missouri 1839. Located at Yelrome, Hancock County, Illinois, in 1839. Cooper by trade. Appointed president of Lima Stake 22 October 1840. After stake disorganized, appointed president of branch of Church at Lima on 11 June 1843. Received endowment 23 December 1843. Moved to Nauvoo 1845. Sealed to Harriet Lenora Snow 1846. No children. Sealed to Hannah Blakesley 14 January

1846. Three children: Joseph Lamoni, Simeon Thomas, and Mary Lenora. Left Nauvoo 1847. Settled at Winter Quarters until 1848; emigrated to Utah. Appointed presiding member of the Salt Lake high council 15 February 1849. Settled Sanpete Valley 1849. Member of general assembly of Provisional State of Deseret. Member of Utah Territorial Legislature 1851-55. Died 24 June 1865 at Fairview, Sanpete County, Utah.[25]

Biographical Note.   John Murdock.

Son of John Murdock and Eleanor Riggs. Born 15 July 1792 in Kortright, Delaware County, New York. Moved to Cuyahoga County, Ohio, about 1820. Joined with Sidney Rigdon in Campbellite movement about 1827. Married Julia Clapp 14 December 1823. Five children: Orrice, John Riggs, Phebe, Joseph, and Julia. Baptized by Parley P. Pratt 5 November 1830. Ordained elder November 1830. Preached numerous times in Western Reserve. Wife, Julia, died 30 April 1831. Appointed by revelation to travel to Jackson County, Missouri, with Hyrum Smith June 1831. Ordained high priest 6 June 1831. Returned to Ohio from Missouri June 1832. Appointed to preach in "eastern countries" August 1832. Preached in Kirtland area September 1832-April 1833. Attended School of Prophets 1833. Left for New York on mission with Zebedee Coltrin 3 April 1833. Returned to Kirtland 28 April 1834. Member of Zion's Camp 1834. Appointed member of Clay County high council 7 July 1834. Left for Ohio 24 September 1834. Arrived in Kirtland January 1835. Received patriarchal blessing 20 February 1835 from Joseph Smith, Sr. Left on mission to Delaware County, New York, 5 March 1835. Left Delaware County, New York, to preach in Vermont 10 November 1835. Married Amoranda Turner 4 February 1836 in New York. No children. Returned to Kirtland 24 February 1836. Left for Missouri 3 June 1836. Arrived in Ray County, Missouri, 14 July 1836. Assisted in settling Far West, Missouri, 1836. Member of Far West high council. Wife, Amoranda, died 16 August 1837. Married Electa Allen 3 May 1838. Three children: Gideon, Rachel, and Hyrum Smith. Appointed to settle DeWitt, Missouri, June 1838. Expelled from Missouri February 1839. Settled near Lima, Illinois; resided until 1841. Moved to Nauvoo in spring of 1841. Ordained bishop of Nauvoo Ward 20 August 1842; served until 29 November 1844. Mission to East November 1844. Wife, Electa, died 16 October 1845. Married Sarah Zuflet 13 March 1846 in Fulton County, Illinois. Two children: George Weire (adopted) and Brigham Young. Left Illinois for West May 1846. Arrived in Salt Lake Valley 24 September 1847. Member of Salt Lake high council. Appointed bishop of Salt Lake Fourteenth Ward 14 February 1849. Left on mission to Australia 12 March 1851. Arrived in Sydney 30 October 1851. Left for Utah 4 June 1852. Arrived in Salt Lake City 23 January 1853. Ordained patriarch 9 April 1854 by Heber C. Kimball. Resided in Lehi, Utah, 1854-67. Moved to Beaver, Utah, 1867. Died 23 December 1871.[26]

Biographical Note.   Simonds Ryder.

Born 20 November 1792 at Hartford, Washington County, Vermont. Moved to Hiram, Ohio, 6 January 1814 with colony from Vermont. Married Mahitable Loomis (born 1799 and also from Vermont) November 1818. Joined Campbellite movement May 1828; appointed to oversee members in Hiram. Baptized into LDS church in spring of 1831. Ordained elder 6 June 1831. In June 1831 instructed to receive calling previously given to Heman Bassett. Appointed to preach gospel during summer of 1831. Letter of appointment and license to preach both misspelled last name. Later used error as pretense to show call was not divinely inspired. Left Church in fall of 1831. Assisted others in tarring and feathering Joseph Smith 24 March 1832 in Hiram, Ohio. Later regained confidence with Campbellites. Remained in Hiram. Farmer of some prominence. Died 1 August 1870 in Hiram, Ohio.[27]

Biographical Note.   Jacob Scott.

Baptized and ordained elder before June 1831. Ordained high priest 3 June 1831. Appointed by revelation to travel to Jackson County, Missouri, with Edson Fuller 6 June 1831; apparently did not go. Left Church 1831. Positive identification cannot be made, but this Jacob Scott did *not* join the Church in Upper Canada.[28]

Biographical Note.   Harvey G. Whitlock.

Born 1809 in Massachusetts. Married Minerva (born 1810 in Connecticut) by 1830. Eight known children: Almon, Sally, Sclota, Herman, Hamer, Oscar, Maloni, and Parintha. Baptized and ordained elder before June 1831. Ordained high priest 3 June 1831 by Joseph Smith. Appointed by revelation to travel to Jackson County, Missouri, with David Whitmer June 1831. Located family in Missouri 1831. Member of Whitmer Branch. Expelled from Jackson County, Missouri, 1833. Stripped of priesthood and membership 1835. In 1835 wrote, "I have fallen from that princely station whereunto our God has called me. . . . I have sunk myself in crimes of the deepest dye." Revelation given 16 November 1835 counseled Whitlock to forsake sins, pursue virtuous life, and go immediately to Kirtland. On 30 January 1836 conference of First Presidency authorized Whitlock to be rebaptized and ordained high priest. Withdrew from Church during Missouri difficulties 1838. Residing in Cedar County, Iowa, 1840. Moved to Salt Lake City, Utah, by 1850; there listed as doctor. In February 1851 arrested as accessory to theft. Rebaptized about 1858. Moved to California by 1864; joined Reorganized LDS church.[29]

Biographical Note.   Lyman Wight.

Son of Levi Wight and Sarah Cardin. Born 9 May 1796 at Fairfield, Herkimer County, New York. Served short time in War of 1812. Married Harriet Benton 5 January 1823 at Henrietta, New York. Six children: Orange Lysander, Anna Christinia, Rosina Minerva, Lyman Lehi, Levi Lamoni, and Loami Limhi. Moved to Warrensville, Ohio, about 1826; remained until 1829. Joined Sidney Rigdon and Campbellite movement May 1829. Entered into covenant of "common stock" with Isaac Morley and Titus Billings. Moved to Kirtland February 1830. Baptized 14 November 1830. Confirmed 18 November 1830. Ordained elder 20 November 1830. Ordained to High Priesthood 3 June 1831. Appointed to travel to Missouri with John Corrill June 1831. Arrived in Jackson County, Missouri, 12 August 1831. With others, mission to Cincinnati, Ohio, 26 January 1832; baptized approximately one hundred. Returned to Independence 14 July 1832. Appointed to preside over Branch Number Seven in Jackson County, Missouri, 11 September 1833. Moved to Clay County, Missouri, late 1833. On 1 January 1834 sent with Parley P. Pratt to Kirtland, Ohio, to counsel with Church leaders concerning Saints' regaining Jackson County lands; arrived about 22 February 1834. Traveled with Joseph Smith, Sidney Rigdon, and others through Pennsylvania and New York to recruit for Zion's Camp. In late March 1834 went with others to Michigan to gather additional volunteers for Zion's Camp. On 5 May 1834, with nineteen men, left Pontiac for Missouri, reaching main body of Zion's Camp in Monroe County, Missouri, 8 June 1834. On 23 June 1834 chosen to receive endowment in Kirtland. Member of Clay County high council 8 July 1834. Left for Cincinnati on mission 13 March 1835. Returned to Clay County 18 May 1835. Left for Kirtland September 1835; arrived 3 November 1835. Attended School of Prophets 1835-36. Received patriarchal blessing 29 December 1835. Sent on mission in early 1836 to raise money for Church. After returning to Kirtland February 1836, left to visit mother in New York. Participated in dedication of Kirtland Temple 27 March 1836. Returned to Missouri in early May 1836. Mission to Illinois in fall of 1836. Moved to Caldwell County, Missouri, February 1837. Moved to Adam-Ondi-Ahman 1 February 1838. Appointed counselor in Adam-Ondi-Ahman Stake presidency 28 June 1838. Arrested for murder and treason November 1838. Incarcerated November 1838-April 1839 at Liberty Jail. No conviction. Escaped from law enforcement officers 16 April 1839. Located temporarily in Quincy, Illinois, in summer of 1839. Received assignment 5 May 1839 to gather affidavits concerning loss of life and damage sustained by Saints in Missouri. Mission to East, June-September 1839. Selected counselor in Zarahemla Stake presidency 19 October 1839 in Lee County, Iowa. Moved family to Augusta, Iowa, 15 November 1839. Appointed one of committee to build temple and Nauvoo House 19 January 1841. Ordained apostle 8 April 1841. Appointed to collect funds for construction of temple and Nauvoo House April 1841. Moved family to Nauvoo in fall of 1841. Traveled to Illinois, Kentucky, Tennessee, and Louisiana to collect money for temple and Nauvoo House during winter of 1841-42. Returned to Nauvoo from New Orleans with group of English Saints 15 March 1842. Initiated into Masonic Order 25 April 1842. Member of Nauvoo Legion and Nauvoo City Council. Assigned to travel east to preach and counter false reports propagated by John C. Bennett 1 September 1842. Met with several branches of Church in Ohio, New York, and Pennsylvania during next several months. Returned to Nauvoo 16 June 1843, having baptized "hundreds." On 22 July 1843 left with family and about one hundred fifty others for Black River (above LaCrosse, Wisconsin); there Nauvoo House committee had purchased pinery to provide lumber for homes, temple, and Nauvoo House. Preached to Indians while in Wisconsin. While on Black River, with others conceived idea of going to Texas to establish gathering place for southern converts. Returned to Nauvoo 1 May 1844. First attended a meeting of Council of Fifty 3 May 1844. Received endowment 14 May 1844. On 21 May 1844 left Nauvoo on mission to advocate Joseph Smith for President of United States. Preached and campaigned in St. Louis, Cincinnati, Pittsburgh, Philadelphia, New York City, Boston, and Baltimore. Arrived in Nauvoo 6 August 1844, after Prophet's death. In accord with decisions of Council of Fifty of 1844-45, spent winter on Black River anticipating move to Texas in spring of 1845. With about one hundred fifty others, left Wisconsin 28 March 1845, traveling down Mississippi for Texas. Arrived in Davenport, Iowa, 13 April 1845; there made preparations for overland journey. Left for Texas 21 May 1845. Spent winter of 1845-46 at evacuated fort called Georgetown in Williamson County, Texas. In April 1846 moved south to point on Colorado River four miles north of Austin, Texas. During summer of 1846 relocated to area called Zodiac, four miles south of Fredericksburg, Gillespie County, Texas, on Perdinales River. Married first plural wife, Mary Hawley, 1845. Two children: Miamomento and Romanon. Married Mary Ann Otis. Three children: Carrina, Rollondo, and infant. Married Margaret Ballentine. One known child: John W. Sustained as member of Quorum of Twelve Apostles until 1848. Cut off from Church 3 December 1848 because of his pamphlet entitled *An Address by way of an abridged account and journal of my life from February 1844, up to April 1848, with an appeal to the Latter-day Saints, scattered abroad in the earth* . . .[Austin, Texas(?), 1848] which rejected leadership of Twelve Apostles. Elected chief justice of Gillespie County, Texas, 1850. In 1851, after floods destroyed colony in Zodiac, group moved to Hamilton's Creek, about eight miles south of Burnet. In 1853 colony moved to site on Medina River, twelve miles south of Bandera, Texas. Called new location Mountain Valley. Died 31 March 1858 at Dexter, Medina County, Texas, about eight miles from San Antonio. Buried at Zodiac.[30]

Section 53

Date.   June 1831 (on or before 19 June).

Joseph Smith left for Missouri on 19 June 1831; thus, section 53 would have been received before that date.

Place.   Kirtland, Geauga County, Ohio.

Historical Note.   This revelation, received in response to A. Sidney Gilbert's request, instructed him to "forsake the world" and preach the gospel. In obedience to verses 4-5, Gilbert traveled, with the Prophet and others, to Independence, Missouri, where he eventually opened a store and was appointed to serve as a Church agent.[1]

Publication Note.   Section 53 was first published as chapter 55 in the Book of Commandments in 1833.

Biographical Note.   Algernon Sidney Gilbert.

Son of Eli Gilbert. Married Elizabeth Van Benthusen 30 September 1823. One known child: Loyal. Merchant and partner of Newel K. Whitney in Kirtland, Ohio, before 1830. Baptized about December 1830. Appointed by revelation to travel to Jackson County, Missouri, with Prophet and others June 1831. Ordained elder 6 June 1831. Arrived in Independence with wife about 25 July 1831. While in Missouri, appointed by revelation to locate in Jackson County and serve as bishop's agent. Returned to Ohio with William W. Phelps August 1831. Arrived before 1 September 1831. Moved to Independence before December 1831. Operated branch of Gilbert-Whitney store in Independence 1831-33. Ordained high priest 26 April 1832. Member of United Firm 26 April 1832. Mission to East June-December 1832. Visited relatives in Connecticut. Returned to Independence before 3 December 1832. Suffered persecution from citizens of Jackson County, Missouri, 1833. Expelled from Jackson County in fall of 1833. Located in Clay County, Missouri, 1833. On 23 June 1834 appointed to receive "endowment" in Kirtland. Died of cholera 29 June 1834 in Clay County, Missouri. Widow died in Utah.[2]

Section 54

Date.   June 1831 (before 19 June).[1]

Place.   Kirtland, Geauga County, Ohio.

Historical Note.   The Saints from Colesville, New York, arrived in the Western Reserve about mid-May 1831[2] and were located in Thompson, Ohio, on property claimed by Leman Copley. Intending to purchase some of Copley's property, Church leaders had made arrangements for members of the Church to occupy and improve the land. Soon after their arrival, the Saints from Colesville began to improve the property by making fences and plowing and planting the fields.[3] When Church members in Thompson were asked to consecrate their property to the Church, Copley refused to do so, and he even reneged on the previous land agreement.[4] With no place to live, members of the Church in Thompson "sent Newel Knight and other Elders" to see Joseph Smith.[5] Responding to their request, the Prophet inquired of the Lord and received section 54. Joseph Knight, Jr., remembering this occasion, stated:

> [After arriving in Thompson, Ohio, we] commenced preparing houses on a brother's land who had a thousand acres, my folks came on, they were called the Colesville church; we planted and sowed a great deal; the man was turned out of the church for bad conduct; his name was Leman Copley, he then began to persecute us and we had to leave his farm and pay sixty dollars damage for fitting up his houses and planting his ground. We then had a revelation to go to the western line of the States.[6]

This revelation instructed the Colesville Saints to "flee the land" and journey to Missouri. This group of about sixty members left Ohio on 3 July 1831 and arrived in Independence on 25 July.[7]

Publication Note.   Section 54 was first published as chapter 56 in the Book of Commandments in 1833.

Section 55

Date. June 1831 (after 6 June and before 19 June).[1]

Place. Kirtland, Geauga County, Ohio.

Historical Note. According to the "Far West Record", William W. Phelps arrived in Kirtland, Ohio, on or before 6 June 1831. He had come from Canandaigua, New York, where for two years he had edited *The Ontario Phoenix,* an anti-Masonic paper. Regarding Phelps's arrival in Kirtland, Joseph Smith noted,

> While we were preparing our journey to Missouri, William W. Phelps and his family arrived among us—"to do the will of the Lord," he said: so I inquired of the Lord concerning him and received [section 55].[2]

The revelation informed Phelps that he would be ordained to assist Oliver Cowdery with the work of printing Church literature and of "selecting and writing books for schools in the church, that little children also may receive instruction."[3] Phelps's expertise as a writer was put to immediate use in the Church (see Historical Note for section 70), and he subsequently became known as "printer unto the Church."[4]

Publication Note. Section 35 was first published as chapter 57 in the Book of Commandments in 1833.

Biographical Note. Joseph Coe.

Born 1785 in New Jersey. Married Sophia. Baptized and ordained elder before June 1831. Appointed by revelation to travel to Jackson County, Missouri, with Joseph Smith and others June 1831. Returned from Missouri 4 September 1831. Moved family to Mentor, Ohio, 22 September 1831. Ordained high priest 1 October 1832 by Joseph Smith. Mission to New York with Ezra Thayer 12 October-28 December 1831. Ordained and set apart as agent to purchase property for Church 18 March 1833. Assisted in laying foundation stones for Kirtland Temple 23 July 1833. Appointed member of Kirtland high council 17 February 1834. Worked on Kirtland Temple. Received blessing for working on Kirtland Temple 8 March 1835. Assisted in purchasing Egyptian mummies, including papyri, 1835. Participated in dedication of Kirtland Temple 1836. Rejected as high councilor 3 September

1837. Disaffected from Church leadership by December 1837. Excommunicated December 1838 by Kirtland high council, John Smith presiding. Farmer residing in Kirtland 1850.[5]

Biographical Note. William Wines Phelps.

Son of Enon Phelps and Mehitabel Goldsmith. Born 17 February 1792 at Hanover, Morris County, New Jersey. Moved with family to Homer, New York, 1800. Married Sally Waterman 28 April 1815. Ten children: William Waterman, Sabrina, Mehitabel, Sarah, Henry Enon, Janes, Jerusha, Lydia, Mary, and Princetta. Employed as editor of *Western Courier*. Moved to Trumansburg, New York, 1823; there commenced publication of *Lake Light*. Moved to Canandaigua, New York, by 1828; there published anti-Masonic *Ontario Phoenix*. Purchased copy of Book of Mormon from Parley P. Pratt 1830. Met Joseph Smith 21 December 1830. Baptized 1831. Moved to Kirtland, Ohio, June 1831. Appointed by revelation to assist Oliver Cowdery in printing Church literature June 1831. Prominent Church leader 1831-38. Traveled to Jackson County, Missouri, in summer of 1831. Directed to reside in Jackson County, Missouri, August 1831. Edited *Evening and Morning Star*. Member of Literary Firm. Printed Book of Commandments 1833. Moved to Clay County, Missouri, late 1833. Chosen counselor in presidency of Church in Missouri 8 July 1834. Directed to return to Kirtland temporarily to assist in Church printing affairs. Left Clay County 25 April 1835. Arrived in Kirtland 16 May 1835. Assisted in compiling 1835 edition of Doctrine and Covenants. Assisted in compiling and printing first Church hymnbook 1836. Participated in dedication of Kirtland Temple. Left Kirtland for Missouri 9 April 1836. During 1836-37, with John Whitmer, began to administer affairs of Church in Missouri—independent of high council. Actions created much confusion; excommunicated 10 March 1838. Moved to Dayton, Ohio, before March 1840. Contacted Orson Hyde and John E. Page June 1840. Repented and was extended hand of fellowship July 1840. Moved to Kirtland by May 1841; there began to strengthen Church. Appointed to preach in Ohio and East 23 May 1841. Located in Nauvoo 1841. Elected mayor's clerk and fire warden for City of Nauvoo 11 February 1843. Assisted Prophet as clerk, scribe, and confidant in wide range of activities 1841-44. Received endowment 9 December 1843. Member of Council of Fifty 11 March 1844. Sealed in Nauvoo Temple to Laura Stowell (born 1825 in New York) 2 February 1846. Sealed in Nauvoo Temple to Elizabeth Dunn (born 1828 in Alabama) 2 February 1846. Left Nauvoo for West 1846. Resided in Winter Quarters until 1849. Appointed to travel east and purchase press and type 31 March 1847. Completed purchase in Boston by August 1847. Returned to Winter Quarters 12 November 1847. Excommunicated 9 December 1847. Rebaptized 11 December 1847. Arrived in Salt Lake City 1849. Constructed adobe house in Old Fort; there resided until death.

Elected to Legislative Assembly of Territory of Utah 1841-57. Elected speaker of House 1851. Appointed member of Board of Regents of University of Deseret. Published *Deseret Almanac* 1851. Admitted to bar 7 October 1851. Died 6 March 1872 in Salt Lake City, Utah.[6]

Section 56

Date.   June 1831 (before leaving for Missouri on 19 June).[1]

Place.   Kirtland, Geauga County, Ohio.

Historical Note.   At the Church conference held in Kirtland the first week of June 1831, Thomas Marsh was appointed to travel to Missouri with Ezra Thayer. As many as 14 pairs of missionaries had been called to journey to the western boundaries of the United States, preaching along the way. Preparations were being made by the elders to leave Kirtland in mid-June.

A small snag developed, prior to the departure of the missionaries, when Elder Marsh's companion, Ezra Thayer, indicated that he would not be making the trip west. It is difficult to ascertain all the details of the problem, but Thayer's investment in a piece of real estate lay at the heart of the matter. The property was being shared by at least three parties, and apparently Thayer was requesting a division be made to secure his interests (see verse 9).

Section 56 was received in response to Thomas Marsh's concern over his mission. The essentials of the problem were later recorded by Elder Marsh:

> In June 1831 I was ordained a High Priest at a Conference held in Kirtland, where I received an appointment to go to Missouri with Ezra Thayer and preach by the way. In consequence of Ezra Thayer delaying so long, I went to Joseph who received the word of the Lord appointing Selah J. Griffin with whom I journeyed to Missouri preaching by the way.[2]

Griffin had earlier been assigned to travel with Newel Knight, but when the Colesville Branch at Thompson, Ohio were ejected from Leman Copley's land, Knight led the group to Jackson County, Missouri.[3]

Verse 8 refers to a "former commandment" which Ezra Thayer had received regarding the property in question. The unpublished revelation, received for Joseph Smith, Sr., and Ezra Thayer, gives insight into the historical setting of section 56:

Hearken unto my words and behold I will make known unto you what ye shall do as it shall be pleasing unto me for verily I say unto you it must needs be that ye let the bargain stand that ye have made concerning those farms until it be so fulfilled behold ye are holden for the one even so likewise thine advisary is holden for the other. Wherefore it must needs be that ye pay no more money for the present time until the contract be fulfilled and let mine aged servant Joseph and his family go into the house after thine advisary is gone and let my servant Ezra board with him and let all the brethren immediately assemble together to put up an house for my servant Ezra and let my servant Fredericks family remain and let the house be prepared and their wants be supplied and when my servant Frederick returns from the west behold and lo he desireth to take his family in mine own due time unto the west let that which belongeth unto my servant Frederick be secured unto him by deed or bond and thus he willeth that the brethren reap the good thereof let mine aged servant Joseph govern the things of the farm and provide for the families and let him have healp in as much as he standeth in need let my servant Ezra humble himself and at the conference meeting he shall be ordained unto power from on high and he shall go from thence (if he be obedient unto my commandments) and proclaim my gospel unto the western regions with my servants that must go forth even unto the borders of the Lamanites for behold I have a great work for them to do and it shall be given unto you to know what ye shall do at the conference meeting even so amen.

What shall the brethren do with the monies. Ye shall go forth and seek dilligently among the brethren and obtain lands and save the money that it may be consecrated to purchase lands in the west for an everlasting inheritance even so Amen.[4]

Missouri

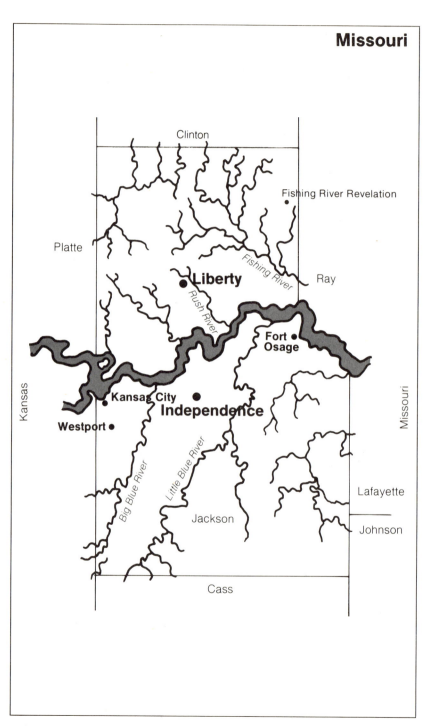

Clinton

Fishing River Revelation

Platte

Fishing River

Ray

Liberty

Rush River

Fort
Osage

Kansas

Kansas City

Independence

Missouri

Westport

Big Blue River

Little Blue River

Lafayette

Johnson

Jackson

Cass

Publication Note.   Section 56 was first published as chapter 58 in the Book of Commandments in 1833.

Section 57

Date.   July 1831 (20 July 1831).[1]

Place.   Jackson County, Missouri (Independence, as per "Kirtland Revelation Book", p. 89).

Historical Note.   Obedient to the instructions of section 52, numerous pairs of missionaries started for Independence, Missouri.[2] Joseph Smith with seven others (Martin Harris, Sidney Rigdon, Edward Partridge, William W. Phelps, Joseph Coe, A. Sidney Gilbert, and his wife, Elizabeth) left Kirtland for Missouri on 19 June 1831. This group traveled to Cincinnati by wagon, canal boat, and stage, from Cincinnati to Louisville, Kentucky, and from Louisville to St. Louis, Missouri by steamer. At St. Louis Sidney Rigdon and the Gilberts waited for water conveyance while the others went on foot to Independence,[3] where they arrived before 17 July 1831.[4] At Independence the Prophet and his party were greeted by Oliver Cowdery, others of the Lamanite Mission, and a handful of Missouri converts. Joseph Smith declared that this "meeting of our brethren, who had long awaited our arrival, was a glorious one, and moistened with many tears."[5] After "viewing the county [and] seeking diligently at the hand of God," Joseph Smith received section 57, which designated "the very spot upon which [the Lord] designed to commence the work of gathering," and the upbuilding of an 'holy city,' even the New Jerusalem.[6] On 2 August 1831, some twelve miles west of Independence, Sidney Rigdon consecrated and dedicated the land for the gathering of the Saints.[7]

The revelation clarified that "the place which is now called Independence is the center place; and a spot for the temple is lying westward, upon a lot which is not far from the court-house." (See verse 3.) On 3 August 1831, the Prophet dedicated a "spot" for the construction of a temple,[8] which was located approximately one-half mile west of the courthouse (the courthouse mentioned in verse 3 was a brick structure erected 1828-32).[9] Bishop Edward Partridge purchased a tract of land consisting of 63 and 43/166 acres from Jones

H. Flournoy on 19 December 1831 for $130. This purchase included the three-acre temple lot dedicated by the Prophet.[10]

Publication Note.   Section 57 was first published as section 27 in the 1835 edition of the Doctrine and Covenants.

Section 58

Date.   1 August 1831.

Place.   Jackson County, Missouri.

Historical Note.   During the last week of July 1831, members of the Colesville Branch as well as Sidney Rigdon and others arrived in Jackson County, Missouri. Section 58 was received shortly after their arrival.

Among other things, this revelation instructed Edward Partridge that Missouri would be "the land of his residence" (verse 24). On 5 August 1831 Partridge informed his wife by letter that some of the brethren were to "plant" their families in Jackson County as soon as possible, but "we are left to our own agreement how we will manage about getting our families here."[1] Verse 49 commanded that an agent be appointed "unto the Church in Ohio, to receive monies to purchase lands" in Missouri. Newel K. Whitney was later appointed to this office.[2]

Verses 35-39 encouraged Martin Harris to be an example to the rest of the Saints and consecrate his properties to the bishop in Missouri. Remembering the occasion, Orson Pratt said:

> [Martin Harris] was among the favored few who went up from the State of Ohio in the summer of 1831, and journeyed nearly a thousand miles to the western part of Missouri, to Jackson County. The Prophet went at the same time . . . . Martin Harris was the first man that the Lord called by name to consecrate his money, and lay the same at the feet of the Bishop in Jackson County, Mo., according to the order of consecration. He willingly did it; he knew the work to be true; he knew that the word of the Lord through the Prophet Joseph was just as sacred as

any word that ever came from the mouth of any Prophet from the foundation of the world. He consecrated his money and his substance, according to the word of the Lord. What for? As the revelation states, as an example to the rest of the Church.[3]

Verse 50 directed Sidney Rigdon to write a description of the land of Missouri. This he did, but the initial draft was not acceptable.[4] Verse 57 instructed Sidney Rigdon to dedicate the land of Zion, which he did on 2 August 1831.[5] Verse 58 directed that a conference be held before the Ohio elders returned home. This meeting was held on 4 August 1831, and the minutes in the "Far West Record" reveal that there were thirty-one members of the Church present. Undoubtedly referring to D&C 52:2 and 58:58, the record affirms that the meeting was held according to "special commandment." After a speech by Sidney Rigdon, the Prophet encouraged the missionaries to perform "acts of righteousness," and promised a blessing upon all that would keep "the commandments of the Lord."[6]

Verse 60 commanded that Ziba Peterson's license as an elder be revoked. After confession and a short period of "chastening," Peterson's priesthood privileges were temporarily restored to him on 4 August 1831.[7]

Publication Note.   Section 58 was first published as chapter 59 in the Book of Commandments in 1833.

Section 59

Date.   7 August 1831 (Sunday).[1]

Place.   Jackson County, Missouri.

Historical Note.   Section 59 is a revelation that speaks of Zion, the Decalogue, and the Sabbath Day. The sixty members of the Colesville Branch of the Church arrived in Jackson County, Missouri, on 25 July 1831. Among their number was Polly Knight (the wife of Joseph Knight, Sr.), who died 6 August 1831 and was buried on 7 August. She was the first member of the Church to die in Missouri. Joseph Knight, Sr., whose account differs slightly with regard to dates, stated that shortly after the arrival of the Colesville Branch,

> Joseph and Sidney and a number of Brotherin came and they looked out and Entered a Considrible of Land, for the People to Settle on. We found it a new Countty with some settlrs on it. There was one Joshua Lewis that had Come into the Church the winter Before, he and his wife. And they ware faithful and good to us and took us in to ther house, my wife Being sick as befor stated. She Died the Seventh Day of August and Joseph and Sidney attended her funeral on the eighth. She was Burried in the woods a spot Chosen and By our selves. I was along By where she was Buried a few Days after and I found the pigs had Begun to root whare she was Burried. I Being verry unwell But I took my ax the next Day and went and Bilt a pen around it. It was the Last I done for her.[2]

Speaking of Polly Knight, Joseph Smith declared, "a worthy member [she] sleeps in Jesus till the resurrection."[3]

Verses 1-2 have specific reference to Polly Knight's death.

Publication Note.   Section 59 was first published in the *Evening and Morning Star* (July 1833) and was included as chapter 60 in the Book of Commandments in 1833.

Section 60

Date.   8 August 1831.

Place.   Jackson County, Missouri.

Historical Note.   Following the dedication of Jackson County, Missouri, as the site of the New Jerusalem, a conference appointed for the Ohio missionaries was convened on 4 August 1831. Thereupon the missionaries prepared for their return to Ohio.[1] Before their departure, the Prophet inquired of the Lord about the return trip and received section 60.

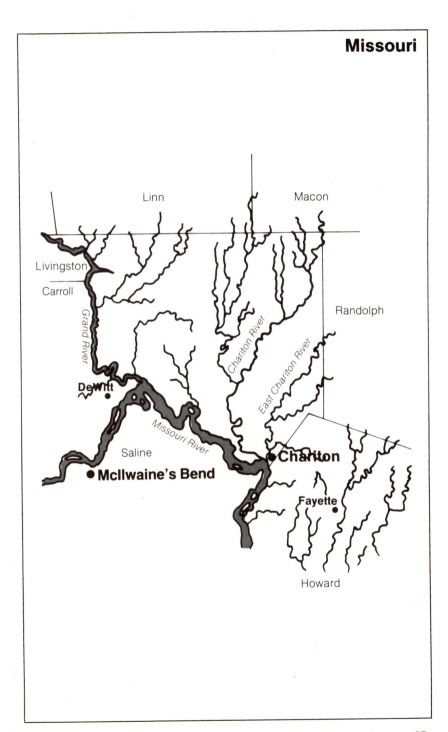

Missouri

Linn

Macon

Livingston

Carroll

Grand River

Randolph

Chariton River

East Chariton River

DeWitt

Missouri River

Saline

Chariton

McIlwaine's Bend

Fayette

Howard

The revelation instructed the elders to make or purchase a "craft" and return to Ohio by way of the Missouri River as far as St. Louis. At St. Louis and Cincinnati, Joseph Smith, Sidney Rigdon, and Oliver Cowdery were to "lift up their voice," while the remainder of the elders were to leave the water route at St. Louis and travel eastward in pairs, preaching along the way.

Elders who had not yet arrived in Jackson County were to hold a conference upon their arrival and then return home.

On 9 August 1831 Joseph Smith and ten others (Oliver Cowdery, Sidney Rigdon, Samuel H. Smith, Reynolds Cahoon, Sidney Gilbert, William W. Phelps, Ezra Booth, Frederick G. Williams, Peter Whitmer, Jr., and Joseph Coe) left Independence in canoes obtained for their conveyance down the Missouri River.[2]

Publication Note.   Section 60 was first published as chapter 61 in the Book of Commandments in 1833.

Section 61

Date.   12 August 1831.

Place.   McIlwaine's Bend, Missouri River (Missouri. See Historical Note.).

Historical Note.   After leaving Independence, Missouri, on 9 August 1831, the Prophet and his party traveled down the Missouri River to Fort Osage, where they spent the first night. Two days later (11 August) an accident occurred: The canoe in which the Prophet and Sidney Rigdon were riding ran into a tree lodged and bobbing in the river. The canoe was upset, and the occupants almost drowned. With this near tragedy, the party of eleven decided to land and encamp at a place called McIlwaine's Bend, some 100 miles from Independence.[1] The location of McIlwaine's Bend is near present-day Miami, Saline County, Missouri (see map). Section 61, which was received the following morning (12 August), while the party still were at McIlwaine's Bend, warned of the dangers of traveling on water. The revelation instructed Joseph Smith, Sidney Rigdon, and Oliver Cowdery to leave the water route and travel by land to Cincinnati, Ohio, where they were to "open their mouths" in preaching the gospel. William W. Phelps and Sidney Gilbert, who were returning to prepare to move to Missouri, were to continue in haste, while the remainder of the elders were to preach along the way.

After receiving the revelation at McIlwaine's Bend, Reynolds Cahoon wrote that the eleven men "then left the water [and] crossed the Misorie at Chariton."[2] A. Sidney Gilbert, also traveling east with the group, prefaced a copy of section 61 with the words: "A Commandment recd the 12th Aug 1831 on the Banks of the Missouri about 40 miles above Chariton on our return from Zion."[3] These references, seen together, assist greatly in locating McIlwaine's Bend, and suggest that the group left the Missouri River at or near the Miami Bend [McIlwaine's Bend], traveled several miles cross-country on the south side of the river, and then crossed the river and entered Chariton, Missouri.[4]

Publication Note. Section 61 was first published in the *Evening and Morning Star* (December 1832) and was included as chapter 62 in the Book of Commandments in 1833.

Section 62

Date. 13 August 1831.

Place. (Chariton, Chariton County, Missouri).[1]

Historical Note. After receiving section 61 at their encampment on McIlwaine's Bend, Joseph Smith and his ten companions crossed to the north side of the Missouri River and stopped at Chariton. Here they were happily surprised to find Hyrum Smith, John Murdock, David Whitmer, and Harvey Whitlock bound for Independence, Missouri. In this joyous setting section 62 was received.

The revelation instructed the four above-named missionaries to continue on to Independence and hold a meeting. These brethren did hold a meeting after their arrival in Jackson County, Missouri, on 24 August 1831.[2]

After this revelation was received, Joseph Smith, Sidney Rigdon, and Oliver Cowdery traveled on foot to Fayette, Missouri, where they took the stage to St. Louis. At St. Louis the trio again boarded a stage, this time for Kirtland, where they arrived 27 August 1831.[3]

Publication Note.   Section 62 was first published as chapter 63 in the Book of Commandments in 1833.

Section 63

Date.   August 1831 (30 August 1831).[1]

Place.   Kirtland, Geauga County, Ohio.

Historical Note.   Joseph Smith, Sidney Rigdon, and Oliver Cowdery arrived in Kirtland, Ohio, from Missouri on 27 August 1831. The following day Oliver was ordained to the High Priesthood.   Two days later section 63 was received. Items contained in this revelation as well as in section 64 (received on 11 September 1831) reflect the uneasy spirit of some of the members of the Church in Kirtland at the time. Joseph's absence from Kirtland during the summer of 1831 left the Mormon community without adequate leadership. This, combined with the dissatisfaction of some of the elders who went to Missouri with the Prophet, resulted in the apostasy of a number of the Saints. Although the dissension appears not to have been widespread, by October 1831 it was being referred to as "the falling away" at Kirtland.[2] The Prophet's preface to this revelation, written several years later, did not comment on the dissension, but focused on the high interest in gathering to Missouri. He noted, "I enquired of the Lord for further information upon the gathering of the saints and the purchase of the land and other matters."[3]

The "other matters" referred to by the Prophet were mentioned in the revelation: (1) Titus Billings was to dispose of property over which he had responsibility, (2) Newel K. Whitney was to retain his store and be ordained an agent for the Church, (3) Oliver Cowdery and Newel K. Whitney were to visit the churches, "expounding the scriptures and commandments, and obtaining moneys" to buy land in Missouri, (4) Sidney Rigdon was to rewrite a description of the land of Zion, the first draft having been unacceptable, and (5) Joseph Smith and Sidney Rigdon were to "seek a home."

Pursuant to the above instructions, Titus Billings made arrangements regarding his property and left for Missouri in the spring of 1832.[4] Newel K. Whitney and Oliver Cowdery visited the churches in the Western Reserve in the fall of 1831 to obtain donations from Church members.[5] Sidney Rigdon wrote another "epistle and subscription." This epistle, not part of the published history of the Church, is included below in its entirety. During the fall of 1831 Joseph Smith and Sidney Rigdon made arrangements to move to Hiram, Ohio, where they remained for nearly a year, the Prophet's family staying at the John Johnson home.

Sidney Rigdon's Epistle, 31 August 1831, Kirtland, Ohio

I Sidney a servant of Jesus Christ by the will of God the Father and through the faith of our Lord Jesus Christ unto the Saints which are scattered abroad in these last days May grace mercy & peace rest upon you from God the Father & from our Lord Jesus Christ who is greatly to be feared among his saints & to be had in reverence of all them who obey him—

Beloved brethren it has pleased God even the Father to make known unto us in these last days the good pleasure of his will concerning his saints & to make known unto us the things which he has decreed upon the nations even wasting and destruction until they are utterly destroyed & the earth made desolate by reason of the wickedness of its inhabitants according as he has made known in times past by the prophets & apostles that such calamities should befal the inhabitants of the earth in the last days unless they should repent & turn to the living God And as the time is now near at hand for the accomplishment of his purposes & the fulfilment of the prophecies which have been spoken by all the holy prophets ever since the world began he has sent & signified unto us by the mouth of his holy prophet that he has raised up in these last days the speedy accomplishment of his purposes which shall be accomplished on the heads of the rebellious of this generation among whom he has been pleased in much mercy & goodness to send forth the fulness of his gospel in order that they might repent & turn to the living God & be made partakers of his holy Spirit but by reason of their wickedness & rebellion against him & stubborn & rebellious hearts the Lord withdraws his spirit from them & gives them up to work all uncleanness with greadiness & to bring swift destruction on themselves & through their wickedness it hastens the day of their calamity that they may be left without excuse in the day of vengenance

But it has pleased our Heavenly Father to make known some better things concerning his saints & those who serve him in fear & rejoice in meekness before him even things which pertain to life everlasting for godliness has the promise of the life that now is & that which is to come even so it has pleased our Heavenly Father to make provision for his saints in these days of tribulation that they through faith & patience & by continuing in well doing may preserve their lives before him & attain unto rest & endless felicity but by no other means than that of a strict observance of his commandments & teachings in all things as there is nor can be no ruler nor lawgiver in the Kingdom of God save it be God even our Savior himself & before him he requires that all his saints & those who have named the name of Jesus should be careful to depart from iniquity & serve him with fear & rejoice with trembling lest he be angry & they perish from the way According to the predictions of the ancient prophets that the Lord would send his messengers in the last days & gather together his elect (which are the elect according to the covenant namely those who like Abraham are faithful to God & the word of his grace) from the four winds even from one end of Heaven to the other as testified of by the Savior himself So in these last days he has commenced to gather them unto a place provided before of God & had in reserve from days of old being kept by the power & providence of God for this purpose & which he now holds in his own hands that they through faith & patience may inherit the promises a land which God by his own commandment has consecrated to himself where he has said that his laws shall be kept & where his saints can dwell in safty through their perservance in well doing & their unfeigned repentance of all their sins our Heavenly Father has provided this land himself because it was the one which was best adapted for his children where Jew & Gentile might dwell together for God has the same respect to all them that call upon him in truth & righteousness whether they be Jew or whether they be gentile for there is no respect of persons with him. This land being sittuated in the centre of the continent on which we dwell with an exceeding fertile soil & cleared ready for the hand of the cultivator bespeaks the goodness of our God in providing so goodly a heritage & its climate suited to persons from every quarter of this continent whether east west north or south yea I think I may say for all consitutions from every part of the world & its productions nearly all the varieties of both grain & vegetables which are common to this country together with the means of cloathing in addition to this it abounds with fountains of pure water the soil climate & surface all adapted to health indeed I may say that the whole properties of the country invite the saints to come & partake in their blessings but what more need I say about a country which our Heavenly Father holds in his hands for if it were unhealthy he could make it healthy & if barren he can make it fruitful Such is the land which God has provided for us in these last days for an inheritance & truly it is a goodly land & none other so well suited for all the saints as this & all those who have faith & confidence in God who has ever seen this land will bear the same testimony. In order that you may understand the will of God respecting this land & the way & means of possessing it I can only refer you to commandments which the Lord has delivered by the mouth of his prophet which will be read to you by our brethren Oliver & Newel whom the Lord has appointed to visit the churches & obtain means for purchasing this the land of our inheritance that we may escape in the day of tribulation which is coming on the earth.

I conclude by exhorting you to hear the voice of the Lord your God who is speaking to you, in much mercy & and who is sending forth his word & his revelations in these last days in order that we may escape impending vengance & the judgements which await this generation & which will speedily overtake them. Brethren pray for me that I may be counted worthy to obtain an inheritance in the land of Zion & to overcome the world through faith & dwell with the sanctified forever & ever Amen.[6]

Publication Note.   Section 63 was first published in the *Evening and Morning Star* (February 1833) and was included as chapter 64 in the Book of Commandments in 1833.

Biographical Note.   Titus Billings.

Son of Ebenezer Billings and Esther Joyce. Born 25 March 1793 in Greenfield, Franklin County, Massachusetts. Married Diantha Morley in Geauga County, Ohio, 16 February 1817. Nine children: Samuel Dwight, Thomas, Ebenezer, Emily, Martha, Alfred Nelson, George Pierce, Eunice, and Titus, Jr. Baptized in Kirtland, Ohio, by Lamanite missionaries about 15 November 1830. Ordained deacon by October 1831. Ordained elder 10 March 1832 by Thomas B. Marsh. Appointed by revelation August 1831 to move to Missouri in spring of 1832. Left for Independence, Missouri, early 1832, arriving before 26 May. Expelled from Jackson County, Missouri, 1833. Settled in Clay County, Missouri, 1833. Ordained high priest and counselor in bishopric in Missouri 1 August 1837. Participated in Battle of Crooked River October 1838. Located in Lima, Adams County, Illinois, after Mormon expulsion from Missouri 1839. Member of Nauvoo Legion 4 February 1841. Moved to Nauvoo 1845. Received endowment 13 December 1845. Sealed in Nauvoo Temple to Diantha Morley 30 January 1846. Moved to Salt Lake Valley 1848. Appointed to settle Sanpete Valley in fall of 1849. One of first settlers of Manti, Utah. Married Mary Ann Tuttle 20 January 1854. Four children: Emily, Titus, Theressa, and Alonzo. Located in Provo, Utah, about 1863. Died in Provo, Utah County, Utah, 6 February 1866.[7]

Biographical Note.   Newel Kimball Whitney.

Son of Samuel Whitney and Susanna Kimball. Born 5 February 1795 at Marlborough, Windham County, Vermont. Located in Painesville, Ohio, about 1817; there employed by merchant A. Sidney Gilbert. Later became junior partner to Gilbert at Kirtland. Married Elizabeth Ann Smith (born 1800 in Connecticut) 20 October 1822. Eleven children: Horace K., Sarah Ann, Franklin K., Mary Elizabeth, Orson K., John K., Joshua K., Ann Maria, Don Carlos, Mary Jane, and Newel Melchizedek. Associated with Sidney Rigdon in Campbellite movement before 1830. Baptized November 1830. Appointed by revelation to be ordained bishop's agent in Kirtland area 31 August 1831. Ordained agent 1 September 1831. Appointed by revelation to be bishop in Kirtland 4 December 1831. Member of United Firm 12 March 1832. Appointed by revelation to travel with Prophet and others to Missouri March 1832. Left Kirtland 1 April 1832. Arrived in Independence 24 April 1832. Left for Ohio 6 May 1832. Detained four weeks in Indiana after breaking leg. Arrived in Kirtland July 1832. Appointed by revelation to take mission to Albany, New York City, and Boston 22 September 1832. Left Kirtland September 1832. Returned 6 November 1832. Attended School of

Prophets 1833. Appointed to take charge of Peter French farm 4 June 1833. Left for New York City to purchase goods to replenish store 1 October 1833. Returned to Kirtland about 1 December 1833. Worked on Kirtland Temple. Received blessing 7 March 1835 for working on Kirtland Temple. Received patriarchal blessing 14 September 1835. Left for New York City with Hyrum Smith to purchase goods for store 7 October 1835. Returned late October 1835. Offered sumptuous feast for Prophet's family 7 January 1836. Participated in dedication of Kirtland Temple March 1836. Charter member of Kirtland Safety Society January 1837. Appointed by revelation to move to Missouri 8 July 1838. Left for Missouri in fall of 1838. Reached St. Louis; there learned of extermination order. Located family temporarily in Carrollton, Greene County, Illinois, 1838. Returned to Kirtland to finish up business during winter of 1838-39. Returned to Carrollton, Illinois, in spring of 1839. Settled in Nauvoo 1839. Appointed bishop of Nauvoo Middle Ward 6 October 1839. Elected alderman for City of Nauvoo 1 February 1841. Received endowment 4 May 1842. Member of Council of Fifty 11 March 1844. Appointed to assume responsibilities of trustee-in-trust for Church 9 August 1844. Married plural wife, Emmeline Belos Woodward, 24 February 1845. Two known children: Isabel Modalena and Melvina Caroline Blanch. Sealed to wife, Elizabeth Ann, on 7 January 1846. Married Olive Maria Bishop 7 January 1846. No known children. Married Anna Houston 7 January 1846. One child: Jethro Houston. Married Elizabeth Mahala Moore 7 January 1846. No known children. Married Elizabeth Almira Pond 7 January 1846. No known children. Married Abigail Augusta Pond 7 January 1846. No known children. Married Henrietta Keys 26 January 1846. No known children. Left Nauvoo for West 1846. Located in Winter Quarters 1846. Arrived in Salt Lake Valley 8 October 1848. Elected justice of peace 12 March 1849. Bishop of Salt Lake Eighteenth Ward. Died 23 September 1850 in Salt Lake City, Utah.[8]

Section 64

Date   11 September 1831.[1]

Place.   Kirtland, Geauga County, Ohio.

Historical Note.   During the early part of September 1831, Joseph Smith made preparations to move to Hiram, Ohio, where he intended to continue the work of the inspired translation of the Bible without interruption.[2] For about one year, during an important period of the Bible translation, the Prophet and his family would reside just outside of the town of Hiram, in the two-story home of John and Elsa Johnson, who had been converted to the Church in early 1831.[3] This revelation was received the day before the Prophet departed for Hiram, Ohio.

As was noted in the Historical Note for section 1, the printing of the Book of Commandments was not completed. A mob destroyed the Church printing press on 20 July 1833, just as the project neared completion. Prior to the destruction of the press, the printer had set type for all of section 64 as we now have it, save the last seven verses—which would have followed on the next page. Consequently, salvaged copies of this first compilation of revelations (roughly sections 1-64) did not contain a complete text of section 64. They were included, however, in the 1835 edition printed in Kirtland.

Verse 20 instructed Isaac Morley to sell his farm, which he did on 12 October 1831. Frederick G. Williams was directed *not* to sell his 144-acre farm.

Publication Note.   Section 64, except for the last seven verses, was first published as chapter 65 in the Book of Commandments in 1833.

Biographical Note.   Frederick Granger Williams.

Son of William Williams and Ruth Granger. Born 28 October 1787 at Suffield, Hartford County, Connecticut. Moved with family to Cleveland, Ohio, about 1799. Worked as pilot on Lake Erie, transporting goods and passengers between Buffalo and Detroit. Married Rebecca Swain late 1815. Four known children: Lovina Susan, Joseph Swain, Lucy Eliza, and Ezra Granger. Located in Warrensville, Ohio, by 1816; there engaged in farming. Studied medicine and moved to Kirtland to practice by 1830. Owned 144 acres of land in Kirtland 1830; subsequently gave land to Church. Baptized November 1830. Ordained elder November 1830. Accompanied Lamanite missionaries to Jackson County, Missouri, late 1830. First met Joseph Smith in Jackson County, Missouri, August 1831. Returned to Kirtland by September 1831. Ordained high priest 25 October 1831. Began serving as scribe for Joseph Smith 20 July 1832. Ordained member of presidency of High Priesthood 18 March 1833. Member of United and Literary firms. Member of Zion's Camp 1834. Attended School of Prophets and Hebrew School in Kirtland. Appointed to edit *Northern Times* (supportive of Democratic Party) May 1835. Worked on Kirtland Temple. Received blessing for working on Kirtland Temple March 1835. Participated in dedication of Kirtland Temple March 1836. Elected justice of peace in Kirtland June 1836. Owned stock in Kirtland Safety Society 1837. Charged with misconduct May 1837. No decision in case. Out of harmony with Prophet over Kirtland Bank 1837. Moved to Far West, Missouri, 1837.

Dropped from First Presidency November 1837; subsequently excommunicated. Rebaptized about July 1838. Expelled from Missouri 1839. Excommunicated *in absentia* 17 March 1839. Located in Quincy, Illinois, 1839. Extended hand of fellowship 8 April 1840. Died in Quincy, Adams County, Illinois, 10 October 1842. Proxy sealing to Rebecca Swain 7 February 1846 in Nauvoo Temple.[4]

Section 65

Date. October 1831 (30 October, according to "Kirtland Revelation Book," p. 87, and *Evening and Morning Star*).

Place. Hiram, Portage County, Ohio.

Historical Note. Section 65 is a prayer, received by revelation, in Hiram, Ohio.[1]

Publication Note. Section 65 was first published in the *Evening and Morning Star* (September 1832) and was included as section 24 in the 1835 edition of the Doctrine and Covenants.

Section 66

Date. 25 October 1831.

Place. Orange, Cuyahoga County, Ohio.

Historical Note. Section 66 is a revelation received by Joseph Smith for William McLellan. An important conference of the Church was held in Orange, Ohio, on 25 October 1831 at the home of Sirenus Burnett. At this meeting many were ordained to various offices of the priesthood, including McLellan, who along with sixteen other elders, was ordained to the High Priesthood by Oliver Cowdery. The conference also served as an opportunity for many of the priesthood brethren to bear their testimonies of the truthfulness of the work in which they were engaged. William E. McLellan, who gave the closing prayer at the conference, stated that "he had the greatest reason to rejoice of any present," and that he "would be subject to the will of God even unto death."[1]

It was at this conference that McLellan first saw and became acquainted with Joseph Smith. Concerning this occasion McLellan wrote,

> On the 25th Oct. I attended a conference. General peace and harmony pervaded the conference and much instruction to me. From thence I went home with Jos. and lived with him about three weeks; and from my acquaintance then and until now I can truely say I believe him to be a man of God. A Prophet, a Seer and Revelator to the church of christ.[2]

McLellan's commission in verse 7 to go and preach the gospel "unto the eastern lands" was revoked on 25 January 1832.[3]

An interesting note in the "Kirtland Revelation Book" states that section 66 is, "a Revelation given to William E. McLelin a true decendent from Joseph that was sold in Egypt down through the loins of Ephraim his son."

Publication Note.   Section 66 was first published as section 74 in the 1835 edition of the Doctrine and Covenants.

Biographical Note.   William E. McLellan.

Son of Charles McLellan. Born 18 January 1806 in Smith County, Tennessee. Married Cynthia Ann 30 July 1829. Wife, Cynthia, died before 1832. School teacher in Paris, Tennessee, 1831. Contacted by Harvey Whitlock and David Whitmer July 1831. Traveled to Independence, Missouri, 30 July-18 August 1831 to see Joseph Smith. Missed seeing Prophet. Baptized about 20 August 1831 in Independence. Ordained elder 24 August 1831. Left Independence for Tennessee with Hyrum Smith 25 August 1831. Preached first sermon as elder 28 August 1831. After arriving in Paris, Tennessee, left with Hyrum Smith for Kirtland; arrived 18 October 1831. Met Joseph Smith 25 October 1831. Through Joseph Smith received revelation 25 October 1831; instructed to take mission to "eastern lands" with Samuel H. Smith. Did preach in Pennsylvania, but mission short-lived because of disobedience and sickness. Appointed by revelation 25 January 1832 to preach in "south countries." Preached in Middlebury, Ohio, 25 February 1832 but did not continue on mission because of illness. Remained in Middlebury until April 1832. Married Emeline Miller (born 4 September 1819 in Vermont) 26 April 1832 in Hiram, Ohio. Three known children: Helen, William Clark, and

Marcus W. Left Ohio for Independence, Missouri, 2 May 1832. Arrived in Independence 16 June 1832. Located in Clay County, Missouri, 1833. Chosen high councilor in Clay County 7 July 1834. Appointed to return to Ohio with Joseph Smith July 1834. Taught in School of Elders in Kirtland. Ordained apostle 15 February 1835. Disfellowshipped summer 1835. Restored 25 September 1835. Attended dedication of Kirtland Temple 1836. Lost confidence in Church leadership August 1836. Publicly opposed Church leaders 11 May 1838 in Far West, Missouri. Excommunicated 1838. Took up practice of medicine after leaving Church. Living in Hampton, Rock Island County, Illinois, January 1845. Attempted to organize new Church in Kirtland January 1847. Published *Ensign of Liberty* in Kirtland 1847. Residing in Linden, Genesse County, Michigan, 1861. Joined Hedrickites 5 June 1869. Left Hedrickites 3 November 1869. Wife joined Reorganized LDS Church. Moved to Independence 1870. Spent remainder of life trying to get David Whitmer to organize new Church. Died in Independence, Jackson County, Missouri, 24 April 1883.[4]

Section 67

Date. November 1831 (1 November).

Circumstantial evidence found in both the *History of the Church* (1:226) and the "Far West Record" (p. 19) reveals that section 67 was received on 1 November 1831.

Place. Hiram, Portage County, Ohio.

Historical Note. Some of the ten elders present at the Hiram Conference (Joseph Smith, Oliver Cowdery, David Whitmer, John Whitmer, Peter Whitmer, Jr., Sidney Rigdon, William E. McLellan, Luke Johnson, Lyman Johnson, and Orson Hyde) expressed concern over the seemingly uneducated language found in the revelations then ready for printing. In response, Joseph Smith received section 67, which challenged the wisest of those present to duplicate any revelation, "even the least that is among them." William E. McLellan, a newly baptized school teacher from Paris, Tennessee, accepted the challenge but failed.

Care should be taken not to condemn McLellan unduly for his participation in this matter. McLellan had met Joseph Smith for the first time only seven days before this meeting. Because he later became a bitter enemy of the Prophet, it is easy to adopt a retroactive interpretation of this circumstance. Consider section 68, which refers to him as one of "the faithful elders of my church."

After McLellan's attempt to write a revelation, Joseph Smith concluded,

> The Elders and all present that witnessed this vain attempt of a man to imitate the language of Jesus Christ, renewed their faith in the fulness of the Gospel, and in the truth of the commandments and revelations which the Lord had given to the Church through my instrumentality.[1]

Publication Note. Section 67 was first published as section 25 in the 1835 edition of the Doctrine and Covenants.

Section 68

Date. November 1831.

The date of reception for section 68 is uncertain. While the *History of the Church* indicates that the revelation came near the commencement of the Hiram Conference (1-3 November 1831), minutes in the "Far West Record" suggest that section 68, or part of it, was received on 11 November 1831. It appears that verses 1-13 were received 1-3 November, and verses 13-35 on 11 November.[1]

The minutes of two different meetings, recorded in the "Far West Record" refer to a revelation received Friday, 11 November 1831, in Hiram, Ohio. First, 3 July 1832 eighteen high priests and elders met at the home of Edward Partridge in Independence, where it was agreed that the "mode and manner of regulating the Church of Christ take effect from this time, according to a Revelation received in Hiram Portage County Ohio Nov. 11, 1831." A second reference to the date of section 68 is recorded in the "Far West Record" under the date 5 October 1832, again in Missouri. A group of fifteen high priests had met in Independence to conduct certain business when it was "moved by br. [William W.] Phelps that a revelation given 11th November be read."[2] It seems clear that the second source is referring to section 68: Matters discussed at the October 1832 meeting concerned the high priests and their responsibilities, topics contained in section 68.

Place. Hiram, Portage County, Ohio.

Historical Note. Section 68 is a composite of two or more revelations. Verses 1-12 were received by Joseph Smith at the request of Orson Hyde, Luke Johnson, Lyman Johnson, and William E. McLellan.[3] Verses 13-35 speak of literal descendants of Aaron, high priests, and their relationship to the office of bishop.

The revelation is significant in that it established the fact that bishops must be high priests,[4] and in cases of alleged wrongdoing, they were accountable only to a "conference of high priests."[5] Additionally, section 68 gave the age of accountability (i.e., age eight).[6]

It is noteworthy that the content of verses 13-35 of section 68 is similar to that of verses 59-100 of section 107, also received in November 1831.[7]

Publication Note. Section 68 was first published in the *Evening and Morning Star* (October 1832) and was included as section 22 in the 1835 edition of the Doctrine and Covenants.

Biographical Note. Orson Hyde.

Son of Nathan Hyde and Sally Thorpe. Born 8 January 1805 in Oxford, New Haven County, Connecticut. Lost both parents by 1817. Resided with Nathan Wheeler family until 1823. Moved to Ohio about 1819. Member of Methodist Church 1827. Resided with Sidney Rigdon for indefinite period. Joined Campbellite movement. Baptized into LDS Church by Sidney Rigdon 2 October 1831. Ordained elder October 1831. Appointed by revelation to accompany Samuel H. Smith on mission to eastern states 25 January 1832; with Samuel H. Smith baptized sixty converts during eleven-month mission. Attended School of Prophets 1833. Mission to Erie County, Pennsylvania, with Hyrum Smith early 1833. Appointed Clerk to First Presidency 6 June 1833. Dispatched to Jackson County, Missouri, with John Gould to inform Missouri Saints to seek redress through law. Left Kirtland mid-August 1833 and returned to Kirtland 25 November 1833. Member of Kirtland high council February 1834-February 1835. Member of Zion's Camp 1834. Married Marinda Nancy Johnson 4 September 1834. Ten children: Nathan, Laura Marinda, Emily Matilda, Orson Washington, Frank Henry, Alonzo Eugene, Delia Ann, Heber John, Mary Lavinia, and Zina Virginia. Ordained apostle 15 February 1835. Mission to eastern states in summer of 1835. Disfellowshipped 4 August 1835 for defaming Sidney Rigdon. Restored 26 September 1835. Received patriarchal blessing 29 December 1835. Attended dedication of Kirtland Temple March 1836. Attended Hebrew School in Kirtland. Mission to Upper Canada in summer of 1836. Sent to Columbus, Ohio, to seek corporate charter for Kirtland Bank from Ohio legislature in late 1836; returned to Kirtland about 1 January 1837 without success. Mission to England 1837-38. Left Kirtland 13 June 1837. Arrived in Liverpool 20 July 1837. With others baptized hundreds into Church. Left Liverpool for United States 20 April 1838. Arrived in Kirtland 21 May 1838. Moved to Far West, Missouri, arriving about mid-July 1838. Signed affidavit against Joseph Smith 24 October 1838. Fellowship withdrawn 1838. Restored to former position 27 June 1839. Settled in Illinois 1839. Left on mission to East 14 November 1839. Met George W. Robinson enroute; decided to assist Robinson in publishing history of Church written by Sidney Rigdon. Returned to Nauvoo January 1840. Appointed to take mission to Jerusalem 6 April 1840. Left Nauvoo 15 April 1840. Arrived in Jerusalem 21 October 1841. Dedicated land of Israel for return of Jews 24 October 1841. Returned to Nauvoo 7 December 1842. Elected to Nauvoo City Council 6 February 1841. Appointed to take mission to Russia June 1843; did not fulfill appointment. Traveled to East in fall of 1843 to gather donations for Russia mission. Received endowment 2 December 1843. Took first plural wife, Martha Rebecca Browett (born 1819 in England), early 1843. No known children. Married Mary Ann Price (born 1816 in England) about April 1843. One child: Urania. Member of Council of Fifty 13 March 1844. Carried petition drafted by Joseph Smith to Washington, D.C., 1844. Left Nauvoo 4 April 1844. Arrived in Washington 23 April 1844. Returned to Nauvoo apparently after 8 August 1844. Left Nauvoo for West 1846. Settled at Council Bluffs. Second mission to England 1846-47. Presided over Church at Winter Quarters 1847-50. Published *Frontier Guardian* in Kanesville, Iowa (1849-52). Moved to Utah 1850. Returned to Kanesville in fall of 1850. Again to Utah and back to Kanesville 1851. Settled in Utah 1852. Married Ann Eliza Vickers. Six known children: Charles Albert, George Lyman, Joseph Smith, Maria Louisa, Melvin Augustus, and Geneva. Married Julia Thomene Reinart. Five known children: Mary Ann, William Arthur, Hyrum Smith, David Victor, and Aurelia Fiducia. Appointed to lead settlers to Fort Supply in Green River 1853. Presided over missionaries and Church in Carson Valley (Nevada). Appointed to preside over affairs in Sanpete County. Took up residence in Spring City, Sanpete County, Utah. Died in Spring City 28 November 1878.[8]

Biographical Note.   Luke Samuel Johnson.

Son of John Johnson and Elsa Jacobs. Born 3 November 1807 in Pomfret, Windsor County, Vermont. Baptized 10 May 1831 by Joseph Smith. Ordained priest by Christian Whitmer soon after baptism. Ordained elder before October 1831. Mission to southern Ohio with Robert Rathburn 1831. Joined with Sidney Rigdon preaching gospel in New Portage, Ohio, area (together baptizing about fifty persons 1831) and in Pittsburgh area (baptizing Rigdon's mother and others of Rigdon family). Ordained high priest 25 October 1831. Mission to Virginia and Kentucky with Seymour

Brunson and Hazen Aldrich 1832-33 (baptizing more than a hundred persons). Married Susan H. Poteet 1 November 1833. Six children: Elsa Mary, Fanny, Eliza, Vashata, James, and Solomon. Member of Kirtland high council 17 February 1834. Member of Zion's Camp 1834. Ordained apostle 15 February 1835. Mission to eastern states in summer of 1835. Returned to Kirtland September 1835. Attended Hebrew School in Kirtland in winter of 1835-36. Attended dedication of Kirtland Temple March 1836. Mission to New York and Upper Canada 1836. Returned to Kirtland in fall of 1836. Charter member of, and owned stock in, Kirtland Safety Society 1837. Alienated from Joseph Smith 1837. Filed charge against Prophet for speaking reproachfully against brethren May 1837. Disfellowshipped 3 September 1837. Excommunicated December 1838. Taught school in Cabell County, Virginia, 1838. Studied medicine. Returned to Kirtland; there practiced medicine. Rebaptized in Nauvoo by Orson Hyde 8 March 1846. Married America Morgan Clark March 1847. Eight children: Susan Marinda, Orson Albert, Mark Anthony, Charlotte Elizabeth, John Joseph, Lovinia Ann, Phebe W., and Luke. Arrived in Salt Lake Valley July 1847. Received endowment 1 April 1854. Settled in St. John, Tooele County, Utah, 1858. Bishop of Church in St. John. Died in home of brother-in-law, Orson Hyde, in Salt Lake City, Utah, 9 December 1861.[9]

Biographical Note.   Lyman Eugene Johnson.

Son of John Johnson and Elsa Jacobs. Born 24 October 1811 at Pomfret, Windsor County, Vermont. Moved to Hiram, Ohio, with family about 1820. Baptized in February 1831 by Sidney Rigdon. Ordained elder 25 October 1831 by Oliver Cowdery. Ordained high priest 1 November 1831. Appointed by revelation to take mission with Orson Pratt 25 January 1832. Left with Pratt for East 3 February 1832. Preached in Pennsylvania, New York, New Jersey, Vermont, New Hampshire, Connecticut, and Massachusetts. Returned to Kirtland about February 1833, having baptized more than one hundred converts. Attended School of Prophets early 1833. Another mission to East with Orson Pratt 1833. Left Kirtland 26 March 1833. Returned 28 September 1833, having baptized fifty persons. Left Kirtland again for East with Pratt 27 November 1833. Returned to Kirtland 13 February 1834. Appointed to take mission to Upper Canada with Milton Holmes 20 February 1834. Member of Zion's Camp 1834. Ordained apostle 14 February 1835. Married Sarah Lang (born 1816 in New Hampshire) before 1836. Two known children: Sarah and John E. Charter member of Kirtland Safety Society 1837. Claimed to have lost $6000 in Kirtland paper 1837. Charged Joseph Smith with slander and lying May 1837. Temporarily disfellowshipped 3 September 1837. Moved to Far West, Missouri, late 1837. Associated with dissenters in Far West area. Excommunicated for apostasy 13 April 1838 in Far West, Missouri. Located in Iowa by 1842. Practiced law in Davenport and Keokuk. Drowned in Mississippi River at Prairie du Chien, Wisconsin, 20 December 1856.[10]

Section 69

Date.   November 1831 (on or before 12 November).[1]

Place.   Hiram, Portage County, Ohio.

Historical Note.   The decision of the Hiram, Ohio, conferences was that Oliver Cowdery should carry the revelations to Independence, Missouri, for printing. So that Cowdery would not have to travel the distance alone with these sacred writings (as well as money to purchase land in Jackson County, Missouri),[2] John Whitmer was appointed to accompany him.

These two men left Ohio on 20 November 1831, stopped in Winchester, Indiana, for about a week (29 November-7 December 1831) to regulate some difficulties in a branch of the Church, and arrived in Independence, Missouri, on 5 January 1832.[3]

Publication Note.   Section 69 was first published as section 28 in the 1835 edition of the Doctrine and Covenants.

Section 70

Date.   November 1831 (After 12 November).[1]

Place.   Kirtland, Geauga County, Ohio.

Historical Note.   Section 70 is a revelation directed specifically to members of the Literary Firm. This firm, organized in November 1831,[2] concerned itself with the printing of official Church literature. On 12 November 1831, the last day of the Hiram, Ohio conferences, it was decided that inasmuch as Joseph Smith, Oliver Cowdery, Sidney Rigdon, John Whitmer, and Martin Harris had played such a conspicuous role in recording, preserving, and preparing the revelations for publication, they should "have claim on the Church for recompense."[3] It was therefore voted by those present that the above-named brethren "be appointed to manage [the sacred writings] according to the Laws of the Church and the Commandments of the Lord."[4] These men who were to "manage" the revelations constituted the membership of the Literary Firm. Members of the partnership were consecrated in their respective responsibilities, and the profits from the sale of the Church publications were to benefit both the individual members as well as the Church at large. Items of specific concern for the Literary Firm were the printing and distribution of

- the New Translation of the Bible[6]
- the Church hymnal[7]
- a Church almanac[8]
- children's literature[9]
- Church newspapers[10]

At the organization of the Literary Firm (mid-November 1831), William W. Phelps was included as a member, and shortly thereafter Jesse Gause was added. In 1833 Frederick G. Williams, who had replaced Gause in the presidency of the High Priesthood, also became a member. Phelps's appointment was natural because he was an experienced newspaper editor and earlier had been designated as a "printer unto the Church."[11] Harris's selection as a charter member of the firm appears to have stemmed from his earlier financial assistance in the printing of the Book of Mormon, but his role in the Literary Firm cannot be determined, though, no doubt, his contribution was monetary, not literary. The appointments of Gause and Williams were related to their position in the presidency.

In September 1831, nearly two months before the creation of the Literary Firm, Phelps had been directed to purchase a printing press and type in Cincinnati on his return to Independence. Leaving Kirtland about mid-October, he obtained the printing apparatus and reached western Missouri no later than December 1831. In late November 1831 Oliver Cowdery and John Whitmer also left for Missouri taking manuscript copies of the revelations for printing. It had been decided at the Hiram, Ohio, conferences that 10,000 copies of the Book of Commandments would be printed in Independence. The cost of such an undertaking, however, later proved prohibitive, and the number was reduced to 3,000—to be sold unbound.[12] The first product of the Literarty Firm was *The Evening and the Morning Star*, printed under the firm name of W.W. Phelps & Co. In February 1832 Phelps issued the prospectus of the monthly, which commenced in June 1832. Just weeks before issuing the first number, the Independence printing office had been dedicated by Edward Partridge for the purpose of spreading divine "truths & revelations in these last days to the inhabitants of the earth."[13]

In March 1832 a companion firm, known as the United Firm, was organized in Ohio. It was determined that where possible, proceeds of the United Firm were to assist in the operation of the Literary Firm.[14]

Although by December 1832 the Book of Commandments was in the press, the May 1833 *Evening and Morning Star* lamented the delay in its completion:

> [It] will be published in the course of the present year, at from 25, to 50 cents a copy. We regret that in consequence of circumstances not within our control, this book will not be offered to our brethren as soon as was anticipated. We beg their forebearance, and solicit an interest in their prayers, promising to use our exertions with all our means to accomplish the work.[15]

It will be remembered, of course, that the Church press in Missouri was destroyed by a mob on 20 July 1833 (during the printing of the Book of Commandments), but members of the firm were determined to start again. Nine days after the printing office had been razed, W. W. Phelps affirmed, "Although the enemy has accomplished his design in demolishing the Printing establishment They cannot demolish the design of our God, for his decrees will stand & his purposes must be accomplished."[16]

Within seven weeks of the destruction of the Missouri press, arrangements were being made to establish another at Kirtland.[17] As a matter of fact, plans for the erection of a printing office at Church headquarters in Kirtland had preceded any knowledge of trouble with the Church press at Independence. A revelation received on 2 August 1833 directed the Saints at Kirtland to establish a printing office for printing the new translation of the Bible.[18] In October of the same year Church leaders agreed to proceed with the construction of the office, but work must have been delayed until the following spring because the wood-frame structure was not completed until the latter part of November 1834. The building, erected adjacent to the Kirtland Temple (then under construction), was occupied upon completion, when the printing materials were moved into the upper story.[19]

At a meeting of the Literary Firm in Kirtland on 11 September 1833 it was decided that the Kirtland "press be established and conducted under the firm of F. G. Williams & Co." Other resolutions were that the firm should continue to print *The Evening and the Morning Star* at Kirtland and start a new paper entitled the *Latter-day Saints' Messenger and Advocate*.[20] On 10 October 1833, with $800,

Oliver Cowdery left for New York to purchase the new press. When he returned, in the latter part of November, all haste was made to ready the equipment for printing, and by 18 December 1833 proof sheets of the *Star* had been printed.[21]

By November 1833 members of the firm had decided to expand their operation to include a political paper that would support Andrew Jackson's administration. Although initial plans suggested that the paper commence in January 1834, other pressures postponed its publication until the following year. This political paper, entitled the *Northern Times*, began officially in February 1835 and continued for more than a year.[22]

By divine command, administrative changes occurred in the Literary Firm in April 1834. Although membership in the company was not altered, Oliver Cowdery and Frederick G. Williams were given direct responsibility for the printing and distribution of the Church literature.[23] In October the first number of the *Latter-day Saints' Messenger and Advocate* appeared, and reprints of the Missouri *Star* began in January 1835.

The year 1835 was particularly busy for members of the firm. In May both Phelps and John Whitmer arrived in Kirtland from Missouri. Immediately Whitmer was appointed editor of the *Messenger and Advocate*, and Phelps was assigned to help with the new edition of the Doctrine and Covenants (and later with the hymnbook). By June 1835 the Doctrine and Covenants was in the press; by August it was ready for binding. In mid-September 1835 the first copies were received from the Cleveland binder and sold at $1 each.[24] The final item on the 1835 agenda for the firm was the printing of the hymnbook. Phelps took primary responsibility for the book, which although dated 1835, was not completed until about February 1836.[25]

Heavy operating expenses (the firm was issuing three monthly newspapers, as well as having printed and bound the Doctrine and Covenants) brought the partnership to the brink of collapse by the fall of 1835. Samuel H. Smith and David Whitmer were appointed agents for the firm on 16 September 1835 to assist in selling subscriptions and collecting subscription monies. Their collections as well as a $600 loan in October 1835 temporarily saved the enterprise.[26]

The expense incurred in binding the Doctrine and Covenants prompted members of the firm to secure materials for their own bookbindery, and in November Cowdery was again sent to New York for that purpose.[27]

In 1836 the Literary Firm began to be dissolved. After the dedication of the Kirtland Temple, Phelps and John Whitmer made preparations to return to their families in Missouri, and on 2 April 1836 they were discharged from their responsibilities as joint partners of the company.[28]In June 1836 Frederick G. Williams also retired as a member. With Williams's withdrawal from the company, publication of Church literature continued under the firm name of "Oliver Cowdery & Co.," until 1 February 1837. During this period the second edition of the Book of Mormon was printed by Cowdery. Upon completion of the Book of Mormon Cowdery sold his interest to Joseph Smith and Sidney Rigdon, the two remaining members of the firm.[29] Finally, in May 1837, Joseph and Sidney, financially unable to operate the business, sold the office, bookbindery, and contents to William Marks with contractual rights to rent or lease the equipment.[30] Under this new arrangement two issues (October and November 1837) of a new Church paper called the *Elders' Journal* appeared in Kirtland, Joseph Smith was editor; Thomas B. Marsh, publisher. But the Prophet's trip to Far West, Missouri, in November 1837 and his permanent departure from Kirtland in January 1838 precluded the issuing of any subsequent numbers from Kirtland. Shortly after Joseph Smith's arrival in Far West in March 1838 arrangements were made to continue the *Elders' Journal*. A printing press at Far West, Missouri, had been obtained by Elisha H. Groves from Kirtland in February or March 1837. W. W. Phelps and John Whitmer, Church leaders in Missouri, had sent Groves to procure the press for their own use at Far West. (It will be remembered that both Phelps and Whitmer had been members of the Literary Firm.) Oliver Cowdery, who was at Kirtland when Groves arrived, helped him obtain the press and type[31] and later was repaid by Phelps and Whitmer. When Cowdery sold his interest in the printing office on 1 February 1837, Joseph and Sidney gave him promissory notes for his equity. Now, with Groves's request, Cowdery asked the Prophet and Rigdon if he could take a "press & some of the type." This they "granted him on conditions that he should give up the notes."[32] Groves transported the press and printing equipment by water from Ohio to Missouri in the spring of 1837.[33] It is clear that Phelps and Whitmer intended on issuing a paper from Far West, for in August 1837 Whitmer advised Cowdery (still in Kirtland) of their plans: "[We] have some timbered land for you, which we will let you have for the Press & type, when you come here we will make all things right . . . .

I think if we are prospered we shall be enabled to issue a paper by the first of Jan. next [1838]. Though we live at a remote distance from materials & will take a long time to accomplish a little."[34] Following their excommunication in March 1838, Phelps and Whitmer lost interest in their printing plans.[35] On 21 April 1838 it was decided to purchase the "printing press, type [and] all the furniture pertaining to the establishment" from John Whitmer for the purpose of printing the *Elders' Journal*. Thomas B. Marsh was to be publisher.[36] Although in early August 1838 plans were made to establish a weekly newspaper for the Saints in Caldwell and Daviess counties,[37] the two final numbers of the *Journal* (July and August 1838) marked the demise of the Literary Firm after nearly seven years.[38]

Publication Note.   Section 70 was first published as section 26 in the 1835 edition of the Doctrine and Covenants.

Section 71

Date.   1 December 1831.

Place.   Hiram, Portage County, Ohio.

Historical Note.   Section 71 directed Joseph Smith and Sidney Rigdon to proclaim the gospel and "confound" their enemies. Ezra Booth, Simonds Ryder, and others had not remained quiet after their defection from the Church. Booth had published nine derogatory letters in the *Ohio Star* (Ravenna), and both Ryder and Booth had denounced Mormonism in local public meetings. In addition, they sought to traduce the character of Joseph Smith.

Following the instructions of section 71, the Prophet and Sidney Rigdon stopped translating the Bible and began traveling and preaching locally, particularly in Shalersville and Ravenna, to mitigate public prejudice against the new Church.[1]

Publication Note.   Section 71 was first published as section 90 in the 1835 edition of the Doctrine and Covenants.

Section 72

Date.   4 December 1831.

Place.   Kirtland, Geauga County, Ohio.

Historical Note.   On 1 December 1831, the Prophet received a revelation (section 71) instructing him and Sidney Rigdon to preach the gospel in the "regions round about." In obedience to this directive, they stopped translating the Bible and on 3 December 1831 journeyed to Kirtland. On the following day several elders and members assembled in Kirtland, Ohio, to learn their duty and be edified. After those assembled had spent some time in conversation, the Prophet received section 72.[1]

The revelation called Newel K. Whitney to be a bishop of the Church in Kirtland and explained his responsibilities in relation to those of Edward Partridge, the bishop in Missouri.

On 10 February 1832 Hyrum Smith and Reynolds Cahoon were called and ordained counselors to Newel K. Whitney.[2]

This revelation appears to be two separate revelations in the "Kirtland Revelation Book."[3] Verses 1-8 constitute one revelation; verses 9-26, the other.

Publication Note.   Section 72 was first published in the *Evening and Morning Star* (December 1832) and was included as section 89 in the 1835 edition of the Doctrine and Covenants.

Sections 1-72 Notes

Section 1

1. "Far West Record," p. 15. At a special conference of the Literary Firm, convened in Independence, Missouri, 30 April 1832, it was decided that the proposed number of the first edition be reduced to three thousand copies ("Far West Record," p. 25).

2. This child's name was Alvin, not Alva as published in some sources. See the family Bible of Joseph and Emma Smith, in possession of Buddy Youngreen.

3. This male child was born 6 February 1842, not 26 December 1842 as recorded in *History of the Church*, 5:209. See family Bible of Joseph and Emma Smith, in possession of Buddy Youngreen. The Prophet's diary entry for 26 December 1842 records that Emma had a "chill," not a "child."

4. Many of the women listed below were sealed to Joseph Smith before his death and, therefore, before marriage sealings were performed in the Nauvoo Temple. In 1846, after the completion of the attic story of the temple, women previously sealed to the Prophet during his lifetime were again sealed, by proxy, as were a number of other women for the first time. One of the women mentioned below was sealed by proxy at Winter Quarters, and two others were sealed at the Endowment House in Salt Lake City, Utah. Sarah Ann Whitney (born 22 March 1825, in Kirtland, Geauga County, Ohio) sealed 12 January 1846. Eliza Maria Partridge (born 20 April 1820, Painesville, Geauga County, Ohio) sealed 13 January 1846. Louisa Beman (born 7 February 1815, Livonia, Livingston County, New York) sealed 14 January 1846. Emily Dow Partridge (born 28 February 1824, Painesville, Geauga County, Ohio) sealed 14 January 1846. Olive Andres (born 24 September 1818, Livermore, Oxford County, Maine) sealed 14 January 1846.

Sarah Merietta Kingsley (born 20 October 1788, Becket, Berkshire County, Massachusetts) sealed 15 January 1846. Lucy Walker (born 30 April 1826, Peacham, Caledonia County, Vermont) sealed 15 January 1846. Jane Tibbets (born 27 August 1804, Gorham, Cumberland County, Maine) sealed 17 January 1846. Phebe Watrous (born 1 October 1805, Sharon, Otsego County, New York) sealed 17 January 1846. Mary Elizabeth Rollins (born 9 April 1818, Lima, Livingston County, New York) sealed 17 January 1846. Elizabeth Davis (born 11 March 1791, Riverhead, Suffolk County, New York) sealed 22 January 1846. Lucinda Pendleton (born 27 September 1801, Washington County, Vermont) sealed 22 January 1846. Mariah Lawrence (born 18 December 1823, Pickering Township, Upper Canada) sealed 24 January 1846. Desdemona Catlin Fullmer (born 6 October 1809, Jefferson, Luzerne County, Pennsylvania) sealed 26 January 1846. Martha McBride (born 17 March 1805, Chester, Warren County, New York) sealed 26 January 1846. Sylvia Porter Sessions (born 31 July 1818, Newry, Oxford County, Maine) sealed 26 January 1846. Sarah Lawrence (born 13 May 1826, Pickering Township, Upper Canada) sealed 26 January 1846. Sophia Woodman Sanburn (born 28 August 1795, Sanburn, New Hampshire) sealed 27 January 1846. Cordelia Calista Morley (born 28 November 1823, Kirtland, Geauga County, Ohio) sealed 27 January 1846. Rhoda Richards (born 8 August 1784, Hopkinton, Middlesex County, Massachusetts) sealed 31 January 1846. Zina Diantha Huntington (born 31 January 1821, Watertown, Jefferson County, New York), sealed 31 January 1846. Nancy Maria Winchester (born 10 August 1828, Black Rock, Erie County, New York) sealed 3 February 1846. Eliza Roxcy Snow (born 21 January 1804, Becket, Berkshire County, Massachusetts) sealed 3 February 1846. Mary Huston (born 11 September 1818, Jackson, Stark County, Ohio) sealed 3 February 1846. Elvira Anna Cowles (born 23 November 1813, Unadilla, Otsego County, New York) sealed 3 February 1846. Helen Mar Kimball (born 25 August 1828, Mendon, Monroe County, New York) sealed 4 February 1846. Presendia Lathrop Huntington (born 7 September 1810, Watertown, Jefferson County, New York) sealed 4 February 1846. Mary Ann Frost (born 14 January 1809, Groton, Caledonia County, Vermont) sealed 6 February 1846. Melissa Lott (born 9 January 1824, Tuchanannock, Luzerne County, Pennsylvania) sealed 8 February 1846. Sally Ann Fuller (born 24 October 1815, Saratoga County, New York) sealed 29 January 1847, Winter Quarters. Marinda Nancy Johnson (born 28 June 1815, Pomfret, Windsor County, Vermont) sealed to the Prophet outside of the Nauvoo Temple in 1843 and by proxy in the Salt Lake Endowment House 31 July 1857. Lydia Dibble, also sealed to the Prophet during his life-time, was sealed a second time in the Salt Lake Endowment House 8 June 1851. Fanny Murray was sealed to Joseph Smith 2 November 1843, but no record of a temple or Endowment House sealing has been found. Research in possession of author.

5. *History of the Church*; Joseph Smith Diaries, Church Archives; Jenson's *Biographical Encyclopedia*, 1:1ff; and Andrew F. Ehat, "Summary of Data on

the Individuals Who Received the Endowment before Ordinance Work Began in the Nauvoo Temple" (1981 revised edition), privately distributed. Hereafter cited as "Endowment Data Summary."

Section 2

1. See Joseph Smith-History, 1:29-47.

Section 3

1. *History of the Church*, 1:21. Joseph Smith undoubtedly felt compelled to satisfy Martin Harris's request because the latter had agreed to finance the printing of the Book of Mormon.
2. *History of Joseph Smith by His Mother*, pp. 128-29.
3. *History of the Church*, 1:28.
4. Wayne C. Gunnell, "Martin Harris, Witness and Benefactor to the Book of Mormon," master's thesis, 1955, Brigham Young University; Richard L. Anderson, *Investigating the Book of Mormon Witnesses* (Salt Lake City: Deseret Book, 1981); *Millennial Star* (15 November 1846); "Journal History," 1 January 1838; Martin Harris LDS family group sheets, Genealogical Society, Salt Lake City, Utah; "Far West Record"; and Jenson's *Biographical Encyclopedia*, 1:271.

Section 4

1. *History of Joseph Smith by His Mother*, p. 135.
2. Larry C. Porter, "A Study of the Origins of The Church of Jesus Christ of Latter-day Saints in the States of New York and Pennsylvania, 1816-31," Ph.D. dissertation, Brigham Young University, 1971, p. 134. Joseph Smith sold this property in June 1833.
3. Dean Jessee, "Joseph Knight's Recollections of Early Mormon History," *Brigham Young University Studies* 16 (Autumn 1976): 29-39. Hereafter cited as Jessee, "Joseph Knight's Recollections."
4. The *History of the Church*, 1:28 gives the date of the visit as February 1829. Joseph Knight, Sr., remembered the month to be January 1829. See Jessee, "Joseph Knight's Recollections."
5. The Prophet's dictated account of this visit names only his father as coming to Harmony in February 1829 (see *History of the Church*, 1:28). Lucy Mack Smith stated that she accompanied her husband to visit Joseph and Emma on this occasion (*History of Joseph Smith by His Mother*, p. 133). Joseph Knight, Sr., remembered that it was Joseph Smith, Sr., and Samuel Smith who visited Joseph and Emma in early 1829 (Jessee, "Joseph Knight's Recollections").
6. *History of the Church*, 1:21-28.
7. *History of the Church*; "Far West Record"; Jenson's *Biographical Encyclopedia*, 1:181; and *History of Joseph Smith by His Mother*.

Section 5

1. Harris's concern over the plates was undoubtedly connected with his previous, yet still binding, agreement to assist in financing the printing of the Book of Mormon.

Section 6

1. Jessee, "Joseph Knight's Recollections."
2. *Messenger and Advocate* 1(October 1834):14 (italics in original).
3. "Kirtland Council Minute Book"; Stanley R. Gunn, *Oliver Cowdery—Second Elder and Scribe* (Salt Lake City: Bookcraft, 1962); Richard L. Anderson, *Investigating the Book of Mormon Witnesses* (Salt Lake City: Deseret Book, 1981); "Pottawatamie High Council Minutes," p. 117; *History of the Church*; "Far West Record"; and Jenson's *Biographical Encyclopedia*, 1:246.

Section 7

1. See *Times and Seasons* 3 (15 July 1842): 853.

Section 8

1. See *Times and Seasons* 3 (15 July 1842):853-54.

Section 9

1. See *Times and Seasons* 3 (15 July 1842):854.

Section 10

1. *History of the Church*, 1:23.
2. My own dating of this revelation would be fall 1828. See Max H. Parkin's thorough study of this dating problem in "A Preliminary Analysis of the Dating of Section 10," *Seventh Annual Sidney B. Sperry Symposium* (Provo: Brigham Young University, 1979), pp. 68-84.

It is interesting to note that the words "by the means of the Urim and Thummim" in verse 1 were not part of this verse in the *Book of Commandments*; nor was section 17, which also makes use of the term *Urim and Thummim*, printed in the *Book of Commandments*. Both section 17 and verse 1 of section 10, as we now have them, first appeared in the 1835 edition. While the retroactive placement of the term in section 10 has led to some speculation relative to the Prophet's having the instrument in his possession, a preponderance of evidence confirms the Prophet's own testimony: "With the records was found a curious instrument, which the ancients called 'Urim and Thummim,' which consisted of two transparent stones set in the rim of a bow fastened to a breastplate" (*History of the Church*, 4:537). The problem here seems to be one of terminology, not whether or not the Prophet had possession of an ancient artifact. Until some time after the translation of the Book of Mormon, the sacred instruments may have been referred to as "Interpreters," or "spectacles." It is possible that Joseph Smith's inspired translation of the Bible played some part in designating the translating instrument "Urim and Thummim." The earliest use of the term *Urim and Thummim* in Mormon literature is in the *Evening and Morning Star* (January 1833). An article on the Book of Mormon, undoubtedly authored by W. W. Phelps, stated, "It was translated by the gift and power of God, by an unlearned man, through the aid of a pair of Interpreters, or spectacles— (known, perhaps in ancient days as Teraphim, or Urim and Thummim)." See also Richard P. Howard, *Restoration Scriptures: A Study of Their Textual Development* (Independence: Herald Publishing House, 1969).

Section 11

1. *History of the Church*, 1:44.
2. *History of the Church*, 5:107-08.
3. Joseph Fielding Smith, *Essentials in Church History* (Salt Lake City: Deseret Book, 1971); *History of Joseph Smith by His Mother*; Hyrum Smith family group sheets, Genealogical Society, Salt Lake City, Utah; *History of the Church*; "Far West Record"; Jenson's *Biographical Encyclopedia*, 1:52; and Ehat, "Endowment Data Summary."

Section 12

1. *History of the Church*, 4:124-25.
2. Jessee, "Joseph Knight's Recollections."
3. Joseph Knight, Sr., family group sheets, Genealogical Society, Salt Lake City, Utah; Jessee, "Joseph Knight's Recollections"; Larry C. Porter dissertation, 1971; and *History of the Church*. Temple ordinance data from Church Archives are in the possession of the author.

Section 13

1. Circumstantial evidence places the restoration of the Melchizedek Priesthood in late May 1829. See Larry C. Porter, "Dating the Restoration of the Melchizedek Priesthood," *Ensign* (June 1979).
2. Patriarchal Blessing Book, vol. 1, September 1835, Church Archives.
3. As reported in Reuben Miller Journal, Church Archives.

Section 14

1. *Kansas City Daily Journal*, 5 June 1881.
2. *The Saints' Herald* (Plano, Illinois), 1 March 1882.
3. Richard L. Anderson, *Investigating the Book of Mormon Witnesses* (Salt Lake City: Deseret Book, 1981); "Far West Record"; "Kirtland Council Minute Book"; D&C, sections 14, 17, 18, 30, and 52; 1850 Federal Census of Missouri; Geauga County, Ohio, Tax Records; Larry C. Porter dissertation, 1971; and Brigham Young discourse in *Journal of Discourses*, 6:320.

Section 15

1. See *Times and Seasons* 3 (15 August 1842):885.
2. Mary Cleora Dear, *Two Hundred Thirty-Eight Years of the Whitmer Family* (Richmond, Missouri: Beck Printing Co., 1976); Larry C. Porter dissertation, 1971; Geauga County, Ohio, Tax Records; Caldwell County, Missouri Land Records; The Book of John Whitmer, microfilm copy in Church Archives; John Whitmer Account Book, Church Archives; "Far West Record"; "Kirtland Council Minute Book"; *History of the Church*; D&C, sections 15, 26, 30, 47, 69, and 70; Jenson's *Biographical Encyclopedia*, 1:251; and Richard L. Anderson, *Investigating the Book of Mormon Witnesses* (Salt Lake City: Deseret Book, 1981).

Section 16

1. *Times and Seasons* 3 (15 August 1842):885.
2. Larry C. Porter dissertation, 1971; "Far West Record"; *History of the Church*; Richard L. Anderson, *Investigating the Book of Mormon Witnesses* (Salt Lake City: Deseret Book, 1981); Peter Whitmer Statement, 13 December 1831, Church Archives; D&C, sections 16, 30, and 32; and Jenson's *Biographical Encyclopedia*, 1:277.

Section 17

1. Ether 5:2-4.
2. *History of the Church*, 1:52-53.
3. In January 1859 Orson Pratt recounted the historical background of section 17: "These three men . . .went and saw Mr. Smith, and inquired of him whether it would be their privilege to behold the plates and know from heaven that the book was true. Joseph Smith inquired of the Lord concerning the matter; and the Lord gave them a promise that if they would sufficiently humble themselves, they should have this privilege . . . . [I was] individually acquainted with the translator and the three witnesses [and] I have seen the place where the angel descended and showed them the plates" (*Journal of Discourses*, 7:29-30).
4. *Kansas City Daily Journal*, 5 June 1881.
5. Remarks by Oliver Cowdery, 21 October 1848, at Council Bluffs, as reported by Reuben Miller, who was present. See Reuben Miller Journal, Church Archives.
6. *The Saints' Herald* (Plano, Illinois), 1 March 1882.
7. *Millennial Star* 21 (20 August 1859):545.
8. Martin Harris to H. B. Emerson, 23 November 1870, cited in *The Saints' Herald* 22 (15 October 1875):630.

Section 18

1. Letter in Joseph Smith Collection, Church Archives.
2. Refering to section 18, Orson Pratt said: "In that early day the prophet

Joseph said to me that the Lord had revealed that twelve men were to be chosen as Apostles. A manuscript revelation to this effect, given in 1829—before the rise of the Church—was laid before me, and I read it. Joseph said to me . . .that I should be one of this Twelve"(*Journal of Discourses*, 12:85-86).

3. See Brigham Young discourse in *Journal of Discourses*, 6:320. Cowdery and Whitmer were apostles in the sense that they were witnesses of Christ and his word as found in the Book of Mormon.

Section 19

1. Copy of mortgage in Wayne C. Gunnell, master's thesis, 1955.

2. Later Harris had to redeem the mortgage (which came due 5 February 1831) by selling 150 acres of his farm to Thomas Lakey on 1 April 1831 for $3000 (see Wayne C. Gunnell, master's thesis, 1955, pp. 38-39).

Section 20

1. Actually sections 20 and 22 were initially both recognized as the "Articles and Covenants" of the Church (see *Evening and Morning Star* [June 1832], p. 1).

2. Section 20 was considered by the early missionaries a very important document. Many of them recorded the revelation in its entirety in their diaries to be quoted in their preaching. Additionally, Priesthood certificates stated that the bearer had been ordained "according to the Articles and Covenants of the Church." When Lincoln Haskin desired to preach the gospel in 1832, a revelation stipulated that he should "be ordained and receive the articles and covenants which I have given unto you and some of the commandments that he may go forth and proclaim my gospel" ("Kirtland Revelation Book," p. 10).

3. See an early draft of section 20, dated 1829 (Joseph Smith Collection, Church Archives), which states that Oliver Cowdery was commanded to write section 20.

4. See "Far West Record," p. 1.

5. Ibid., pp. 1-2. See also Lyndon W. Cook, "The Far West Record and the Doctrine and Covenants," *Seventh Annual Sidney B. Sperry Symposium* (Provo: Brigham Young University, 1979), pp. 129-39.

6. Section 20, with some minor modifications, was published in the *Painesville Telegraph*, 19 April 1831. The editor of the *Telegraph* indicated that he had obtained a copy of the "Mormon Creed" from Martin Harris. Sections 22 and 27:1-4 were also published at the same time.

Section 21

1. See Richard L. Anderson, "Who were the six who organized the Church on 6 April 1830?" *Ensign* (June 1980).

2. Larry C. Porter dissertation, 1971, p. 385. The certificate of incorporation has not been found.

3. *Evening and Morning Star* (May 1834).
4. D&C 115:3.
5. Jessee, "Joseph Knight's Recollections."

Section 22

1. See *Evening and Morning Star* (June 1832) and "Book of Commandments, Laws, and Covenants," Book B (first entry), where section 22 is included as part of the "Articles and Covenants" of the Church.

2. *Journal of Discourses*, 16:293-94.

3. Section 22 was published in the *Painesville Telegraph*, 19 April 1831. The revelation was included with sections 20 and 27:1-4 (see Historical Note for section 20, note 6).

Section 23

1. Dean Jarman, "The Life and Contributions of Samuel Harrison Smith," master's thesis, Brigham Young University, 1961; Samuel H. Smith Journal (1831-32), Church Archives; Reynolds Cahoon Journal (1831-32), Church Archives; Orson Hyde Journal (1831-32), Church Archives; Jenson's *Biographical Encyclopedia*, 1:278; D&C, sections 23, 52, 66, 75, and 124; *History of the Church*; "Far West Record"; "Kirtland Council Minute Book"; "Nauvoo High Council Minutes"; and Ehat, "Endowment Data Summary."

Section 24

1. *History of the Church*, 1:89-96.

Section 25

1. *History of the Church*, 1:270. See also "Far West Record, " p. 26.

2. See "Kirtland Council Minute Book," p. 108.

3. Although the publication date of this first hymnbook is 1835, it was not completed until early 1836. The second edition was printed in Nauvoo in 1841.

4. Peter Crawley, "A Bibliography of The Church of Jesus Christ of Latter-day Saints in New York, Ohio, and Missouri," *Brigham Young University Studies* 12 (Summer 1972): 503-05.

5. See *Times and Seasons* 4 (1 February 1843): 95.

6. *History of the Church*, 5:107.

7. *History of the Church*; D&C, section 25; Jenson's *Biographical Encyclopedia*, 1:692-93; Newel Knight Journal, Church Archives; Emma Smith Correspondence, RLDS Library-Archives, The Auditorium, Independence, Missouri; Ehat, "Endowment Data Summary"; and Larry C. Porter dissertation, 1971, p. 202.

Section 26

1. *Times and Seasons* 4 (15 February 1843): 108.

Section 27

1. Although as Brigham Young said, "The Lord told Joseph that he would accept of water [instead of wine]," pure wine, prepared by the Saints, was acceptable, and was not completely and officially abandoned until July 1906 (*Journal of Discourses*, 10:245 and 19:92). See John Henry Smith Diary (July 1906), Manuscripts Division, J. Willard Marriott Library, University of Utah, Salt Lake City, Utah.
2. Newel Knight Journal, Church Archives.
3. Ibid.
4. Verses 1-4 were published in the *Painesville Telegraph*, 19 April 1831. The revelation was included with sections 20 and 22 (see Historical Note for section 20, note 6).

Section 28

1. *History of the Church*, 1:109 and Newel Knight Journal, Church Archives.
2. Newel Knight Journal, Church Archives.
3. See D&C 48:5 and 52:5.
4. *History of the Church*; D&C 28; "Far West Record"; Mary Cleora Dear, *Two Hundred Thirty-Eight Years of the Whitmer Family* (Richmond, Missouri: Beck Printing, 1976); "List of Residents of the South Quarter of Far West, Missouri," in Teacher's Quorum Minutes (1838), Church Archives; 1850 Federal Census of Missouri; Richard L. Anderson, *Investigating the Book of Mormon Witnesses* (Salt Lake City: Deseret Book, 1981), pp. 126-33; and Jenson's *Biographical Encyclopedia*, 1:277.

Section 29

1. *History of the Church*, 1:110; see also Newel Knight Journal, Church Archives.

Section 30

1. *Autobiography of Parley P. Pratt*, p. 42; Samuel H. Smith Journal, 1831-32, Church Archives; Orson Hyde Journal, 1831-32, Church Archives; 1820 and 1830 Federal Census of New York; "Junius Town Meeting Records," Genealogical Society, Salt Lake City, Utah; and Probate Court Records, Seneca County, New York. Samuel H. Smith noted, "He was glad to see us, and Sister Burroughs was strong in the faith." Orson Hyde recorded, "Brother B. [was] rather low, but left him about persuaded to go to Zion."

Section 31

1. See "History of Thomas B. Marsh, Written by Himself (November 1857)," manuscript located in Church Archives.

2. See *Utah Genealogical and Historical Magazine* (January 1836).

3. "History of Thomas B. Marsh, Written by Himself (November 1857)," Church Archives; Walter C. Lichfield, "Thomas B. Marsh, Physician to the Church," master's thesis, Brigham Young University, 1956; "Far West Record"; *History of the Church*; D&C, sections 31, 52, 56, 75, and 112; Edward Partridge Journal, Church Archives; Jenson's *Biographical Encyclopedia*, 1:74; Caldwell County, Missouri Land Records; 1860 Federal Census of Utah Territory; and Lyndon W. Cook, " 'I Have Sinned Against Heaven, and Am Unworthy of Your Confidence, But I Cannot Live without a Reconciliation': Thomas B. Marsh Returns to the Church," *Brigham Young University Studies* 20 (Summer 1980):389-400.

Section 32

1. The "Kirtland Revelation Book," pp. 83-84, includes this revelation with the following notation: "Revelation to Parley Pratt to go to the wilderness . . .Manchester October 1830."

2. *Times and Seasons* 4 (15 April 1843):172.

3. Letter of Ezra Booth to Rev. Ira Eddy, 24 November 1831, Nelson, Ohio, cited in the *Ohio Star* (Ravenna), 8 December 1831. The originals of these two covenant documents have not survived.

4. A very detailed account of the first leg of the "Lamanite mission" is found in Richard L. Anderson, "The Impact of the First Preaching in Ohio," *Brigham Young University Studies* 11 (Summer 1971):474-96.

5. Variously known as "Richard B." (see *History of the Church*, 1:81), "Ziba B." (see 1840 Federal Census of Missouri), and "William Z." (see Death Record of Ziba Peterson's son, George Washington Peterson, 14 January 1909, California State Board of Health, Bureau of Vital Statistics, Napa County, California).

6. LaFayette County, Missouri, Marriage Records (1831); D&C, sections 32 and 58; "Far West Record"; *History of the Church*; Peter Whitmer, Jr., statement, 13 December 1831, Church Archives; Inez Smith Davis, *The Story of the Church* (Independence: Herald Publishing House, 1961); Eber D. Howe, *Mormonism Unvailed* (Painesville, Ohio, 1834); Richard L. Anderson, "The Impact of the First Preaching in Ohio," *Brigham Young University Studies* 11 (Summer 1971); Register of Deaths, Rebekah Peterson (Ziba's widow), 21 April 1896, County Recorder, Napa County, California; Oliver Cowdery to Joseph Smith, 8 April 1831, Church Archives; *Autobiography of Parley P. Pratt*; and Death Record of George Washington Peterson, 14 January 1909, California State Board of Health, Bureau of Vital Statistics, Napa County, California). My thanks to Irene E. Johnson for some of this data.

7. *History of the Church*; D&C, sections 32, 49, 52, 97, and 124; "Far West Record"; "Kirtland Council Minute Book"; *Autobiography of Parley P. Pratt*; Steven Pratt, "Eleanor McLean and the Murder of Parley P. Pratt," *Brigham Young University Studies* 15 (Winter 1975):225-56; Jenson's *Biographical Encyclopedia*, 1:83; and Ehat, "Endowment Data Summary."

Section 33

1. *The Saints' Herald* (July 1862).
2. "Kirtland Revelation Book," pp. 91-92. The revelation, received May 1831, concerned itself with Frederick G. Williams's farm and the responsibilities of Joseph Smith, Sen. and Ezra Thayer. See p. 89.
3. *History of the Church*; "Far West Record"; "Kirtland Council Minute Book"; D & C, sections 33, 52, and 56; 1820 and 1830 Federal Census of New York; Inez Smith Davis, *The Story of the Church* (Independence: Herald Publishing House, 1961); *The Saints' Herald* (July 1862); William Swartzell, *Mormonism Exposed, Being a Journal of a Residence in Missouri from the 28th of May to the 20th of August, 1838* (Pekin, Ohio: By the Author, 1840); Thayer family group sheet, Genealogical Society, Salt Lake City, Utah; and D. Michael Quinn, "The Council of Fifty and Its Members, 1844-1945," *Brigham Young University Studies* 20 (Winter 1980):163-97.
4. "Far West Record"; D&C 33; Emer Harris family group sheet, Genealogical Society, Salt Lake City, Utah; 1830 Federal Census of New York; 1840 Federal Census of Ohio; 1850, 1860, 1870, and 1880 Federal Census of Michigan; Marriage Records, Branch County, Michigan; Geauga County, Ohio, Tax Records; *The Saints' Herald* (July 1862); and *Journal of Discourses*, 7:114.

Section 34

1. *Autobiography of Parley P. Pratt*, p. 43.
2. "Journal History," 4 November 1830.
3. *Journal of Discourses*, 12:85 and 88.
4. *Journal of Discourses*, 7:311.
5. *History of the Church*; Elden J. Watson, *The Orson Pratt Journals* (Salt Lake City: Elden J. Watson, 1975); "Far West Record"; "Kirtland Council Minute Book"; D&C, sections 34, 52, 75, 124, and 136; Jenson's *Biographical Encyclopedia*, 1:87; and Ehat, "Endowment Data Summary."

Section 35

1. *Times and Seasons* (15 September 1843).
2. See Historical Note for section 37.
3. *History of the Church*; "Far West Record"; "Kirtland Council Minute Book"; Stephen Post Papers, Church Archives; *Times and Seasons* 4 (1 May 1843): 177ff; D&C, sections 35, 37, 40, 44, 49, 52, 58, 61, 70, 73, 76, 100, 103,

104, and 124; 1850, 1860, 1870 Federal Census of New York; Jenson's *Biographical Encyclopedia*, 1:31; Daryl Chase, "Sidney Rigdon: Early Mormon," Ph.D. dissertation, University of Chicago, 1931; F. Mark McKiernan, *The Voice of One Crying in the Wilderness: Sidney Rigdon, Religious Reformer 1793-1876* (Lawrence, Kansas: Coronado Press, 1971); Milton V. Backman, Jr., "The Quest for a Restoration: The Birth of Mormonism in Ohio," *Brigham Young University Studies* 11 (Summer 1972); Ehat, "Endowment Data Summary"; Hans Rollmann, "The Early Baptist Career of Sidney Rigdon in Warren, Ohio," *Brigham Young University Studies* 21 (Winter 1981); and Thomas J. Gregory, "Sidney Rigdon: Post Nauvoo," *Brigham Young University Studies* 21 (Winter 1981).

Section 36

1. See dating for section 35.
2. *History of the Church*, 1:148.
3. Edward Partridge Journal, Church Archives; "Far West Record"; D&C, sections 36, 41, 42, 50, 51, 52, 57, 58, 60, 64, 115, and 124; Jenson's *Biographical Encyclopedia*, 1:218; *Utah Genealogical and Historical Magazine* (October 1936); *History of the Church*; and "A Book of Proxey" (Nauvoo Temple proxy sealings), Church Archives.

Section 37

1. See dating for section 35.
2. See Historical Note for section 38.
3. See Robert J. Matthews, *A Plainer Translation: Joseph Smith's Translation of the Bible* (Provo: Brigham Young University Press, 1975).
4. Scriptural language refers to the Prophet's inspired work on the Bible as "the fullness of my scriptures" (see D&C 42:15 and 104:58), "the translation of my scriptures" (see D&C 94:10), and "the new translation of my holy word" (see D&C 124:89).
5. See Robert J. Matthews, *A Plainer Translation*.

Section 38

1. *Deseret News* (22 February 1860). See also *Journal of Discourses*, 7:372.
2. The Book of John Whitmer, microfilm copy at Church Archives.
3. Newel Knight Journal, Church Archives.
4. See *Palmyra Reflector* (1 February 1831), and Eber D. Howe, *Mormonism Unvailed* (Painesville, Ohio: 1834), pp. 112-13.
5. *Painesville Telegraph* (17 May 1831).

Section 39

1. *Times and Seasons* 4 (15 October 1843): 353-54.
2. Mrs. T.S. Chisholm, "Covell Family in America," film #230615, Genealogical Society, Salt Lake City, Utah; *History of the Church*; and 1790,

1800, 1820, and 1830 Federal Census of New York. These census records, like the family record, use the spelling "Covell."

Section 40

1. *Times and Seasons* 4 (15 October 1843): 354.

Section 41

1. The traditional date of Joseph Smith's arrival in Kirtland, Ohio is 1 February 1831 (*History of the Church*, 1:145). However, the *Painesville Telegraph* (Painesville, Ohio), 15 February 1831, shows that Sidney Rigdon (who accompanied the Prophet), had arrived in the Kirtland area by 30 January 1831, and possibly earlier.

2. See verse 3. Use of the term "my law" (specifically meaning the law of consecration), is also found in D&C 38:32, 44:6, 51:2, and 58:19.

3. An undated certificate of appointment and ordination (undoubtedly created in the fall of 1831), signed by eighteen elders, is located in the Joseph Smith Collection, Church Archives. Edward Partridge is the only man in this dispensation to have been ordained a bishop without first being ordained a high priest. His ordination as high priest occurred on 3 June 1831.

Section 42

1. See manuscript copy of section 42 in Revelations Collections, Ms. f 490, Church Archives. This manuscript, which appears to be in the hand of Oliver Cowdery, states the following: "February 23d, 1831 the rules and regulations of the Law. How the Elders of the church of Christ are to act upon the points of the Law given by Jesus Christ to the Church in the presence of twelve Elders February 9th 1831 as agreed upon by Seven Elders 23 d 1831 according to the Commandment of God."

2. Manuscript copy of section 42, Ms. f 490, Church Archives.

3. Ibid. See sections 48 and 51 which address this problem.

4. *Book of Commandments*, chap. 44, verse 57.

5. "Book of Commandments, Laws and Covenants," Book B, Church Archives.

6. *Book of Commandments*, chap. 44, verse 57. Bracketed words are in manuscript copy of section 42, Ms. f 490, Church Archives. This instruction suggests that the whole effort to establish a truly God-like community would depend on maintaining a close compact pattern of settlement.

7. Manuscript copy of section 42, Ms. f 490, Church Archives.

8. Ibid. See also *Book of Commandments*, chap. 44, verse 57.

9. "Book of Commandments, Laws and Covenants," Book B, Church Archives.

10. Manuscript copy of section 42, Ms. f 490, Church Archives.

11. Ibid.

12. Ibid.

13. Oliver Cowdery, referring to section 42 in 1835, wrote the following to Newel K. Whitney: "Will you have the kindness to send us, by the bearer the original copy of the revelation given to 12 elders Feb. 1831 called 'The Law of the Church?' We are preparing the old Star for re-printing, and have no copy from which to correct, and kno[w] of no other besides yours" (Oliver Cowdery to Newel K. Whitney, 4 February 1835, in Newel K. Whitney Collection, Brigham Young University).

14. Joseph Smith to Martin Harris, 22 February 1831, Joseph Smith Collection, Church Archives.

15. The Book of John Whitmer, microfilm copy in Church Archives.

16. Verses 12-77 of section 42 were published in the *Painesville Telegraph,* 13 September 1831, and entitled "The Laws of the Church of Christ. Kirtland, Geauga Co. May 23d, A.D. 1831. A Commandment to the Elders."

Section 43

1. The Book of John Whitmer, microfilm copy in Church Archives.
2. Statement of Ezra Booth, *Painesville Telegraph* (20 December 1831).

Section 44

1. *Times and Seasons* 5 (1 January 1844): 385.

Section 45

1. The Book of John Whitmer, microfilm copy at Church Archives.
2. Robert J. Matthews, *A Plainer Translation,* pp. 66 and 73. The fact that section 45 gives attention to Matthew 24 suggests the possibility that the Prophet's curiosity had led the Bible translation into the New Testament prior to 8 March.
3. Robert J. Woodford, "The Historical Development of the Doctrine and Covenants," Ph.D. dissertation, 1974, Brigham Young University, pp. 590 and 594.

Section 46

1. The Book of John Whitmer, microfilm copy at Church Archives. Whitmer indicated that certain Book of Mormon passages (undoubtedly 3 Nephi 18:30-33 and Moroni 6:7-9) also were quoted to point up the need to resolve this issue.
2. Ibid.
3. This was only the beginning of instructions regarding the discerning of spirits. "Subsequent revelations through Joseph Smith gave greater detail concerning keys to detecting the adversary. D&C 50:30-35 gave instructions that if after prayer a spirit would not manifest itself, the individuals involved would have power to rebuke the spirit. Joseph Smith had experience himself with this type of manifestation. On the banks of the Susquehanna River, Michael appeared to intervene and detect the devil when he appeared as an angel of light (D&C 128:20), indicating another

dimension to this question of detection. Because the adversary apparently can take light and truth away from the disobedient (D & C 93:39), he can attempt to pass as an angel of glory (2 Corinthians 11:14, D & C 129:8; Moses 1:2, 9, 11-25)." See Andrew F. Ehat and Lyndon W. Cook, *The Words of Joseph Smith: The Contemporary Accounts of the Nauvoo Discourses of the Prophet Joseph* (Provo, Utah: Religious Studies Center, 1980), p. 20. Also see Historical Note for section 129.

Section 47

1. The date is either 7 or 9 March in the "Kirtland Revelation Book," p. 12.

2. The place of reception for section 47 in the "Kirtland Revelation Book" (undoubtedly an error), is Hiram, Portage County, Ohio (see p. 12).

3. The Book of John Whitmer, microfilm copy at Church Archives.

4. "Far West Record," p. 3.

5. Joseph Smith to William W. Phelps, 31 July 1832, Joseph Smith Collection, Church Archives.

6. John Whitmer to Oliver Cowdery, 29 July 1833, Joseph Smith Collection, Church Archives.

7. See *History of the Church*, 3:15, where Joseph Smith condemns Whitmer for refusing to surrender the history.

Section 48

1. The Book of John Whitmer mentions the reception of section 48: "The time drew near for the brethren from the state of New York to arrive at Kirtland, Ohio. And some had supposed that it was the place of gathering, even the place of the New Jerusalem spoken of in the Book of Mormon, according to the visions and revelations received in the last days. There was no preparation made for the reception of the Saints from the East. The Bishop being anxious to know something concerning the matter, therefore the Lord spake unto Joseph Smith, Junior, as follows: [section 48]." See The Book of John Whitmer, microfilm copy at Church Archives.

2. *Times and Seasons* 5 (15 January 1844): 401.

Section 49

1. The actual date of reception may have been 7 March. See Journal of Ashbel Kitchel, copied by Elisha D. Blakeman, manuscript on file at the Shaker Museum, Old Chatham, New York (I am indebted to Richard L. Anderson for this information).

2. See The Book of John Whitmer, microfilm copy at Church Archives and *History of the Church*, 1:167.

3. Journal of Ashbel Kitchel (see note 1). See also *Autobiography of Parley P. Pratt*, p. 61.

4. *History of the Church*; D&C 49; Robert Meader, "The Shakers and the Mormons," *The Shaker Quarterly* 2 (Fall 1962):87; 1800 Federal Census of

Vermont; 1820, 1830, 1840, 1850, and 1860 Federal Census of Ohio; Zebedee Coltrin Journal, Church Archives; Newel Knight Journal, Church Archives; and Jessee, "Joseph Knight's Recollections."

Section 50

1. *Autobiography of Parley P. Pratt*, p. 61. For additional references to this difficulty with false spirits, see Levi W. Hancock Journal, Church Archives; Jared Carter Journal, Church Archives; John Corrill, *A Brief History of the Church of Christ of Latter Day Saints, (Commonly Called Mormons) Including An Account of Their Doctrine and Discipline; with the Reasons of the Author for Leaving the Church* (St. Louis: Printed For the Author, 1839); *Painesville Telegraph* (15 February 1831); and The Book of John Whitmer, microfilm copy at Church Archives.

2. The historical setting of section 50 is noted by John Whitmer:

> For a perpetual memory to the same and confusion of the devil permit me, to say a few things, respecting the proceedings of some of those who were disciples, and some remain among us, and will, and have come from under the error and enthusiasm, which they had fallen. Some had visions and could not tell what they saw, some would fancy to themselves that they had the sword of Laban, and would wield it as expert as a light dragon, some would act like an Indian in the act of scalping, some would slide or scoop on the floor, with the rapidity of a serpent, which they termed sailing in the boat to the Lamanites, preaching the gospel. And many other vain and foolish manoevers that are unseeming and unprofitable to mention . . . . These things grieved the servants of the Lord, and some conversed together on this subject, and others came in and we were at Joseph Smith, Jr. the Seer, and made it a matter of consultation, for many would not turn from their folly, unless God would give a revelation, therefore the Lord spoke to Joseph (The Book of John Whitmer, pp. 26-27).

3. *Autobiography of Parley P. Pratt*, p. 61.

4. See Historical Note for section 46, note 3. Also Historical Note for section 129.

5. John Corrill, *A Brief History of the Church of Christ*; Jenson's *Biographical Encyclopedia*, 1:241; "Far West Record"; "Kirtland Council Minute Book"; *History of the Church*; D&C 50 and 52; 1830 Federal Census of Ohio; 1840 Federal Census of Illinois; "John Corrill Affidavit," Mss. 942, Brigham Young University, Manuscripts; "Joseph Smith Scriptory Book," Church Archives; 1833 Jackson County List of Mormons, Church Archives; Clay County, Missouri, Land Records; and Caldwell County, Missouri, Land Records.

6. *Autobiography of Parley P. Pratt*, p. 65; "Journal History," 10 January 1858, Church Archives; *Painesville Telegraph* (31 January 1834); *History of the Church*; D&C 50 and 52; 1820 and 1830 Federal Census of New York.

Section 51

1. Both the "Kirtland Revelation Book," (p. 87) and "Book of Commandments, Laws and Covenants," Book B, give the date of reception as 20 May 1831. The date in the former source was originally "20 August 1831," but has been altered to read "20 May 1831."

2. *Times and Seasons* 5 (1 February 1844): 416.

3. Orson Pratt discourse, 28 June 1874, Brigham City, Utah, *Millennial Star* 32 (11 August 1874): 498.

4. "Kirtland Revelation Book," p. 87.

5. *History of the Church*, 1:366-67.

6. Joseph Smith to Edward Partridge, 2 May 1833, Joseph Smith Collection, Church Archives. For reference to the challenging of the legality of these proceedings, see *History of the Church*, 1:380, cited from *Evening and Morning* 2 (July 1833): 110. The *Painesville Telegraph* (26 April 1833) also reported the lawsuit:

> We perceive by a letter from Independence, Missouri, to the Editor of the Cincinnati Journal, that difficulties have already began in the Mormon community, at Mount Zion, in that quarter; one of the members having sued the Bishop, in a court of justice, for fifty dollars, which had been sent by the plaintiff to the said Bishop, from Ohio, *"to purchase an inheritance for himself and the saints of God in Zion in these last days."* This was certainly a most impious act, but "nevertheless and notwithstanding," the jury found for the plaintiff; it appearing that though the good bishop had indeed appropriated the money "to the purchase of an inheritance," yet he had, unthoughtedly no doubt, procured the deed to be drawn in his own name, to his heirs, &c. and no one else in Zion nor out of it. The writer states that on this decision several other members are ready to make similar demands on the good bishop.

Although modifications were made to convey legal title for consecrated properties, the 1833-38 phase of the law of consecration was not characterized by this process, but simply by the consecration of surplus properties. Stewardships, therefore, were not deeded since individual owners retained title to their properties.

7. See section 51:5, which was modified to reflect the change of policy and the *Evening and Morning Star* (July 1833), which states: "Members of the Church have, or *will* have, 'deeds' in their own name" (emphasis mine).

Section 52

1. *History of the Church*, 1:175.

2. The Book of John Whitmer, microfilm copy at Church Archives. Pages 27-29 of this document report the June 1831 conference and the reception of section 52:

June 3, 1831, A general conference was called, and a blessing promised, if the elders were faithful and humble before him. Therefore the elders assembled from the East, and the West, from the North and the South, And also many members. Conference was opened by prayer and ex[h]ortation by Joseph Smith Jr. the Revelator. After the business of the church was attended to according to the Covenants, the Lord made manifest to Joseph that it was necessary that such of the elders as were considered worthy, should be ordained to the high priesthood.

The Spirit of the Lord fell upon Joseph in an unusual manner, And prophesied that John the Revelator was then among the ten tribes of Israel who had been led away by Salmanaser, King of Israel, to prepare them for their return from their long dispersion, to again possess the land of their fathers. He prophesied many more things [nine words struck out] that I have not written. After he had prophesied, he laid his hands upon Lyman Wight [and ordained him] to the High priesthood after the holy order of God. And the Spirit fell upon Lyman and he prophesied, concerning the coming of Christ . . . .

June 6 1831, Received a Revelation what to do [section 52].

3. Levi W. Hancock Journal (typescript), Brigham Young University, Special Collections.

4. John Smith Journal, 1831-32 (not the Prophet's uncle), Church Archives.

5. "Far West Record," pp. 3-5.

6. The significance of these ordinations to the high priesthood can be appreciated only if one understands that for several years the office of high priest was recognized as the highest priesthood office in the Church (see Alma 13:5-18 which undoubtedly served as the basis for this idea). Joseph Smith and his associates did *not* equate high priesthood with Melchizedek Priesthood. Only high priests held the high priesthood; as such they were recognized as the elite of the priesthood. In January 1832 Joseph Smith was sustained as President of the High Priesthood (i.e., president of all the high priests), and two months later he appointed two counselors to assist him (see Historical Note for section 81). Section 84:63 (given to ten high priests) clearly identifies the early prominence of the high priests: "And as I said unto mine apostles, even so I say unto you, for you are mine apostles, even God's high priests; ye are they whom my Father hath given me; ye are my friends." The affairs of the Church were governed by two bodies of high priests, one in Kirtland and one in Missouri, until the organization of the Church high councils in 1834, when a small number of high priests, with additional powers, were selected to administer and adjudicate Church matters. The quorum of the First Presidency grew out of the Presidency of the High Priesthood by 1834. Although it retained its supremacy as a presiding body, the title (First Presidency) more clearly identified the body as the supreme quorum over the whole Church rather than merely an organizational presidency. (Additionally, the title "Presidency of the High Priesthood" was considered obnoxious by some who feared elitism and

authoritarianism.) Whereas the Quorum of Twelve Apostles would eventually assume greater authority than that of the high councils, this did not occur immediately following the appointments to the quorum in 1835, instead it developed gradually. By 1841 the Twelve had begun to take their place next to the First Presidency. Until at least 1841, elders, seventies, and apostles were recognized as "elders," and high priests were high priests— the elite. (See for example, *History of the Church*, 4:105.) Subsequently, priesthood supremacy was given to those who had received temple ordinances, because receiving all such ordinances extended to man the "fulness" of the priesthood. After the Prophet's death the significance began to diminish, and eventually the term *high priesthood* became synonymous with Melchizedek Priesthood and "higher priesthood." (See Heber C. Kimball Journal, 14 December 1845, Church Archives, where Brigham Young declared that a seventy can ordain high priests.)

7. Minutes of the Missouri meeting, convened 4 August 1831, are in the "Far West Record."

8. *History of the Church*, 1: 188. The anti-Mormon *Painesville Telegraph* (14 June 1831) reported the events of the Kirtland conference:

> After all the good followers of Jo. Smith from York state had got fairly settled down in this vicinity, which Rigdon had declared to be their "eternal inheritance," Jo. must needs invent another "command from God." At a meeting of the tribe on the 3d inst. the fact was made known to them that 28 elders must be selected and ordained, to start immediately, for Missouri. Jo accordingly asked the Lord in the assembly whom he should select, and the Lord named them over to him as he made them believe. The ceremony of endowing them with miraculous gifts, or supernatural power, was then performed, and they were commanded to take up a line of march; preaching their gospel, (Jo's Bible) raising the dead, healing the sick, casting out devils, &c. This squad comprises Jo himself, Rigdon, Martin Harris, Gilbert, Morley, Murdock, Partridge, and all the other leading and influential men among them. The flock are to be left to *shirk* for themselves the best way they can. It is said they are about to commence an establishment some 500 miles up the Missouri, where they contemplate building the New Jerusalem, and they have expressed doubts whether few if any of them will ever return to *this* "land of promise" . . . . The chosen few are to be off during the present week, going by pairs in different routes, all on foot, except Jo., Rigdon, and Harris.

9. See Historical Note for section 56. For additional information on section 52 and the labors of the missionaries named therein, see Levi W. Hancock Journal (typescript), Brigham Young University, Special Collections; William E. McLellan to Samuel McLellan, 4 August 1832, located at RLDS Library-Archives, Independence, Missouri; The Book of John Whitmer, microfilm copy at Church Archives; *Autobiography of Parley*

P.Pratt; "Journal History"; and John Corrill, *A Brief History of the Church of Christ*.

10. 1830 Federal Census of Ohio; 1840 Federal Census of Iowa Territory; *History of the Church*; D&C 52; "Kirtland Council Minute Book"; "Far West Record"; "Nauvoo Temple Endowment Register," Genealogical Society, Salt Lake City, Utah; and *The Saints' Herald* 6 (1 November 1864): 138.

11. Levi W. Hancock Journal (typescript), Brigham Young University Library, Special Collections; *Painesville Telegraph* (24 May 1831); D&C 52; and Heman Bassett genealogical records, Genealogical Society, Salt Lake City, Utah.

12. *History of the Church*; "Far West Record"; D&C sections 52 and 64; 1830, 1850, and 1860 Federal Census of Ohio; Portage County, Ohio, Marriage Records; *The Ohio Star* (Ravenna); and Eber D. Howe, *Mormonism Unvailed* (Painesville, Ohio: 1834).

13. "Journal History"; "Far West Record"; *History of the Church*; D&C, sections 52, 61, 75, and 94; Reynolds Cahoon Journal, Church Archives; "Kirtland Council Minute Book"; "Record of Sealings" (Nauvoo Temple), Church Archives; Ehat, "Endowment Data Summary"; Stella Cahoon Shurtleff, *Reynolds Cahoon and his Stalwart Sons* (Salt Lake City: Paragon Press, 1960); and Hyrum Smith Journal (1831-35), Church Archives.

14. *History of the Church*; "Far West Record"; D&C, sections 52 and 79; "Kirtland Council Minute Book"; "Journal History"; Jared Carter Journal, Church Archives; "List of Saints Residing in Far West, Missouri in 1838," in Teachers' Quorum Minutes (1838), Church Archives; 1850 Federal Census of Illinois; and *Nauvoo Neighbor* (25 September 1844). Carter's wife and children were residing in DeKalb County, Illinois, in 1850.

15. 1790 Federal Census of Connecticut; 1800, 1810, and 1820 Federal Census of Massachusetts; 1830 Federal Census of Ohio; 1840 Federal Census of Iowa Territory; "Far West Record"; *History of the Church*; D&C 52; "Journal History"; and "Record of Sealings" (Nauvoo Temple), Church Archives.

16. "Far West Record"; and D&C 52.

17. "Far West Record"; Zebedee Coltrin Journals, Church Archives; Jenson's *Biographical Encyclopedia*, 1:190; "Journal History"; "Record of Sealings" (Nauvoo Temple), Church Archives; "Kirtland Council Minute Book"; D&C 52; *Messenger and Advocate*; *Painesville Telegraph* (18 April 1828); and *History of the Church*.

18. "Far West Record"; Jared Carter Journal, Church Archives; Levi W. Hancock Journal (typescript), Brigham Young University Library, Special Collections; D&C 52; 1830 and 1840 Federal Census of Ohio; *Painesville Telegraph* (26 April 1831); and 1850 Federal Census of Michigan.

19. 1820, 1830, and 1850 Federal Census of Ohio; 1840 Federal Census of Illinois; Selah J. Griffin Affidavit, Mss. 942, Brigham Young University Library, Manuscripts; "General Record of the Seventies," Book A, Church Archives; William W. Phelps Letters, Church Archives; Geauga County,

Ohio, Land Records; Reynolds Cahoon Journal, Church Archives; "Far West Record"; *History of the Church*; D&C 52; and "Journal History."

20. *History of the Church*; Jenson's *Biographical Encyclopedia*; "Far West Record"; Levi W. Hancock Journal (typescript), Brigham Young University Library, Special Collections; Levi W. Hancock family group sheets, Genealogical Society, Salt Lake City, Utah; "Record of Sealings" (Nauvoo Temple), Church Archives; D&C 52; and "Journal History."

21. *History of the Church*; "Far West Record"; Levi W. Hancock Journal (typescript), Brigham Young University Library, Special Collections; D&C 52; "Journal History"; and Solomon Hancock family group sheet, Genealogical Society, Salt Lake City, Utah.

22. *History of the Church*; D&C 52; 1810, 1820, and 1830 Federal Census of New York; Solomon Humphrey family group sheet, Genealogical Society, Salt Lake City, Utah; and Jenson's *Biographical Encyclopedia*.

23. Cuyahoga County, Ohio, Probate Records; *History of the Church*; "Journal History"; and D&C 52.

24. *History of the Church*; *Nauvoo Neighbor*; "Far West Record"; D&C 52; "Record of Sealings" (Nauvoo Temple), Church Archives; Newel Knight Journal, Church Archives; *Scraps of Biography—Tenth Book of the Faith Promoting Series*, Juvenile Instructor Office (Salt Lake City: 1883); Larry C. Porter, "The Colesville Branch and the Coming Forth of the Book of Mormon," *Brigham Young University Studies* 10 (Spring 1970):365-85; "Journal History"; Joseph Holbrook Journal (1846), Church Archives; and "Nauvoo High Council Minutes."

25. *History of the Church*; "Far West Record"; D&C, sections 52 and 64; Jenson's *Biographical Encyclopedia*; "Journal History"; Isaac Morley family group sheet, Genealogical Society, Salt Lake City, Utah; "Record of Sealings" (Nauvoo Temple), Church Archives; "Nauvoo High Council Minutes"; and Ehat, "Endowment Data Summary."

26. John Murdock Journal, Church Archives; Jenson's *Biographical Encyclopedia*, 2:362; "Far West Record"; D&C, sections 52 and 99; "Journal History"; "Kirtland Council Minute Book"; "Nauvoo High Council Minutes"; and "Pottawatamie High Council Minutes."

27. 1820, 1830, 1840, 1850, and 1860 Federal Census of Ohio; "Far West Record"; *History of the Church*; D&C 52; Amos Sutton Hayden, *Early History of the Disciples in the Western Reserve, Ohio* (Cincinnati, 1876); Portage County, Ohio, Probate Records; and Portage County, Ohio, Marriage Records.

28. "Far West Record"; and D&C 52.

29. *History of the Church*; "Far West Record"; D&C 52; "Journal History"; and 1850 Federal Census of Utah Territory.

30. *History of the Church*; Philip C. Wightman, "The Life and Contribution of Lyman Wight," master's thesis, Brigham Young University, 1971; D&C, sections 52 and 124; Ehat, "Endowment Data Summary"; *Times and Seasons*; Jenson's *Biographical Encyclopedia*; "Journal History"; "Kirtland Council Minute Book"; "Far West Record"; "Record of Adoptions and

Sealings of Parents and Children" (Nauvoo Temple), Church Archives; and H.W. Mills, "De Tal Palo Tal Astilla," *Annual Publications—the Historical Society of Southern California* 10 (1917):86-172.

Section 53

1. *Times and Seasons* 5 (15 February 1844):432. See also D&C 57:8.
2. *History of the Church*; *Messenger and Advocate* (November 1834); "Far West Record"; D&C, sections 53, 57, 64, and 90; "Journal History"; Joseph Smith to William W. Phelps, 31 July 1832, Joseph Smith Collection, Church Archives; and "Autobiography of Mary Elizabeth Rollins Lightner," in *The Utah Genealogical and Historical Magazine* (July 1926).

Section 54

1. See dating for section 53.
2. The unfriendly *Painesville Telegraph* (17 May 1831) announced the arrival of the New York Saints: "About two hundred men, women and children, of the deluded followers of Jo Smith's Bible speculation, have arrived on our coast during the last week, from the state of New-York, & are about seating themselves down upon the 'promised land' in this county."
3. Jessee, "Joseph Knight's Recollections."
4. Ibid. Also see Historical Note for section 49.
5. *History of the Church*, 1:180.
6. Joseph Knight, Jr., "Incidents of History 1827-1844," Church Archives.
7. See *Scraps of Biography—Tenth Book of the Faith Promoting Series*, Juvenile Instructor Office (Salt Lake City: 1883). On 28 June 1831 the *Telegraph* gave its version of the historical setting of section 54:

> We mentioned two weeks since that the Mormon speculators on the souls of men, were about to take up a line of march for Missourie. The leaders have already departed. Before Jo left, he had a special command for all those of his followers who had located themselves in the township of Thompson, to depart forthwith for Missourie, and all those who did not obey were to be deprived of all the blessings of Mormonism. There were in that township about twenty families, the most of whom started last week for the Ohio River, leaving their spring crops all upon the ground.

Section 55

1. See dating for section 53.
2. *History of the Church*, 1:184-85.
3. Though William W. Phelps did assist the Church greatly in printing scripture and Church literature, he did not write any books for little children. At the October conference in 1845 Phelps recalled section 55 and his commission regarding this assignment: "By revelation, in 1831, I was appointed to do the work of printing . . . and writing books for schools in

this church, that little children might receive instruction . . . . We will instruct our children in the paths of righteousness; and we want that instruction compiled in a book. Moved that W. W. Phelps write some books for the use of children; seconded and carried" (*History of the Church*, 7:474-75). It appears that this was never carried into action.

4. See "Far West Record," 26 April 1832; and D&C 57:11.

5. Joseph Coe Journal (1831), in Newel K. Whitney Collection, Brigham Young University, Manuscripts; "Far West Record"; *History of the Church*; Joseph Coe Letters in Joseph Smith Collection, Church Archives; 1850 Federal Census of Ohio; "Kirtland Council Minute Book"; and D&C, sections 55 and 102.

6. *History of the Church*; Jenson's *Biographical Encyclopedia*; Walter D. Bowen, "The Versatile W. W. Phelps—Mormon Leader, Educator, and Pioneer," master's thesis, Brigham Young University, 1958; "Kirtland Council Minute Book"; "Far West Record"; "Journal History"; Juanita Brooks, ed., *On the Mormon Frontier: The Diary of Hosea Stout, 1844-1861* (Salt Lake City: Utah State Historical Society, 1964); Ehat, "Endowment Data Summary"; "Record of Sealings" (Nauvoo Temple), Church Archives; and D&C, sections 55, 57, 58, and 70.

Section 56

1. See dating of section 53.

2. "History of Thomas B. Marsh, Written by Himself," (November 1857), Church Archives. The "Far West Record" affirms that Marsh and Griffin traveled to Missouri and attended the conference in Independence.

3. See Historical Note for section 54.

4. "Kirtland Revelation Book," pp. 91-92.

Section 57

1. Three different sources affirm the date of reception as 20 July 1831: "Far West Record," p. 20; "Kirtland Revelation Book," p. 89; and "Book of Commandents, Laws and Covenants," Book B. The third source notes: "Commandment recd at Missouri after the arrival of Joseph Smith Junr- M. Harris Edwd Partridge- Joseph Coe & W. W. Phelps July 20, 1831."

2. See Historical Note for section 52.

3. *Times and Seasons* 5 (15 February 1844): 434.

4. See William W. Phelps to Brigham Young, 12 August 1861, Church Archives. Phelps, who accompanied the Prophet to Missouri, reported that a revelation was received west of Independence (in present-day Kansas), on 17 July 1831.

5. *Times and Seasons* 5 (15 February 1844): 434.

6. See *Messenger and Advocate* (September 1835): 179-80.

7. The Book of John Whitmer, microfilm copy at Church Archives.

8. John Whitmer wrote the following concerning the dedication of the new Zion and the temple site:

And by the special protection of the Lord, Bro. Joseph Smith, Junior, and Sidney Rigdon, in company with eight other elders, with the church from Colesville, New York, consisting of about sixty souls, arrived in the month of July and by revelation the place was made known where the temple shall stand and the city should commence. . . .

On the second day of August, 1831, Brother Sidney Rigdon stood up and asked, saying, Do you receive this land for the land of your inheritance with thankful hearts from the Lord? Answer from all, We do. Do you pledge yourselves to keep the laws of God on this land which you have never kept in your own land? We do.

Do you pledge yourselves to see that others of your brethren who shall come hither do keep the laws of God? We do. After prayer he arose and said, I now pronounce this land consecrated and dedicated to the Lord for a possession and inheritance for the Saints, (in the name of Jesus Christ, having authority from him.) And for all the faithful servants of the Lord to the remotest ages of time. Amen.

The day following eight elders, viz., Joseph Smith, Junior, Oliver Cowdery, Sidney Rigdon, Peter Whitmer, Junior, Frederick G. Williams, William W. Phelps, Martin Harris, and Joseph Coe, assembled together where the temple is to be erected. Sidney Rigdon dedicated the ground where the city is to stand, and Joseph Smith, Junior, laid a stone at the northeast corner of the contemplated temple in the name of the Lord Jesus of Nazareth. After all present had rendered thanks to the Great Ruler of the universe, Sidney Rigdon pronounced this spot of ground wholly dedicated unto the Lord for ever. Amen (Book of John Whitmer, chap. 9).

Whitmer claimed that the foregoing account was first written by Oliver Cowdery (see Ibid). Although the *History of the Church*, 1:199, notes that Joseph Smith dedicated the temple spot, John Whitmer's account (above), credits Rigdon with that action, and the *Times and Seasons* 5 (1 March 1844):450, does not identify the individual that dedicated the site.

9. Max H. Parkin, "The Courthouse Mentioned in the Revelation on Zion," *Brigham Young University Studies* 14 (Summer 1974): 451-57.

10. Jackson County, Missouri, Deed Record, Book B, p. 1.

Section 58

1. Emily Partridge Papers, Church Archives.

2. See D&C 63:45.

3. *Journal of Discourses*, 18:160-61.

4. See D&C 63:55-56.

5. See Historical Note for section 57; Historical Note for section 63; and *History of the Church*, 1:196.

6. "Far West Record," p. 5.

7. Ibid.

Section 59

1. A prefatory note for section 59 in "Book of Commandments, Laws and Covenants" Book A, states: "Given by Joseph the translator & written by Oliver Cowdery August 7, 1831 in the land of Zion."
2. Jessee, "Joseph Knight's Recollections."
3. *Times and Seasons* 5 (1 March 1844): 450.

Section 60

1. See Historical Note for section 58.
2. See *History of the Church*, 1:206 and Reynolds Cahoon Journal, Church Archives. An account of the return trip in the *Times and Seasons* 5 (15 March 1844):464 suggests the group traveled in sixteen canoes. Possibly some of the canoes were used for baggage.

Section 61

1. See *Times and Seasons* 5 (15 March 1844):464. Also see Ezra Booth's account of this return trip in E. D. Howe, *Mormonism Unvailed* (Painesville, Ohio: 1834), pp. 204-06.
2. Reynolds Cahoon Journal, Church Archives.
3. See headnote for section 61 (in handwriting of A. Sidney Gilbert), "Book of Commandments, Laws and Covenants," Book B, Church Archives.
4. The writer is indebted to Max H. Parkin for assisting in the location of McIlwaine's Bend.

Section 62

1. The place of reception for section 62 is found in the Reynolds Cahoon Journal and in the John Murdock Journal, both in Church Archives. The little town of Chariton no longer exists.
2. Minutes of this meeting are recorded in the "Far West Record." Present were David Whitmer, Hyrum Smith, Harvey Whitlock, and a few others. The meeting opened by "singing [and] prayer by br. Hyrum Smith. br. Edward Partridge made certain remarks from the 3rd Chapter of Malichi. br. Whitlock made remarks upon the second coming of Christ, br. Hyrum Smith gave an exhortation, spoke of Zion & the gathering of the saints into her, &c. & read a part of the 102 Psalm." After remarks from David Whitmer, Isaac Morley, and John Corrill, William E. McLellan was ordained an elder and the meeting closed ("Far West Record," pp. 6-7).
3. *Times and Seasons* 5 (15 March 1844): 465.

Section 63

1. Three different sources give the date of reception as 30 August 1831: The Book of John Whitmer; *Evening and Morning Star* (February 1833); and

"Book of Commandments, Laws and Covenants," Book B. The third source states: "Given by Joseph the Seer in Kirtland Augt 30, 1831 & written by Oliver."

2. "Far West Record," p. 12.

3. *Times and Seasons* 5 (15 March 1844): 465.

4. On 10 March 1832 Billings was "authorized to take the leave of the Kirtland Church whilst traveling to the land of Zion" (Hyrum Smith Journal, under date, Church Archives).

5. See "Far West Record," pp. 8-9.

6. Sidney Rigdon Papers, Church Archives.

7. *History of the Church*; Jenson's *Biographical Encyclopedia*, 1:242; Geauga County, Ohio, Marriage Records; family group sheets, Genealogical Society, Salt Lake City, Utah; "Far West Record"; "Record of Sealings" (Nauvoo Temple), Church Archives; "Nauvoo Temple Endowment Register," Genealogical Society, Salt Lake City, Utah; and D&C 63.

8. *History of the Church*; "Journal History"; Jenson's *Biographical Encyclopedia*, 1:222-27; "Far West Record"; D&C, sections 63, 72, 78, 84, 93, 96, 104, and 117; Geauga County, Ohio, Marriage Records; "Record of Sealings" (Nauvoo Temple), Church Archives; Ehat, "Endowment Data Summary"; "Kirtland Council Minute Book"; "Nauvoo High Council Minutes"; and "Record of Adoptions and Sealings of Parents and Children" (Nauvoo Temple), Church Archives.

Section 64

1. "Book of Commandments, Laws and Covenants," Book B., Church Archives, gives the date of reception as 12 September 1831. However, many other early manuscript copies are dated "11 September 1831."

2. *Times and Seasons* 5 (1 April 1844)): 480. Minutes of meetings recorded in the "Far West Record" (pp. 8, 9 and 13), show that the elders were appointed to secure funds to assist the Prophet and Sidney during this period of Bible translation.

3. See Luke S. Johnson Statement, Church Archives, regarding the Prophet's stay at the Johnson home in Hiram, Ohio.

4. *History of the Church*; "Kirtland Council Minute Book"; "Far West Record"; D&C, sections 90 and 93; Jenson's *Biographical Encyclopedia*, 1:51; Frederick G. Williams Papers, Church Archives; Frederick G. Williams, "Frederick Granger Williams of the First Presidency of the Church," *Brigham Young University Studies* 12 (Spring 1972); *Utah Genealogical and Historical Magazine* (January 1937); and Nauvoo Temple Records, research in possession of author.

Section 65

1. *Times and Seasons* 5 (1 April 1844): 482.

Section 66

1. "Far West Record," p. 11.
2. William E. McLellan to Samuel McLellan, 4 August 1832, RLDS Library-Archives, Independence, Missouri.
3. See section 75:6.
4. Though William E. McLellan varied the spelling of his surname at different periods during his life (as witnessed in extant autographed letters), the above usage will be maintained throughout this work. This spelling is clearly preferred by him in later life and was also used by his relatives from Smith County, Tennessee. *History of the Church*; "Far West Record"; "Kirtland Council Minute Book"; "Journal History"; Jenson's *Biographical Encyclopedia*, 1:82; and McLellan correspondence, RLDS Library-Archives.

Section 67

1. *Times and Seasons* 5(15 April 1844):496.

Section 68

1. Actually, verses 16-21 were not originally part of this revelation, and were first published in the *Evening and Morning Star* (Kirtland reprint) in June 1835. Use of the term "First Presidency of the Melchizedek Priesthood" (rather than Presidency of the High Priesthood) in these verses reflects title changes which occurred sometime in 1834-35.
2. "Far West Record," pp. 28 and 32.
3. Section 68 is the first latter-day revelation to address the notion of being sealed up unto eternal life (verse 12). This was a topic of considerable importance during the Prophet's life-time. Shortly after the Orange, Ohio, conference (25 October 1831) high priests began sealing the Saints to eternal life. These early priesthood sealings (1831-35) were not unimportant, but it was later determined that they were insufficient. Although the Prophet received the greater keys of sealing from Elijah in April 1836, he delayed administering the higher (temple) ordinances until the 1840s. The first priesthood (eternal) marriage was performed in April 1841, and the priesthood endowment was administered for the first time in May 1842. Having received these prerequisite ordinances, the faithful could continue on and receive the fulness of the priesthood wherein they were sealed up unto eternal. (The fulness of the priesthood began to be administered in September 1843.) Thus, a complete understanding of the nature of making one's calling and election sure (i.e., being sealed up unto eternal) developed over a ten-year period, and achieved its fullest expression during the Nauvoo period.
4. Edward Partridge had been ordained bishop while still an elder. It was later decided to make an exception for literal, first born descendants of Aaron.

5. See section 68 as published in *Evening and Morning Star* (October 1832).

6. Robert J. Matthews has pointed out that the age of accountability was revealed to Joseph Smith earlier than November 1831 and seems to have been received while Joseph was working on the inspired translation of the book of Genesis, sometime between 1 December and 4 April 1831 (see Robert J. Matthews, "The 'New Translation' of the Bible, 1830-1833: Doctrinal Development During the Kirtland Era," *Brigham Young University Studies* 11 [Summer 1971]: 409-10).

7. See Historical Note for section 107.

8. *History of the Church*; D&C, sections 68, 75, 102, 103, 124; "Far West Record"; "Kirtland Council Minute Book"; Jenson's *Biographical Encyclopedia*, 1: 80; "Journal History"; *Frontier Guardian* (1849-52); Orson Hyde correspondence in "Brigham Young Incoming Correspondence Collection," Church Archives; and Ehat, "Endowment Data Summary."

9. *History of the Church*; D&C sections 68, 75, and 102; "Far West Record"; "Kirtland Council Minute Book"; "Journal History"; Jenson's *Biographical Encyclopedia*, 1:85; Luke S. Johnson family group sheet, Genealogical Society, Salt Lake City, Utah; Newel K. Whitney Collection, Brigham Young University Library, Manuscripts; and "General Record of the Seventies," Book A, Church Archives.

10. *History of the Church*; "Far West Record"; "Kirtland Council Minute Book"; Jenson's *Biographical Encyclopedia*, 1:91; D&C, sections 68 and 75; "Journal History"; and 1850 Federal Census of Iowa. The writer is indebted to Keith Perkins for assisting on some of this information.

Section 69

1. At a special conference in Hiram, Ohio on 12 November 1831 Joseph Smith dedicated (to the Lord) "brs. Oliver Cowdery & John Whitmer & the sacred writings which they have entrusted to them to carry to Zion [by the] prayer of faith" ("Far West Record," p. 18).

2. See D&C 63: 46 and Historical Note for section 63.

3. See The Book of John Whitmer, microfilm copy at Church Archives. The "Far West Record" (pp. 19-21), contains the minutes of five meetings held in Winchester, Indiana (29 November-7 December 1831). A branch of the Church had been organized at Winchester by Levi W. Hancock and Zebedee Coltrin during the summer of 1831.

Section 70

1. Section 70 was received at Kirtland, Ohio, and after the Hiram, Ohio, conferences, which were held 1-12 November 1831.

2. It is difficult to ascertain the exact date of the organization of the Literary Firm, but it occurred sometime between 12 November and 20 November 1831—the day Cowdery and Whitmer left for Missouri. Initial plans for the creation of this firm were made on 12 November 1831 in Hiram,

Ohio. Minutes of the meeting stated, "In consequence of the dilligence of our brethren, Joseph Smith jr. Oliver Cowdery John Whitmer & Sidney Rigdon in bringing to light by the grace of God these sacred things, [approved that they] be appointed to manage them according to the Laws of the Church & the Commandments of the Lord" ("Far West Record," p. 18). The "managing" of the sacred writings was the responsibility of the Literary Firm.

3. "Far West Record," pp. 18 and 26.
4. "Far West Record," p. 18.
5. See D&C 70: 3; *History of the Church*, 2: 434; and William W. Phelps to Sally Phelps, 16 September 1835, William W. Phelps Collection, Church Archives.
6. D&C 70: 3 and 94: 10
7. "Far West Record," p. 26.
8. Ibid.
9. D&C 55: 4.
10. "Kirtland Council Minute Book," p. 24.
11. D&C 57: 11. See also D&C 55: 4.
12. See "Far West Record," p. 26, and *History of the Church*, 1: 362.
13. "Far West Record," pp. 27-28. The dedication occurred on 29 May 1832. Phelps and his family occupied the lower story of the printing office at Independence. The office was located on lot 76, which had been purchased by Edward Partridge from James Gray on 8 August 1831 for $50. It was a two-story brick structure.
14. See D&C 72: 20-21; D&C 96: 8; and Historical Note for section 78. "The order of the Literary Firm is a matter of stewardship, which is of the greatest importance, and the mercantile establishment [United Firm], God commanded to be devoted to the support thereof" (*History of the Church*, 1: 365-66).
15. *Evening and Morning Star* (May 1833).
16. William W. Phelps to "Dear Brethren," 20 July 1833, Joseph Smith Collection, Church Archives.
17. "Kirtland Council Minute Book," p. 24.
18. D&C 94: 10.
19. See Historical Note for section 94.
20. "Kirtland Council Minute Book," p. 24.
21. *History of the Church*, 1: 465.
22. The political paper was intended to be called the *Democrat*, but the proposed title was changed by the fall of 1834. Some reports suggest that a couple of issues, under the title of *Northern Times*, were printed in the fall of 1834 (see Max H Parkin, "Mormon Political Involvement in Ohio," *Brigham Young University Studies* 9 (Summer 1969):484-502; and Peter Crawley, "A Bibliography of The Church of Jesus Christ of Latter-day Saints in New York, Ohio, and Missouri," *Brigham Young University Studies* 12 (Summer 1972): 496.
23. See D&C 104: 28-30 and 58.

24. William W. Phelps to Sally Phelps, 16 September 1835, Church Archives.

25. See Historical Note for section 25.

26. See "Kirtland Council Minute Book," p. 108, and *History of the Church*, 2:273 and 287. A letter from Joseph Smith to "Dear Brethren," dated 15 June 1835, mentioned the projects then being printed by the firm as well as the need for money: "We are now commencing to prepare and print the New Translation [of the Bible], together with all the revelations [1835 edition of the Doctrine and Covenants] which God has been pleased to give us in these last days, and as we are in want of funds to go on with so great and glorious a work, brethren we want you should donate and loan us all the means or money you can that we may be enable[d] to accomplish the work as a great means towards the Salvation of Men" (letter in Joseph Smith Collection, Church Archives).

27. See *History of the Church*, 2: 300 and 318. Also William W. Phelps to Sally Phelps, 14 November 1835, William W. Phelps Collection, Church Archives.

28. See *History of the Church*, 2: 434.

29. *History of the Church*, 2: 475. Further reference to Cowdery's selling out his share in the partnership is found in "Far West Record," p. 125 (at his trial of excommunication).

30. See *History of the Church*, 2: 487.

31. See "An Account of the Life of Elisha Hurd Groves," written by Groves, Church Archives.

32. "Far West Record," p. 125. The minutes indicate that Cowdery did not give up the notes.

33. "An Account of the Life of Elisha Hurd Groves."

34. John Whitmer to Oliver Cowdery, 20 August 1837, Brigham Young University Library, Manuscripts.

35. John Whitmer may also have contemplated printing his history of the Church, which he had been keeping since June 1831. It is clear that the Prophet wanted it published. See "The Scriptory Book of Joseph Smith," p. 28.

36. "Far West Record," p. 136. D&C 118:2 also mentions Marsh's responsibility regarding the printing establishment.

37. On 6 August 1838 the subject of establishing a weekly paper was discussed. The Prophet is recorded as having said that "the time had come when it was necessary that we should have some thing of this nature to unite the people and aid in giving us the news of the day &c. Thereupon it was unanimously agreed that Prest. S. Rigdon should edit the same" ("The Scriptory Book of Joseph Smith," p. 65).

38. Before the war of expulsion against the Saints in Missouri in the fall of 1838, the Church press and type were boxed and buried near Far West at night to prevent their being destroyed. In the spring of 1839 the printing equipment was dug up and hauled to Nauvoo, where it would be used to print the *Times and Seasons*.

Section 71

1. The *Painesville Telegraph* (20 December 1831) announced Rigdon's decision to refute the acrimonious orations of Booth and Ryder:

> Sidney Rigdon, the vicegerant and champion of Jo. Smith, has thrown out a challenge, in the Ohio Star, to Mr. Booth and Deacon Rider, who have renounced the Mormon faith, to meet him in mortal combat (of words) on the subject of the Gold Bible.

In Ravenna, Ohio, on 26 December 1831, Sidney Rigdon gave a public rebuttal to Booth's claims (see Hyrum Smith Journal and Reynolds Cahoon Journal, both in Church Archives), but Ryder refused to engage in public debate with the talented Mormon spokesman. On 6 January 1832 Sidney Rigdon wrote a letter which was published in the *Ohio Star* (12 January 1832) regarding Ryder's trepidation:

> Simons, like the worker of iniquity, has sought a hiding place. Let the public remember, when he goes forth again to proclaim his assertions against the book of Mormon, that he has been invited upon honorable principles to investigate its merits, and dare not do it.

Section 72

1. *Times and Seasons* 5 (1 May 1844): 513.
2. Reynolds Cahoon Journal, and Hyrum Smith Journal, both in Church Archives.
3. See "Kirtland Revelation Book," pp. 13-15. The index of this record notes: "A revelation given to choose a Bishop N.K. Whitney was chosen & was sanctioned by the Lord and also another [revelation] in addition to the Law [section 42] making known the duty of the Bishop."

By March 1832, yet another revelation was received regarding the duty of the Church bishops:

> Verily thus saith the Lord unto you my servant Sidney and Joseph I reveal unto you for your own prophet [profit] and instruction concerning the Bishops of my church what is their duty in the church behold it is their duty to stand in the office of their Bishoprick and to fill the judgement seat which I have appointed unto them to administer the benefits of the church or the overpluss of all who are in their stewardships according to the Commandments as they are sever[al]ly appointed and the property or that which they receive of the church is not their own but belongeth to the church wherefore it is the property of the Lord and it is for the poor of the church to be administered according to the law for it is the will of the Lord that the church should be made equal in all things wherefore the bishops are accountable before the Lord for their stewardships to administer of their stewardship in the which they are appointed by commandment jointly

with you my servents unto the Lord as well as you my servents or the rest of the church that the benef[i]ts of all may be dedicated unto the Lord that the Lords storehouse may be filled always that ye may all grow in temporal as well as spiritual things and now verily I say unto you the bishops must needs be seperated unto their bishoppricks and judgement seats from care of business but not from claim neither from council Wherefore I have given unto you commandment that you should be joined together by covenant and bond wherefore see that ye do even as I have commanded and unto the office of the presidency of the high Priesthood I have given authority to preside with the assistence of his councellers over all the concerns of the church wherefore stand ye fast claim your Priesthood in authority yet in meekness and I am able to make you abound and be fruitfull and you shall never fall for unto you I have given the keys of the kingdom and if you transgress not they shall never be taken from you. Wherefore feed my sheep even so Amen (Original in Newel K. Whitney Collection, Brigham Young University Library, Manuscripts).

Sections 73-138

Section 73

Date. 10 January 1832.

Place. Hiram, Portage County, Ohio.

Historical Note. On 1 December 1831 a revelation (section 71) had instructed Joseph Smith and Sidney Rigdon to preach the gospel in the regions round about.[1] On their return they received section 73, which instructed them to resume their work of translation until the upcoming conference. The conference referred to was convened in Amherst, Ohio, on 25 January 1832.[2]

Publication Note. Section 73 was first published as section 29 in the 1835 edition of the Doctrine and Covenants.

Section 74

Date. January 1832 (after 10 January and before 25 January. See Historical Note.).

Place. Hiram, Portage County, Ohio.

Historical Note. Section 73, received 10 January 1832, had commanded Joseph Smith and Sidney Rigdon to resume the translation of the Bible. They had done so. While no available statement definitely connects section 74 with the translation of the Bible, the implication is certainly very strong: Section 74 is an explanation of 1 Cor. 7:14.[1]

Publication Note. Section 74 was first published as section 73 in the 1835 edition of the Doctrine and Covenants.

Section 75

Date.   25 January 1832.

Place.   Amherst, Lorain County, Ohio.

Amherst, Ohio, is about fifty miles west of Kirtland.

Historical Note. On 25 January 1832 an important priesthood conference was convened in Amherst, Ohio,[1] the home of several Church members, notably the Carters, the Johnsons, and Sylvester Smith.[2] At this meeting Joseph Smith was ordained and sustained president of the High Priesthood.[3]

The elders in attendance at this conference were anxious for Joseph Smith to inquire of the Lord "that they might know His will, or learn what would be most pleasing to Him for them to do."[4] Pursuant to this request by the brethren, "a revelation was given and written in the presence of the whole assembly, appointing many of the Elders to missions."[5]

Edson Barney, an early convert, stated that he "became personally acquainted with the Prophet Joseph in January 1832 at a Conference in Lorraine Co at that Conference a Revelation was received by Joseph in [Barney's] presence and Sidney Rigdon wrote it down."[6]

Section 75 is a composite of two revelations.[7] Verses 1-22 ("a command given to 10 Elders"[8]) called four elders to go south (William E. McLellan, Luke S. Johnson, Major N. Ashley, and Burr Riggs), four to go east (Orson Hyde, Samuel H. Smith, Orson Pratt, and Lyman E. Johnson), and two to go west (Asa Doods and Calves Wilson).

Verses 23-36 (the second part of the revelation) named fourteen elders who were given a general call to preach the gospel.[9]

Publication Note. Section 75 was first published as section 87 in the 1835 edition of the Doctrine and Covenants.

Biographical Note. Major Noble Ashley.

Son of Oliver Ashley and Tabitha Baker. Born 3 March 1798 in Sheffield, Berkshire County, Massachusetts. Living in Strongsville, Ohio, 1831. Baptized and ordained priest before June 1831. Ordained elder before 25 October 1831. Ordained high priest 25 October 1831. Appointed to preach gospel with Burr Riggs in "south country" 25 January 1832. Resided in Jackson County, Missouri, 1832-33. Tanner by profession. Left church before 1838. Residing in Tallmadge, Summitt County, Ohio, 1840.[10]

Biographical Note. Seymour Brunson.

Son of Reuben Brunson and Sally Clark. Born 18 September 1799 in Virginia. Served in War of 1812. Residing in Mantua, Portage County, Ohio, 1830. Married Harriet Gould before 1830. Four known children: Reuben, Lewis, Joseph, and Seymour. Baptized by Solomon Hancock January 1831. Ordained elder 25 January 1831 by John Whitmer. Appointed by revelation to preach gospel with Daniel Stanton 25 January 1832. Mission with Luke Johnson 1832. After establishing branch of Church in Windsor, Ohio, moved family there. Residing in Kirtland 1835. Temporary member of high council in Far West, Missouri, 1838. Expelled from Missouri 1839. Located in Nauvoo 1839. Appointed member of Nauvoo high council 6 October 1839. Appointed by high council 1 December 1839 to obtain signatures for petition to legislature to define new boundary lines in City of Nauvoo. Colonel in Hancock County Militia. Died 10 August 1840 in Nauvoo, Hancock County, Illinois. At funeral Joseph Smith first publicly announced doctrine of baptism for dead.[11]

Biographical Note. Stephen Burnett.

Son of Sirenus and Jane Burnett. Born 1814 in Ohio. Married to Leonora. Six children: Stephen, Jane, R. (female child), Charles, Emily, and Mary. Long-time resident of Orange, Ohio; there owned property and farmed with father. Baptized about 28 November 1830 by John Murdock. Ordained priest before June 1831. Ordained elder 11 October 1831 by John Whitmer. Conference of Church held in home 25 October 1831. Ordained high priest 25 October 1831 by Oliver Cowdery. Appointed by revelation to take mission with Ruggles Eames 25 January 1832. Appointed by revelation to take mission with Eden Smith March 1832. Preached with Horace Cowen in

New Hampshire 14 June-8 July 1833. Became disaffected from Church leadership by late 1837. Publicly denounced Joseph Smith in spring of 1838. In Church publication called "an ignorant little blockhead" 1838. Residing in Orange, Ohio, 1850.[12]

Biographical Note.   Gideon Hayden Carter.

Son of Gideon Carter and Johanah Sims. Born 1798 in Killingworth, Connecticut. Residing in Amherst, Ohio, 1831. Baptized 25 October 1831 by Joseph Smith at Orange, Ohio. Ordained priest by Oliver Cowdery 25 October 1831. Married Hilda Burwell. Six known children: Moses, Gideon, Philo, Ervin, Rosella, and Matilda. Ordained elder 25 January 1832. Appointed by revelation to preach with Sylvester Smith 25 January 1832 at Amherst Conference; with Smith traveled to Vermont, leaving Kirtland 5 April 1832 and returning August 1832. Married Charlotte Woods (born 1814 in New York) about 1835. Charter member of and owned stock in Kirtland Safety Society January 1837. Served on Kirtland high council 1837. Moved to Far West, Missouri 1838. Killed at Battle of Crooked River in Ray County, Missouri, 25 October 1838. Proxy sealing to Charlotte Woods in Nauvoo Temple 30 January 1846.[13]

Biographical Note.   Asa Dodds.

Born 1793 in New York. Mason by trade. Baptized and ordained to priesthood before January 1832. Appointed by revelation to preach gospel with Calves Wilson 25 January 1832 at Amherst Conference. Joined Orson Pratt on mission to Ohio from Missouri October 1831. Stopped in Indiana. Ordained high priest by Hyrum Smith 2 February 1832. Residing in Farmington, Trumball County, Ohio, 1850.[14]

Biographical Note.   Ruggles Eames.

Married Charlotte Rose 27 June 1830 in Mayfield, Ohio. Residing in Medina, Medina County, Ohio, 1831. Missionaries held meetings in Eames's home September 1831. Baptized and ordained priest before October 1831. Appointed by revelation to preach gospel with Stephen Burnett 25 January 1832. Residing in VanBuren County, Iowa, 1840.[15]

Biographical Note.   Emer Harris.

Son of Nathan Harris and Rhoda Lapham. Born 29 May 1781 in Cambridge, Washington County, New York. Married Roxana Peas 22 July 1802. Six known children: Selina, Elathan, Alvira, Sophronia, Nathan, and Ruth. Married Deborah Lott 16 January 1819. Four known children: Emer, Martin Henderson, Harriet, and Denison. Married Parna Chapel 29 March 1826. Four known children: Fauna, Joseph, Alma, and Charles. Residing in Luzerne County, Pennsylvania, 1820. Baptized 10 February 1831. Moved to

Kirtland, Ohio, 1831. Ordained elder before June 1831. Appointed member of committee to obtain money for Prophet to continue inspired translation of Bible 25 October 1831. Ordained high priest 25 October 1831. Appointed by revelation to preach gospel with Simeon Carter 25 January 1832. Mission to Susquehanna County, Pennsylvania, with Martin Harris 1832. Located in Huron County, Ohio, about December 1833. Worked on Kirtland Temple 1835. In spring of 1836 moved to farm three miles from Kirtland. Traveled to Pennsylvania in spring of 1838 to receive pay for farm there. Returned July 1838. Left for Missouri 5 September 1838. Arrived in Far West, Missouri, about 12 October 1838. Forced to leave Caldwell County 17 October 1838. Arrived in Adams County, Illinois, about 22 December 1838. Carpenter by trade. Purchased property about three miles northeast of Nauvoo 1840. Moved family to new farm in spring of 1841. Member of Nauvoo Legion. Married Polly Chamberlain 11 January 1846. Received endowment 30 January 1846. Moved to Utah 1850. Married Martha Allen 10 September 1850. Located in Provo. Appointed to be ordained patriarch 8 October 1853. Appointed to preside over high priests in Provo area 5 September 1855. Died 28 November 1869 in Logan, Cache County, Utah.[16]

Biographical Note.   Burr Riggs.

Born 17 April 1811 at New Haven, New Haven County, Connecticut. Baptized and ordained elder before June 1831. Ordained high priest 25 October 1831. Appointed by revelation to preach gospel with Major Ashley in "south country" 25 January 1832. Excommunicated 26 February 1833 for not magnifying high calling. Rebaptized by 1834. Member of Zion's Camp 1834. Married Lovina Williams (daughter of Frederick G. Williams) 19 November 1834. Three known children: George Washington, Adeline, and Lucy. Physician by profession. Moved to Clay County, Missouri, 1836. Located in Far West, Missouri, by 1837; there owned city lot as well as large acreage in Caldwell County. Became disaffected from Church 1838. Moved to Quincy, Illinois, 1839. Excommunicated 17 March 1839 for apostasy. Wife, Lovina Williams, died in Quincy, Illinois, November 1846 or 1847. Residing in Quincy 1850. Married Eunice Stone (born 1825 in Pennsylvania) 8 March 1851, in Adams County, Illinois. Died 8 June 1860.[17]

Biographical Note.   Eden Smith.

Son of John Smith. Born 1806 in Indiana. Married Elizabeth (baptized 9 August 1831). Residing in Portage County, Ohio, 1831. Baptized 1831. Ordained priest 11 September 1831 by Joseph Coe. Ordained elder 17 November 1831 by Reynolds Cahoon. Preached frequently in Western Reserve 1831-32. Appointed by revelation to accompany Stephen Burnett on mission in March 1832. Appointed branch president in Eugene, Vermillion

County, Indiana, about late 1832. Joined with Charles C. Rich in preaching near Eugene November 1832. Disfellowshipped 2 July 1833 for possessing a contentious spirit. Subsequently restored to fellowship. Appointed to travel with Benjamin Leland on mission to Erie County, Pennsylvania, 10-12 April 1843. Married Sobrina (born 1806 in Vermont). Two known children: Isaac and Hannah. Moved to Pottawatamie County, Iowa, by 1850. Died 7 December 1851 in Vermillion County, Indiana.[18]

Biographical Note.   Sylvester Smith.

Born about 1805. Resident of Amherst, Lorain County, Ohio, 1830. Baptized and ordained elder before June 1831. Ordained high priest 25 October 1831 by Oliver Cowdery. Appointed by revelation to preach gospel with Gideon Carter 25 January 1832; traveled together from Ohio to Vermont, preaching along way. Left Kirtland area 5 April 1832. Returned August 1832, having baptized several converts. Assisted in laying foundation stones for Kirtland Temple 23 July 1833. Member of Zion's Camp 1834. Tried for traducing character of Joseph Smith August 1834. Subsequently forgiven upon confession. Appointed member of Kirtland high council 17 February 1835. Ordained seventy 28 February 1835. Ordained president of First Quorum of Seventy 1 March 1835. Served as clerk for high council August-September 1835. Appointed acting scribe for Joseph Smith on 25 January 1836. Attended Hebrew School in Kirtland. Attended School of Prophets. Attended solemn assembly January 1836. Attended dedication of Kirtland Temple March 1836. Charter member of Kirtland Safety Society January 1837. Released from Kirtland high council 13 January 1836. Released as president of Seventy 6 April 1837. Became disaffected from Church leadership 1837. Left church by 1838.[19]

Biographical Note.   Daniel Stanton.

Son of Amos Stanton and Elizabeth Wyman. Born 28 May 1795 at Manlius, Onondaga County, New York. Married Clarina Graves (born 8 March 1797) about 1818. Four known children: Daniel, Lucy, Jonathan, and Constance. Fought in War of 1812. Moved to Ohio 1819. Baptized 3 November 1830 by Parley P. Pratt. Ordained priest January 1831 by Lyman Wight. Ordained elder 6 June 1831. Ordained high priest 25 October 1831. Appointed by revelation to preach gospel with Semour Brunson 25 January 1832. Moved to Jackson County, Missouri, by February 1833. Member of Prairie Branch in Jackson County, Missouri. Appointed to preside over Branch Number Two 11 September 1833. After Mormon troubles in Jackson County, Missouri, moved north into Clay and Caldwell counties. Located in Adam-Ondi-Ahman area 1838. Member of Adam-Ondi-Ahman high council June 1838. Moved to Quincy, Illinois, 1839. Appointed president of the Quincy Stake 25 October 1840. Appointed member of Lima high council 11 June 1843.

Received endowment 25 December 1845 in Nauvoo Temple. Emigrated to Utah and settled in Springville. Died 26 October 1872 at Panaca, Lincoln County, Nevada.[20]

Biographical Note.   Micah Baldwin Welton.

Son of Eliakim Welton and Loly Barnes. Born 13 August 1794 in Watertown, Litchfield County, Connecticut. Residing in Portage County by 1831. Married Wealthy Upson. Later married Keziah. Known children: Sarah Elizabeth and Rachel. Baptized 23 June 1831 at Northampton, Ohio, by John Smith (not the Prophet's uncle). Ordained priest by Oliver Cowdery 25 October 1831 at Orange, Ohio. Ordained elder 17 November 1831 by Reynolds Cahoon. Appointed to preach gospel with Eden Smith 25 January 1832. Residing in Clay County, Missouri, 1836. After Mormon expulsion from Missouri, located in Pike County, Illinois, 1839. Ordained seventy on or before 6 May 1839 at Quincy, Illinois. Member of Third Quorum of Seventy in Nauvoo. Appointed to preach in Kentucky April 1844. Received endowment in Nauvoo Temple 29 January 1846.[21]

Biographical Note.   Calves Wilson.

Baptized before 25 October 1831. Ordained priest by Oliver Cowdery 25 October 1831 at Orange, Ohio. Appointed by revelation to preach gospel with Asa Dodds in "western countries" 25 January 1832 at Amherst, Ohio. (It is not known if Dodds accompanied Wilson on this mission.) In company with Lyman Wight in spring of 1832 in Cincinnati, Ohio, where scores were baptized into Church. Baptized John S. Higbee May 1832 in Cincinnati area.[22]

Section 76

Date.   16 February 1832.

Place.   Hiram, Portage County, Ohio.

Historical Note.   After returning to Hiram from the Amherst conference, Joseph Smith and Sidney Rigdon resumed the translation of the New Testament. Section 76 was received while they were translating John 5:29. Known as "The Vision,"[1] this section is of major doctrinal importance.[2]

Philo Dibble, one of a dozen brethren present when this vision was received, indicated that he saw the glory and felt the power but did not see the vision. Referring to the occasion, Dibble stated,

> Joseph would, at intervals, say: "What do I see?" Then he would relate what he had seen or what he was looking at. Then Sidney replied, "I see the same." Presently Sidney would say, "What do I see?" and would repeat what he had seen or was seeing, and Joseph would reply, "I see the same." This manner of conversation was repeated at short intervals to the end of the vision, and during the whole time not a word was spoken by any other person. Not a sound nor motion made by anyone but Joseph and Sidney, and it seemed to me that they never moved a joint or limb during the time I was there, which I think was over an hour, and to the end of the vision. Joseph sat firmly and calmly all the time in the midst of a magnificent glory, but Sidney sat limp and pale, apparently as limber as a rag, observing which Joseph remarked, smilingly, "Sidney is not used to it as I am."[3]

According to some of the early journals, this revelation was not well received by all members of the Church because it conflicted with their previous notions of heaven and hell; much missionary work was required to keep unity among the Saints.[4]

In February 1843, as a rejoinder to a poem written by William W. Phelps, Joseph Smith wrote a poetic version of section 76. This important writing, which clarified some passages in this revelation, was published in Nauvoo, Illinois, in February 1843. It is here included in its entirety.[5]

A Vision

1. I will go, I will go, to the home of the Saints,
Where the virtue's the value, and life the reward;
But before I return to my former estate
I must fulfil the mission I had from the Lord.

2. Wherefore, hear, O ye heavens, and give ear O ye earth;
And rejoice ye inhabitants truly again;
For the Lord he is God, and his life never ends,
And besides him there ne'er was a Saviour of men.

3. His ways are a wonder; his wisdom is great;
The extent of his doings, there's none can unveil;
His purposes fail not; from age unto age
He still is the same, and his years never fail.

4. His throne is the heavens, his life time is all
Of eternity *now*, and eternity *then*;
His union is power, and none stays his hand,—
The Alpha, Omega, for ever: Amen.

5. For thus saith the Lord, in the spirit of truth,
I am merciful, gracious, and good unto those
That fear me, and live for the life that's to come;
My delight is to honor the saints with repose;

6. That serve me in righteousness true to the end;
Eternal's their glory, and great their reward;
I'll surely reveal all my myst'ries to them,—
The great hidden myst'ries in my kingdom stor'd—

7. From the council in Kolob, to time on the earth.
And for ages to come unto them I will show
My pleasure & will, what my kingdom will do:
Eternity's wonders they truly shall know.

8. Great things of the future I'll show unto them,
Yea, things of the vast generations to rise;
For their wisdom and glory shall be very great,
And their pure understanding extend to the skies:

9. And before them the wisdom of wise men shall cease,
And the nice understanding of prudent ones fail!
For the light of my spirit shall light mine elect,
And the truth is so mighty 't will ever prevail.

10. And the secrets and plans of my will I'll reveal;
The sanctified pleasures when earth is renew'd,
What the eye hath not seen, nor the ear hath yet heard;
Nor the heart of the natural man ever hath view'd.

11. I, Joseph, the prophet, in spirit beheld,
And the eyes of the inner man truly did see
Eternity sketch'd in a vision from God.
Of what was, and now is, and yet is to be.

12. Those things which the Father ordained of old,
Before the world was, or a system had run,—
Through Jesus the Maker and Savior of all;
The only begotten, (Messiah) his son.

13. Of whom I bear record, as all prophets have,
And the record I bear is the fulness,—yea even
The truth of the gospel of Jesus—*the Christ,*
With whom I convers'd, in the vision of heav'n.

14. For while in the act of translating his word,
Which the Lord in his grace had appointed to me,
I came to the gospel recorded by John,
Chapter fifth and the twenty ninth verse, which you'll see.
Which was given as follows:

Speaking of the resurrection of the dead,—
Concerning those who shall hear the voice of the son of man—
And shall come forth:—
They who have done good in the resurrection of the just.
And they who have done evil in the resurrection of the unjust."

15. I marvel'd at these resurrections, indeed!
For it came unto me by the spirit direct:—
And while I did meditate what it all meant,
The Lord touch'd the eyes of my own intellect:—

16. Hosanna forever! they open'd anon,
And the glory of God shone around where I was;
And there was the Son, at the Father's right hand,
In a fulness of glory, and holy applause.

17. I beheld round the throne, holy angels and hosts,
And sanctified beings from worlds that have been,
In holiness worshipping God and the Lamb,
Forever and ever, amen and amen!

18. And now after all of the proofs made of him,
By witnesses truly, by whom he was known,
This is mine, last of all, that he lives; yea he lives!
And sits at the right hand of God, on his throne.

19. And I heard a great voice, bearing record from heav'n,
He's the Saviour, and only begotten of God—
By him, of him, and through him, the worlds were all made,
Even all that career in the heavens so broad,

20. Whose inhabitants, too, from the first to the last,
Are sav'd by the very same Saviour of ours;
And, of course, are begotten God's daughters and sons,
By the very same truths, and the very same pow'rs.

21. And I saw and bear record of warfare in heav'n;
For an angel of light, in authority great,

Rebell'd against Jesus, and sought for his pow'r,
But was thrust down to woe from his Godified state.

22. And the heavens all wept, and the tears drop'd like dew,
That Lucifer, son of the morning had fell!
Yea, is fallen! is fall'n, and become, Oh, alas!
The son of Perdition; the devil of hell!

23. And while I was yet in the spirit of truth,
The commandment was: write ye the vision all out;
For Satan, old serpent, the devil 's for war,—
And yet will encompass the saints round about.

24. And I saw, too, the suff'ring and mis'ry of those,
(Overcome by the devil, in warfare and fight,)
In hell-fire, and vengeance, the doom of the damn'd;
For the Lord said, the vision is further: so write.

25. For thus saith the Lord, now concerning all those
Who know of my power and partake of the same;
And suffer themselves, that they be overcome
By the power of Satan; despising my name:—

26. Defying my power, and denying the truth;—
They are they—of the world, or of men, most forlorn,
The Sons of Perdition, of whom, ah! I say,
'T were better for them had they never been born!

27. They're vessels of wrath, and dishonor to God,
Doom'd to suffer his wrath, in the regions of woe,
Through the terrific night of eternity's round,
With the devil and all of his angels below:

28. Of whom it is said, no forgiveness is giv'n,
In this world, alas! nor the world that's to come;
For they have denied the spirit of God.
After having receiv'd it: and mis'ry's their doom.

29. And denying the only begotten of God,—
And crucify him to themselves, as they do,
And openly put him to shame in their flesh,
By gospel they cannot repentance renew.

30. They are they, who must go to the great lake of fire,
Which burneth with brimstone, yet never consumes,
And dwell with the devil, and angels of his,
While eternity goes and eternity comes.

31. They are they, who must groan through the great second death,
And are not redeemed in the time of the Lord;

While all the rest are, through the triumph of Christ,
Made partakers of grace, by the power of his word

32. The myst'ry of Godliness truly is great;—
The past, and the present, and what is to be;
And this is the gospel—glad tidings to all,
Which the voice from the heavens bore record to me:

33. That he came to the world in the middle of time,
To lay down his life for his friends and his foes,
And bear away sin as a mission of love;
And sanctify earth for a blessed repose.

34. 'Tis decreed, that he'll save all the work of his hands,
And sanctify them by his own precious blood;
And purify earth for the Sabbath of rest,
By the agent of fire, as it was by the flood.

35. The Savior will save all his Father did give,
Even all that he gave in the regions abroad.
Save the Sons of Perdition: They're lost; ever lost
And can never return to the presence of God.

36. They are they, who must reign with the devil in hell,
In eternity now, and eternity then,
Where the worm dieth not, and the fire is not quench'd;—
And the punishment still, is eternal. Amen.

37. And which is the torment apostates receive,
But the end, or the place where the torment began,
Save to them who are made to partake of the same,
Was never, nor will be, revealed unto man.

38. Yet God shows by vision a glimpse of their fate,
And straightway he closes the scene that was shown:
So the width, or the depth, or the misery thereof,
Save to those that partake, is forever unknown.

39. And while I was pondering, the vision was closed;
And the voice said to me, write the vision: for lo!
'Tis the end of the scene of the sufferings of those,
Who remain filthy still in their anguish and woe.

40. And again I bear record of heavenly things,
Where virtue's the value, above all that's pric'd—
Of the truth of the gospel concerning the just,
That rise in the first resurrection of Christ.

41. Who receiv'd and believ'd, and repented likewise,
And then were baptis'd, as a man always was,

Who ask'd and receiv'd a remission of sin,
And honored the kingdom by keeping its laws.

42. Being buried in water, as Jesus had been,
And keeping the whole of his holy commands,
They received the gift of the spirit of truth,
By the ordinance truly of laying on hands.

43. For these overcome, by their faith and their works,
Being tried in their life-time, as purified gold,
And seal'd by the spirit of promise, to life,
By men called of God, as was Aaron of old.

44. They are they, of the church of the first born of God,—
And unto whose hands he committeth all things;
For they hold the keys of the kingdom of heav'n,
And reign with the Savior, as priests, and as kings.

45. They're priests of the order of Melchisedek,
Like Jesus, (from whom is this highest reward,)
Receiving a fulness of glory and light;
As written: They're Gods; even sons of the Lord.

46. So all things are theirs; yea, of life, or of death;
Yea, whether things now, or to come, all are theirs,
And they are the Savior's, and he is the Lord's,
Having overcome all, as eternity's heirs.

47. 'Tis wisdom that man never glory in man,
But give God the glory for all that he hath;
For the righteous will walk in the presence of God,
While the wicked are trod under foot in his wrath.

48. Yea, the righteous shall dwell in the presence of God,
And of Jesus, forever, from earth's second birth—
For when he comes down in the splendor of heav'n,
All these he'll bring with him, to reign on the earth.

49. These are they that arise in their bodies of flesh,
When the trump of the first resurrection shall sound;
These are they that come up to Mount Zion, in life,
Where the blessings and gifts of the spirit abound.

50. These are they that have come to the heavenly place;
To the numberless courses of angels above:
To the city of God; e'en the holiest of all,
And to the home of the blessed, the fountain of love:

51. To the church of old Enoch, and of the first born:
And gen'ral assembly of ancient renown'd.

Whose names are all kept in the archives of heav'n,
As chosen and faithful, and fit to be crown'd.

52. These are they that are perfect through Jesus' own blood,
Whose bodies celestial are mention'd by Paul,
Where the sun is the typical glory thereof,
And God, and his Christ, are the true judge of all.

53. Again I beheld the terrestrial world,
In the order and glory of Jesus, go on;
'Twas not as the church of the first born of God,
But shone in its place, as the moon to the sun.

54. Behold, these are they that have died without law;
The heathen of ages that never had hope,
And those of the region and shadow of death,
The spirits in prison, that light has brought up.

55. To spirits in prison the Savior once preach'd,
And taught them the gospel, with powers afresh;
And then were the living baptiz'd for their dead,
That they might be judg'd as if men in the flesh.

56. These are they that are hon'rable men of the earth;
Who were blinded and dup'd by the cunning of men:
They receiv'd not the truth of the Savior at first;
But did, when they heard it in prison, again.

57. Not valiant for truth, they obtain'd not the crown,
But are of that glory that's typ'd by the moon:
They are they, that come into the presence of Christ,
But not to the fulness of God, on his throne.

58. Again I beheld the telestial, as third,
The lesser, or starry world, next in its place,
For the leaven must leaven three measures of meal,
And every knee bow that is subject to grace.

59. These are they that receiv'd not the gospel of Christ,
Or evidence, either, that he ever was;
As the stars are all diff'rent in glory and light.
So differs the glory of these by the laws.

60. These are they that deny not the spirit of God,
But are thrust down to hell, with the devil, for sins,
As hypocrites, liars, whoremongers, and thieves,
And stay 'till the last resurrection begins.

61. 'Till the Lamb shall have finish'd the work he begun;
Shall have trodden the wine press, in fury alone,

And overcome all by the pow'r of his might:
He conquers to conquer, and save all his own.

62. These are they that receive not a fulness of light,
From Christ, in eternity's world, where they are,
The terrestrial sends them the Comforter, though;
And minist'ring angels, to happify there.

63. And so the telestial is minister'd to,
By ministers from the terrestrial one,
As terrestrial is, from the celestial throne;
And the great, greater, greatest, seem's stars, moon, and sun.

64. And thus I beheld, in the vision of heav'n,
The telestial glory, dominion and bliss,
Surpassing the great understanding of men,—
Unknown, save reveal'd, in a world vain as this.

65. And lo, I beheld the terrestrial, too,
Which excels the telestial in glory and light,
In splendor, and knowledge, and wisdom, and joy,
In blessings, and graces, dominion and might.

66. I beheld the celestial, in glory sublime;
Which is the most excellent kingdom that is,—
Where God, e'en the Father, in harmony reigns;
Almighty, supreme, and eternal, in bliss.

67. Where the church of the first born in union reside,
And they see as they're seen, and they know as they're known;
Being equal in power, dominion and might,
With a fulness of glory and grace, round his throne.

68. The glory celestial is one like the sun;
The glory terrestrial is one like the moon;
The glory telestial is one like the stars,
And all harmonize like the parts of a tune.

69. As the stars are all different in lustre and size,
So the telestial region, is mingled in bliss;
From least unto greatest, and greatest to least,
The reward is exactly as promis'd in this.

70. These are they that came out for Apollos and Paul;
For Cephas and Jesus, in all kinds of hope;
For Enoch and Moses, and Peter, and John;
For Luther and Calvin, and even the Pope.

71. For they never received the gospel of Christ,
Nor the prophetic spirit that came from the Lord;

Nor the covenant neither, which Jacob once had;
They went their own way, and they have their reward.

72. By the order of God, last of all, these are they,
That will not be gather'd with saints here below,
To be caught up to Jesus, and meet in the cloud:—
In darkness they worshipp'd; to darkness they go.

73. These are they that are sinful, the wicked at large,
That glutted their passion by meanness or worth;
All liars, adulterers, sorc'rers, and proud;
And suffer, as promis'd, God's wrath on the earth.

74. These are they that must suffer the vengeance of hell,
'Till Christ shall have trodden all enemies down,
And perfected his work, in the fulness of times:
And is crown'd on his throne with his glorious crown.

75. The vast multitude of the telestial world—
As the stars of the skies, or the sands of the sea;—
The voice of Jehovah echo'd far and wide,
Ev'ry tongue shall confess, and they all bow the knee.

76. Ev'ry man shall be judg'd by the works of his life,
And receive a reward in the mansion prepar'd;
For his judgments are just, and his works never end,
As his prophets and servants have always declar'd.

77. But the great things of God, which he show'd unto me,
Unlawful to utter, I dare not declare;
They surpass all the wisdom and greatness of men,
And only are seen, as has Paul, where they are.

78. I will go, I will go, while the secret of life,
Is blooming in heaven, and blasting in hell;
Is leaving on earth, and a budding in space:—
I will go, I will go, with you, brother, farewell.

JOSEPH SMITH

Nauvoo, Feb. 1843.

Publication Note. Section 76 was first published in the *Evening and Morning Star* (July 1832) and was included as section 91 in the 1835 edition of the Doctrine and Covenants.

Section 77

Date.   March 1832.[1]

Place.   Hiram, Portage County, Ohio.

Historical Note.   Section 77, which explains several topics found in the book of Revelation, was received by Joseph Smith while he was working on the inspired translation of the Bible. The Prophet's history notes the following concerning its reception, "In connexion with the translation of the scriptures, I received the following explanation of the revelations of St. John."[2]

Publication Note.   Section 77 was first published in the *Times and Seasons* (1 August 1844) and was included as section 77 in the 1876 edition of the Doctrine and Covenants.

Section 78

Date.   March 1832 (1 March).[1]

Place.   Hiram, Portage County, Ohio (Kirtland).[2]

Historical Note.   Section 78 was received by Joseph Smith while he was visiting the Saints in Kirtland, Ohio. The revelation calls for an "order" to be established according to a "bond" or "covenant" that cannot be broken. This order, variously known as the "United Order," the "Order of Enoch," and the "United Firm," was created at this time.[3]

The United Firm was a business partnership consisting of about a dozen Church leaders. Members of the firm were either land-owners or merchants whose purpose was to work in concert, using the financial means at their disposal, to generate profits. Inasmuch as the members of the partnership were also presiding Church leaders, it is difficult to determine which of their financial transactions were purely personal and which were Church-related. This dual relationship has led some writers to erroneously conclude that the United Firm administered the law of consecration. Specifically, the Church bishop administered the program of consecration. The United Order was essentially a private business concern.

The nucleus from which the United Firm grew was the Gilbert-Whitney mercantile establishment in Kirtland, Ohio. The Gilbert-Whitney store, as it was called, expanded to two branches (one in Kirtland and one in Independence) after Newel K. Whitney and Sidney Gilbert joined the Church and Gilbert was called by revelation to reside in Missouri.[4] Other Church brethren who had financial means, namely Martin Harris, Frederick G. Williams, and John Johnson, were called by revelation to be part of this order.

Section 78 directed that the order be formed and commanded that Joseph Smith, Sidney Rigdon, and Newel K. Whitney "sit in council with the Saints . . . in Zion," to regulate the affairs of the poor. Obeying the command, Joseph Smith, Sidney Rigdon, Jesse Gause, and Newel K. Whitney left Ohio on 1 April 1832 and traveled to Independence, Missouri, arriving 24 April.[5] During their visit in Missouri, a meeting of the United Firm essentially incorporated the Missouri branch of the Gilbert-Whitney Store into the firm.[6]

William E. McLellan stated on more than one occasion that there were nine members of the United Firm, but there may have been more.[7] The following are known to have been members in 1832: Joseph Smith, Sidney Rigdon, Jesse Gause, Oliver Cowdery, Martin Harris, A. Sidney Gilbert, Newel K. Whitney; undoubtedly Edward Partridge, William W. Phelps, and John Whitmer were also members in that year.[8] Frederick G. Williams and John Johnson became members of the order in 1833.[9]

The members of the United Firm were consecrated in their respective responsibilities, and although they were to benefit personally from the profits of the firm, the surplus profits were to be used for the operation and blessing of the whole Church.

The United Firm was short-lived. On 10 April 1834 members of the firm met and decided that the order should be dissolved,[10] and on 23 April 1834 a revelation (section 104), commanded that the two branches of the firm become separate entities and that the members discontinue operating jointly.[11]

The coded names in section 78 and subsequent revelations dealing with the United Firm (i.e., sections 82, 92, 96, and 104) were used to prevent enemies of the Church from taking advantage of the brethren after the revelations were published. It was decided that the financial affairs of the Church, administered by the firm, should be kept confidential.[12]

Publication Note. Section 78 was first published as section 75 in the 1835 edition of the Doctrine and Covenants.

Section 79

Date. March 1832 (12 March, as per "Kirtland Revelation Book," p. 12).

Place. Hiram, Portage County, Ohio.

Historical Note. Section 79, a revelation received by Joseph Smith, instructed Jared Carter to take a mission to the "eastern countries."[1] A prominent elder and missionary during the 1830s, Carter recorded in his journal the following concerning section 79:

> I at length went to Hiram [Ohio] to the Seer to inquire the will of the Lord concerning my ministry the ensuing season; and the word of the Lord came forth that showed that it was his will that I should go forth to the Eastern countries in the power of the ordinance wherewith I had been ordained, which was to the high privilege of administering in the name of Jesus Christ even to seal on earth and to build up the Church of Christ and to work miracles in the name of Christ....Now I have received a revelation of the will of the Lord to me by the mouth of Joseph the Seer, that I should not only preach the gospel from place to place, but from city to city.

Upon returning from his mission in October 1832, Carter continued,

> Now while I make this record, I remember the goodness of the Lord to me in the mission that I have lately been to the East. I have enjoyed my health continually and the Lord, notwithstanding the great opposition to this glorious work, he has blessed me....I have been gone 6 months and 2 days. The Lord permitted me to administer the gospel to 79 souls, and many others by my instrumentality have been convinced of this most glorious

work. All that have been baptized while I have been in the regions where I have been in this mission is 98, and many others have been convinced of the work that sooner or later I think will obey the work.[2]

Publication Note.   Section 79 was first published as section 76 in the 1835 edition of the Doctrine and Covenants.

Section 80

Date.   March 1832 (7 March, as per "Kirtland Revelation Book," p. 18).

Place.   Hiram, Portage County, Ohio.

Historical Note.   Section 80 was received in March 1832, a very busy month for Joseph Smith. The revelation instructed Stephen Burnett to preach the gospel and take Eden Smith as a companion.[1] It is not known if these two missionaries served this mission. On 22 March 1832 Stephen Burnett and John Smith (Eden's father) left for southern Ohio to preach to John Smith's relatives.[2]

Publication Note.   Section 80 was first published as section 77 in the 1835 edition of the Doctrine and Covenants.

Section 81

Date.   March 1832 (15 March, as per "Kirtland Revelation Book," p. 10).

Place.   Hiram, Portage County, Ohio.

Historical Note.   At a priesthood conference held in Amherst, Ohio, on 25 January 1832, Joseph Smith was ordained and sustained President of the High Priesthood.[1] Less than two months later the Prophet appointed two men to stand with him in the Presidency of the High Priesthood. During the Prophet's lifetime, the terms *High Priesthood* and *Melchizedek Priesthood* were not identical. Only high priests possessed the High Priesthood; thus, during the 1830s, they held the highest ordained priesthood office in the Church.[2] Although the "Presidency" of the High Priesthood (an organizational title)[3] was to preside over all ordained high priests, by 1834 this body had become the First Presidency of the Church.[4]

While traditional Church histories indicate that the Presidency of the High Priesthood was first organized in March 1833, minutes recorded in the "Kirtland Revelation Book" for 8 March 1832 state the following:

> Chose this day and ordained brother Jesse Gause and Broth Sidney [Rigdon] to be my councellers of the ministry of the presidency of the high Priesthood.[5]

The above entry and other minutes, principally in the "Far West Record", affirm that as early as March 1832 Joseph Smith appointed and ordained two counselors to assist him in the Presidency of the High Priesthood.[6]

While the recipient of Section 81 has traditionally been believed to be Frederick G. Williams, the "Kirtland Revelation Book" discloses that the revelation was intended for Jesse Gause. The page index for the record book notes the following for Section 81: "Revelation to Jesse Gause March 15, 1832." The "Kirtland Revelation Book" further reveals that the words "my servant Jesse" have been altered to read "my servant Frederick G. Williams."[7] Because Williams later replaced Gause as counselor in the Presidency, liberty has been taken to substitute the names.

Publication Note.   Section 81 was first published as section 79 in the 1835 edition of the Doctrine and Covenants.

Biographical Note.   Jesse Gause.

Son of William Gause and Mary Beverly. Born about 1785 in Pennsylvania. Married Martha Cuntry before 1825. Five known children: Harriett, Amelia, Hannah, Owen Beverly, and Martha. Active in Quaker movement in Fayette and Chester counties in Pennsylvania and also in Ohio along Ohio River. Wife, Martha, died 1828. Married Minerva before 1832. One known child. Resigned as Quaker preacher 26 April 1830. Converted to United Society of Believers of Christ's Second Appearing (Shakers) by 1830. Associated with Shaker community in Hancock, Essex County, Massachusetts, by 1831. Located in Shaker community in Cleveland, Ohio, area by October 1831. Baptized by Mormon elders after 22 October 1831. Ordained high priest on or before 8 March 1832. Ordained member of original Presidency of High Priesthood 8 March 1832. Revelation dated 15 March 1832 confirmed above appointment. Member of United and Literary firms 1832. Traveled to Independence, Missouri, with Joseph Smith and others April 1832. Remained in Independence area after Prophet's departure for Ohio May 1832. Taught John Whitmer grammar while in Jackson County, Missouri. Returned to Kirtland by August 1832. Mission to Pennsylvania August 1832 with Zebedee Coltrin. Left Kirtland 1 August 1832. Parted company with Coltrin about 19 August 1832, apparently enroute to Fayette County, Pennsylvania—Gause's preaching area as Quaker. Left Church by December 1832. Excommunicated 3 December 1832.[8]

Section 82

Date.   26 April 1832.

Place.   Jackson County, Missouri (Independence as per "Far West Record," p. 30).

Historical Note.   A revelation given to Joseph Smith on 1 March 1832 (section 78) instructed Joseph Smith, Sidney Rigdon, and Newel K. Whitney to "sit in council" with the Saints in Jackson County, Missouri, then numbering about four hundred.[1] In response, these brethren, accompanied by Jesse Gause, left Ohio on 1 April 1832 and arrived in Jackson County on 24 April. It was a busy and difficult time for the Church leaders, intensified by the sickness of the Prophet's and Sidney's children who had the measles. Recounting the inauspicious occasion the Prophet wrote,

> [We left] our familys in afflication admidst of death [and] upon the mercy of mobs & of brethern who you know sometimes are found to be unstable unbelieving, unmerciful and in this trying situation to keep the commandment of God we took our lives in our hands and traveled through every combination of wickedness to your country for your salvation.[2]

Two days after their arrival in Independence, 26 April 1832, a general council of the Church was convened in which the Missouri Saints acknowledged Joseph Smith as President of the High Priesthood.[3] At the close of the conference, the Prophet received section 82. The minutes of the meeting, dated 26 April 1832, state,

> Joseph Smith acknowledged by the High priests in the land of Zion to be President of the High Priesthood according to commandment and ordination in Ohio, at the Conference held in Amherst January 25, 1832 . . . .Br. Sidney Rigdon then stated the items embraced in a Revelation received in Ohio [section 78] & the reason why we were commanded to come to this land & sit in Council with the high priests here, for the particulars of which read the Commandment . . . .All differences settled & the hearts of all run together in love A Revelation received through him whom the Church has appointed respecting organization.[4]

Section 82 concerns itself with the organization of a branch of the United Firm in Missouri and the responsibilities of the members of the firm to "manage the affairs of the poor."[5]

Verse 1 specifically refers to difficulties between Joseph Smith and Church leaders in Missouri and an eight-month-old disagreement between Sidney Rigdon and Edward Partridge. The former problem was referred to in a letter from Orson Hyde and Hyrum Smith to Church leaders in Missouri, 14 January 1833:

> At the time Joseph, Sidney, and Newel left Zion, all matters of hardness and misunderstanding were settled and buried (as they supposed), and you gave them the hand of fellowship; but, afterwards, you brought up all these things again, in a censorious spirit, accusing Brother Joseph in rather an indirect way of seeking after monarchial power and authority . . . .We are sensible that this is not the thing Brother Joseph is seeking after, but to magnify the high office and calling whereunto he has been called and appointed by the command of God, and the united voice of this Church [i.e., President of the High Priesthood].[6]

We lack some details of the latter problem, but the factors involved were "money," Ridgon's near drowning in the Missouri River on his return trip to Ohio from Missouri in 1831, and inconveniences suffered on the 1831 Missouri trip.[7] Although the matter was considered resolved at the 26 April 1832 meeting, it surfaced again after Rigdon's return to Kirtland in May 1832. Sidney became so disturbed over this affair that he became mentally depressed and preached falsely in public in Kirtland. On Sunday, 10 June 1832, Rigdon delivered "a disgrace upon the privaleg of Jew & Gentile he determined there was no difference nor respect to persons with God."[8] And at a meeting held in Kirtland on Thursday, 5 July 1832, Sidney Rigdon informed his hearers of a revelation he had received.[9] According to Charles C. Rich, present on this occasion, Rigdon

> came into the meeting and told the congregation they might as well go home as God had rejected them. He left the meeting but shortly returned and gave the meeting another speech, telling them it was useless to pray or do anything, that the Kingdom was sent from the people. This caused confusion in the congregation both before and after dismissal. Hyrum Smith said he did not believe a word of it and said if he had a horse he would go and see the Prophet, then in the town of Hyrum [Hiram].[10]

On the following day, Friday, Hyrum Smith took Charles Rich's horse to Hiram, Ohio, to notify the Prophet of Rigdon's statements and actions. Both Joseph and Hyrum Smith returned to Kirtland on Saturday, 7 July 1832. On Sunday, the following day, "Everybody turned out to meeting—Joseph preached, denouncing the doctrine of Rigdon's as being false, took his licence from him and said, "The Devil would handle him as one man handles another—the less authority he had the better."

Rigdon quickly became aware of his error, sought forgiveness, and on 28 July was reordained as a member of the Presidency of the High Priesthood.[12] A letter from Joseph Smith, to William W. Phelps dated 31 July 1832, mentioned the Rigdon-Partridge controversy, the trip to and from Missouri in 1832, and Rigdon's fall from grace:

Our object in going to Zion was altogether to keep the commandment of the most high [section 78]. when bro Sidney learned the feelings of the Brethren in whom he had placed so much confidence for whom he had endured so much fatiague and suffering & whom he loved with so much love his heart was grieved his spirit failed & for a moment he became frantic & the adversary taking the advantage, he spake unadviseable with his lips. after receiving severe chastisement [he] resigned his commision and became a private member in the church, but has since repented . . . . and after a little suffering by the buffetings of Satan has been restored to his high standing in the church of God.[13]

Publication Note.   Section 82 was first published as section 85 in the 1835 edition of the Doctrine and Covenants.

Section 83

Date.   30 April 1832.

Place.   Independence, Jackson County, Missouri.

Historical Note.   Section 83 was received during Joseph Smith's visit to Jackson County, Missouri, in the spring of 1832. The Prophet's party, consisting of himself, Sidney Rigdon, Jesse Gause, and Newel K. Whitney, had traveled to Independence (1) to incorporate the Missouri branch of the Gilbert-Whitney store into the United Firm, (2) to coordinate the printing activities of the Literary Firm, and (3) to assist local Missouri elders in establishing the law of consecration and stewardship.[1]

Joseph Smith, Rigdon, and Whitney left Independence for Ohio on 6 May 1832. Rigdon arrived in Kirtland on 26 May, but the Prophet and Bishop Whitney were detained about four weeks in Greenville, Indiana, while Whitney recovered from a broken leg.[2]

Section 83, received prior to the Prophet's departure for Ohio, gave instructions concerning the rights of widows and their children to the benefits of the Church storehouse.

Regarding verse 3 of this revelation, the Prophet later wrote,

Again concerning inheritances, you are bound by the law of the Lord, to give a deed, securing to him who receives inheritances his inheritance, for an everlasting inheritance, or in other words to be his own property, his private stewardship, and if found in transgression & should be cut off, out of the church, his inheritance is his still and he is delivered over to the buffetings of satan.[3]

Publication Note.   Section 83 was first published in the *Evening and Morning Star* (January 1833) and was included as section 88 in the 1835 edition of the Doctrine and Covenants.

Section 84

Date.   22 and 23 September 1832.

Place.   Kirtland, Geauga County, Ohio.

Historical Note.   Section 84 is a revelation of major doctrinal importance; parts of it may well have been received in conjunction with the inspired translation of the Bible. The revelation appears to be a composite of several somewhat interrelated ideas that were recorded in their present form on at least two different days (i.e., 22-23 September 1832). It is difficult to determine which verses were received on which day, but some evidence suggests that verses 1-41 constitute parts of the revelation received on 22 September, and that verses 42-120 were received on 23 September. Whereas verse 1 indicates that the revelation was received in the presence of six elders (undoubtedly high priests), an unpublished note (dated 23 September 1832) that appears in the "Kirtland Revelation Book" after verse 42 affirms that that verse (42) was specifically intended for ten high priests, then present. It is also worthy of note that there is a change of tense in verse 42 from the third to the first person.[1]

Verses 1-5 concern themselves with the building of the New Jerusalem in Jackson County, Missouri (particularly the construction of a temple). This divine injunction was rescinded in 1841. (See D&C 124:49 and 51.)[2] Verse 76 directed that the "brethren in Zion" be upbraided for their "rebellion against you at the time I sent you." This alludes to the Prophet's trip to Jackson County, Missouri, in the spring of 1832 (see Historical Note for section 82). In accordance with this verse, a council of High Priests appointed Orson Hyde and Hyrum Smith to draft a letter to be sent to Missouri Church leaders. The letter, dated 14 January 1833, accuses the Missouri leaders of harboring a rebellious spirit and threatening insinuations against Joseph Smith, Sidney Rigdon and Newel K. Whitney. The summary of the epistle was: "Repent, repent, or Zion must suffer."[3]

Throughout the remainder of the revelation are found several variations of biblical and Book of Mormon passages. (For example, compare verses 65-73 with Mark 16:17-18, and compare verses 81-85 with Matthew 6 and 3 Nephi 13). Verses 99-102 contain prophetic poetry regarding the Millennium.

Pursuant to the instructions in verse 114, Joseph Smith and Newel K. Whitney traveled to Albany, New York, and Boston in the fall of 1832. These two men left Kirtland in the latter part of September and arrived in New York City before 13 October 1832. Much of their time in the East was spent transacting business, but Newel K. Whitney later stated that the trip "was taken to fulfill the Revelation."[4]

While in New York City, the Prophet and Bishop Whitney made contact with the distinguished Bishop Onderdock of the Episcopal Church of New York. They also traveled to Boston, where Joseph Smith "prophecied unto that city."[5] And although evidence is lacking, it is probable that contacts were made in Albany in accord with the instructions of the revelation. These two men arrived back in Kirtland on 6 November 1832.[6]

Concerning the three cities mentioned in verse 114, Wilford Woodruff prophesied in 1863 that New York City would be destroyed by an earthquake, Boston by a tidal wave, and Albany by fire.[7]

Publication Note.   Section 84 was first published as section 4 in the 1835 edition of the Doctrine and Covenants.

Section 85

Date.   27 November 1832.

Place.   Kirtland, Geauga County, Ohio.

Historical Note.   Section 85 consists of an extract from a letter written by Joseph Smith to William W. Phelps on 27 November

1832.[1] Many of the instructions found in this revelation were specifically intended for John Whitmer, the Church historian.

Verses 5, 7, 8, and 11 make mention of the book of the law of God or the book of remembrance. This book, which was to have recorded in it the law of the Lord (i.e., section 42 and possibly related revelations), was to serve as a membership record for the Church. No known record book, kept in Missouri or Ohio, fits the description of the book mentioned in section 85. Moreover, in Nauvoo a record was commenced in 1841, called the "Book of the Law of the Lord," which seems to have served a purpose similar to that specified in the Prophet's 1832 letter.[2]

In response to several letters John Whitmer had sent to Kirtland concerning his responsibilities as historian, Oliver Cowdery communicated with him in January 1834. Among other matters, Cowdery discussed questions regarding the contents of section 85. As will be seen in the following citation, the Prophet envisioned at least three levels at which the book of remembrance would be kept (i.e., family, community, and general church):

> You have requested instruction on the subject of Church Records: I have just conversed with bro. Joseph concerning the same; and he has given me instruction upon his letter [section 85] published in the 8th No. of the Star; but says that we shall probably receive more on the same, and then we will communicate it. I will say, however, that it is necessary to keep the names of the Saints, & when a child is brought forward to be blessed by the Elders, it is then necessary to take their name upon the Church Record. Put down the name of the man, his place of birth, and when, &c. and also of his family . . . . If he apostatises write opposite his name that he has. If he begets children after that and they do not come into the Church their names are not known with their brethren in the book of remembrance. The names of the Saints are to be kept in a book that contains the law of God, this is what is meant in bro. Joseph's letter . . . . Each family will have its record with the law of the Lord in it; each branch of the Church the same in every city; and each city one general record kept by a general clerk.

Cowdery's letter also sheds new light on verse 8, which traditionally has been thought to refer to Edward Partridge:

Brother Joseph says, that the item in his letter that says, that the man that is called &c. and puts forth his hand to steady the ark of God, does not mean that any one had at the time, but it was given for a caution to those in high standing to be ware, lest they should fall by the shaft of death.[3]

Publication Note.   Section 85 was first published in the *Evening and Morning Star* (January 1833), and was included as section 85 in the 1876 edition of the Doctrine and Covenants.

Section 86

Date.   6 December 1832.

Place.   Kirtland, Geauga County, Ohio.

Historical Note.   Section 86 further explains the Parable of the Wheat and the Tares, found in Matthew chapter 13.[1] The first draft of this parable in the Prophet's translation of the Bible retained the wording found in the King James Version, namely, that the *tares* would first be gathered. This initial draft was written sometime between 7 April and 19 June 1831. Subsequently, however, the passage was revised (probably on 6 December 1832) to correspond with section 86—the *wheat* would first be gathered.[2]

That the reception of section 86 was closely connected with the inspired translation of the Bible is affirmed by a statement in Joseph Smith's journal: "December 6th translating and received a revelation explaining the Parable the Wheat and the Tears &c."[3]

Publication Note.   Section 86 was first published as section 6 in the 1835 edition of the Doctrine and Covenants.

Section 87

Date.   25 December 1832.

Place.   Kirtland, Geauga County, Ohio.

Historical Note.   Section 87, commonly known as "the prophecy on war," was received on Christmas Day 1832, some twenty-eight years before the American Civil War commenced at Fort Sumter on Charleston Bay in South Carolina.

In November 1832, before the reception of this revelation, South Carolina had adopted a States' Rights position intended to nullify federal regulations not in their interests (specifically, high tariffs on foreign imports, which protected northern manufacturing interests). In addition to the economic problems of the upcountry cotton planters, the wealthy rice aristocracy of the lowcountry had become sensitive to the beginnings of northern antislavery movements. Reacting to the protective tariffs and the agitation against slavery, radical South Carolinians saw nullification as the logical defense to the "tyranny" of the majority. On 24 November 1832 a special convention passed an Ordinanace of Nullification that prohibited the collecting of tariff duties in the state after 1 February 1833. Students of the period generally agree that the situation in South Carolina was explosive, and the passage in early March 1833 of a compromise tariff temporarily averted civil war.[1]

Although Joseph Smith considered this action on the part of the South Carolina convention a "rebellion," he later clarified that the commencement of warfare prior to the Second Coming would arise through the slave question.[2]

Brigham Young, who noted that section 87 was intentionally left out of the 1835 edition of the Doctrine and Covenants, indicated that this revelation was received "when the brethren were reflecting and reasoning with regard to African slavery on this continent, and the slavery of the children of men throughout the world."[3]

Publication Note.   Section 87 was first published in the Pearl of Great Price in 1851 and was included as section 87 in the 1876 edition of the Doctrine and Covenants.

Section 88

Date. 27 December 1832 (27-28 December 1832 and 3 January 1833, as per "Kirtland Council Minute Book," pp. 3-4, and "Kirtland Revelation Book," pp. 47-48. Verses 1-126 were received 27-28 December 1832, and verses 127-141 were received 3 January 1833.).

Place. Kirtland, Geauga County, Ohio.

Historical Note. Section 88 is a revelation of major doctrinal importance. Known as the "Olive Leaf," this revelation was received in the Prophet's translating room in the Whitney Store. Present were Joseph Smith, Jr., Joseph Smith, Sr., Sidney Rigdon, Orson Hyde, Hyrum Smith, Samuel H. Smith,[1] Newel K. Whitney, Frederick G. Williams, Ezra Thayer, and John Murdock. Frederick G. Williams, who took minutes on this occasion, recorded the following:

> Bro Joseph arose and said, to receive revelation and the blessing of heaven it was necessary to have our minds on god and exercise faith and become of one heart and of one mind. therefore he recommended all present to pray separatly and vocally to the Lord for to reveal his will unto us concerning the upbuilding of Zion & for the benifit of the saints and for the duty and employment of the Elders. Accordingly we all bowed down before the Lord, after which each one arose and spoke in his turn his feelings, and determination to keep the commandments of God. And then proceeded to receive a revelation concerning the duty [of the Elders as] above stated. 9 oclock P.M. the revelation not being finished the conference adjourned till tomorrow morning 9 oclock A.M. [28th] met according to adjournment and commenced by Prayer thus proceded to receive the residue of the above revelation and it being finished and there being no further business before the conference closed the meeting by prayer in harmony with the brethren and gratitude to our heavenly Father for the great manifestation of his holy Spirit during the setting of the conference.[2]

In addition to the items of doctrine contained in this revelation, there are references to a number of topics which would have great significance to the Church at Kirtland: a solemn assembly, the construction of a house of worship, and the organization of the School of the Prophets.

Solemn Assembly.   Reference to a solemn assembly, D&C 88:70, called the elders "to tarry in this place, and call a solemn assembly." Those to be invited to this solemn meeting were called the "first laborers," (also known as "first elders") of this "last kingdom"— namely, the leading brethren of the Church. The solemn assembly was intended to be another day of Pentecost for the latter-day elders. An "endowment" of spiritual power was to be poured out upon the faithful at the assembly—but much preparation was to precede the occasion. First the elders were to be schooled both spiritually and secularly; later they were to be washed and anointed to cleanse them from the sins of this world. The final preparation, the ordinance of washing of feet, was to occur on the day of the sacred meeting when the righteous would see the face of the Lord. On 12 November 1835 the Prophet stated,

> We must have all things prepared, and call our solemn assembly as the Lord has commanded us, that we may be able to accomplish His great work, and it must be done in God's own way. The house of the Lord must be prepared, and the solemn assembly called and organized in it, according to the order of the house of God; and in it we must attend to the ordinance of washing of feet . . . . All who are prepared, and are sufficiently pure to abide the presence of the Savior, will see Him in the solemn assembly.[3]

On 30 March 1836, three days after the temple dedication, three hundred brethren assembled for the long-awaited meeting. The time was spent in administering the ordinances of washing of feet and partaking of the sacrament. Many witnessed remarkable spiritual manifestations.[4]

On 6 April 1837 another solemn assembly was held in the Kirtland Temple especially for those elders who had not been washed and anointed the previous year.[5] On both occasions the Prophet sought to fill up vacancies in the quorums of the priesthood and "set them in order." Having the priesthood quorums thus organized, and having been purified through the ordinances, the brethren sought to receive a rich outpouring of the Lord's spirit.

The House of Worship. The first scriptural reference to the erection of a sacred house in Kirtland, Ohio, recorded 28 December 1832, directed the Saints to "establish a house, even a house of prayer, a house of fasting, a house of faith, a house of learning, a house of glory, a house of order, a house of God" (verse 119). Although the building subsequently would be referred to as a "temple," early appellations were simply "house of God," or "school." Evidence shows that the Prophet initially conceived the primary function of the sacred edifice to be that of a schoolhouse for those called to the ministry. A revelation dated 3 January 1833 stated, "The order of the house prepared for the presidency of the school of the prophets [was] for their instruction in all things, even for all the officers of the church, or in other words, those who are called to the ministry in the church, beginning at the high priests, even down to the deacons" (verse 127). It is unclear when the decision to build a house of worship was made public, but by 14 January 1833 the Prophet had written to Church leaders in Missouri regarding the project: "The Lord commanded us, in Kirtland, to build a house of God, and establish a school of Prophets [and] the Lord helping us, we will obey."[6] On 8 March 1833 a revelation mentioned the School of the Prophets (section 90), and on 23 March 1833 a committee was appointed to purchase land for the purpose of erecting a school.[7] The property upon which the house of God would be built was purchased from Peter French—initially the deed was in the name of Joseph Coe, one of the committee. The French farm was of particular interest because there was a brick kiln on the property. On 4 May 1833, high priests in Kirtland appointed a committee of three (Hyrum Smith, Reynolds Cahoon, and Jared Carter) "to obtain subscriptions for the purpose of erecting" the schoolhouse;[8] by the first week in June a revelation was received which gave the dimensions of the house of worship but stated that the architecture would be revealed later to three (i.e., the Presidency of the High Priesthood).[9] The revelation further clarified that the house of worship should have two levels—the lower for preaching, fasting, and praying and the upper for the school—and promised that in the building the Lord would "endow those whom I have chosen with power from on high."[10] In accordance with divine will, work on the sacred edifice commenced immediately. George A. Smith hauled the first load of stone for the temple on 5 June 1833, and Hyrum Smith and Reynolds Cahoon began excavating the foundation.[11] On 6 June the building committee were directed to obtain materials—stone, brick, and lumber—in order to proceed without delay.[12] Work on the basement of the building progresed rapidly, and on 25 July 1833 the foundation stones of the temple were laid by the Prophet and twenty-three elders.

Although the sacred edifice was to be constructed of brick (manufactured at the brick kiln on the newly purchased French farm), the furnace was found to be defective, and locally cut sandstone, covered with plaster, was used. The original plaster was most unusual for the Western Reserve, being made of crushed glassware. The stucco was "a variation of a very old building technique known as rough cast, a method for achieving a textured wall surface by mixing extraneous material" into the plaster.[13] While there was no single architect for the temple, the master builder appears to have been Artemus Millett of Upper Canada, who took charge of the construction in the spring of 1834. Others known to have worked extensively on the temple, in addition to the temple committee, were Jacob Bump and Alpheus Cutler. On 7-8 March 1835, some 119 men received a blessing for either directly laboring on or contributing to the construction of the house.[14]

The temple is of high rectangular shape with double rows of windows and a tower rising from the main body. The dimensions are impressive: the structure measures 78' x 58', and from the basement to the tower the height is about 110 feet. The building is divided into three levels—two almost identical stories of equal height and an attic—and is lighted with thirty-two Gothic, three Venetian, ten dormer, one circular, and two square-gable windows. The ground floor was specially intended for worship, and the upper floor for classroom use. The attic was partitioned into ten small rooms, five on either side of a hall. Both main levels had two complete sets of pulpits, one at either end. The western pulpits were for the Melchizedek Priesthood, and the eastern pulpits for the Aaronic. Each pulpit group had a compartment with a lectern behind which rose three tiers of pulpits. Eight wooden columns supported a ceiling that was flat over the aisles and arched over the center. Sets of ropes and pulleys concealed within the columns operated curtains (veils) that could be lowered to divide each hall and each row of pulpits into smaller compartments.

The site upon which the temple stands, one of the highest in the area, overlooks the east Chagrin Valley. From the belfry it is possible to see Lake Erie, a distance of six miles.

Constructing the building took some thirty-three months and required enormous sacrifice of the Saints. A conservative estimate of the cost of construction is $60,000.[15] On 6 April 1837 Sidney Rigdon was recorded as stating that the then "unliquidated debt" on the temple was $13,000.[16]

The building was not completely finished when first occupied by a Hebrew school on 4 January 1836. This group occupied a room designated the "translating room" in the attic story, and two weeks later the entire School of Elders moved from the printing office to an adjoining room to the Hebrew class in the temple attic.

The sacred building was dedicated on 27 March 1836 in the presence of some one thousand persons. After singing, praying, and preaching, the dedicatory prayer (section 109) was read aloud.[17]

Following its dedication, the House of the Lord remained in constant use for several years with Sunday worship, weekly sermons, public discourses, high council meetings, priesthood quorum meetings, special councils, solemn assemblies, choir presentations, and secular studies. However, the Saints did not enjoy permanent use of the sacred house because a majority of those in the Kirtland area had left Ohio for Missouri by mid-1838, and the remainder by 1845. Although title to the temple appears to have been transferred to one of the Church's creditors in 1837, members remaining in Kirtland maintained use of the building until about 1845, when preparations were being made to migrate to the West. In 1880 the Reorganized LDS Church was awarded title to the building by "adverse possession"—that is, although they did not hold legal title to it, their use and possession of the building over several years constituted ownership.

School of the Prophets.   Section 88 called for the organization of a school for all of those called to the ministry, for "their instruction in all things" (verse 127). A subsequent revelation detailed the meaning of "all things" when it directed members of the school to "study and learn, and become acquainted with all good books, and with languages, tongues and people" (D&C 90:15). The school, variously known as the "School of the Prophets," the "School of the Elders," and the "school of mine apostles," was intended to teach doctrine as well as secular topics to the Elders in order to properly "qualify themselves as messengers of Jesus Christ."[18] Instruction for the "Elders" was offered during four winter sessions in Kirtland: January-April 1833, 1834-35, 1835-36, and 1836-37. Evidence also affirms that at least one session of the school was held in Missouri, during the summer of 1833.

The 1833 School: Kirtland Phase.   On January 23 a small number of men convened to organize the School of the Prophets. The event which predominated the meeting was the washing of feet. Following is an extract from the minutes of the meeting:

> Opened with Prayer by the President [Joseph Smith] and after much speaking praying and singing, all done in Tongues proceded to washing hands faces feet in the name of the Lord . . . each one washing his own after which the president girded himself with a towel and again washed the feet of all the Elders wiping them with the towel . . . . The President said after he had washed the feet of the Elders, as I have done so do ye wash ye therefore one anothers feet pronouncing at the same time through the power of the Holy Ghost that the Elders were all clean from the blood of this generation but that those among them who should sin wilfully after they were thus cleansed and sealed up unto eternal life should be given over unto the buffettings of Satan until the day of redemption. Having continued all day in fasting & prayer before the Lord at the close they partook of the Lords supper.[19]

Consisting primarily of high priests, members of the school met regularly for nearly ten weeks (23 January to about 1 April 1833) in Kirtland, Ohio. The school was held in a small (10' x 14') room in the upper story of Newel K. Whitney's store, at a time when the entire upper level of the store was being used by the Prophet and his wife as a residence. The "school room," as it was called, had served earlier as a porch but had been enclosed by Levi Hancock, a carpenter, for use by the school. Regulations for the operation of the School of the Prophets were received by revelation and adhered to during the 1833 school season. Although Joseph Smith presided over the school, Orson Hyde was appointed the teacher. The number composing the 1833 school probably never exceeded twenty-five. Known members were: Joseph Smith, Sidney Rigdon, Frederick G. Williams, Joseph Smith, Sr., Hyrum Smith, Samuel H. Smith, William Smith, Ezra Thayer, Newel K. Whitney, Martin Harris, Zebedee Coltrin, John Murdock, Lyman Johnson, Orson

Hyde, Solomon Humphrey, Sylvester Smith, Orson Pratt, and Levi Hancock. The salutation recorded in D&C 88:133 was given each time the group came together. The teacher "saluted the brethren [with uplifted hands] as they came in," remembered Zebedee Coltrin, one of the original school, and "they also answered with uplifted hands." Coltrin also stated, "Before going to school we washed ourselves and put on clean linen."[20] Members of school came fasting at sunrise and normally continued until near 4:00 P.M.

The Sacrament was "administered at times when Joseph appointed, after the ancient order; that is, warm bread to break easy was provided, and broken into pieces as large as [a] fist and each person had a glass of wine."[21] At the conclusion of each meeting, the scholars were dismissed following a prayer with uplifted hands. Although the school was primarily intended for "revelation and doctrine," time was also given for "learning English grammer," and Sidney Rigdon "lectured on grammer sometimes."[22]

Several accounts of spiritual manifestations in the school are available. Zebedee Coltrin, however, is the author of the most dramatic. The following is from Coltrin's account:

> About the time the school was first organized some wished to see an angel, and a number joined in a circle, and prayed when the vision came, two of the brethren shrank and called for the vision to close or they would perish, they were Bros. Hancock and Humphries.
>
> At one of these meetings after the organization of the school, on the 23rd January, 1833, when we were all together, Joseph having given instructions, and while engaged in silent prayer, kneeling, with our hands uplifted each one praying in silence, no one whispered above his breath, a personage walked through the room from East to west, and Joseph asked if we saw him. I saw him and suppose the others did, and Joseph answered that is Jesus, the Son of God, our elder brother. Afterward Joseph told us to resume our former position in prayer, which we did. Another person came through; He was surrounded as with a flame of fire. He (Bro. C[oltrin]) experienced a sensation that it might destroy the tabernacle as it was of consuming fire of great brightness. The Prophet Joseph said this was the Father of our Lord Jesus Christ. I saw Him . . . . This appearance was so grand and overwhelming that it seemed I should

melt down in His presence, and the sensation was so powerful that it thrilled through my whole system and I felt it in the marrow of my bones. The Prophet Joseph said: Brethren now you are prepared to be Apostles of Jesus Christ, for you have seen both the Father and the Son.[23]

The 1833 School: Missouri Phase. According to directions received from the Prophet and others in Kirtland, Church leaders in Jackson County, Missouri, organized a school for the Elders in 1833. Although it is not clear when the school commenced, evidence shows that it was operating during the summer of 1833. Parley P. Pratt, who was designated to preside over and instruct the school, recorded the following concerning his responsibilities:

A school of Elders was also organized, over which I was called to preside. This class, to the number of about sixty, met for instruction once a week. The place of meeting was in the open air, under some tall trees, in a retired place in the wilderness, where we prayed, preached and prophesied, and exercised ourselves in the gifts of the Holy Spirit. Here great blessings were poured out, and many great and marvelous things were manifested and taught. The Lord gave me great wisdom, and enabled me to teach and edify the Elders, and comfort and encourage them in their preparations for the great work which lay before us. I was also much edified and strengthened. To attend this school I had to travel on foot, and sometimes with bare feet at that, about six miles.[24]

The School of the Elders (Missouri) was intended to serve as a counterpart to the School of the Prophets (Kirtland) in preparing and instructing those called to the ministry. Though accounts of spiritual manifestations in the Kirtland school are more numerous, there is evidence that the Missouri school enjoyed spiritual gifts. Writing from Independence in July 1833, John Whitmer noted the following concerning the School of the Elders: "God is pouring out his Spirit upon his people so that most all on last thursday at the school received the gift of tongues & spake & prophesied."[25]

The 1833-34 School: Kirtland. There was no classroom instruction during the winter of 1833-34.[26] Although the Prophet offered no explanation, four considerations appear to have played a significant role in precluding such a course: (1) the lack of an appropriate facility in which to house the students, (2) the indebtedness and failure of the United Firm, (3) a preoccupation with the difficulties of the Missouri Saints, and (4) the apostasy of Dr. Philastus Hurlburt and subsequent litigation involving the Prophet and Hurlburt.

1834-35 School: Kirtland.   About the first of November 1834, arrangements were made to resume the instruction of the Elders in the Kirtland area for the coming winter. A special room, on the ground floor of the newly finished printing office in Kirtland was designated as the school room. Classwork began in early December 1834 and continued until late March 1835, nearly sixteen weeks. A school board (also known as the Kirtland School Committee) consisting of Joseph Smith, Sidney Rigdon, Oliver Cowdery, and Frederick G. Williams directed the operation and instruction of the school. Though the purpose of instruction was aimed at better preparing the Elders for the ministry, the initial enrollment included nearly fifty adolescents. The resultant overcrowding forced the school board to dismiss the younger students in favor of the Elders. The study of penmanship, arithmetic, English grammar, and geography complemented the theological discussions. It was during this 1834-35 school season that the Lectures on Faith were delivered to and studied by the elders. Several instructors may have been hired by the trustees, but it is known that William E. McLellan played a significant role in teaching the secular topics.

1835-36 School: Kirtland.   The 1835-36 Elders' School (also called the School of the Prophets) may well have been the most significant period of Church instruction in Kirtland. The impending temple dedication and solemn assembly brought several elders—particularly some Church leaders from Missouri—to Kirtland. The primary purpose of the school was to prepare the elders for the "glorious endowment" to be poured out upon the faithful at the solemn assembly on 30 March 1836. According to the direction of the school committee, instruction commenced on 2 November 1835 and continued until 29 March 1836. Most classes were held in the Church printing office, but possibly they convened at other locations too. Orson Hyde appears to have had primary responsibility for teaching the regular courses of reading, writing, and arithmetic. The 1835-36 curriculum also included the study of Hebrew.

Although his qualifications were in doubt, a Dr. Piexotto had been contracted to teach the Hebrew class as soon as a room could be finished in the attic of the temple.[27] In anticipation of Piexotto's arrival, Oliver Cowdery had purchased Hebrew Bibles in New York. With the completion of the room in early January 1836, Piexotto was accordingly notified, but he advised the school committee that he would necessarily be delayed some few days. Prompted by their anxiety to begin on the one hand, and their fear of his not being qualified on the other, the committee opted to dismiss the gentleman, and dispatched William E. McLellan and Orson Hyde to the Hudson Seminary in Hudson, Ohio, to find another teacher. Arrangements were soon made, and Mr. Joshua Seixas of Hudson was hired for seven weeks at $320.[28]

Although without an instructor, the Hebrew class began on 4 January and continued until Seixas's arrival on 26 January 1836. Seixas was given an office in the printing office and immediately began giving one-hour lectures to the forty-five Hebrew students. By 4 February 1836, two more classes had been created and placed under Seixas's tutelage. Both before and after the lectures, the students would improve their time by reading and reciting passages from their Hebrew Bibles. All instruction ceased on 29 March 1836, the day before the solemn assembly.

1836-37 School: Kirtland. Under the direction of the school trustees, the Kirtland High School commenced classwork in the attic story of the temple in November 1836; with some interruptions, it continued until at least the first week of April 1837. Nearly one hundred and fifty students met regularly for instruction under the tutelage of H. M. Hawes, professor of Greek and Latin. Actually Hawes was assisted by two instructors, Elias Smith and Marcellus F. Cowdery, who taught English, arithmetic, and geography. Elias Smith was responsible for teaching the regular courses to the juveniles; Cowdery was given the more advanced students; and Hawes taught the classical languages. The texts included Kirkham's Grammar, Olney's Geography, Whelphey's History, and Jacob's Latin Grammar. On 4 January 1837, at the termination of the first quarter, the students were given a three-hour final examination and recessed until 1 February 1837, when the second quarter began.

Publication Note. Verses 117-126 were published in the *Evening and Morning Star* (February 1833); verses 127-137 were first published in the *Evening and Morning Star* (March 1833); and verses

1-116 were first published on a broadsheet in December 1833 or January 1834. The entire revelation was included as section 7 in the 1835 edition of the Doctrine and Covenants.

Section 89

Date.   27 February 1833.

Place.   Kirtland, Geauga County, Ohio.

Historical Note.   Section 89, known as the "Word of Wisdom," was received at a meeting of the School of the Prophets in the upper level of the Whitney store. Zebedee Coltrin, present when this revelation was received, clarified that although twenty-two brethren were in attendance that day, section 89 was received in an adjoining room, in the presence of two or three brethren.[1]

Although not in attendance on 27 February 1833, Brigham Young later stated that he was well acquainted with the circumstances surrounding the reception of section 89. In 1868 President Young declared,

> The first school of the prophets was held in a small room situated over the Prophet Joseph's kitchen, in a house which belonged to Bishop Whitney, and which was attached to his store, which store probably might be about fifteen feet square. In the rear of this building was a kitchen, probably ten by fourteen feet, containing rooms and pantries. Over this kitchen was situated the room in which the Prophet received revelations and in which he instructed his brethren. The brethren came to that place for hundreds of miles to attend school in a little room probably no larger than eleven by fourteen. When they assembled together in this room after breakfast, the first they did was to light their pipes, and, while smoking, talk about the great things of the kingdom, and spit all over the room, and as soon as the pipe was out of their mouths a large chew of tobacco would then be taken. Often when the Prophet entered the room to give the school instructions he would find himself in a cloud of tobacco smoke. This, and the complaints of his wife at

having to clean so filthy a floor, made the Prophet think upon the matter, and he inquired of the Lord relating to the conduct of the Elders in using tobacco, and the revelation known as the Word of Wisdom was the result.[2]

Publication Note. Section 89 was first published on a broadsheet in December 1833 or January 1834 and was included as section 80 in the 1835 edition of the Doctrine and Covenants.[3]

Section 90

Date.   8 March 1833.

Place.   Kirtland, Geauga County, Ohio.

Historical Note.   Jesse Gause, who had served with Sidney Rigdon as counselor to the Prophet in the presidency of the high priesthood, was excommunicated in December 1832.[1] The vacancy was filled by Frederick G. Williams. A fairly well-to-do farmer from Kirtland, Williams had served as Joseph Smith's scribe since 20 July 1832.[2] As a clerk to the presidency Williams had the Prophet's confidence, and was a natural choice. On 5 January 1833 a revelation called Frederick G. Williams to be "a Councillor and scribe unto my servant Joseph."[3] Among other things, section 90 directed that Rigdon and Williams be made equal with Joseph Smith in "holding the keys of this last kingdom."[4]

At an assembly of high priests convened at the School of the Prophets (18 March 1833), Sidney Rigdon requested that he and Frederick G. Williams be ordained to the office to which they had been called. "Accordingly Bro. Joseph preceded to and ordained them by the laying on of the hands to be equal with him in holding the Keys of the Kingdom and also to the Presidency of the high Priesthood."[5] Two days later, 20 March 1833, Williams was given a certificate of ordination which stated that he, "was regularly ordained to the Presidency of the High Priesthood under the hands of Joseph Smith, Jr. after the holy order of God according to a commandment given the 8th day of March AD 1833."[6]

Publication Note. Section 90 was first published as section 84 in the 1835 edition of the Doctrine and Covenants.

Biographical Note. Vienna Jaques.

Daughter of Henry and Lucinda Jaques (Father born in France). Born 10 June 1787 in Beverly, Essex County, Massachusetts. Baptized near Boston before July 1832. Came to Kirtland before 30 April 1833. Directed to consecrate property to Church and receive inheritance in Zion 8 March 1833. Moved to Missouri in company with William Hobart 1833. Married to Daniel Shearer. No known children. Received Patriarchal Blessing from William Smith in Nauvoo 25 July 1845. Received endowment 22 January 1846 in Nauvoo Temple. Died in Salt Lake City, Utah, 7 February 1884.[7]

Section 91

Date. 9 March 1833.

Place. Kirtland, Geauga County, Ohio.

Historical Note. Section 91 was received as a direct result of Joseph Smith's inspired translation of the Bible. The *History of the Church* notes the following: "Having come to that portion of the ancient writings called the Apocrypha, I received [section 91]."[1] The Apocrypha consists of fourteen books found at the end of earlier editions of the King James Version of the Old Testament, and are in the Catholic (Douay) version of the Bible.[2]

A few months after the reception of this revelation, Sidney Rigdon wrote the following to William W. Phelps:

> Respecting the Apocrypha, the Lord said to us that there were many things in it which were true, and there were many things in it which were not true, and to those who desire it, should be given by the Spirit to know the true from the false.[3]

Publication Note. Section 91 was first published as section 92 in the 1835 edition of the Doctrine and Covenants.

Section 92

Date.   15 March 1833.

Place.   Kirtland, Geauga County, Ohio.

Historical Note.   Section 92 instructed Frederick G. Williams to become a member of the United Firm. The terms *United Order* and *United Firm* were used interchangeably by members of the firm; consequently, both terms are found in minutes and published revelations.[1] A copy of this revelation in the Frederick G. Williams Papers at the Church Archives is identical to section 92 with one exception: "United firm" is used instead of "united order."[2]

On the same day, 15 March 1833, Frederick G. Williams apparently was admitted to the firm. An entry in the "Kirtland Council Minute Book" for 15 March 1833 records the following:

> Thirsday received a revelation making known that F.G.W. Should be received into the United firm in full partnership agreeable to the specification of the bond. [The bond is mentioned in D&C 78:11 and 82:11][3]

Publication Note.   Section 92 was first published as section 93 in the 1835 edition of the Doctrine and Covenants.

Section 93

Date.   6 May 1833.

Place.   Kirtland, Geauga County, Ohio.

Historical Note.   The inspired translation of the New Testament was temporarily completed on 2 February 1833, but work on the Old Testament continued until 2 July 1833. Verse 53 of section 93 directed the Prophet to "hasten" the translation of the scriptures. This revelation is of major doctrinal importance. The headnote of section 93 in the 1921 edition of the Doctrine and Covenants (and all subsequent reprints, 1921-1980) suggests that the text of the revelation contains a portion of the record of John the Apostle. Both John Taylor and Orson Pratt believed the record to be that of John the Baptist.[1]

Publication Note.   Section 93 was first published as section 82 in the 1835 edition of the Doctrine and Covenants.

Section 94

Date.   6 May 1833 (2 August 1833).

Both the "Kirtland Revelation Book" and a letter from the Prophet and others to Church leaders in Missouri, dated 6 August 1833, give the date of reception for section 94 as 2 August 1833.[1] Moreover, the 6 August 1833 letter makes it clear that sections 97 and 94 were received together and appear to be either two parts of one revelation or two revelations joined together—section 94 constituting the latter half. Internal evidence also suggests that section 94 was received after section 95: verses 1-2 of section 94 indicate that the pattern for constructing the Kirtland Temple had already been given, but section 95 gave the dimensions for the temple[2] and added that the "manner" (i.e., architecture) would be later shown to three.[3]

Place.   Kirtland, Geauga County, Ohio.

Historical Note.   Section 94 gave specific attention to two sacred buildings to be constructed in Kirtland: the house for the Presidency and a house for printing. The revelation also mentioned that the three-member committee who had been commissioned earlier to supervise the receiving of subscriptions for the erection of these sacred edifices were to be given city lots in Kirtland.

The above-mentioned letter gave instructions to the Missouri members of the Church regarding the content of the revelation (i.e., sections 97 and 94). The letter, in the hand of Sidney Rigdon, stated in part,

> Having received br Oliver's letter of July 9th as well as one from the breatheren composing the school we now answer them both in one letter as relates to the school of Zion according to your request we inquired of the Lord

and send in this letter the communication which we received from the Lord concerning the school in Zion It was obtained August 2nd and reads thus [here follow sections 97 and 94 respectively]. You will see by these revelations that we have to print the new translation here in Kirtland for which we will prepare as soon as possable. here follows another revelation received to day Kirtland August 6th 1833 [section 98 follows]. Having here given you two revelations we accompany them with the following explanations 1) the revelation respecting the two houses to be built in Kirtland in addition to the one we are now building [i.e., the temple] one for the presidency and the other for the printing are also bending upon on you that is you at Zion have to build two houses as well as the one of which we have sent the pattern [i.e., the Jackson County temple, see "Kirtland Council Minute Book," p. 22] and mentioned in the first revelation above written you are also in addition to this one to build two others one for the presidency and one for the printing they are to be of the same size in the inner court of the one of which you have received the pattern they will therefore be larger than the ones we are to build in Kirtland 2) you are to print an Edition of the schriptures [i.e., the New Translation of the Bible] there at the same time we do here so that two additions [editions] will be struck at the same time the one here and the other there, the two last mentioned houses are to be built as soon after the other as means can be obtained so to do The pattern of the last mentioned houses as yet to be given see revelation 1 above [see D&C 94:5-6 and 11].[4]

> Sidney Rigdon
> F.G. Williams
> Joseph Smith Jr.

Pursuant to the instructions of section 94, a printing office was erected adjacent to the temple in Kirtland. On 10 October 1833, nearly two months after receiving section 94, it was decided to proceed with the construction of a printing office (30' × 38'), somewhat smaller than specified in the revelation, and it was determined that the building, at least temporarily, would serve as both a printing office and a office for the presidency (of the School of the Prophets).[5] The structure was completed the latter part of

November 1834 and was put to immediate use. The first story was used for the school of the elders (prophets) and the upper story for the printing press. Other rooms on both levels as well as the attic were used as offices for the Church Presidency and for all types of meetings. The building was attached to satisfy a judgment in late 1837, and on 16 January 1838 the whole printing apparatus and office were burned to the ground.[6]

Publication Note.   Section 94 was first published as section 83 in the 1835 edition of the Doctrine and Covenants.

Section 95

Date.   1 June 1833 (3 June ?).[1]

Place.   Kirtland, Geauga County, Ohio.

Historical Note.   On 4 May 1833 a conference of high preists met in Kirtland, Ohio, to take into consideration the commandment in section 88 to build a house for the School of the Prophets. Hyrum Smith, Jared Carter, and Reynolds Cahoon were appointed by the conference as a committee to obtain subscriptions for the above-named purpose.[2]

On 1 June 1833 this committe issued a circular in which they urged the Saints to fulfill the commandment of the Lord to build a house wherein they could call a solemn asembly and "treasure up words of wisdom."[3]

Two days later, 3 June 1833, during another conference of high priests in Kirtland, it was decided that the dimensions of the sacred edifice should be specified. Thereupon the Prophet

received a revelation on the size of the house the word of the Lord was that it shall be fifty five feet wide and sixty five feet long in the inner court and the conference appointed Bro Joseph Jr Sidney Rigdon and Frederick G. Williams to obtain a draft or construction of the inner court of the house.[4]

Verse 14 of the revelation directed that the building be erected "after the manner which I shall show unto three of you."

Accordingly Joseph Smith, Sidney Rigdon, and Frederick G. Williams, members of the First Presidency, were privileged to see the house in vision prior to its construction. Concerning this vision, Frederick G. Williams stated,

> Joseph received the word of the Lord for him to take his two counsellors Williams and Rigdon and come before the Lord, and he would show them the plan or model of the House to be built. We went upon our knees, called on the Lord, and the Building appeared within viewing distance: I being the first to discover it. Then all of us viewed it together. After we had taken a good look at the exterior, the building seemed to come right over us, and the Makeup of this Hall seems to coincide with what I there saw to a minutia.[5]

Publication Note   Section 95 was first published as section 95 in the 1835 edition of the Doctrine and Covenants.

Section 96

Date.   4 June 1833.

Place.   Kirtland, Geauga County, Ohio.

Historical Note.   On 23 March 1833 a council of high priests and elders was convened in Kirtland to discuss the matter of purchasing certain properties in the city. Zebedee Coltrin recorded that on this day "a council of high Priests [met] to investigate the subject of Purch[as]ing the brick tavern and farm owned by Pete French."[1] Brethren were dispatched during the meeting to ascertain the terms upon which three farms could be purchased. Their report was that, "Elijah Smith would sell his farm for four thousand dollars and that Mr. Morley [Moore?] would sell his farm for twenty one hundred dollars, and . . . . that Peter French would sell his farm for five thousand dollars."[2] After hearing the above report, the assembled brethren voted to buy the properties and authorized Ezra Thayer and Joseph Coe to negotiate the purchase. Coltrin's summary of the meeting was, "It was agreed to buy it [the tavern] and several other farms which made it necessary to call the Elders out of School [of the

Prophets] for the purpose of going again into the world and procuring means for paying for the farms."³

On 4 June 1833 a group of high priests met in the Prophet's translating room in Kirtland to determine who should take responsibility for the French farm.⁴

> The council could not agree who should take charge of it but all agreed to enquire of the lord accordinly we received a revilation [section 96] which decided that Broth N K Whitney should take the charge thereof and also that brother John Johnson be admited as a member of the united firm accordingly he was ordained unto the high Priesthood and admited.⁵

Three weeks later Sidney Rigdon wrote to William W. Phelps concerning part of this revelation: "Zombre has been received as a member of the [United] firm by commandment, and has just come to Kirtland to live."⁶

Publication Note. Section 96 was first published as section 96 in the 1835 edition of the Doctrine and Covenants.

Biographical Note. John Johnson.

Son of Israel Johnson and Abigail Higgins. Born 11 April 1778 in Chesterfield, Cheshire County, New Hampshire. Resided in Pomfret, Vermont, from about 1803 to 1818; there owned large farm. Married Elsa Jacobs 22 June 1800. Nine children: Elsa, Fanny, John, Jr., Luke S., Olmsted, Lyman E., Emily, Marinda Nancy, and Mary. Moved to Hiram, Ohio, about 1818; there owned farm. Baptized in spring of 1831. Joseph Smith's family lived in Johnson home in Hiram September 1831-September 1832. Ordained elder 17 February 1833. Appointed by revelation to become member of United Firm 4 June 1833. Ordained high priest 4 June 1833. Moved to Kirtland, Ohio, 1833. Appointed member of Kirtland high council 17 February 1834. Served as member of high council 1834-37. Worked on Kirtland Temple. Received blessing 8 March 1835 for working on Kirtland Temple. Charter member of and owned stock in Kirtland Safety Society 1837. Rejected as high councilor 4 September 1837. Became disaffected from Church leaders 1837-38. Withdrew from Church by 1838. Died 30 July 1843, in Kirtland, Lake County, Ohio.⁷

Section 97

Date.   2 August 1833.

Place.   Kirtland, Geauga county, Ohio.

Historical Note.   A letter from Joseph Smith and others to Church leaders in Jackson County, Missouri, explains the setting in which section 97 was received:

> Having received br Oliver's letter of July 9th as well as one from the breatheren composing the school in Zion according to your request we now answer them both in one letter as relates to the school in Zion according to your request we enquired of the Lord and send this letter the communication which we received from the Lord concerning the school in Zion. It was obtained August 2 and reads thus [section 97].[1]

Concerning verses 3-6 Parley P. Pratt later wrote,

> A school of Elders was also organized, over which I was called to preside. This class, to the number of about sixty, met for instruction once a week. The place of meeting was in the open air, under some tall trees, in a retired place in the wilderness, where we prayed, preached and prophesied, and exercised ourselves in the gifts of the Holy Spirit.[2]

The command to build a house in Zion (verses 10-17) was also discussed in the Prophet's above-mentioned letter (6 August 1833). The Prophet instructed that three sacred edifices were to be erected in Zion, namely, a temple, a house for printing, and a house for the Presidency.

Publication Note.   Section 97 was first published as section 81 in the 1835 edition of the Doctrine and Covenants.

Section 98

Date.   6 August 1833.

Place.   Kirtland, Geauga County, Ohio.

Historical Note.   Although there is little available background information for section 98, the content of the revelation suggests the possibility that some news of the anti-Mormon sentiment in Jackson County, Missouri, had reached Kirtland. Although it is improbable that Church leaders in Kirtland were aware of the 20 July 1833 mobbings in Independence, a now-lost letter from Oliver Cowdery to Joseph Smith, dated 9 July 1833,[1] undoubtedly carried news of the growing antagonism in Jackson County.[2] Conflicts between Mormons and non-Mormons in Missouri undoubtedly provided the background for this revelation.

Publication Note.   Section 98 was first published as section 85 in the 1835 edition of the Doctrine and Covenants.

Section 99

Date.   August 1833 (29 August 1832).

The date of reception for section 99 is August 1832, *not* August 1833. The "Kirtland Revelation Book" headnote lists the date as 29 August 1832,[1] and John Murdock's journal affirms the date as August 1832. All published copies of section 99 prior to the 1876 edition of the Doctrine and Covenants have the date as August 1832.

Place.   Kirtland, Geauga County, Ohio (Hiram, Portage County, Ohio as per "Kirtland Revelation Book").[2]

The place of reception for this revelation may well have been Hiram, Ohio, because the Prophet and his family did not move back to Kirtland until about 12 September 1832.[3]

Historical Note.   John Murdock has recorded the following with regard to section 99:

> I then continued with the church preaching to them and strengthening them and regaining my health till the

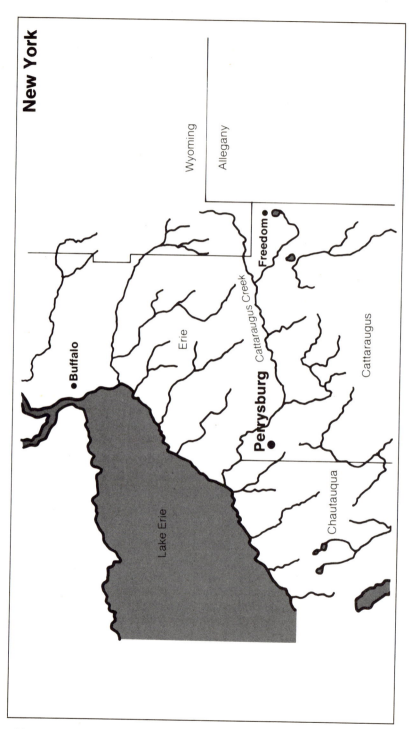

New York

Wyoming

Allegany

Freedom

Cattaraugus Creek

Erie

Buffalo

Perrysburg

Cattaraugus

Chautauqua

Lake Erie

month of Aug. [1832] when I received the Revelation
[section 99], at which time I immediately commenced to
arrange my business and provide for my children and
sent them up to the Bishop in Zion, which I did by the
hand of Bro. Caleb Baldwin in Sept [1832]. I gave him 10
Dollars a head for carrying up my three eldest children
[Orrice C., John R., and Phebe C.].[4]

Publication Note.   Section 99 was first published as section 78 in
the 1835 edition of the Doctrine and Covenants.

Section 100

Date.   12 October 1833.

Place.   Perrysburg, Cattaraugus County, New York.

Historical Note.   On 5 October 1833, Joseph Smith and Sidney
Rigdon, accompanied by Freeman Nickerson, started east from
Kirtland on a preaching mission. The Prophet's party traveled down
Lake Erie to Niagara, then westward through Ontario to Mt.
Pleasant (near present-day Brantford, Ontario, Canada).[1]
   While en route to Upper Canada, the party stopped two days in
Perrysburg, New York, the residence of Freeman Nickerson, who
had been baptized the previous April. John P. Greene, who met the
Prophet in Perrysburg, recorded the following in his journal:

> 13 Sundy   I went to Br Nickersons in Perresburg & met
> Brs. Joseph Smith & Sidny Rigdon & Sidney Preached in
> the demmonstr[a]tion of the Spirrit & after ward I . . .
> Spent the eveni[n]g with the Breth with grate satisfaction
> in company with Joseph . . . .
> 14 day monday we went to Lodi & Sidney preached 15
> the next morning the people desired to hear again & Esq
> McKer gave out word that Sidney would preach at 10 ock.
> in the Presbyterian house one man who had the key of to
> house would not suffur the door opened; & so we came
> off & left them all in confusion; & in the after noon came
> to Collings and parted with my Bratheren & they went on
> to Canada.[2]

Section 100 was received in answer to a great concern the Prophet had for his family's welfare.[3] In the Prophet's journal, kept during this trip, an entry for 12 October 1833 states, "Came Saturday the 12th [to] the house of father Nickerson I feel very well in my mind the Lord is with us but have much anxiety about my family &c."[4] This revelation informed the Prophet and Sidney Rigdon that their families were well and that Sidney should be a spokesman for Joseph Smith.[5]

In addition to the above, section 100 revealed that Orson Hyde and John Gould would be taken care of. Hyde and Gould had been sent to Jackson County, Missouri, to inform Church leaders there that legal measures should be taken immediately to seek redress for wrongs they had suffered at the hands of Missourians. These two men left Kirtland in late August and returned 25 November 1833.[6]

On 4 November 1833 Joseph Smith arrived home from Upper Canada. His journal entry for that day states, "Left Buffalo, N.Y. at 8 o'clock A.M. and arrived at home Monday, the 4th at 10 A.M. found my family all well according to the promise of the Lord for which blessings I feel to thank his holy name."[7]

Publication Note.   Section 100 was first published as section 94 in the 1835 edition of the Doctrine and Covenants.

Biographical Note.   John Gould.

Born 11 May 1808 in Ontario, Canada. Baptized by June 1833. Appointed to travel to Jackson County, Missouri, with Orson Hyde 21 August 1833 to inform Church leaders in Missouri to seek redress at law. Left Kirtland about 31 August 1833 and arrived in Independence about 28 September 1833. Revelation received by Joseph Smith 12 October 1833 assured Prophet that Orson Hyde and John Gould were safe and well. Arrived back in Kirtland 25 November 1833. Accompanied Joseph Smith and others to seek volunteers for Zion's Camp March 1834. Joined with Evan M. Greene in New York to preach gospel 16 June 1834. Assisted in establishing branches of Church in Freedom, New York, area 1834. Mission in Catteraugaus County, New York 1834-35. Ordained seventy 1836. Attended solemn assembly in Kirtland April 1837. Ordained and set apart 25 President of First Quorum of Seventy 6 April 1837; dropped from position 3 September 1838. Reinstated 1838. Located in Nauvoo. Received endowment 3 February 1846. Married to Abigail Harrington. Known children: John, Jr., Magor G. Left Detroit, Michigan, for Illinois with William Burton 2 May 1846. Settled at Cooley's Mill in Pottawatamie County, Iowa where he died 9 May 1851.[8]

Section 101

Date. 16 December 1833.

Place. Kirtland, Geauga County, Ohio.

Historical Note. In accordance with a "secret constitution" authored and circulated by anti-Mormons in Jackson County, Missouri, a mob gathered in Independence Square on Saturday, 20 July 1833, and demanded "the discontinuance of the Church printing establishment," the closing of the Gilbert-Whitney store, and "the cessation of all mechanical labors."

When Church members refused to comply, the rabble destroyed the Church printing office and tarred and feathered two Mormons. Three days later, Church leaders were forced to sign a written agreement to leave the county by 1 January 1834. Oliver Cowdery was promptly sent to Kirtland to inform the Prophet of the riot. Upon his arrival, sometime before 18 August 1833,[1] a meeting was convened to hear the matter. It was decided "that measures should be immediately taken to seek redress by the laws of our country."[2] After dispatching Orson Hyde and John Gould to Independence with the decision of the council, the Prophet corresponded with leaders of the Church in Missouri concerning their plight:

> In fellowship and love towards you, but with a broken heart and contrite spirit I take the pen to adress you, but I know not what to say to you and the thought that this letter will be so long coming to you my hearts faints within me ....The Church in Kirtland concluded with one accord to die with you or redeem you and never at any time have I felt as I now feel that pure love and for you my brethren the warmth and zeal for your safety .... Brother Oliver is now sitting before me and is faithful and true and his heart bleeds as it were for Zion, yea, never did the heart pant for the cooling stream as doth the heart of thy Brother Oliver for thy salvation ....This affliction is sent upon us not for your sins, but for the sins of the Church and that all the ends of earth may know that you are not speculating with them for lucre, but you are willing to die for the Church you have espoused.[3]

Upon petitioning the Missouri governor for assistance, Church leaders were urged by the state attorney-general to seek both redress and protection under the law. This attempt to normalize conditions produced a vehement response from members of the opposition. The intransigence of non-Mormons in Jackson County was immediately made manifest when, on 31 October 1833, citizens demolished houses and whipped several Mormon men. Violence continued, and judges repeatedly refused to issue warrants against the mobsters. On 4 November 1833 a skirmish on the Big Blue River caused the deaths of one Mormon and two Missourians.[4]

As early as 25 November 1833 Hyde and Gould had returned to Kirtland bearing the tragic news of the Missouri mobbings and bloodshed. And on 10 December 1833 the Prophet learned by letter of the Saints' flight from Jackson County by force.

Section 101, received on 16 December 1833, explained the reasons for the Saints' expulsion from Zion. Moreover, it reiterated the command to purchase land in Jackson and adjoining counties[5] and contained a parable which adumbrated the march of Zion's Camp to rescue the homeless Saints.

Publication Note.   Section 101 was first published in December 1833 or January 1834 on a broadside and was included as section 97 in the 1835 edition of the Doctrine and Covenants.[6]

Section 102

Date.   17 February 1834.

Place.   Kirtland, Geauga County, Ohio.

Historical Note.   Section 102 consists of the final revised and corrected minutes of the organization and rules of procedure for the Kirtland high council. On 12 February 1834 Joseph Smith met with a group of high priests and elders to discuss the function of Church councils. The Prophet instructed those present that

> no man was capable of judging a matter in council without his own heart was pure....In ancient days councils were conducted with such strict propriety, that

no one was allowed to whisper, be weary, leave the room, or get uneasy in the least, until [a decision had been reached].[1]

Joseph Smith declared that Church councils or courts were to be conducted according to an ancient pattern which had been "shown to him by vision." "Jerusalem was the seat of the Church Council in ancient days," said the Prophet; "the apostle, Peter, was the president of the Council and held the keys of the Kingdom of God on earth."[2] To clarify the matter of guilt, the Prophet added,

> It was not the order of heaven in ancient councils to plead for and against the guilty as in our judicial courts (so called) but that every counsellor when he arose to speak, should speak precisely according to evidence and according to the teaching of the Spirit of the Lord, that no counsellor should attempt to screen the guilty when his guilt was manifest.[3]

The formal organization of the Kirtland high council occurred on 17 February 1834, and a companion high council was organized in Clay County, Missouri, on 7 July 1834.[4] The Kirtland high council, and the high council in Clay County, Missouri, held wide judicial and administrative powers. This pattern remained consistent for several years with regard to a high council situated at Church headquarters (i.e., Kirtland, Far West, Nauvoo, and Salt Lake City). Although their authority and jurisdiction would subsequently diminish, members of these early councils (ordained high priests), were clearly recognized as "general authorities." Whether officially or unofficially, these high councils held the status of a "High Council in Zion"[5] and, as such, were in their respective right and turn, a presiding quorum of the Church. Although these early Church high councils rarely convened to hear criminal cases, Church courts did adjudicate controversies between member and member—matters that today would be settled by civil courts. An important feature of the high council court was that the rights of the accused were protected by at least half of the participating high councilors.

Publication Note. Section 102 was first published as section 5 in the 1835 edition of the Doctrine and Covenants.

Biographical Note.   John Sims Carter.

Son of Gideon Carter and Johanah Sims. Born 1796 in Killingworth, Middlesex County, Connecticut. Married Elizabeth Kenyon 28 February 1813. One known child: William. Baptized and ordained elder by 1832. Ordained high priest 24 May 1832. Mission with brother Jared May-July 1832 in Vermont area. On 20 February 1834 appointed by Kirtland high council to accompany Jesse Smith on mission to "east." Traveled to Clay County, Missouri, with Zion's Camp 1834. Died of cholera 26 June 1834 in Clay County, Missouri.[6]

Biographical Note.   John Smith.

Son of Asahel Smith and Mary Duty. Born 16 July 1781 in Derryfield, Rockingham County, New Hampshire. Married Clarissa Lyman 11 September 1815. Four children: Female child, George Albert, Caroline, and John Lyman. Baptized 9 January 1832. Ordained elder 1832. Moved to Kirtland, arriving 25 May 1833. Ordained high priest 21 June 1833. Appointed member of Kirtland high council 17 February 1834. Worked on Kirtland Temple. Received blessing for working on Kirtland Temple 8 March 1835. Mission to eastern states with Joseph Smith, Sr., 1836. Left Kirtland 22 June 1836. Preached in Pennsylvania, New York, Vermont, and New Hampshire. Returned to Kirtland 2 October 1836. Left Kirtland for Far West, Missouri, 5 April 1838. Arrived 16 June 1838. Subsequently settled in Daviess County. Appointed president of Adam-Ondi-Ahman Stake 28 June 1838. Expelled from Missouri 1839. Located at Green Plains, Illinois, in spring of 1839. Moved to Commerce June 1839. Appointed president of Church in Lee County, Iowa, 5 October 1839. Moved to Nashville, Iowa, 12 October 1839. Moved to Hawley Settlement near Nashville, 20 January 1840. Appointed to move to Keokuk, Iowa, 15 September 1842. Received endowment by 28 September 1843. Directed to move to Ramus, Illinois, October 1843. Presided over branch of Church in Ramus until October 1844. Ramus Branch requested he be ordained patriarch 12 December 1843. Ordained patriarch 10 January 1844 by Joseph Smith. Member of Council of Fifty by 3 May 1844. Directed to move to Nauvoo 9 August 1844. Appointed president of Nauvoo Stake 7 October 1844. Sealed to Ann Carr (born 1790 in Connecticut) 15 January 1846. Sealed to Miranda Jones (born 1784 in Massachusetts) 15 January 1846. Sealed to Mary Aiken (born 1797 in Vermont) for time, 15 January 1846. Sealed to Julia Hills (mother of Benjamin F. Johnson and born 1783 in Massachusetts) 24 January 1846. Sealed to Asenath Hulbert (mother of Lyman Sherman and born 1780 in Massachusetts) 24 January 1846. Sealed to Rebecca Smith (born 1788 in Massachusetts) 24 January 1846. Left Nauvoo for West 9 February 1846. To Winter Quarters 1846. To Salt Lake Valley 23 September 1847. President of Salt Lake Stake 1847-48. Ordained Presiding Patriarch of Church 1 January 1849. Gave 5,560 patriarchal blessings. Died in Salt Lake City, Utah, 23 May 1854.[7]

Section 103

Date. 24 February 1834.

Place. Kirtland, Geauga County, Ohio.

Historical Note. On 1 January 1834, Church leaders in Clay County, Missouri, voted that Lyman Wight and Parley P. Pratt "be sent as special messengers, to represent the situation of the scattered brethren in Missouri, to the Presidency and Church in Kirtland, and ask their advice."[1] Wight and Pratt left Clay County for Ohio on 12 January and arrived in Kirtland on Saturday, 22 February 1834. After hearing a recital of the meager conditions and sufferings of the Saints in Missouri, the Prophet received section 103, which, alluding to the parable in section 101, directed Joseph Smith to organize a body of men to journey to Missouri and "redeem the land." Eight men, named in the revelation, were to enlist volunteers to make the trip to Missouri.[2] An entry from Heber C. Kimball's journal captures the historical setting:

> Brother Joseph received a revelation concerning the redemption of Zion, part of which remains yet to be fulfilled. He sent Messengers to the East and to the North, to the West and to the South to gather up the Elders and, He gathered together as many of the brethren as he conveniently could, with what means they could spare to go up to Zion to render all the assistance that we could to our afflicted brethren. We gathered clothing and other necessaries to carry up to our brethren and sisters who had been plundered; and putting our horses to the wagons and taking our firelocks and ammunition, we started on our journey; leaving only Oliver Cowdery, Sidney Rigdon and a few aged workmen who were engaged at the Temple; so that there were very few men left in Kirtland.[3]

This body, known as Zion's Camp, grew to approximately 205 members. The plan of this armed body of men was to return the Missouri Saints to their homes in Jackson County in cooperation with state authorities and under state protection.[4] The advance guard left Kirtland on 5 May 1834.[5]

Publication Note.   Section 103 was first published as section 101 in the 1844 edition of the Doctrine and Covenants.

Section 104

Date.   23 April 1834.

Place.   (Kirtland, Geauga County, Ohio).

Historical Note.   Section 104 is an important revelation giving instructions to members of the United Firm.[1] The headnote for section 104 in the "Kirtland Revelation Book" states that the section is a "revelation given April 23d 1834, appointing to each member of the United firm their stewardships."[2]

Prior to the Prophet's leaving for Missouri in May 1834, he desperately sought to borrow or collect by donation two thousand dollars to pay pressing debts incurred by the United Firm.

On 26 February 1834 Joseph Smith and others journeyed to New York to seek volunteers to help redeem the Jackson County Saints and to obtain money "for the relief of the brethren in Kirtland." While the Prophet's group was in Avon, New York, a Church council voted that several elders should "exert themselves to obtain two thousand dollars for the present relief of Kirtland," and that Orson Hyde should "tarry and preach in the regions round about, till the money should be obtained." On 7 April 1834, having returned to Kirtland unsuccessful in obtaining the needed money, the Prophet met with Newel K. Whitney, Frederick G. Williams, Oliver Cowdery, and Heber C. Kimball and prayed that the Lord would "furnish the means to deliver the [United] Firm from debt." That same day, in a letter to Orson Hyde, Joseph Smith wrote that unless the money could be obtained, he could not go to Missouri.

On 10 April 1834, unable to secure the needed funds, members of the United Firm met and agreed that the "Order" should be dissolved and each member have his stewardship set off to him.[3]

Section 104 gives the particulars of the division of the United Firm among the members living in Kirtland, and also directs the two branches of the firm (i.e., the Missouri branch and the Kirtland branch) to become separate entities.

Focusing on the Kirtland branch of the United Firm, section 104, verses 20-45, explains the procedure of division:

1. Sidney Rigdon was to have the place where he resides plus the lot of the tannery.

2. Martin Harris was to have the lot that John Johnson received in exchange for his former inheritance.

3. F.G. Williams was to have the place where he dwells.

4. Oliver Cowdery was to have both the lot which adjoins the printing house and the lot where his father dwells.

5. Oliver Cowdery and F.G. Williams were to have the printing house and accessories.

6. John Johnson was to have the house in which he lives plus "the inheritance" except for the lots which have been designated for sacred buildings and the lots given to O. Cowdery.

7. Newel K. Whitney was to have the houses and the lot where he now resides plus the lot and building on which the mercantile establishment stands, plus the lot which is on the corner south of the mercantile establishment, plus the lot on which the ashery is located.

8. Joseph Smith was to have the lot on which "my house" is to be built: 40 rods long and twelve rods wide, plus the inheritance upon which his father resides.

As a further step in the dissolution of the United Firm, another revelation, received the same day (23 April 1834) required "every one of what was then called the firm to give up all notes & demands that they had against each other and all be equal."[4]

A document in the Newel K. Whitney collection reveals the amounts of the notes in question:

Amt. of Balances due from the following persons the 23d day of Apl. 1834 at which time Joseph said it was the will of the Lord the accounts v.s. [against] those persons should be balanced (up to the above date) in full without any value recd; amts as follows Viz.

Balance due from F.G. Williams & Co	23d Apl 1834 was	$ 584.14
Balance due from Joseph Smith Jr.	do do	1151.31
Balance due from Oliver Cowdery	do do	68.57
Balance due from Sidney Rigdon	do do	777.98
Balance due from F.G. Williams	do do	485.67
Balance due from Jno. Johnson	do do	567.68
		$3635.35[5]

Concerning the division of the Kirtland branch and the Missouri branch of the United Firm, an unpublished revelation dated Kirtland, 28 April 1834, further explains the nature of the division:

> Verily thus saith the Lord concerning the division and settlement of the United Firm. Let there be reserved three thousand Dollars for the right and claim of the Firm in Kirtland for inheritances in due time, even when the Lord will, and with this claim, to be had in remembrance when the Lord shall reveal it for a right of inheritance, ye are made free from the Firm of Zion, and the Firm in Zion is made free from the Firm in Kirtland: Thus saith the Lord. Amen.[6]

Textual Note.   The following lines, which follow verse 59 in the "Kirtland Revelation Book," are not part of the present text of section 104 of the Doctrine and Covenants:

Therefore, a commandment I give unto you, that ye shall take the books of Mormon and also the copy-right, and also the copy-right which shall be secured of the Articles and Covenants in which covenants all my commandments which it is my will should be printed, shall be printed, as it shall be made known unto you; and also the copy-right of the new translation of the scripture; and this I say that others may not take the blessings away from you which I have conferred upon you.[7]

Publication Note.   Section 104 was first published as section 98 in the 1835 edition of the Doctrine and Covenants.

Section 105

Date.   22 June 1834.

Place.   Fishing River, Clay County, Missouri.

Historical Note.   Zion's Camp marched out of Kirtland on 5 May 1834. The plight of the Missouri Saints engaged the attention of the approximately two hundred Mormons who joined the camp to defend the rights of their brethren. With a pledge from the Missouri

governor to give the homeless Mormons a military escort back to
their lands in Jackson County, members of Zion's Camp traveled
one thousand miles to protect and defend the Missouri Saints from
local harassment after their return. The plan was published and sent
to the eastern branches of the Church on a broadside authored by
Oliver Cowdery and Sidney Rigdon. Upon the arrival of Zion's
Camp in Missouri, the persecuted Saints were

> To inform the Governor of that state that they are ready to
> go back to their lands. The Governor is bound to call out
> the Militia and take them back, and has informed our
> brethren of his readiness so to do . . . .When orders arrive
> from the Governor to the Military Commanding Officers
> in that vicinity to guard our brethren back, then it is
> expected that all will march over, the former residents as
> well as those now on the way. When they are on their
> own possessions, they have a right to defend themselves
> and property from destruction and spoilation, and be
> justified. in the right of the laws of heaven and men. The
> company now on the way, with the scattered brethren
> when collected, will be sufficiently strong in the strength
> of the Lord to maintain the ground, after the Militia have
> been discharged.[1]

The Mormon army crossed the Mississippi River in early June,
arriving at the Salt River Branch of the Church in Monroe County,
Missouri, on 7 June 1834. After a short respite the camp resumed its
march on 12 June. Three days later Orson Hyde and Parley P. Pratt
returned to the camp from Jefferson City with news that Governor
Daniel Dunklin had "refused to fulfill his promise of reinstating"
the Mormons on their lands in Jackson County. Dunklin apparently
made his earlier promise in good faith; however, in the intervening
six months, as Mormon-non-Mormon conditions worsened, he
perceived that an armed conflict would inevitably ensue if the
Mormons returned to their lands, and "pragmatically withdrew his
promise in order to avert a civil war."[2]

Inasmuch as the camp intended only to work in concert with state
authorities and under state protection, the governor's refusal
insured that Zion's Camp would not enter Jackson County. With its
primary objective out of reach, all that remained for the camp was to
move into Clay County, where the body of the Church was residing,
and discuss possible compromises.

Section 105, received after Zion's Camp had arrived in Clay County, gave reasons why Zion would not be redeemed in 1834 and explained what must be done to effect that redemption.[3]

John Whitmer, who had been expelled from Jackson County, reported that the failure of the mission of Zion's Camp "blasted" his fondest hopes:

> Received a revelation that it was not wisdom to go to Jackson county at this time and that the armies of Israel should become very great and terrable first. and the servants of the Lord be endowed with power from on high previous to the redemption of Zion. Thus our fond hopes of being redeemed at this time were blasted at least for a season.[4]

Publication Note.   Section 105 was first published as section 102 in the 1844 edition of the Doctrine and Covenants.

Section 106

Date.   25 November 1834.

Place.   Kirtland, Geauga County, Ohio.

Historical Note.   During the month of November 1834, Joseph Smith was occupied in making preparations for the School of the Elders. "No month," he said, "ever found me more busily engaged than November; but as my life consisted of activity and unyielding exertions, I made this my rule: *When the Lord commands, do it.*"[1]

Section 106 directed Warren A. Cowdery to preside over the branch of the Church in Freedom, Cattaraugus County, New York.

Publication Note.   Section 106 was first published as section 99 in the 1835 edition of the Doctrine and Covenants.

Biographical Note.   Warren A. Cowdery.

Son of William Cowdery and Rebecca Fuller. Born 5 October 1788 in Poultney, Rutland County, Vermont. (Elder brother of Oliver Cowdery.) Married Patience Simonds 22 September 1814 in Paulet, Vermont. Eleven children: Marcellus F., Warren F., Martius D., Lyman, Mary, Martha, Oliver P., Eleanor C., Jay William, John Simonds, and Sarah E. Resident and early physician of Paulet, Vermont. Moved from Vermont to Freedom, New York, about 1816; there continued to practice medicine and operated apothecary business. First postmaster of Freedom, New York, 1824; there built first brick house 1828. Joined Church before November 1831. Appointed presiding high priest of Freedom, New York, Branch 25 November 1834. Arrived with family in Kirtland, Ohio, 25 February 1836; resided there until death. Assisted in writing dedicatory prayer for Kirtland Temple 1836. Paid personal property tax on two cows in Kirtland 1837. Served as scribe and assistant recorder for Church 1836-37. Served as member of Kirtland high council May 1837. Edited *Messenger and Advocate* July-September 1837. Disaffected from Church leadership 1838. In 1850 Federal Census for Ohio listed with wife and six children as residents of Kirtland; there had assets of $700. Died in Kirtland, Ohio, 23 February 1851.[2]

Section 107

Date.   28 March 1835 (and November 1831).
Verses 1-58 were received 28 March 1835. Verses 59-100, except 61, 70, 73, 76-78, part of 92, and 93-98, were received in November 1831.[1]

Place.   Kirtland, Geauga County, Ohio. (The verses received in November 1831 were received in Cuyahoga County, Ohio.)

Historical Note.   In February 1835, members of the first Quorum of Twelve Apostles were chosen by the Three Witnesses to the Book of Mormon, in Kirtland, Ohio. The Prophet met periodically with the quorum after its organization and gave instruction to them. At one such meeting, held on 12 March 1835, it was decided that the Twelve should "take their first mission through the eastern States to the Atlantic Ocean and hold conferences in the vicinity of the several branches of the Church."[2] Section 107, known as the "Revelation on Priesthood," is a composite of two revelations, and verses 1-58 were received while the Prophet met with members of the Twelve on 28 March 1835. In the late afternoon of the day, members of the quorum confessed their sins, committed themselves to greater service, and received instruction from Joseph Smith. Knowing that they would soon depart for the East, members of the quorum requested that the Prophet "enquire of God for us and obtain a written revelation (if consistent) that we may look upon it when we are separated that our hearts may be comforted."[3] Pursuant to their request, section 107 (verses 1-58) was recieved.[4] Some evidence suggests that Oliver Cowdery served as scribe.[5]

Organizationally, verses 21-37 were significant because they tempered the earlier supremacy of the presidency of the high priesthood by equally dispersing presiding priesthood authority among five quorums of church government. Verses 76 and 82 established the machinery of Church government by which a member of the presidency of the high priesthood could be tried for misconduct. The revelation specified that such a case must be heard by the "common council" (i.e., a bishop, his counselors, and twelve high priests).[6]

Publication Note.   Section 107 was first published as section 3 in the 1835 edition of the Doctrine and Covenants.

Section 108

Date.   26 December 1835.

Place.   Kirtland, Geauga County, Ohio.

Historical Note.   The day after Christmas in 1835, Lyman Sherman approached the Prophet Joseph Smith and said, "I have been wrought upon to make known to you my feelings and desires, and was promised that I should have a revelation which should make known my duty."[1] The Lord's promise was fulfilled to Sherman, for Joseph Smith received a revelation for him that very hour. The revelation informed Sherman that he would receive an ordination in conjunction with the "first of mine elders," a term which referred to a chosen few who were to receive an "endowment." The Kirtland endowment was to consist of a rich outpouring of God's spirit upon the faithful elders. Preparation for the "endowment" occupied much of the Church leaders' time during the early months of 1836. Brethren who had been selected to participate in this important event met regularly in the Kirtland Temple during January and February 1836. This preparation, intended to sanctify the brethren, involved the following:[2]

1.   Confessing of sins and asking forgiveness,

2. Covenanting to be faithful to God,

3. Having one's body washed and bathed with cinnamon-perfumed whiskey,

4. Washing one's own body with pure water and perfume,

5. Having one's head anointed with holy oil,

6. Having the anointing blessing sealed with uplifted hands (the sealing blessing consisting of three parts: solemn prayer, a sealing prayer, and the hosanna shout), and

7. Washing of faces and feet and partaking of the Lord's Supper.

Publication Note. Section 108 was first published in the *Deseret News* (10 July 1852) and was included as section 108 in the 1876 edition of the Doctrine and Covenants.

Biographical Note. Lyman Royal Sherman.

Son of Elkanah Sherman and Aseneth Hulbert. Born 22 May 1804, at Monkton, Addison County, Vermont. Married Delcena Didamia Johnson 16 January 1829. Six children: Alvira, Mary E., Albey Lyman, Seth, Daniel, and Susan Julia. Baptized January 1832. Moved to Kirtland, Ohio, 1833. Member of Zion's Camp. Ordained president of Seventy 28 February 1835. Received revelation through Joseph Smith 26 December 1835. Participated in Kirtland Temple dedication 1836. Called to fill vacancy in Kirtland high council 10 October 1837. Moved to Far West, Missouri, by October 1838. Called as temporary high councilor in Far West, Missouri, 13 December 1838. Called to apostleship 16 January 1839, but not notified or ordained before death February 1839, in Far West, Caldwell County, Missouri. Proxy sealing to Delcena Johnson in Nauvoo Temple 24 January 1846.[3]

Section 109

Date. 27 March 1836.

Place. Kirtland, Geauga County, Ohio.

Historical Note. Section 109 is a prayer that was read at the dedication of the Kirtland Temple on 27 March 1836.[1] The dedication of this temple and the numerous meetings and other activities associated with it both before and after the actual dedication were clearly the acme of Church activity in Kirtland, Ohio. A revelation given to Joseph Smith on 11 September 1831 noted that the Lord would "retain a strong hold in the land of Kirtland, for the space of five years" (D&C 64:21). The history of the Church during this early period affirms that the year 1836 indeed marked both the spiritual climax of the Church as well as the beginning of the end of Kirtland as a stronghold.

Approximately one thousand Saints crowded into the Kirtland Temple on the morning of 27 March 1836 to participate in the dedication of that sacred edifice.[2] Prayers were offered, hymns sung, and sermons preached. The dedicatory prayer was pronounced by Joseph Smith in the afternoon, when he announced that Peter the apostle had been in their midst to accept the dedication.[3]

After the prayer had been read, the several quorums, as well as the entire congregation, voted unanimously to accept it.

Under the direction of the Prophet, some leading brethren of the Church prepared the prayer of dedication in Kirtland prior to 27 March 1836. Oliver Cowdery recorded in his journal the following regarding section 109:

> From Saturday 19th. attended Heb. School, up to Saturday the 26. Nothing of note transpiring. This day our school did not keep, We prepared for the dedication of the Lord's house. I met in the presidents room pres. J. Smith, jr. S. Rigdon, my brother W.A. Cowdery & Elder W. Parrish, and assisted in writing a prayer for the dedication of the house.[4]

Publication Note. Section 109 was first published in the *Messenger and Advocate* (March 1836) and was included as section 109 in the 1876 edition of the Doctrine and Covenants.

Section 110

Date.   3 April 1836.

Place.   Kirtland, Geauga County, Ohio.

Historical Note.   On Sunday, 3 April 1836, one week after the dedication of the Kirtland Temple, Church members in Kirtland

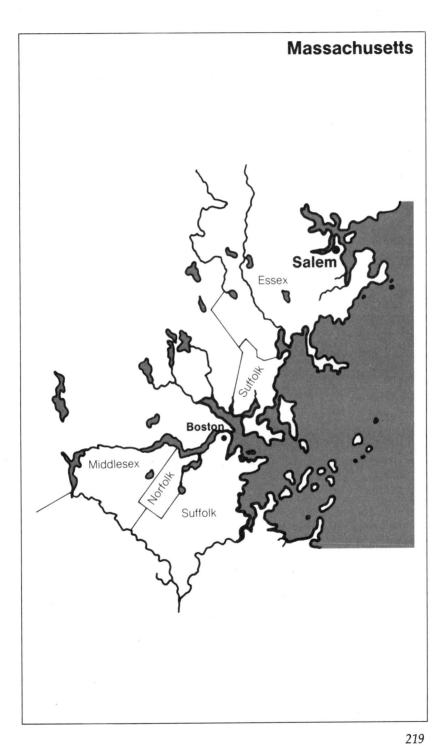

Massachusetts

Salem

Essex

Suffolk

Boston

Middlesex

Norfolk

Suffolk

assembled in the sacred edifice to worship. In the afternoon the sacrament was adminstered and distributed to those present, after which Joseph Smith and Oliver Cowdery secluded themselves from the congregation by means of curtain partitions. After being engaged in silent prayer Joseph and Oliver saw a series of visions wherein four heavenly messengers appeared unto them: The Lord Jesus Christ, Moses, Elias, and Elijah. The Lord accepted the temple as his house, and the latter three dispensed keys that would assist in the restoration of all things.[1] Although this revelation was not published until 1852, it was recorded contemporaneously in the Prophet's diary in the hand of Warren A. Cowdery:

> Sabbath April 3d He [Joseph Smith] attended meeting in the Lords House assisted the other Presidents of the Church in seating the congregation and then became an attentive listener to the preaching from the Stand. T.B. Marsh & D.W. Patten spoke in the A.M. to an attentive audience of about 1000 persons. In the P.M. he assisted the other presidents in distributing the elements of the Lords Supper to the church, receiving them from the Twelve, whose privilege it was to officiate in the sacred desk this day. After having performed this service to his brethren, he retired to the pulpit, the vails being dropped, and bowed himself with O. Cowdery, in solemn but silent prayer to the Most High. After rising from prayer the following vision was opened to both of them [here follows section 110].[2]

Publication Note. Section 110 was first published in the *Deseret News* (6 November 1852) and included as section 110 in the 1876 edition of the Doctrine and Covenants.

Section 111

Date. 6 August 1836.

Place. Salem, Essex County, Massachusetts.

Historical Note. On 25 July 1836, Joseph Smith, his brother Hyrum, Oliver Cowdery, and Sidney Rigdon left Kirtland, Ohio, for the East. Indebtedness plagued church leaders in Ohio. With the rapid increase of membership, constant travel to regulate Church branches, the purchase and development of several properties (including the temple), and the purchase and/or operation of several business enterprises (including the Whitney store and the printing office), Church leaders desperately sought every available opportunity to obtain money. Private discussions had already addressed the topic of founding a bank in Kirtland.

A major factor that encouraged this trip east was the affirmation of a Massachusetts member of the Church named Burgess that a "large amount of money had been secreted in the cellar of a certain house in Salem, Massachusetts." Sufficient credence was given to the statement of this brother, undoubtedly Jonathan Burgess of Barnstable, Massachusetts, that "steps were taken to try and secure the treasure."[1]

Arriving in New York City the last day of July, these Church authorities made business contacts, inquired about plates and dies for printing notes for the Church bank, and went sightseeing. The foursome left New York City on 3 August for Salem, where they arrived the following day.[2] According to one account, "Brother Burgess met them in Salem, evidently according to appointment, but time had wrought such a change that he could not for a certainty point out the house and soon left."[3]

Section 111, received on Sunday, 6 August 1836, mentioned the "follies" of the party for giving too much attention to earthly "treasures." Moreover, the revelation emphasized that the city had "more treasures than one," meaning prospective converts to the gospel message. As a consequence, Elder Rigdon filled at least two preaching assignments in Salem.[4]

After remaining approximately three weeks, the Prophet, Cowdery, and Rigdon departed for Kirtland, about 25 August 1836. (Hyrum Smith had departed for Ohio the previous week.) The trio arrived back in Kirtland sometime in September 1836. Verse two implies that many people would be gathered out of the Salem area. It is significant to note that over one hundred converts were baptized in 1841 through the labors of Erastus Snow.[5]

Publication Note. Section 111 was first published in the *Deseret News* (25 December 1852) and was included as section 111 in the 1876 edition of the Doctrine and Covenants.

Section 112

Date.   23 July 1837.

Place.   Kirtland, Geauga County, Ohio.

Historical Note.   Section 112 was received by the Prophet Joseph Smith for Thomas B. Marsh, President of the Quorum of Twelve Apostles. In the spring of 1837, while residing in Missouri, Marsh was experiencing frustration relative to his position as president of his quorum. Although an 1835 revelation (section 107) seemed to place his quorum next to the First Presidency in the Church government, in reality, the Presidency of the Church in Missouri (David Whitmer, William W. Phelps, and John Whitmer) and the two Church high councils had retained their supremacy (having been organized before the Twelve) next to the First Presidency. Furthermore, Thomas lamented that his quorum had not maintained close contact since their 1835 mission to the Eastern States, nor had they been unified in fulfilling their divine calling as special missionaries. Of a more serious nature was news which had reached Marsh that members of his quorum had fallen into apostasy, and he was likewise mortified upon learning that Parley P. Pratt, one of his quorum, was planning a mission to England.

On 10 May 1837, Marsh and David W. Patten, first and second respectively in seniority among the Twelve, and both residing in Missouri, dispatched word to Parley requesting him to defer his mission across the Atlantic until the quorum could convene. Marsh considered taking the gospel abroad an act of such magnitude that no one of the quorum should attempt such an action independently. In the letter Marsh called a meeting of the entire quorum for 24 July 1837 in Kirtland.[1] Marsh and Patten left for Ohio sometime the following month.

In the meantime, however, Joseph Smith had directed Heber C. Kimball and Orson Hyde of the Twelve to travel to England to introduce the gospel.[2] It is not known when Marsh and Patten learned of the departure of these missionaries, but it seems clear that the news angered them and shattered their hopes of unifying the quorum. Brigham Young, remembering their arrival in Kirtland, said, "As soon as they came I got Marsh to go to Joseph But Patten would [not] . . . .He got his mind prejudiced & when He went to see Joseph David insulted Joseph & Joseph slaped him in the face

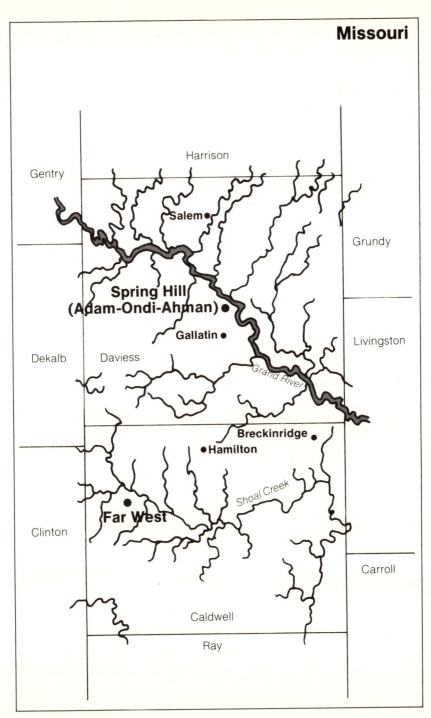

Missouri

Gentry

Harrison

Salem ●

Grundy

Spring Hill
(Adam-Ondi-Ahman) ●

Gallatin ●

Dekalb

Daviess

Grand River

Livingston

● Breckinridge ●

● Hamilton

● Far West

Shoal Creek

Clinton

Carroll

Caldwell

Ray

223

& kicked him out of the yard this done David good."[3] It appears that Marsh himself desired to introduce the gospel abroad.[4]

Section 112, received one day before the scheduled meeting of the Quorum of the Twelve, gave instructions to Marsh regarding his responsibilities in relation to other members of his quorum and the First Presidency.[5] According to one source, Thomas B. Marsh served as scribe.[6]

Publication Note.   Section 112 was first published as section 104 in the 1844 edition of the Doctrine and Covenants.

Section 113

Date.   March 1838 (after 14 March).

Place.   (Far West, Caldwell County, Missouri).

Historical Note.   On 12 January 1838 Joseph Smith received a revelation that said in part, "Thus saith the Lord, let the Presidency of my Church, take their families as soon as it is practicable, and a door is open for them, and moove unto the west, as fast as the way is made plain before their faces."[1] In response to this command and the pending threats on his life, Joseph Smith left Kirtland later that same evening (12 January 1838) for Far West, Missouri, where he arrived 14 March 1838.

The earliest record of the questions and answers in section 113 (written in the hand of George W. Robinson, clerk for the First Presidency) is found in "The Scriptory Book of Joseph Smith, Jr."[2] The "Scriptory Book," an 1838 record book, was begun on 12 April 1838 in Far West, Missouri.[3] Although no date is attached to the questions and answers on scripture, items entered in the record book, both before and after what is now section 113, indicate that the revelation was recorded soon after the Prophet's arrival in Far West.

Section 113 consists of answers to questions concerning passages of scripture in the book of Isaiah, chapters 11 and 52. Some of these questions were asked by Elias Higbee, who was a member of the high council and a resident of Far West.

Publication Note.   Section 113 was first published in the *Deseret News* (5 March 1853) and was included as section 113 in the 1876 edition of the Doctrine and Covenants.

Biographical Note.   Elias Higbee.

Son of Isaac Higbee and Sophia Somers. Born 23 October 1795, at Galloway, Gloucester County, New Jersey. Moved with parents to Clermont County, Ohio, in 1803. Married Sarah Elizabeth Ward 10 September 1818 in Clermont County. Eight children: Francis Marion, Chauncy Lawson, Andrew Jackson, William, DeWitt Clinton, Elizabeth, Sarah, and Elias Keryle. Residing in Tate Township, Clermont County, Ohio, 1820. Residing in Fulton, Hamilton County, Ohio, 1830. Baptized in spring of 1832. Traveled to Jackson County, Missouri, in summer of 1832. Returned to Cincinnati area by 20 February 1833; there ordained elder by brother, Isaac Higbee. Moved to Jackson County March 1833. Expelled from Jackson County in fall of 1833. Located in Clay County, Missouri, in fall of 1833. Appointed to be ordained high priest 26 September 1833. Ordained high priest 7 August 1834. Mission to Ohio 1835. Left Clay County 26 March 1835. Worked on Kirtland Temple 1835. Set apart as member of Clay County high council in Kirtland 6 January 1836. Participated in washings and anointings in Kirtland Temple 1836. Attended dedication of Kirtland Temple March 1836. Settled in Caldwell County, Missouri, 1836. Purchased property in Caldwell County January 1837. Elected senior county judge of Caldwell County, Missouri. Appointed member of Far West high council 7 November 1837. Expelled from Missouri 1838. Left Far West for Illinois before 13 December 1838. Located in Quincy, Illinois, area before February 1839. On 9 March 1839, appointed member of committee to view Isaac Galland properties in Lee County, Iowa, and Commerce, Illinois. Subsequently settled in Nauvoo. Appointed 6 October 1839 to travel to Washington, D.C., with Joseph Smith and others to seek redress for wrongs committed against Saints in Missouri. Left Nauvoo 29 October 1839. Arrived in Washington, D.C., 28 November 1839. Met with President Martin Van Buren 29 November 1839. Remained in Washington after Prophet's departure for Nauvoo to lobby for redress. Left Washington for Nauvoo 23 March 1840. Arrived in Nauvoo by May 1840. On 3 October 1840 appointed one of committee to build Nauvoo Temple and appointed to continue seeking redress for Missouri injustices. With Robert B. Thompson, wrote petition to Congress 28 November 1840 for redress of grievances. Served as temporary member of Nauvoo high council 1840-42. Reproved by Joseph Smith for lack of diligence in raising children and building Nauvoo Temple 28 January 1842. Died of cholera 8 June 1843 in Nauvoo, Hancock County, Illinois. Following written in "Book of the Law of the Lord" (p. 315): "His loss will be universally lamented, not only by his family, but by a large circle of brethren who have long witnessed his integrity and uprightness, as well as a life of devotedness to the cause of truth." Joseph Smith preached funeral sermon 13 August 1843 at Nauvoo.[4]

Section 114

Date.   17 April 1838.

Place.   Far West, Caldwell County, Missouri.

Historical Note.   Joseph Smith received two revelations on 17 April 1838—one for Brigham Young and one for David W. Patten.[1] Section 114, the revelation for Elder Patten, directs him to arrange his affairs in preparation for traveling with others of the Twelve to Great Britain.

Publication Note.   Section 114 was first published in the *Deseret News* (19 March 1853) and was included as section 114 in the 1876 edition of the Doctrine and Covenants.

Biographical Note.   David Wyman Patten.

Son of Benoni Patten and Abigail Cole. Born 17 November 1799 in Vermont. Settled in Monroe County, Michigan; there married Phoebe Ann Babcock 1828. No known children. Converted by brother, John Patten. Traveled from Michigan to Fairplay, Indiana, 1832. Baptized 15 June 1832. Ordained elder 17 June 1832 by Elisha H. Groves. Mission to Michigan 1832. Traveled to Kirtland September-October 1832. Ordained high priest 2 September 1832 by Hyrum Smith. Mission to Pennsylvania October 1832-February 1833. Mission to eastern states with Reynolds Cahoon March 1833. Established several branches of Church in New York. Returned to Kirtland in fall of 1833. Worked on Kirtland Temple. Moved from Michigan to Florence, Ohio, 1833. With William Pratt, sent to Clay County, Missouri, 19 December 1833 bearing dispatches to Church leaders in Missouri. Remained in Missouri until arrival of Zion's Camp June 1834. Mission to Tennessee with Warren Parrish in fall of 1834. Ordained apostle 15 February 1835. Mission to eastern states with Twelve in summer of 1835. In revelation dated 3 November 1835 chastised for commission of certain sins. Participated in solemn assembly and dedication of Kirtland Temple early 1836. Mission to Kentucky and Tennessee 1836. Moved to Far West, Missouri, with wife 1836. Mission to East in spring of 1837. With Thomas B. Marsh appointed President pro tem of Church in Missouri 10 February 1838. Authorized to lead body of Caldwell County militia to rescue kidnaped Mormons in Ray County, Missouri, 24 October 1838. Mortally wounded 25 October 1838 at Battle of Crooked River. Died at home of Stephen Winchester, three miles from Far West, Missouri, 25 October 1838. Buried in Far West, Missouri, 27 October 1838. Widow died in Nauvoo 5 January 1841.[2]

Section 115

Date.   26 April 1838.

Place.   Far West, Caldwell County, Missouri.

Historical Note.   Section 115 is best known as the revelation that gives the official name of the Church. Previously the Church had been called "The Church of Christ" (6 April 1830 to 3 May 1834) and "The Church of the Latter Day Saints" (3 May 1834 to 26 April 1838). This revelation gave the final designation for the Church, which has remained unchanged to the present time.[1]

Soon after section 115 had been received, Thomas B. Marsh wrote a letter to Wilford Woodruff explaining the contents of the revelation. Consider the following excerpt from Marsh's letter:

> Since Br. Joseph came to this place, we have been favored with a lengthy revelation in which many important items are shown forth. First that the Church, shall hereafter be called. "The Church of Jesus Christ of Latter-day Saints." Second it saith "Let the City Farwest be a holy and a consecrated land unto me, and it shall be called most holy, for the ground upon which thou standest is holy: Therefore, I command you to build a house unto me, for the gathering together of my Saints, that they may worship me." 3d. It also teaches, that the foundation stone must be laid on the 4th of July next [1838], and that a commencement must be made in this following season; and in one year from that time, to continue the work until it is finished. Thus we see that the Lord is more wise than men, for Phelps & Whitmer thought to commence it long before this, but it was not the Lords time, therefore, he over threw it, and has appointed his own time. The plan is yet to be shown to the first presidency, and all the Saints, in all the world, are commanded to assist in building the house.[2]

The city of Far West was laid out in August 1836. By late 1838 the population was nearly five thousand, almost entirely Mormon. The corner stones of the Far West Temple were laid 4 July 1838, but even though walls for the building were at one time nearly three feet high, the edifice was never completed.

Verse 18 addressed the subject of organizing additional stakes of Zion. Particularly was this a sensitive issue at the time. William W. Phelps and John Whitmer earlier had designated Far West, Missouri, as a stake of Zion without the approval of the First Presidency.[3] An unpublished revelation, received 12 January 1838, explained that only the presidency of the Church had that authority.[4]

Publication Note.   Section 115 was first published in the *Elders' Journal* (August 1838) and was included as section 115 in the 1876 edition of the Doctrine and Covenants.

Section 116

Date.   19 May 1838 (11 June 1838?).[1]

Place.   Spring Hill, Daviess County, Missouri.

Historical Note.   Daviess County, created in December 1836, was a sparsely populated area during the Mormon occupation of Northern Missouri. Bordering Caldwell County on the north, Daviess County offered some excellent sites for further Mormon settlement, particularly on the Grand River. Lyman Wight and others had settled on the Grand River in the spring of 1837, but official Church exploration parties did not scout the area until November 1837. In December 1837 Oliver Cowdery, Frederick G. Williams, David W. Patten, and Lyman Wight were appointed to explore Daviess County and select sites for additional settlements. Although the full extent of the activities and deliberations of the committee on explorations are not known, Cowdery later wrote that they had identified "between forty and fifty locations" north of Far West.[2]

In mid-May 1838, two months after his arrival in Far West, Joseph Smith accompanied others to Wight's settlement at Spring Hill, where they laid out a city.[3] The city was given the name "Adam-Ondi-Ahman" in keeping with the Prophet's statement that the area had been so named by the Lord.[4] Although the land in Adam-Ondi-Ahman was not available for purchase from the federal government until 12 November 1838, many Saints who settled there had purchased preemption rights on the property. The name *Adam-*

Ondi-Ahman was in use as early as 1835 (see D&C 107:53). A hymn authored by William W. Phelps, entitled "Adam-Ondi-Ahman," was published in the *Messenger and Advocate* in June 1835, and section 78 (as published in the 1835 edition of the Doctrine and Covenants) spoke of establishing the "foundations of Adam-Ondi-Ahman."[5]

Publication Note.   Section 116 was first published in the *Deseret News* (2 April 1853) and was included as section 116 in the 1876 edition of the Doctrine and Covenants.

Section 117

Date.   8 July 1838.

Place.   Far West, Caldwell County, Missouri.

Historical Note.   After a very eventful Independence Day celebration, a three-day Church conference was held, 6-8 July 1838, in Far West, Missouri.[1] On the final day of the conference, the Prophet Joseph Smith received several revelations.

Section 117, received on the morning of 8 July, instructed William Marks, president of the Kirtland Stake, and Newel K. Whitney, bishop, to sell the remaining Church properties, liquidate Church debts, and move posthaste to Far West, Missouri.

Oliver Granger was to return to Kirtland, Ohio, commissioned as the Prophet's attorney-in-fact to "settle up his business affairs." Concerning Granger's responsibility the Prophet later stated, "As I was driven from Kirtland without the privilege of settling up my business, I had ... employed Colonel Oliver Granger as my agent, to close all my affairs in the east."[2]

A letter to Marks and Whitney, bearing the date 8 July 1838 and signed by the First Presidency, stated the following:

> We send you by the hand of br O. Granger a revelation recd this morning. By this you will understand the will of the Lord concerning you & will doubtless act accordingly—It would be wisdom for all the Saints that can come this Summer to come....If they cannot sell their property let them turn it out for the debts....There

needs be no fear in the Saints coming up here there are Provisions or will be in great abundance of all kinds.[3]

Publication Note.   Section 117 was first published in the *Deseret News* (2 April 1853) and was included as section 117 in the 1876 edition of the Doctrine and Covenants.

Biographical Note.   Oliver Granger.

Son of Pierce and Clarissa Granger. Born 7 February 1794 in Phelps, Ontario County, New York. Married Lydia Dibble (born 5 April 1790) 8 September 1818. Three known children: Lydia, Gilbert, and Carlos. Lost much of sight from cold and exposure 1827. Sheriff of Ontario County, New York. Baptized and ordained elder in Wayne County, New York, by Brigham and Joseph Young. Moved to Kirtland 1833. Mission to East with Samuel Newcomb 1833. Appointed to take mission alone "eastward" 20 February 1834. Worked on Kirtland Temple. Received blessing for working on Kirtland Temple 8 March 1835. Mission to East with John P. Greene 1836. Established branches of Church in Huntsburg, Geauga County, and in Perry, Richland County, Ohio, 1836. Ordained high priest 29 April 1836. Appointed member of Kirtland high council 4 September 1837. Ordained 9 September 1837 as high councilor. Moved to Far West, Missouri, June 1838. Appointed by revelation on 8 July 1838 to return to Kirtland as Prophet's attorney-in-fact to settle up Church business. Arrived in Kirtland August 1838. Left Kirtland to return to Far West October 1838; precluded from doing so by Bogg's extermination order. Located in Nauvoo 1839. During summer of 1839, served as Church land agent, acquiring property in Lee County, Iowa, for Saints. Moved to Kirtland 1840. Appointed to make land exchanges to Church members by First Presidency as being "a man of the most strict integrity and moral virtue; and in fine, a man of God." Died 25 August 1841 in Kirtland, Lake County, Ohio.[4]

Biographical Note.   William Marks.

Born 15 November 1792, in Rutland, Rutland County, Vermont. Married Rosannah (born 1796 in Vermont). Five known children: Ephraim, Goodrich, Sophia, William, Jr., and Llewellen. Residing in Portage, Alleghany County, New York, before 1830. Baptized before April 1835 in Portage, New York. Ordained priest before 3 April 1835. Ordained elder before 3 June 1836. Took ownership of office of *Messenger and Advocate* May 1837. Moved to Kirtland before September 1837. Appointed member of Kirtland high council 3 September 1837. Ordained high councilor 9 September 1835. Appointed agent to Bishop Newel K. Whitney 17 September 1837. President of Kirtland Stake 1838. Appointed by revelation to be president of stake at Far West, Missouri, 8 July 1838. Did not assume position because of Mormon expulsion from Missouri. Located temporarily in Quincy, Illinois, 1839. Appointed to preside over Church in Commerce, Illinois, 6 May 1839. Appointed president of Nauvoo Stake 5 October 1839. Elected alderman for City of Nauvoo 1 February 1841. Chosen one of regents of University of Nauvoo 3 February 1841. Assisted in laying corner stones of Nauvoo Temple April 1841. Initiated into Masonry 20 April 1842. Received endowment 4 May 1842. Member of Council of Fifty 19 March 1844. Expressed ambivalence concerning right of Twelve to govern Church after Prophet's death. Sympathized with Sidney Rigdon's claims. Dropped by high council 10 September 1844. Rejected as president of Nauvoo Stake 7 October 1844. Left Nauvoo about 12 March 1845. Located in Fulton City, Whiteside County, Illinois, 1845. Appointed counselor to James J. Strang 6 March 1846. Assumed position 6 April 1847 at Voree, Wisconsin. Counselor to Strang until 6 June 1850. Residing in Shabbona, DeKalb County, Illinois, 1850. By April 1852, joined with Charles B. Thompson in organizing new church. Withdrew from Thompson in 1853. Searching for legitimate successor to Joseph Smith 1853-59. Postmaster and justice of peace of Shabbona, Illinois. Supported proponents of reorganization 1859. Assisted in founding Reorganized LDS Church 1860. Assisted in ordination of Joseph Smith III as president of Reorganization. Appointed counselor to Joseph Smith III April 1863. Died in Plano, Kendall County, Illinois, 22 May 1872.[5]

Section 118

Date. 8 July 1838.

Place. Far West, Caldwell County, Missouri.

Historical Note. Section 118 was received by Joseph Smith in the presence of Sidney Rigdon, Hyrum Smith, Edward Partridge, Isaac Morley, Jared Carter, Samson Avard, Thomas B. Marsh, and George W. Robinson. Because four members of the original Quorum of Twelve Apostles had fallen into apostasy, the above brethren inquired of the Lord, saying, "Show unto us thy will O Lord concerning the Twelve."[1]

Section 118 revealed that John Taylor, John E. Page, Wilford Woodruff, and Willard Richards should fill the vacancies in the Quorum of the Twelve. A letter written by Thomas B. Marsh, dated 14 July 1838, explained the contents of the revelation to Wilford Woodruff:

A few days since, Prest. Joseph Smith Jr. [and] others assembled together to attend to some church business, when it was thought proper to select those who were designed of the Lord to fill the places of those of the twelve who had fallen; namely Wm. E. Mclellin, Lyman E. Johnson, Luke Johnson, and John F. Boynton. The persons selected were John E. Page, John Taylor, Wilford Woodruff and Willard Richards. On the following day [9 July] five of the twelve with President Rigdon and some others met and resolved that President Rigdon write to Br. Richards, who is now in England, and inform him of his appointment, and that P.P. Pratt write to Orson Pratt and inform him that the Lord has commanded that the 12 assemble in this place as soon as possible and that I should write to yourself.[2]

Section 118 also instructed the Twelve to "take leave of my saints in the city of Far West" on 26 April 1839 and "go over the great waters, and there promulgate my gospel." By April 1839 the Mormon people had been expelled from Missouri, and in order to fulfill the instructions of section 118, members of the Twelve, with others, secretly assembled in Far West, Missouri, on 26 April 1839, held a meeting, and labored a few hours in erecting the walls of the Far West Temple. In accordance with verse 2, Thomas B. Marsh was appointed to edit the *Elders' Journal*, an official Church organ.[3]

Publication Note.   Section 118 was first published in the *Deseret News* (2 April 1853) and was included as section 118 in the 1876 edition of the Doctrine and Covenants.

Biographical Note.   John Edward Page.

Son of Ebenezer and Rachel Page. Born 25 February 1799 in Trenton Township, Oneida County, New York. Baptized by Emer Harris 18 August 1833 in Brownhelm, Ohio. Ordained elder 12 September 1833. Married Lorain Stevens 26 December 1833. Moved to Kirtland, Ohio, in fall of 1835. Mission to Bathurst District, Upper Canada, May-December 1836. Second mission to Upper Canada February 1837. Baptized nearly six hundred converts during two missions. Led Canadian converts to Missouri 1838. Joined Kirtland Camp en route May 1838. Arrived in DeWitt, Missouri, late September 1838. Later located in Far West. Appointed by revelation to fill vacancy in Quorum of Twelve Apostles 8 July 1838. Ordained apostle 19 December 1838. After death of first wife and two children in Missouri, married Mary Judd about January 1839. Three known children: John S., Justin, and Jerome. Expelled from Missouri 1839. Located in Warsaw, Illinois, 1839. Failed to take mission to England with others of Twelve 1839. Appointed to accompany Orson Hyde to Jerusalem 8 April 1840. Did not complete mission but did travel east and preach in eastern states 1841-42. Reproved by First Presidency for delaying mission to Jerusalem 15 January 1841. Returned to Nauvoo by spring of 1842. Initiated into Masonry 21 April 1842. Appointed to organize Church in Pittsburgh, Pennsylvania, 6 April 1842. Resided in Pittsburgh 8 May 1842-8 June 1843. Edited and published *The Gospel Light* in Pittsburgh and Philadelphia 1843-44. Conflict with other members of Twelve 1843. In 1843 revelation directed to leave Boston area and preach in Washington, D.C. Returned to Nauvoo by December 1844. Received endowment 26 January 1845. Disfellowshipped 9 February 1846. Supported James Jesse Strang's claim as lawful successor to Joseph Smith 1846. Excommunicated 26 June 1846. Cut off from Council of Fifty on 12 November 1846. Residing in Walworth County, Wisconsin, 1850; there listed occupation as "Mormon Clergyman." Ordained Granville Hedrick apostle and "president of the high Priesthood" 17-18 May 1863. Helped Hedrickites gain possession of Independence Temple lot. Resided several years near Sycamore, DeKalb County, Illinois; died there 14 October 1867. Widow married William Eaton.[4]

Biographical Note.   Willard Richards

Son of Joseph Richards and Rhoda Howe. Born 24 June 1804 at Hopkinton, Middlesex County, Massachusetts. Practiced medicine in Massachusetts before 1835. Learned of Book of Mormon 1835. Traveled to Kirtland, Ohio, October 1836. Baptized by cousin Brigham Young 31 December 1836. Ordained elder by Alva Beman 6 March 1837. Short mission to eastern states 11 March-11 June 1837. Appointed to take mission to England June 1837. Left Kirtland 13 June 1837. Arrived in England 20 July 1837. Ordained high priest in Preston, England, 1 April 1838. Counselor to Joseph Fielding in presiding over Church in England 1838-40. Married Jennetta Richards (born 1817) 24 September 1838. Three children: Heber John, Heber John, and Rhoda Ann. Ordained apostle in Preston, England, by Brigham Young 14 April 1840. Moved from Preston to Manchester February 1841. Left England for Illinois April 1841. Arrived in Nauvoo 16 August 1841. Located in Warsaw, Illinois, 1841. Elected member of Nauvoo City Council 30 October 1841. Moved to Nauvoo December 1841. Appointed temple recorder and private secretary to Joseph Smith 13 December 1841. Initiated into Masonry 7 April 1842. Received endowment 4 May 1842. Mission to New England 1842. Left Nauvoo 1 July 1842. Returned with family 29 November 1842. Appointed General Church Recorder 30 July 1843. Member of Council of Fifty 11 March 1844. Present at martyrdom of Prophet 27 June 1844. Sealed to Jennetta Richards 22 January 1846. Sealed to Amelia Elizabeth Pierson (born 1825 in Massachusetts) 22 January 1846. Sealed to Sarah Longstroth (born

1826 in England) 22 January 1846. Four children: Willard Brigham, Joseph Smith, Sarah Ellen, and Paulina. Sealed to Nancy Longstroth (born 1828 in England) 24 January 1846. Three children: Alice Ann, Mary Asenath, and Stephen Longstroth. Sealed to Mary Thompson (born 1827 in England) 27 January 1846. Two children: Phebe Amelia and Jennetta. Sealed to Jane Hall (born 1826 in England) 6 February 1846. Sealed to Ann Reed (born 1794 in England) 6 February 1846. Married Susan Bayliss about 1847. One child: Mary Ann. Entered Salt Lake Valley July 1847. Sustained as counselor to Brigham Young in First Presidency 27 December 1847. Married Rhoda Harriet Foss 21 November 1851. One child: Calvin Willard. Died 11 March 1854, in Salt Lake City, Utah.[5]

Biographical Note.   John Taylor.

Son of James Taylor and Agnes Taylor. Born 1 November 1808 in Milnthorpe, Westmoreland County, England. Joined Methodist Church about 1823; subsequently appointed preacher. Emigrated to Toronto, Canada, 1828-29. Married Leonora Cannon (born 1796 at Isle of Man) 28 January 1833 in Toronto. Four children: George John, Mary Ann, Joseph James, and Leonora Agnes. Baptized 9 May 1836 by Parley P. Pratt, and ordained elder shortly thereafter. Visited Kirtland March 1837. Ordained high priest 21 August 1837. Appointed by revelation 8 July 1838 to be ordained apostle. Moved to Missouri in fall of 1838. Ordained apostle 19 December 1838 in Far West, Missouri. Located temporarily in Quincy, Illinois, 1839. Accompanied others of Twelve to Far West, Missouri, 26 April 1838. Located family at Montrose, Iowa, 1839. Mission to England 1839-41. Left Montrose 8 August 1839. Arrived Liverpool 11 January 1840. Left Liverpool for United States 20 April 1841. Arrived in Nauvoo 1 July 1841. Elected member of Nauvoo City Council and Nauvoo Legion, and regent of Nauvoo University. Appointed associate editor of the *Times and Seasons* 3 February 1842. Initiated into Masonry 22 April 1842. Editor-in-chief of *Times and Seasons* 1842-1846. Editor and proprietor of *Nauvoo Neighbor* May 1843-October 1845. Received endowment 28 September 1843. Sealed to Elizabeth Kaighin 12 December 1843. Three children: Josephine, Thomas Edward, and Arthur Bruce. Sealed to Jane Ballantyne 25 February 1844. Three children: Richard James, Annie Maria, and David John. Member of Council of Fifty 10 March 1844. Accompanied Prophet to Carthage Jail June 1844. Received four balls into body from guns of mob 27 June 1844. Sealed to Mary Ann Oakley April 1845. Five children: Henry Edgar, Mary Elizabeth, Brigham John, Ida Oakley, and Ezra Oakley. Nauvoo Temple sealing to Leonora Cannon 7 January 1846. Nauvoo Temple sealing to Elizabeth Kaighin (born 1811 in Isle of Man) 14 January 1846. Nauvoo Temple sealing to Jane Ballantyne (born 1813 in Scotland) 14 January 1846. Nauvoo Temple sealing to Mary Ann Oakley (born 1826 in New York) 14 January 1846. Nauvoo Temple sealing to Mary Rainsbottom (born 1826 in England) 23

January 1846. Nauvoo Temple sealing for time to Lydia Dibble 30 January 1846. Left Nauvoo for West in spring of 1846. To Winter Quarters 1846. Mission to England 1846-47. Arrived in England 3 October 1846. Sealed to Sophia Whitaker (born 1825 in England) 23 April 1847 at Winter Quarters. Seven children: Harriet Ann Whitaker, James Whitaker, Hyrum Whitaker, John Whitaker, Helena Whitaker, Moses Whitaker, and Frederick Whitaker. To Salt Lake Valley in fall of 1847. Sealed to Harriet Whitaker (born 1825 in England) 4 December 1847 in Salt Lake Valley. Three children: Sophia Elizabeth, William Whitaker, and John. Elected associate judge of provisional State of Deseret 12 March 1849. Called on mission to France October 1849. Arrived in Liverpool 27 May 1850. Arrived in Boulogne, France, 18 June 1850. Left England for United States 6 March 1852. Arrived in Salt Lake City 20 August 1852. Appointed to preside over branches of Church in eastern states and publish paper 1854. Sealed to Margaret Young (born 1837 in Connecticut) 26 September 1856 in Salt Lake City. Nine children: Ebenezer Young, Frank Young, Leonora Young, Robert Young, Maggie Young, Nephi Young, Mary Young, Abraham Young, and Samuel Young. Published *The Mormon* in New York City February 1855-May 1857. Returned to Salt Lake City 7 August 1857. Member of Utah Territorial Legislature 1857-76. Speaker of house for five successive sessions, beginning 1857. Probate judge of Utah County 1868-70. Elected territorial superintendent of district schools in Utah 1877. Elected director of ZCMI 7 October 1877. Elected president of ZCMI 5 October 1883. President of Church 10 October 1880-25 July 1887. Died at Kaysville, Davis County, Utah, 25 July 1887.[6]

Biographical Note.   Wilford Woodruff.

Son of Aphek Woodruff and Beulah Thompson. Born 1 March 1807 at Farmington, Hartford County, Connecticut. Baptized by Zerah Pulsipher 31 December 1833 at Richland, New York. Ordained teacher 25 January 1834. Directed by Parley P. Pratt to join Zion's Camp 1 April 1834. Left Richland for Kirtland 11 April 1834. Arrived in Kirtland 25 April 1834. Member of Zion's Camp 1834. Worked in Clay County, Missouri, June-November 1834. Ordained priest 5 November 1834. Mission to Arkansas, Tennessee, and Kentucky November 1834-December 1836. Preached with Warren Parrish, Abraham O. Smoot, and David W. Patten. Ordained elder 1835. Ordained seventy 31 May 1836. Attended solemn assembly in Kirtland Temple April 1837. Charter member of and owned stock in Kirtland Safety Society 1837. Married Phoebe Whitmore Carter 13 April 1837. Nine children: Sarah Emma, Wilford, Jr., Phoebe Amelia, Susan Cornelia, Joseph, Ezra, Sarah Carter, Beulah Augusta, and Aphek. Received patriarchal blessing 15 April 1837. Mission with Jonathan H. Hale to Fox Islands May-October 1837. Left Kirtland May 1837. Arrived at North Fox Islands 20 August 1837. Left Fox Islands for Maine 2 October 1837. Parted company with Hale October 1837. Returned to Fox Island 1 November 1837.

Revelation dated 8 July 1838 called Woodruff to apostleship. Helped Saints from Fox Islands prepare to gather to Missouri 1838. Left for Missouri October 1838; frustrated by Boggs's extermination order. Located temporarily in Quincy, Illinois, in spring of 1839. Accompanied members of Twelve to Far West, Missouri, April 1839. Ordained apostle by Brigham Young 26 April 1839 at Far West, Missouri. Located family in Montrose, Iowa, 18 May 1839. Mission to England 1839-41. Left for England 8 August 1839. Arrived in Liverpool 11 January 1840. Left for America 20 April 1841. Arrived in Nauvoo 6 October 1841. Elected to Nauvoo City Council 30 October 1841. Mission to eastern states to collect funds for construction of Nauvoo House and Temple 7 July-4 November 1843. Sealed to wife, Phoebe, 11 November 1843. Received endowment 2 December 1843. Mission to eastern states May-August 1844 to campaign for Joseph Smith as President of United States. Returned to Nauvoo 6 August 1844. Appointed to preside over European mission 12 August 1844. Left Nauvoo 28 August 1844. Arrived in Liverpool 3 January 1845. Left Liverpool for United States 15 January 1846. Returned to Nauvoo 13 April 1846. Sealed to Mary Ann Jackson 15 April 1846. One child: James Jackson. Left Nauvoo for West May 1846. Reached Council Bluffs 7 July 1846. Crossed Missouri River to Nebraska 25 July 1846. To Salt Lake Valley July 1847. Returned to Winter Quarters late 1847. Mission to New England 1848. Left Winter Quarters 21 June 1848. Returned to Council Bluffs 16 May 1850. Left for Salt Lake Valley 21 May 1850. Arrived in Salt Lake Valley 14 October 1850. Accompanied First Presidency on tour of southern Utah in spring and summer 1852. Member of Utah Territorial Legislature. Sealed to Emma Smith 13 March 1853. Eight children: Hyrum Smith, Emma Manella, Asahel Hart, Ann Thompson, Clara Martisha, Abraham Owen, Winnifred Blanch, and Mary Alice. Sealed to Sarah Brown 13 March 1853. Eight children: David Patten, Brigham Young, Phoebe Arabella, Sylvia Melvina, Newton, Mary, Charles Henry, and Edward Randolph. Chosen president of Salt Lake Horticulture Society 13 September 1853. Appointed assistant historian of Church 7 April 1856. Played major role in compiling and writing Manuscript History of the Church. Sealed to Sarah Delight Stocking 31 July 1857. Seven children: Marion, Emeline, Ensign, Jeremiah, Rosanna, John Jay, and Julia Delight Stocking. Traveled to California to attend California State Fair 1872. President of Deseret Agricultural and Manufacturing Society of Utah. Offered dedicatory prayer at St. George Temple January 1877. Appointed to preside over St. George Temple 1877. Mission to Arizona March 1879-March 1880. Appointed President of Quorum of Twelve Apostles 10 October 1880. Mission to Colorado 1883. Mission to Snake River and Teton Valley in Idaho 1884. President of Church 7 April 1889-2 September 1898. Traveled to California September 1890. Issued "Manifesto" 24 September 1890. Dedicated Salt Lake Temple 6 April 1893. Traveled to Alaska in summer of 1895. Left Utah for California 13 August 1898. Died 2 September 1898 at San Francisco, San Francisco County, California.[7]

Section 119

Date.   8 July 1838.

Place.   Far West, Caldwell County, Missouri.

Historical Note.   On 6 December 1837, seven months prior to the reception of section 119, Edward Partridge, John Corrill, and Isaac Morley were appointed as a committee to adopt a plan whereby revenue could be raised to defray Church expenses. Their report, given the following day, proposed a voluntary tithing program to assist the poor, compensate Church leaders for services while attending to Church business, and pay for other related Church expenses. The donation, which was to be based on assets, not income, considered widows not having assets over $75 exempt, and it provided for a yearly inventory with the Church bishop.[1]

This voluntary contribution initiative apparently was never implemented, but it undoubtedly served as a prelude to section 119.

On 8 July 1838 Joseph Smith and others inquired of the Lord, saying, "O Lord, show unto thy servants how much thou requirest of the properties of thy people for a tithing."[2] The language of this revelation makes it clear that "tithing" did not simply connote ten per cent, but contribution. The proposed tithing of 1837, the language of section 119, and the history of the period affirm that this revelation was establishing the requirements of the law of consecration as it was then understood. To "be tithed" was to comply with the requirements of the law of consecration—a one-time donation of one's "surplus" properties (i.e., real and personal properties that could be reasonably sacrificed), and subsequently, ten per cent of one's "interest" (i.e., profits).

The 1833-1838 phase of the law of consecration (essentially devoid of deeded stewardships) was characterized by a contribution of surplus (real and personal) property. Because times were meager and members could exercise discretion in assessing their "surplus," the collection of an absolute ten per cent of one's profits was seen as necessary for the economic survival of the Church.

Concerning section 119 and the consecration of surplus properties, Brigham Young later stated,

> When the revelation [was] given in 1838, I was present, and recollect the feelings of the brethren. A number of

revelations were given on the same day. The brethren wished me to go among the Churches, and find out what surplus property the people had, with which to forward the building of the Temple we were commencing at Far West. I accordingly went from place to place through the country. Before I started, I asked brother Joseph, "Who shall be the judge of what is surplus property?" Said he, "Let them be the judges themselves . . . ." [I found] upon asking them about their surplus property, most of the men who owned land and cattle would say, "I have got so many hundred acres of land, and I have got so many boys, and I want each one of them to have eighty acres, therefore this is not surplus property.[3]

Publication Note.   Section 119 was first published as section 107 in the 1844 edition of the Doctrine and Covenants.

Section 120

Date.   18 July 1838 (8 July).
The correct date of reception for Section 120 is 8 July 1838. "The Scriptory Book of Joseph Smith" notes, "Revelation given the same day July 8th 1838 making known the disposition of the properties tithed as named in the proceeding revelation."[1]

Place.   Far West, Caldwell County, Missouri.

Historical Note.   Whereas prior to this time consecrated monies and properties were generally controlled and administered by the bishop of the Church, section 120 gave this responsibility to a Church council consisting of the First Presidency, the bishopric, and the high council.
On 26 July 1838 the First Presidency, the bishopric, and the high council met in Far West, Missouri to

Take into concideration the disposing of the publick properties in the hands of the Bishop, in Zion, for the people of Zion have commenced liberally to consecrate agreeably to the revelations, and commandments of the Great I Am of their surpluss properties &c

It was agreed that the first presidency keep all their properties, that they can dispose of to their advantage and support and the remainder be put into the hands of the Bishop or Bishops, agreeably to the commandments, and revelations.[2]

Publication Note. Section 120 was first published in the *Deseret News* (2 April 1853) and was included as section 120 in the 1876 edition of the Doctrine and Covenants.

Section 121

Date.   20 March 1839 (20-25 March. See Historical Note.).

Place.   Liberty, Clay County, Missouri (Liberty Jail).

Historical Note.   At Far West, Missouri, on 31 October 1838, Joseph Smith and approximately fifty others were arrested and charged with breaking the law. Although within three weeks of their arrest most of the prisoners had been either released or admitted to bail, six of them (Joseph Smith, Hyrum Smith, Sidney Rigdon, Lyman Wight, Caleb Baldwin, and Alexander McRae) were finally sent to Liberty Jail to stand trial for treason and murder.

It was during his incarceration in Liberty Jail that Joseph Smith dictated a letter to Church leaders in Quincy, Illinois. Sections 121, 122, and 123 consist of extracts from this letter, which was written between 20 and 25 March 1839.[1]

Publication Note.   Section 121 was first published in the *Times and Seasons* (May and July 1840) and was included as section 121 in the 1876 edition of the Doctrine and Covenants.

Section 122

Date.   March 1839 (20-25 March. See Historical Note for section 121.).

Place.   Liberty, Clay County, Missouri (Liberty Jail).

Historical Note.   See Historical Note for section 121. Verse 6 refers to the Prophet's arrest and heart-rending departure from his family at Far West, Missouri in November 1838. Lyman Wight described the inhumane scene:

> About the hour the prisoners were to have been shot on the public square in Far West, they were exhibited in a wagon in the town, all of them having families there, but myself; and it would have broken the heart of any person possessing an ordinary share of humanity, to have seen the separation. The aged father and mother of Joseph Smith were not permitted to see his face, but to reach their hands through the curtains of the wagon, and thus take leave of him. When passing his own house, he was taken out of the wagon and permitted to go into the house, but not without a strong guard, and not permitted to speak with his family but in the presence of his guard and his eldest son, Joseph, about six or eight years old, hanging to the tail of his coat, crying father, is the mob going to kill you? The guard said to him, "you damned little brat, go back, you will see your father no more."[1]

Publication Note.   Section 122 was first published in the *Times and Seasons* (July 1840) and was included as section 122 in the 1876 edition of the Doctrine and Covenants.

Section 123

Date.   March 1839 (20-25 March. See Section 121.).

Place.   Liberty, Clay County, Missouri (Liberty Jail).

Historical Note.   See Historical Note for section 121.
On 4 May 1839, pursuant to the instructions of section 123, Almon

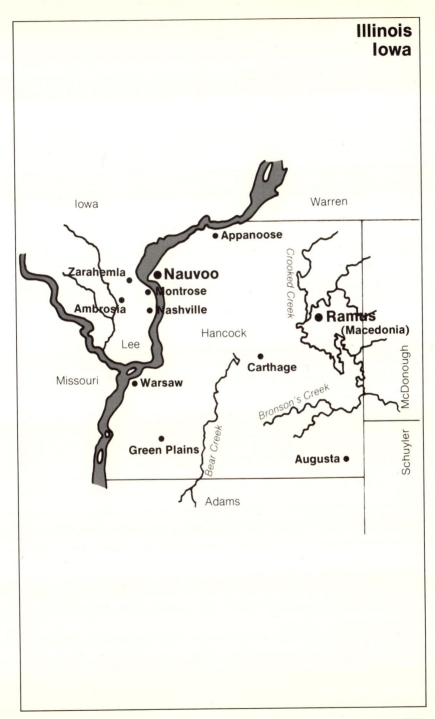

Illinois
Iowa

Iowa

Warren

Appanoose

Zarahemla

Nauvoo

Montrose

Ambrosia

Nashville

Lee

Hancock

Crooked Creek

Ramus
(Macedonia)

Missouri

Carthage

McDonough

Warsaw

Bronson's Creek

Schuyler

Green Plains

Bear Creek

Augusta

Adams

241

W. Babbitt, Erastus Snow, and Robert B. Thompson were appointed "a traveling committee to gather up and obtain all the libelous reports and publications which have been circulated against the Church" as well as "other historical matter connected with said Church, which they can possibly obtain."[1] Referring to this assignment, Erastus Snow wrote,

> [On 4 May 1839] I was appointed by the conference one of three committee to collect the libilous publications of all kinds that had been published against the saints and to insert and refute them in a church history which should be compiled by us after the conference.[2]

Joseph Smith advised that Erastus Snow and Almon W. Babbitt each travel and preach as their circumstances would permit and "gather in our travels what publications we could and send them to Elder [Robert B.] Thomson who should be writing and compiling the history which should be subject to our inspection."[3]

Publication Note.   Section 123 was first published in the *Times and Seasons* (July 1840) and was included as section 123 in the 1876 edition of the Doctrine and Covenants.

Section 124

Date.   19 January 1841.

Place.   Nauvoo, Hancock County, Illinois.

Historical Note.   After the Prophet was freed from his Missouri imprisonment (16 April 1839), immediate plans were made to locate the Saints at another gathering place. Upon viewing properties in Lee County, Iowa, and Hancock County, Illinois, Church land agents purchased thousands of acres of unimproved land in these two counties, and soon Nauvoo (Commerce) became the headquarters of the Church.

With the land problem temporarily solved, Joseph Smith turned his attention to balancing accounts for wrongs suffered in Missouri. With others, the Prophet traveled to Washington, D.C., November 1839-March 1840, where he held audience with President Martin

Van Buren, presented Congress with claims against the State of Missouri, and lobbied for redress of Missouri grievances. After achieving little or no success in the East, Joseph Smith returned to Nauvoo, where he began to build up and strengthen the Church. Section 124, the first known revelation since July 1838, was received about four weeks after the governor of Illinois had signed charters for the city of Nauvoo, the University of Nauvoo, the Nauvoo House Association, the Nauvoo Agricultural and Mechanical Association, and the Nauvoo Legion. The revelation had monumental importance to the Prophet and his associates because its fulfillment engaged nearly every waking moment of the Prophet's time until his death. Following is a discussion of the major topics contained in this "famous revelation."[1]

The proclamation to the kings of the earth.   (See verses 2-14, 16, and 107.) The revelation specified that Robert B. Thompson, the Prophet's scribe, was to help write the document, and that John C. Bennett should assist in its dissemination. However, Thompson's premature death and Bennett's apostasy precluded either contributing to the project. The Prophet first gave attention to the proclamation on 22 December 1841, when he "commenced giving instructions to the scribe [Willard Richards] concerning writing the proclamation to the kings of the earth,"[2] but it appears that other pressures took precedence: by 15 November 1843 the Prophet still spoke of the writing as a future work.[3] On 21 November 1843 Joseph Smith directed Willard Richards, Orson Hyde, John Taylor and William W. Phelps to proceed with the writing,[4] but again other demands hindered any significant progress. In January 1844 a branch of the Church was invited to donate means to forward the writing of the proclamation,[5] and finally, in the spring of 1844, one of Joseph's scribes was able to proceed in earnest. William W. Phelps reported in 1863 that he was specially commissioned in May 1844 to write the "great proclamation" under the direction of the Prophet and that he had in his possession twenty-two manuscript pages that Joseph Smith had approved. He lamented, however, that the project was dropped after the martyrdom.[6] In 1845 the Quorum of the Twelve Apostles essentially fulfilled the instructions of section 124 by publishing their proclamation to the kings of the world.[7]

The construction of the Nauvoo House.   (See verses 22-24, 56-82, 111-12, 117, and 119-22.) Before the reception of section 124, a bill had already been presented to the Illinois state legislature for the incorporation of an association to sell stock for the purpose of constructing a hotel in the city of Nauvoo. An act to incorporate the Nauvoo House Association, approved on 23 February 1841, named four trustees: George Miller, Lyman Wight, John Snyder, and Peter Haws. These men were duly authorized to sell $150,000 worth of stock from which proceeds the hotel would be built. Each share was valued at $50, and no stockholder could own more than 300 shares (i.e., $15,000). Since the edifice was to be constructed on land donated by Joseph Smith, the Prophet and his heirs were to retain a set of rooms in the building for their use. Sale of spirituous liquors in the house was to be prohibited.[8]

The Prophet considered the construction of the Nauvoo House just as urgent and sacred as the completion of the Nauvoo Temple. George Miller was appointed president of the association with John Snyder as secretary. Lucian Woodworth was the architect. The hotel was to be in the form of an "L"—having a 120-foot front on each of two streets, a depth of 40 feet, and a height of three stories (exclusive of the basement). The construction was to be principally of brick, and the total cost of the project was estimated at from $100,000 to $150,000. Encouragement for the completion of the Nauvoo House came from the pulpit constantly.[9] The cornerstone of the building was laid by Joseph Smith on 2 October 1841, and several records were deposited therein. Of particular note among these records was a manuscript copy of section 124 and a copy of the twenty-third issue of the *Times and Seasons* (1 April 1841) which printed the charter of the Nauvoo House Association.[10] The Nauvoo House, situated as it was on the bank of the Mississippi River was intended to accommodate distinguished visitors in a facility "unrivaled in the western country."[11] Joseph Smith envisioned the Nauvoo House as a means whereby the Saints could entertain "men of wealth, character and influence" and "teach them the truth."[12]

On 20 March 1841 William Allred and Henry W. Miller were directed by revelation to buy stock in the house and serve as agents in the selling of stock.[13] For nearly four years the trustees busily engaged themselves in selling stock and collecting donations from branches of the Church throughout the United States. In the summer of 1841 it was decided that the best plan for procuring lumber for the building of the temple and the Nauvoo House was to purchase sawmills located on the Black River, a tributary of the Mississippi in Wisconsin. Trustees of the association in concert with members of the Temple committee spent untold hours in the pineries on the Black River 1841-44. Characterizing the work of these men, George Miller said, "Too much cannot be said in praise of these faithful brethren. They really performed wonders."[14] Despite the efforts of the four trustees and their hired help, however, work progressed very slowly on the hotel because means were meager.

Recognizing that the project was an excessive burden for the members of the association, Joseph Smith, on 6 April 1843, directed the Twelve Apostles to take responsibility for collecting funds, and were sent to the East in the summer and fall of 1843 for that purpose.[15] Ultimately the desire to finish the temple led to a decision (on 4 March 1844) to postpone completion of the Nauvoo House.[16] The following year (on 7 April 1845) Wight and Snyder were released as trustees, and George A. Smith and Amasa M. Lyman were appointed in their place, and in the summer of 1845 William Weeks replaced Woodworth as architect.[17] After these appointments, construction of the house resumed, and a large-scale effort was made to manufacture its bricks. On 18 August 1845 the Saints met at the Nauvoo House and dedicated the finished portion to the Lord; afterward the first brick was laid. During the next four weeks, work on the building progressed rapidly: the walls were laid up to the second story.[18] However, on 16 September 1845, work on the house was once more discontinued, because Church leaders sensed a renewed urgency to complete the temple.[19] Although the Saints intended at least to enclose the house, their exodus in the spring of 1846 precluded further progress.

With the settlement of the Prophet's estate and the liquidation of Mormon properties in Nauvoo, title to the Nauvoo House was retained by Emma Smith. Lewis C. Bidamon, Emma's second husband, later dismantled a large portion of the walls of the Nauvoo House down to the stonework of the basement and erected a two-story structure on the southwest corner of the original foundation. This building, known as the Riverside Mansion, was used as a residence by the family beginning in 1871.[20] The lot and building are now owned by the Reorganized LDS Church.

The construction of the Nauvoo Temple.   Prior to the reception of section 124, plans for the erection of a temple in Nauvoo had been disclosed by the Prophet. The official public announcement came at a general conference of the Church on 3 October 1840 in Nauvoo. At the meeting a temple committee, consisting of Reynolds Cahoon, Alpheus Cutler, and Elias Higbee, was appointed to supervise the construction of the sacred edifice. All three of this committee had worked on the Kirtland Temple. Cahoon, a veteran at this sort of work, had served as a member of the Kirtland Temple committee, and Cutler had had important responsibilities as master mason of the uncompleted temple at Far West, Missouri. Land for the temple, acquired from Daniel H. Wells, was located on the east bench of the new city, overlooking the Mississippi River. Grandest of all Nauvoo construction projects, the building of the temple would dominate the activities of the Mormon city for nearly five years. At the 3 October meeting the Prophet asked that work on the temple begin within ten days and that every tenth day be given to labor on the building. The construction plans of architect William Weeks won acceptance by Joseph Smith, and although the former would be recognized as the chief architect of the temple, his work was always subject to the latter's approval.

Excavation of the foundation began immediately, and on 12 October 1840 a quarry was opened on the outskirts of the city. Albert P. Rockwood, assisted by Charles Drury, supervised the stone-cutting from beginning to end. Work at the quarry often continued during the winter months. The walls of the temple consisted of solid blocks of cut limestone—from four to six feet thick. The stones were roughly cut at the quarry, then dressed and polished at the temple site. Mostly uniform in size and shape, some of the stones were said to have weighed as much as two tons. William W. Player, a convert from England, had come to Nauvoo specifically to direct the stone setting. He began work on 8 June 1842 and continued as principal stone-setter until the last stone was set, on 24 May 1845. The stones were moved into place by means of specially made cranes. As many as three cranes were in use by 1844. One man, Moses Horn, was killed while blasting at the quarry on 14 March 1845.

The foundation of the temple was laid out by the temple committee in early February 1840, and digging of the basement began on 18 February. To better organize the donated labor, the city was divided into wards on 22 February 1841, and each ward was assigned a particular day for working on the building.

By 8 March 1841 workers began laying the foundation stones, and by 5 April 1841 the walls were five feet high and ready for the placing of the cornerstones. April 6, 1841, was a day of much festivity in Nauvoo. Anticipating the anniversary of the organization of the Church, the Prophet had given instructions to have all things in readiness for the laying of the cornerstones. Great ceremony attended the placing of the four stones. The Nauvoo Legion paraded, bands played, a prayer of dedication was offered, and Sidney Rigdon delivered an able address to an estimated congregation of 10,000. The following day Joseph called for contributions of labor, money, and materials for the temple, and on 9 April he informed the elders that labor on the temple was as acceptable as preaching. The same day eight agents were appointed to collect funds for the building of the edifice.

Following the April conference, work on the temple progressed rapidly as the Saints began to give more liberally of their time and means. Although labor had been essentially donated up to that time, the increase in contributions allowed the temple committee to hire a number of skilled craftsmen on a permanent basis.

By July 1841 plans were under way to erect a pinewood baptistry in the basement of the temple. Plans drafted by Weeks for the font were approved, and work began on 8 August 1841. The font was constructed promptly and was dedicated on 8 November 1841 by Joseph Smith. The baptistry was approximately sixteen feet long, twelve feet wide, and seven feet high from the foundation, and the basin was four feet deep. Twelve life-sized wooden oxen, carved by Elijah Fordham, supported the font. Water for the baptistry was drawn from a thirty-foot well in the east end of the basement. In 1845 the wooden font was replaced with one of stone.

As has been mentioned elsewhere, timber for the temple interior was acquired from the forests of Wisconsin. Alpheus Cutler, Peter Haws, and others left Nauvoo to cut timber in the "pineries" on 25 September 1841. In late April of the following year, another company left to join the original group; a third party, consisting of some fifty men with keel boats and provisions, departed Nauvoo on 6 July 1842.

The first lumber reached the Mormon city on 4 August 1842, consisting of 100,000 board feet of sawed lumber, and 192,000 square feet of rough timber. Alpheus Cutler returned to Nauvoo on 13 August 1842 with a second raft containing 90,000 board feet and 288,000 square feet of timber. George Miller, Nauvoo House Association member, led another group to the Wisconsin pineries in late 1842. Their work yielded at least three loads of lumber in 1843 consisting of some 650,000 board feet of lumber and seventy thousand shingles. Two additional rafts, laden with 155,684 board feet of lumber, arrived in Nauvoo in July 1844. One man, named Cunningham, was drowned while rafting logs in the summer of 1843.

The Nauvoo Temple, not unlike the Kirtland Temple, was of a high rectangular shape with double rows of windows and with a tower rising from the main body. The dimensions were imposing:

188 feet long by 88 feet wide, and from the basement to the tower the height was about 159 feet. The building was divided into four levels—a basement, two almost identical stories, and an attic.

The basement was divided off into thirteen rooms—six along either side, and one lage room (100 feet by 50 feet) running through the center. The baptismal font was in the center of the main room, and at the east end was the well.

The first story, entered by the main entrance on the west, was not completed, but the plan was to divide it into fifteen rooms—a large central auditorium (100 feet by 50 feet) with smaller rooms along each side. The ceiling was of an arched design, plastered and painted. Tiered pulpits, for the Melchizedek and Aaronic priesthoods, were located at either end of the hall. The second level, nearly identical in size, was intended to be a duplicate of the first.

Rising above the temple's massive limestone walls was the attic. The western section, called the "half-story," was more than eighty feet long and forty feet wide. Accessed by either of two large, circular staircases, the half-story was divided into a number of rooms. Passing the outer and inner courts, one could gain access to the Council Chamber, a long hall running the remaining length of the attic to the east. This hall was partitioned off for temple ordinance work. Along each side of the Council Chamber were six small rooms assigned to individuals or priesthood quorums.

On 13 December 1841 Willard Richards was appointed recorder of temple donations. His office was located in the "counting room" of the Prophet's red-brick store. Before this, Elias Higbee had occupied nearly all his time issuing receipts for donations. But earlier that year, when Joseph became sole Trustee-in-Trust for the Church, it was decided that all donations should come through his office.

Donors and amounts were logged into a special record book called the "Book of the Law of the Lord." The Saints were to contribute one tenth of all they possessed at the commencement of the temple construction, and one tenth of all increase from that time until its completion. On 10 February 1842 William Clayton was called to assist Richards, and on 3 September 1842, after the latter's departure to the eastern states, the Prophet appointed Clayton official Temple Recorder. James Whitehead became Clayton's assistant on 11 June 1842. In the fall of 1842 it was agreed that the recorder's office should be moved to better accommodate the interests of the committee and the recorders. Accordingly, the temple committee directed the construction of a small brick recorder's office near the temple, and on 2 November 1842 Clayton moved his records and other materials into the new building. A new tithing office was opened in December 1844 at Parley P. Pratt's new store one block north of the temple.

Members of the temple committee commanded an important but rather thankless job. They had the enormous task of coordinating the entire work force. Although the number of workers fluctuated over a five year period, the committee would hire at least 1,221 men—885 of whom worked at least one month. Nor do these figures include the donated labor of literally hundreds of workers during the same period. Nearly always under attack, the committee was criticized by the employees for poor working conditions, lack of tools, insufficient wages, favoritism, unequal distribution of provisions, and misappropriation of funds. Members of the committee were several times summoned to Church courts to give testimony relative to their actions but were always exonerated.

On 8 June 1843 Elias Higbee died, leaving a vacancy in the committee. Jared Carter, a member of the temple committee at Kirtland, immediately applied for the position, but because he was rebellious, the Prophet chose his own brother, Hyrum, also one of the Kirtland temple committee.

In August 1844, after the Prophet's death, Bishops Newel K. Whitney and George Miller were appointed Trustees-in-Trust for the Church and accordingly were given general oversight of temple construction. By December of the same year, following an administrative reorganization among the Trustees and the temple committee, the bishops and their staff assumed greater responsibility over the project.

In December 1844, before the completion of the stonework, the Twelve and the Trustees decided to employ fifteen carpenters to prepare the timber works for the interior of the temple as soon as the stonework was finished. A makeshift shop was fixed up by weather-boarding the south side of the lower story.

After completion of the stonework in May 1845, attention was promptly given to the roof. By 13 August 1845 the last shingle had been laid, and before the end of August Brigham Young reported that the dome and cap of the temple tower had been raised. The structure now being properly enclosed, the October 1845 general conference was held inside.

As the interior work continued feverishly, the attic story took precedence. On 26 November 1845 the painters finished their work, and on 30 November Brigham Young dedicated the attic for temple work. Immediately thereafter special furniture was obtained to prepare the attic for the administering of endowment ceremonies. Ordinance work began on 10 December 1845 and continued until 8 February 1846.

Although the Saints began to leave Nauvoo for the west in February 1846, construction workers continued to work on the temple interior until 1 May 1846, when it was publicly dedicated (though not totally completed). After the departure of most of the Mormon population in 1846, a committee unsuccessfully attempted to sell the temple, but concern for the sacred edifice ended on 9 October 1848, when it was completely destroyed by fire. The temple lot in Nauvoo is now owned by the Church.

The Priesthood ordinances of the temple. (See verses 28, 40-42, 55, 95, and 97). Whereas the term *endowment* has come to be known as the embodiment of certain priesthood ordinances performed in the temple, Kirtland usage of the term connoted, not the ordinances themselves, but rather the outpouring of the spirit upon those who had participated in the ordinances. (See discussion under section 108). In Nauvoo the temple ordinances (wherein the Saints performed washings, and anointings and received signs and tokens of the Holy Priesthood), were known as the "ancient order of the Priesthood" or simply as the "endowment," there being no particular attempt to distinguish between the ceremony and the spiritual outpouring. On 4 May 1842, before the completion of the temple, the Prophet initiated nine men into the ancient order. Though Joseph had expected to administer these sacred ordinances only after the temple was finished, yet a sense that he might not live to see its completion urged him to proceed earlier. By June 1844, just before his death, the Prophet had selected twenty-five males and thirty-two females to receive the ordinances of the endowment. After his death, but before the completion of the attic of the temple, another twenty also received the endowment. On 10 December 1845 endowment work commenced in the attic story of the temple. There, during the next eight weeks, nearly 5,600 members (males and females) participated in these ceremonies. Related ordinances administered by the Prophet before the completion of the temple included eternal marriages, baptisms for the dead, and conferring the fulness of the priesthood. Approximately one hundred fifty people were eternally sealed to their companions under the direction of Joseph Smith beginning 5 April 1841. Baptisms for the dead commenced about 15 August 1840. Initially these ordinances were performed in the Mississippi River and local streams, but with few exceptions proxy baptisms were performed only in the temple baptistry after 21 November 1841. Some of these early baptisms were not properly recorded, but extant records indicate that at least 15,626 proxy baptisms were performed in Nauvoo (either in the baptistry or in rivers or streams). Of forty-four men and women who received the fulness of the Priesthood before the completion of the Nauvoo Temple, thirty-five received the blessing from Joseph Smith.[22]

The reorganization of priesthood quorums. Apostasy, death, and other changes necessitated the reorganization of the various quorums and offices in the Church government at Nauvoo. The death of Patriarch Joseph Smith, Sr., in 1840 left a vacancy which was filled by his son, Hyrum (see verse 124). The latter also assumed the "same blessing, and glory, and honor, and priesthood" that Oliver Cowdery had held before his excommunication in 1838 (see verse 95). The vacancy left in the First Presidency by Hyrum Smith's new appointment was filled by William Law (verse 126). Brigham Young was named president of the Quorum of the Twelve Apostles (verse 127). (Although only eleven are named in the revelation, Lyman Wight was called to complete the quorum in April 1841.)[23] The Nauvoo High Council had been organized on 6 October 1839 with William Marks as president. Seymour Brunson, one of the High Council, had died in August 1840, and the vacancy was filled by Aaron Johnson (verse 132). Oddly enough William Marks is not named in the revelation, though he was the president of the Nauvoo Stake. He selected Charles C. Rich and Austin Cowles as counselors on 29 March 1841.[24] Samuel Rolfe, named president of the priests' quorum, chose Stephen Markham and Hezekiah Peck as his counselors on 21 March 1841.[25] The presidencies of the teachers and deacons quorums were also appointed on 21 March 1841. The presidency of the former comprised Elisha Everett, James W. Huntsman, and James Hendricks; the presidency of the latter was Phinehas R. Bird, David Wood, and William W. Lane.[26]

Publication Note.   Section 124 was first published in the *Times and Seasons* (1 June 1841) and was included as section 103 in the 1844 edition of the Doctrine and Covenants.

Biographical Note.   Almon Whiting Babbitt.

Son of Ira and Nancy Babbitt. Born 1 October 1812 in Cheshire, Berkshire County, Massachusetts. Baptized 1833. Member of Zion's Camp 1834.

Ordained seventy February 1835. Tried before Kirtland high council 19
August 1835 for not keeping Word of Wisdom and for stating that Book of
Mormon not essential to salvation of Saints but that Bible was only scripture
of their faith. Forgiven upon confession. Tried before Kirtland High
Council on 28 December 1835 for traducing character of Joseph Smith.
Forgiven upon confession 2 January 1836. Mission to Upper Canada 1837-
38. Arrived in Caldwell County, Missouri, with company of Canadian
Saints July 1838. Expelled from Missouri 1839. Appointed with others 4 May
1839 to gather libelous reports and publications against Church. Tried by
Nauvoo high council on 5 September 1840 for making false statements
against Joseph Smith. Acquitted 6 September 1840. Appointed president of
Kirtland Stake 22 May 1841. Disfellowshipped 2 October 1841 for teaching
and promoting building up of Kirtland as place of gathering, instead of
Nauvoo, Illinois. Subsequently made satisfaction. Moved to Illinois in 1842.
Appointed presiding elder of Ramus, Illinois, branch of Church 13 March
1843. Disfellowshipped March-April 1843 for impropriety. Restored to
fellowship 10 April 1843. Appointed to serve mission to France 6 May 1844;
did not fulfill assignment. Elected to state legislature, representing Hancock
County, Illinois, 1844. Received endowment 12 May 1844. Member of
Council of Fifty by 11 April 1844. Attorney by profession. Frequently
employed as counsel for Church. Sealed to Julia Ann Johnson (born 1809 in
Vermont) 24 January 1846. Date of civil marriage not known. Three known
children: Don Carlos, Almon W., and Julia. Sealed to Mary Tulley (born 1810
in England) 24 January 1846. Sealed to Dulcena Didamia Johnson Sherman
for time 24 January 1846. Remained in Nauvoo after Mormon exodus to take
charge of Mormon property there. Involved in battle at Nauvoo in
September 1846. Signed treaty by which Saints agreed to surrender city to
non-Mormons. To Utah 1848. Elected delegate to Congress for provisional
State of Deseret 1849. Left for Washington, D.C., in fall of 1849. Not seated.
Residing in Nauvoo 1850. Disfellowshipped in Kanesville, Iowa, May 1851
for immorality and intemperance. Appointed secretary of Utah Territory
1852. Left Utah for Washington, D.C., 22 April 1856 to purchase supplies for
new statehouse in Salt Lake City. Returning to Utah, killed 7 September
1856 by Cheyenne Indians at Ash Hollow, Nebraska.[27]

Biographical Note.   Jesse Baker.

Born 23 January 1778. Married Sarah (born 22 May 1782). Joined Church by
1837. Ordained elder 1837. Charter member of and owned stock in Kirtland
Safety Society January 1837. Member of Kirtland Camp 1838. Expelled from
Missouri 1838-39. Signed petition to Congress for redress of Missouri
grievances 29 November 1839. Appointed by revelation 19 January 1841 to
be counselor to John A. Hicks in elders quorum in Nauvoo. Received
endowment 15 December 1845.[28]

Biographical Note. John Cook Bennett.

Son of John Bennett and Abagail Cooke. Born 4 August 1804 at Fairhaven, Bristol County, Massachusetts. Early childhood in Washington County, Ohio. Married Mary A. Barker of Washington County, Ohio. Two known children: one son, who graduated from West Point, and one daughter. Later separated. Studied medicine under Dr. Samuel Preston Hildreth of Marietta, Ohio. Licensed as physician by Twelfth District Medical Society 1 November 1825. Practiced medicine in Ohio and West Virginia 1825-32. Initiated into Masonry in Ohio 1826. After obtaining charter, with others founded nonsectarian Christian College in New Albany, Indiana. Name of college changed to Indiana University. Gave instruction, but sold many diplomas. After two years in Indiana, returned to Ohio. Married Sarah Ryder (born 1809 to Job Ryder and Sarah Cassidy). Published articles in the *Western Journal of the Medical and Physical Sciences* 1830. In 1834 employed as agent to solicit funds for Willoughby University of Lake Erie, incorporated March 1834. Assisted in founding medical college at Willoughby in fall of 1834. Dismissed by March 1835 but retained title of Professor of Midwifery, Diseases of Women and Children, and Medical Jurisprudence. Published *The Accouchers Vade Mecum* in 1837. Moved to Illinois 1838; practiced medicine for two years at Fairfield, Wayne County. Appointed brigadier general of Second Division of Illinois Militia by Governor Thomas Carlin 20 February 1839. Appointed quartermaster general of State of Illinois by Carlin 20 July 1840. Active in founding Illinois State Medical Society 1840. Moved to Nauvoo September 1840. Baptized about September 1840. Instrumental in obtaining charters for City of Nauvoo, Nauvoo Legion, and University of Nauvoo in December 1840. Elected first mayor of Nauvoo, chancellor of University of Nauvoo, and major-general of Nauvoo Legion. Appointed assistant president to Joseph Smith 8 April 1841. (This position to be temporary, until Sidney Rigdon recovered from illness.) Appointed master in chancery for Hancock County, Illinois, by Stephen A. Douglas 6 May 1841. Interested in tomato for medicinal use. Resigned office of mayor of Nauvoo 17 May 1842. Excommunicated 25 May 1842 for adultery and teaching that illicit intercourse was condoned by Church leaders. While in Nauvoo wrote articles defending Church under pen name of Joab. Left Nauvoo by June 1842. Published *The History of the Saints; or, An Expose of Joe Smith and Mormonism* (Boston: Leland & Whiting, 1842). Lectured against Church after excommunication. Associated with James J. Strang after Prophet's death. Organized poultry show in Boston 1849. Had moved to Plymouth, Massachusetts, by 1850. Originated Plymouth Rock chicken. Published *The Poultry Book: A Treatise on Breeding and General Management of Domestic Fowls* (Boston: Phillips, Sampson and Co., 1856). Moved to Madison Township, Polk County, Iowa, by 1860; there practiced medicine. Wife died 15 July 1863 and buried at Polk City, Iowa. Died 5 August 1867; buried at Polk City, Polk County, Iowa.[29]

Biographical Note.   Samuel Bent.

Son of Joel Bent. Born 19 July 1778 at Barre, Worcester County, Massachusetts. Married Mary Hilbourne (born 1785 in Vermont) about 1805. Four known children: William, Joseph, Horatio, and Mary. Member of Congregationalist and Presbyterian churches before conversion to Mormonism. Colonel in Massachusetts Militia. Learned of Mormonism from Elmira Scobie. Baptized by Jared Carter in Pontiac, Michigan, January 1833. Ordained elder day of baptism. Mission to Michigan January 1833. Visited Kirtland 1833. Member of Zion's Camp 1834. Attended School of Prophets 1835. Attended Kirtland Temple dedication March 1836. Moved to Clay County, Missouri, 1836. After death of wife, Mary, married Lettice Palmer (widow of Ambrose Palmer) September 1837. Located near Far West, Missouri, 1836. Appointed member of Far West high council 6 October 1838. Expelled from Missouri 1839. Located in Nauvoo 1839. Appointed member of Nauvoo high council 6 October 1839. Sent on mission to collect money for printing purposes 17 July 1840. Traveled in Illinois, Indiana, and Ohio. Member of Nauvoo Legion. Member of Council of Fifty 19 March 1844. Mission to Michigan 1844. Received endowment 13 December 1845. Sealed to Lettice Palmer for time 14 January 1846. Sealed in Nauvoo Temple to Cynthia Noble (born 1806 in New York) 14 January 1846. Sealed in Nauvoo Temple to Mariah Thompson (born 1808 in Vermont) 14 January 1846. Sealed to Asenath Slafter (born 1796 in Connecticut) 28 January 1846. Sealed to Elizabeth Burgess (born 1789 in Massachusetts) 28 January 1846. Sealed to Polly Smith for time 30 January 1846. Left Nauvoo for West 1846. Appointed to preside over Church at Garden Grove, Iowa. Died 16 August 1846 at Garden Grove, Iowa.[30]

Biographical Note.   Josiah Butterfield.

Son of Abel and Mercy Butterfield. Born 13 March 1795 at Dunstable, Middlesex County, Massachusetts. Married Polly Moulton 30 October 1819. One known child: Josiah. Residing in Buxton, Maine, 1820-30. Baptized in Maine 1 October 1833 by John F. Boynton and Evan M. Greene. Moved to Kirtland, Ohio, about 1834. Worked on Kirtland Temple. Received blessing 7 March 1835 for working on Kirtland Temple. Ordained elder before 1836. Ordained seventy 1836. Charter member of and owned stock in Kirtland Safety Society January 1837. Ordained president of First Quorum of Seventy 6 April 1837. Owned property in Kirtland 1837-38. Member of Kirtland high council 1837; functioning simultaneously as seventy. Assisted in leading Kirtland Camp to Missouri 1838. Expelled from Missouri 1839. Located at Bear Creek, Adams County, Illinois, 1839. Wife, Polly, died 28 October 1840 at Bear Creek. Married Margaret Lawrence (mother of Sarah and Maria Lawrence). Margaret born 29 April 1801 in Toronto, Canada. Argued with

Joseph Smith over Lawrence estate. Appointed to preach in Maine April 1844. Excommunicated 7 October 1844. Later rebaptized. Received endowment 20 January 1846 in Nauvoo Temple. Remained in Midwest until about 1850. Moved to California by 1853. Married Clarinda. Two known children: Mary and Charles. Died 3 March 1871 at Watsonville, Santa Cruz County, California.[31]

Biographical Note. John Alpheus Cutler.

Son of Knight Cutler and Elizabeth Boyd. Born 29 February 1784 in Plainfield, Cheshire County, New Hampshire. Married Lois Lathrop (born 1788 in New Hampshire) in 1808. Ten children: Thaddeus, Libbeus, Louisa Elizabeth, Sally, William, Benjamin F., Clarissa, Emily, Edwin H., and Betsy A. Moved to New York about 1809. Served in War of 1812. Moved to Wayne County, New York, about 1821. Baptized 20 January 1833. Ordained elder shortly thereafter. Moved to Kirtland, Ohio, by summer of 1834. Worked on Kirtland Temple. Received blessing 7 March 1835 for working on Kirtland Temple. Participated with elders quorum in washings and anointings in Kirtland Temple January 1836. Attended dedication of Kirtland Temple March 1836. Ordained high priest 29 April 1836. Moved to Caldwell County, Missouri, 1836; there purchased land October 1836. Later settled in Ray County, Missouri. Appointed master workman of temple at Far West, Missouri. Expelled from Missouri 1839. Located in Nauvoo in summer of 1839. Appointed member of Nauvoo high council 6 October 1839. Designated as architect for contemplated stone schoolhouse in Nauvoo 28 October 1839. Appointed member of Committee to build Nauvoo Temple 3 October 1840. On Black River in Wisconsin, obtained lumber for construction of Nauvoo House and Temple 1841-42. Received endowment 12 October 1843. Member of Council of Fifty 11 March 1844. Sealed to Luana Hart Beebe Rockwell 14 January 1846. Sealed in Nauvoo Temple to Margaret Carr (born 1771 in North Carolina) 3 February 1846. Sealed in Nauvoo Temple to Abigail Carr (born 1780 in North Carolina) 3 February 1846. Sealed in Nauvoo Temple to Sally Cox (born 1794 in New Jersey) 3 February 1846. Sealed in Nauvoo Temple to Disey Caroline McCall (born 1802 in North Carolina) 3 February 1846. Sealed in Nauvoo Temple to Henrietta Clarinda Miller (born 1822 in New York) 3 February 1846. Left Nauvoo for West February 1846. Located in Cutler's Park, Nebraska. Appointed presiding member of "Municipal High Council" in Cutler's Park 9 August 1846. Appointed to locate site for Winter Quarters 8 September 1846. Site found 11 September 1846. Rejected leadership of Brigham Young. Settled on Spring Creek, Mills County, Iowa, 1848. Moved to Manti, Fremont County, Iowa, about 1853. Organized "The True Church of Jesus Christ" 19 September 1853. Died 10 August 1864 at Manti, Iowa.[32]

Biographical Note.   Amos Davis.

Son of Wells and Mary Davis. Born 20 September 1813 at Hopkinton, Rockingham County, New Hampshire. Residing in Illinois by 1837. Merchant and landowner in Nauvoo. Married Elvira Maria Hibbard 1 January 1837. Three known children: Orin Wales, Robert, and Isabell Elvira. Appointed postmaster of Commerce 27 July 1839. Baptized between 5 and 9 April 1840. Traveled to Vermont to visit relatives June-September 1840. Appointed by revelation to pay stock into Nauvoo House 19 January 1841. Traveled to Philadelphia April-September 1843. Issued six-month license to sell merchandise 25 December 1843. Did not migrate west with Saints 1846. Divorced Elvira Hibbard April 1847. Married Catherine Cormack in Hancock County, Illinois, 26 July 1848. Married Harriet Louisa Andrus 27 January 1850. Five known children: Infant, Ethan Culver, George Edmund, Dick Herbert, and Chloe Elisa. Traveled to California in summer of 1850 to dig for gold. Residing in Michigan 1853. Returned to Illinois by 1858. Wife Harriett died 4 February 1866. Married Mary Jane Isenberger 12 April 1866. Four known children: Amos, Jacob Wells, Mary Jane, and Guy. Died 22 March 1872 at Big Mound, Hancock County, Illinois.[33]

Biographical Note.   David Dort.

Born in 1793. Residing in Gilsum, New Hampshire, 1820. Moved to Pontiac, Michigan, by 1830. Converted to Mormonism through Lucy Mack Smith 1831. Accompanied Michigan Saints to Missouri 1834. Joined Zion's Camp 8 June 1834 in Monroe County, Missouri. Member of Zion's Camp. Returned to Michigan by 1835. Located in Kirtland by 1836. Paid personal property tax on livestock in Kirtland 1837. Charter member of Kirtland Safety Society January 1837. Member of Kirtland high council September 1837. Moved to Far West, Missouri, 1838. Member of high council at Far West, Missouri, 1838-39. Located in Nauvoo 1839. Member of Nauvoo high council 1839-41. Died 10 March 1841 at Nauvoo, Hancock County, Illinois.[34]

Biographical Note.   James Foster.

Born 1 April 1775. Baptized before 1834. Member of Zion's Camp 1834. Ordained elder by 1835. Participated in solemn assembly in Kirtland Temple 1837. Ordained President of First Quorum of Seventy 6 April 1837. Temporary member of Kirtland high council simultaneous with calling as seventy 1837. Assisted in organization and march of Kirtland Camp 1838. Moved to Missouri with Kirtland Camp 1838. Expelled from Missouri 1839. Tried for impropriety at April 1841 general conference in Nauvoo. Acquitted and retained office 9 April 1841. Located in Jacksonville, Morgan County, Illinois; there died 21 September 1841. (One source notes that Foster was dropped from the First Quorum of the Seventy prior to his death.)[35]

Biographical Note.   Robert D. Foster.

Son of John and Jane Foster. Born 14 March 1811, in Braunston, Northampton County, England. Married Sarah (born 1812 in Massachusetts). Two known children: Nicodin and Adaline. Licensed physician. Baptized before October 1839. Ordained elder 6 October 1839. Traveled to Washington, D.C., and back to Nauvoo with Joseph Smith 1 November 1839-4 March 1840. With others appointed 7 April 1840 to draft resolutions pursuant to report of Senate Committee of Judiciary, who heard Mormon memorial on Missouri persecutions. Resolutions presented to Church conference 8 April 1840. Received patriarchal blessing from Joseph Smith, Sr., 20 July 1840. Called before Nauvoo high council 13 December and 20 December 1840 for "lying, profane swearing, and slandering the authorities of the Church." Acquitted 20 December 1840. Appointed one of regents of University of Nauvoo 3 February 1841. Member of Nauvoo Agricultural and Manufacturing Association 23 February 1841. Appointed county magistrate for Hancock County, Illinois. Appointed surgeon-in-chief and brevet brigadier-general of Nauvoo Legion. Purchased land for speculation in Nauvoo. Traveled to New York City with wife 1842, arriving 30 August. Returned to Nauvoo by January 1843. Appointed to take mission with Jonathan Allen to Tioga County, New York, 10 April 1843. Sworn in as school commissioner at Carthage, Illinois, 12 August 1843. Attended opening festivities of the Nauvoo Mansion 3 October 1843. Appointed chairman for evening; read resolution that stated in part, "Resolved, [that] General Joseph Smith, whether we view him as a Prophet at the head of the Church, a General at the head of the Legion, a Mayor at the head of the City Council, or as a landlord at the head of his table, if he has equals, he has no superiors." Joined dissident Mormons in Nauvoo during winter of 1843-44. Fined for gambling in Nauvoo April 1844. Excommunicated 18 April 1844 for adultery and apostasy. Chosen apostle in schismatic group headed by William Law 28 April 1844. Court-martialed for conduct unbecoming an officer 10 May 1844. Charges sustained. Assited in writing and printing of *Nauvoo Expositor* 7 June 1844. Reported to have been accessory to murder of Joseph and Hyrum Smith 27 June 1844. Residing in Canandaigua, Ontario County, New York, by 1850; there practicing medicine. Later settled at Loda, Iroquois County, Illinois.[36]

Biographical Note.   David Fullmer.

Son of Peter Fullmer and Susannah Zerfoss. Born 7 July 1803 at Chillisquaque, Northumberland County, Pennsylvania. Married Rhoda Ann Marvin (born 1813 in Pennsylvania) 18 September 1831. Eleven children: Eugene Bertrand, Junius Sextus, Hannibal Octavius, Elvira Martha, Hortensia Jane, Susannah, Rhoda Ann, David, Don Peter, Mary Vilate, and Esther. Moved to Richmond County, Ohio, 1835. Baptized 16

September 1836 by Henry G. Sherwood. Ordained elder 22 February 1837 by Reuben Hedlock. Moved to Caldwell County, Missouri, September 1837. Located in Daviess County, Missouri, in spring of 1838. Expelled from Missouri 1839. Located in Illinois 1839. Traveled to Ohio 1839 to bring father to Illinois. Ordained high priest 1839. Appointed member of Nauvoo high council 6 October 1839. Appointed 1844 to campaign in Michigan for Joseph Smith as President of United States. Member of Nauvoo City Council. Elected to town council of Nauvoo after city charter repealed. Member of Council of Fifty. Received endowment 15 December 1845. Sealed to wife Rhoda 19 January 1846. Sealed to Margaret Phillips (born 1800 in New York) 19 January 1846. No known children. Sealed to Sarah Sophronia Oysser Bank (born 1822 in Connecticut) 19 January 1846. Nine children: Sarah Jane, Samuel, Juliette, Ellen, Margaret Ann, Janette, John Williams, Isabella, and James Montgomery. Left Nauvoo for West 1846. Settled in Garden Grove, Iowa, 1846. Appointed to assist Samuel Bent in presiding over Church members in Garden Grove 1846. Assumed presidency of Garden Grove after Bent's death. Later settled in Winter Quarters. To Utah 1847. Member of legislature of provisional State of Deseret. Appointed first counselor to Daniel Spencer, president of Salt Lake Stake 1849. Acting president of Salt Lake Stake 1852-56. Elected member of legislature of Territorial Government of Utah for Salt Lake County. Treasurer *pro tem* of Salt Lake County. Treasurer of Salt Lake City. Released from Salt Lake Stake presidency April 1866. Ordained patriarch several years before death. Died in Salt Lake City, Utah, 21 October 1879.[37]

Biographical Note.   Isaac Galland.

Son of Matthew Galland and Hannah Fenno. Born 15 May 1791 in Somerset County, Pennsylvania. Spent early years in Washington County, Ohio. Married Nancy Harris 22 March 1811. Married Margaret Knight by 1816. Two known children: Sophia and Eliza. Residing in Owen County, Indiana, 1820; there owned land for speculation. Began studying and practicing medicine in Indiana. Acquired title of "doctor." Moved to Edgar County, Illinois, about 1821. Settled in Horselick Grove, Illinois, about 1824. Married Hannah Kinney 5 October 1826. Two known children: Washington and Eleanor. Moved to Oquawka, Henderson County, Illinois, 1827; there built first cabin and established trading post. Located in Lee County, Iowa, 1829; founded town of Nashville. Fought in Black Hawk War 1832. Wife Hannah died 17 March 1831. Married Elizabeth Wilcox 25 April 1833. Purchased land in Half-breed Tract in Lee County; sold land to Church members 1839. Residing in Commerce, Illinois, 1839. Baptized 3 July 1839. Ordained elder 3 July 1839. Left for Chillicothe, Ohio, 4 July 1839. Authored *Galland's Iowa Emigrant* 1840. Appointed by revelation to buy stock for Nauvoo House 19 January 1841. Also directed to travel with Hyrum Smith to East to obtain monies for Nauvoo House and Temple. Arrived in Pennsylvania late March

1841. Authored *Doctor Galland's Reply to Various Falsehoods, Misstatements and Misrepresentations Concerning the Latter Day Saints, Reproachfully Called Mormons* July 1841. Withdrew from Church activity 1842. Resided in Keokuk, Iowa, 1842-53. Traveled to California 1853. Resided in Petaluma, California, 1853-56. Returned to Ft. Madison, Iowa, 1856; remained there until death 27 September 1858.[38]

Biographical Note.   Thomas Grover.

Son of Thomas Grover and Polly Spaulding. Born 22 July 1807 at Whitehall, Washington County, New York. Employed as cabin boy on Erie Canal about 1819. Later became captain of boat. Married Caroline Whiting 1828. Seven children: Jane, Emeline, Mary E., Adeline, Caroline, Eliza Ann, and Emma. Moved to Freedom, New York, in early 1830s. Baptized by Warren A. Cowdery September 1834. Moved to Kirtland by 1835. Appointed to be ordained elder 2 January 1836. Ordained high priest January 1836. Appointed member of Kirtland high council 13 January 1836. Moved to Far West, Missouri, by December 1836. Appointed member of Far West high council 1 August 1837. Expelled from Missouri 1839. Moved to Nauvoo 1839. Appointed member of Nauvoo high council 6 October 1839. Wife, Caroline, died October 1840. Married Carolina Eliza Nickerson 20 February 1841. Four children: Percia Cornelia, Marshall, Leonard, and Data. Later divorced. Member of Nauvoo Legion 1841. Mission to southern states from about June to October 1841. Another mission from about September 1842 to January 1843; area unknown. Assisted in rescuing Prophet from Dixon arrest 1843. Mission to Michigan 1844. Married Hannah Tupper 17 December 1844. Fifteen children: Thomas, Hannah, Joel, Pauline, Jedediah Morgan Grant, James, Evelyn, Hyrum Smith, Silas, Josephine, Jerome, Maria Louisa, Ezra, John Ladd, 2nd Charles Coulson Rich. Received endowment 15 December 1845. Married Lodoiska Tupper 20 January 1846. Seven children: Lucy, Moroni, Jacob, Napoleon, Edward Partridge, Inez, and Don Carlos. Left Nauvoo February 1846. Arrived in Council Bluffs 23 July 1846. Appointed member of Council Bluffs high council 21 July 1846. Did not accept calling. Appointed member of "Municipal High Council" in Cutler's Park 9 August 1846. Arrived in Salt Lake Valley 3 October 1847. Moved to Centerville in spring of 1848. Moved to Farmington, Utah, about fall of 1848. To California 1848-49. Traveled to Missouri 1850 to purchase cattle. Returned to Salt Lake area in spring of 1853 with 150 head of cattle. Resided in Farmington remainder of life. Member of Utah Legislature. Probate judge of Davis County. Married Elizabeth Walker 1856. Nine children: Clara, Walter L., Nettie, Zeruah, Enoch, Pollie, Alma Fredrick, Samuel, Lafayette. Married Emma Walker in 1857. Nine children: Keturah, Rosella, Henry A., Amy Blanche, Vernisha, William Frank, Abner, David, and Albert Isaiah. Assisted emigrating Saints from Missouri River 1861. Mission to eastern states 1874-75. Died 19 February 1886 at Farmington, Davis County, Utah.[39]

Biographical Note.   George Washington Harris.

Son of James Harris. Born 1 April 1780 in Berkshire County, Massachusetts. Married Margaret. Wife, Margaret, died 1828. Residing in Batavia, New York, 1830. Had purchased property in Terre Haute, Indiana, 1817-21 while residing in New York. A renouncing mason, married Lucinda Pendleton Morgan, widow of Masonic martyr William Morgan, 30 November 1830. Moved to Terre Haute, Indiana, before 1834. Baptized by Orson Pratt in fall of 1834 in Terre Haute. Moved to Far West, Missouri, by September 1836; there owned property. Appointed member of high council in Far West 3 March 1838. Ordained high priest 3 March 1838. Located in Illinois 1839. Chosen member of Nauvoo high council 6 October 1839. On 17 July 1840 appointed to travel eastward collecting funds and materials for Church publications. In Cincinnati, Ohio, in September 1840 and in New York in 1841. Returned to Nauvoo before September 1841. Prominent Church leader 1840-50. Elected alderman in Nauvoo 30 October 1841. Received endowment 12 December 1845. Wife, Lucinda, sealed to Joseph Smith. President of the Nauvoo Coach and Carriage Manufacturing Association. Left Nauvoo 1846. Located in Council Bluffs, Iowa. Bishop in Council Bluffs 17 July 1846. Appointed member of high council in Council Bluffs 21 July 1846. Did not move west with Saints. Informed Church leaders in Utah of intent to remain in Iowa until Saints returned to redeem Zion in Missouri. Died 1857 in Council Bluffs, Pottawattamie County, Iowa.[40]

Biographical Note.   Peter Haws.

Son of Edward and Polly Haws. Born 17 February 1796 in Young Township, Leeds County, Upper Canada, Johnstown District. Married Charlotte Harrington (born 8 April 1798). Six known children: Alpheus, Abigail, Albert, Loly Ann, Catherine, and Charlotte. Miller by trade. Converted to Church in Canada. Moved to Illinois by 1839. Traveled on short mission with Erastus Snow to Illinois 1839. On 19 January 1841 appointed by revelation to be member of Nauvoo House Committee with Lyman Wight, George Miller, and John Snider. Member of Nauvoo Agricultural and Manufacturing Association 23 February 1841. Owned steam-operated sawmill near Nauvoo. Served as alternate high councilor for Nauvoo high council 1840-44. Member of Council of Fifty 11 March 1844. Received endowment 13 December 1845. Sealed in Nauvoo to wife, Charlotte, 10 January 1846. Sealed in Nauvoo Temple to Betsy Harrington (born 1790 in New York) 10 January 1846. Sealed in Nauvoo Temple to Mary Quard (born 1806 in Ireland) 26 January 1846. Sealed in Nauvoo Temple to Sarah Morris (born 1810 in Ohio) 26 January 1846. Moved west to Council Bluffs, Iowa, with Saints 1846. Traveled to Texas with Lucian Woodworth to visit Lyman

Wight's colony 1848. Returned to Council Bluffs, Iowa, by January 1849. Criticized leadership of Quorum of Twelve in January 1849. Argued that no revelation binding on Church without sanction of Council of Fifty. Tried by Pottawattamie High Council January-February 1849 for selling whiskey to Indians and speaking against Brigham Young. Claimed Council of Fifty held powers superior to those of Twelve Apostles. Cut off from Church February-March 1849 for refusing to retract statements and clear up pending case. Residing in Pottawattamie County, Iowa, 1850. Settled on branch of Humboldt River (Nevada) 1854; there raised grain, vegetables, and cattle for overland emigrants. Moved to California about 1855; died there 1862. Two or more of children joined Reorganized LDS Church. Haws may have joined also.[41]

Biographical Note.   Henry Herriman.

Son of Enoch Herriman and Sarah Brocklebank. Born 9 June 1804 in Bradford, Essex County, Massachusetts. Married Clarissa Boynton (born 1807 in Massachusetts) 26 April 1827. No known children. Baptized 29 August 1832 by Orson Hyde. Ordained elder 8 June 1833 in Bath, New Hampshire. Moved to Kirtland, Ohio, 1834. Member of Zion's Camp 1834. Ordained seventy March 1835. Ordained president of First Quorum of Seventy 6 February 1838; held position for fifty-three years (1838-91). Assisted in organizing Kirtland Camp March 1838. Left Kirtland for Missouri July 1838. Located in Adam-Ondi-Ahman October 1838. Expelled from Missouri 1839. Located in Nauvoo 1839. Captain in Nauvoo Legion. Elected lieutenant colonel in Legion 18 September 1845. Received endowment 12 December 1845. Sealed to Clarissa Boynton 16 January 1846. Sealed to Eliza Elizabeth Jones 16 January 1846. Nine known Children: Henry H., Mary, Benjamin, Emily E., Olive Hale, Lydia Ellen, Eliza Ann, Hyrum Smith, and Clarissa. Left Nauvoo for West early 1846. Located in Council Bluffs 1846. Arrived in Salt Lake Valley 1848. Assisted in settling Herriman, Utah (named in his honor). Mission to Great Britain 1857-58. Arrived in Liverpool 4 August 1857. Required to return home early because of Utah War. Left Liverpool 21 January 1858. Mission to Dixie about 1862. Settled in Huntington, Emery County, Utah, December 1887. Died 17 May 1891.[42]

Biographical Note.   John A. Hicks.

Born 1810 in New York. Married Malinda. Four known children: Eliza, Mirah, Charlotte, and Francelia. Undoubtedly converted in Upper Canada. Residing at Crooked Creek Branch near Ramus, Illinois, 1840. Charged for slandering John P. Greene and lying 19 April 1840. After confessing and promising to make restitution, was extended the hand of fellowship by Nauvoo high council 2 May 1840. Appointed by revelation to preside over elders quorum in Nauvoo area 19 January 1841. Not sustained at April 1841 general conference by various priesthood quorums. Tried by the elders quorum in Nauvoo 1841 for stating falsehoods, engaging in schismatical conversation, and breaching Nauvoo City ordinances. Appealed October 1841 general conference in Nauvoo. Excommunicated 5 October 1841. Associated with apostates in Nauvoo after 1841. Sought to traduce character of Joseph Smith and have him murdered.[43]

Biographical Note.   William Huntington.

Son of William Huntington and Prescinda Lathrop. Born 28 March 1784 in Grantham, Cheshire County, New Hampshire. Moved in 1804 with family to Watertown, New York. Returned to New Hampshire 1806; there married Zina Baker 28 December 1806. Nine children: Chauncey Dyer, Nancy, Dimick Baker, Prescinda Lathrop, Adaline Elizabeth, William Dresser, Zina Diantha, Oliver Boardman, and John Dickenson. Farmed in Watertown 1806-11; there owned several parcels of property. Served in War of 1812. Baptized 1835. Ordained elder 1836. Left New York for Kirtland, Ohio, 1 October 1836. Arrived in Kirtland 11 October 1836. Charter member of and owned stock in Kirtland Safety Society 1837. Ordained high priest 8 October 1837. Member of Kirtland high council 1837. Left Kirtland for Missouri 21 May 1838. Settled in Adam-Ondi-Ahman. Assisted Mormon families moving from Missouri 1838-39. Located in Commerce, Illinois, 14 May 1839. Wife, Zina, died July 1839. Appointed member of Nauvoo high council 6 October 1839. Married Lydia Partridge, widow of Edward Partridge, 28 August 1840. Worked as stonecutter on Nauvoo Temple. Sexton of Nauvoo Cemetery. Fifer in Nauvoo Band. Received endowment 12 December 1845. Sealed in Nauvoo Temple to Zina Baker (born 1786 in New Hampshire) 14 January 1846. Sealed in Nauvoo Temple to Lydia Clisby Partridge (born 1793 in Massachusetts) for time 14 January 1846. Sealed in Nauvoo Temple to Mary Anner Armstrong (born 1784 in New York) 24 January 1846. Sealed in Nauvoo Temple to Mary Johnson (born 1792 in New York) 24 January 1846. Left Nauvoo for West February 1846. Appointed to preside over Church members at Mt. Pisgah, Iowa, 22 May 1846. Died 19 August 1846, at Mt. Pisgah, Iowa.[44]

Biographical Note.   Aaron Johnson.

Son of Didymus Johnson and Rheuama Stevens. Born 22 June 1806 at Haddam, Middlesex County, Connecticut. Bound out at the age of fourteen to learn gunsmithing; continued in this trade until about 1827. Joined

Methodist Church 1824. Married Polly Zerviah Kelsey 13 September 1827. Four known children: Willis, Marilla, Mary Ann, and Emma Maria. Baptized 15 April 1836. Moved to Kirtland, Ohio, in spring of 1837. Purchased land in Kirtland at suggestion of Joseph Smith. Member of Kirtland Camp 1838. Ordained seventy in Far West, Missouri 28 December 1838. Moved to Nauvoo 1839. Justice of peace in Nauvoo. Appointed member of Nauvoo high council 19 January 1841; acknowledged in position 6 February 1841. Served as high councilor 1841-45. Received endowment 21 December 1845. Sealed to Jane Scott 12 July 1845. Six known children: Don Carlos, Aaron, Sophia, Stephen, Moses, and Heber. Sealed to Sarah Maria Johnson 22 December 1845. Two children. Sealed to Mary Ann Johnson 18 May 1846. No known children. Left Nauvoo 1846. Settled in Garden Grove, Iowa, May 1846. Bishop in Garden Grove. Resided in Iowa until spring of 1850; then left for Utah. Arrived in Salt Lake City September 1850. Directed to settle in Springville, Utah. First bishop of Springville served there 1850-72. Chief justice for Utah County for eight years. Major general of Utah Militia. Member of Utah Legislature for twenty years. Postmaster of Springville for twenty-six years. Sealed to Rachel Ford 22 April 1852. Three known children: Marion, Rachel Ann, and Rose Emmeline. Sealed to Harriet Fedelia Johnson 16 December 1852. Five known children: Ida, Eugenia, George, Christabelle, and Alexander. Sealed to Eunice Lucinda Johnson 14 June 1853. No known children. Sealed to Margaret Jane Ford. Six known children: Montezuma, Quetlavaka, Zina, Girilda, Gotamoses, and Daniel. Sealed to Julia Maria Johnson 1 March 1857. Two known children: William and Isabelle. Sealed to Sarah James 1 March 1857. Five known children: Winfred, Edward, Ambrose, Brigham Young, and Annabella. Sealed to Cecelia Almina Sanford 1 March 1857. Eight known children: Lafayette, Sulvia, Armenta, Arminia, Cecelia, Silas, Cyrus, and Maude. Married Jemina Davis Johnson, brother's widow, for time 6 April 1857. Died 10 May 1877 in Springville, Utah County, Utah.[45]

Biographical Note.   Heber Chase Kimball.

Son of Solomon Kimball and Anna Spaulding. Born 14 June 1801 at Sheldon, Franklin County, Vermont. Moved with family to West Bloomfield, Ontario County, New York, 1811. Learned blacksmithing from father. Learned potter's trade from brother Charles about 1820-22. Moved to Mendon, New York, by 1822. Married Vilate Murray November 1822. Ten children: Judith M., William H., Helen Mar, Roswell H., Heber P., David P., Charles S., Brigham W., Solomon F., and Murray G. Inititated into Masonry in Victor, New York, 1823. Baptized April 1832 by Alpheus Gifford; ordained elder shortly thereafter. Traveled to Kirtland, Ohio, to see Joseph Smith October-November 1832. Moved to Kirtland in fall of 1833. Member of Zion's Camp 1834. Left Missouri for Kirtland 20 June 1834. Arrived in Kirtland 26 July

1834. Established pottery in Kirtland area August 1834. Attended School of Prophets in winter of 1834-35. Ordained apostle 14 February 1835. Mission to eastern states in summer of 1835. Returned to Kirtland 25 September 1835. Attended dedication of Kirtland Temple March 1836. Left Kirtland on mission to upstate New York and Vermont 10 May 1836. Returned to Kirtland 2 October 1836. Charter member of and owned stock in Kirtland Safety Society January 1837. Appointed to preach in England 4 June 1837. Left Kirtland 13 June 1837. Arrived in Liverpool 20 July 1837. Returned to Kirtland 22 May 1838. With companions baptized nearly fifteen hundred. Moved to Missouri 1838. Arrived in Far West 25 June 1838. Expelled from Missouri 1839. Located temporarily in Quincy, Illinois, 1839. Moved to Nauvoo in summer of 1839. Left for mission to England September 1839. Arrived in England 6 April 1840. Returned to Nauvoo 1 July 1841. Elected member of Nauvoo City Council 23 October 1841. Received endowment 4 May 1842. Mission in Illinois September-November 1842. Married Sarah Noon 1842. Three children: Adelbert Henry, Sarah H., and Heber. Mission to eastern states July-October 1843. Member of Council of Fifty 11 March 1844. Mission to East May 1844 to campaign for Joseph Smith as President of United States. Returned to Nauvoo 6 August 1844. Assisted in preparing Saints to leave Nauvoo 1845. Married Sarah Ann Whitney 1846. Seven children: David, David O., David Heber, Newel W., Horace H., Maria, and Joshua. Married Lucy Walker 1846. Nine children: Rachael S., John H., Willard H., Lydia H., Anna S., Eliza, Washington, Franklin H., and Joshua H. Married Prescinda Huntington 1846. Two children: Prescinda C. and Joseph. Left Nauvoo 1846. Located in Winter Quarters until 1847. Married Clarrisa Cutler about 1846. One child: Abram A. Married Emily Cutler about 1846. One child: Isaac A. Married Mary Ellen Abel. One child: Peter. Married Ruth Reese. Three children: Susannah R., Jacob R., and Enoch H. Married Christeen Golden. Four children: Cornelia C., Jonathan Golden, Elias Smith, and Mary M. Married Anna Gheen. Five children: Samuel H., Daniel H., Andrew H., Alice, and Sarah. Married Amanda Green. Four children: William G., Albert H., Jeremiah, and Moroni. Married Harriet Sanders. Three children: Harriet, Hyrum, and Eugene. Married Ellen Sanders. Five children: Samuel, Joseph, Augusta, Jedediah, and Rosalia. Married Frances Swan. One child: Frances. Married Martha Knight. One child: Son. Married Mary Smithies. Five children: Melvina, James, Wilford, Lorenzo, and Abbie. In all sixty-five children. Arrived in Salt Lake Valley 24 July 1847. Returned to Winter Quarters 31 October 1847. Sustained as member of First Presidency 27 December 1847. Member of First Presidency 1847-68. Left for Salt Lake Valley May 1848. Arrived in Salt Lake Valley September 1848. Elected lieutenant-governor of provisional State of Deseret 1849. Until death served faithfully in First Presidency. Assisted in organizing wards, stakes, missions, and colonies and preached throughout Church. Died 22 June 1868 in Salt Lake City, Utah.[46]

Biographical Note.   Vinson Knight.

Son of Rudolphus Knight and Rizpah Lee. Born 14 March 1804 in Chester, Washington County, New York. Married Martha McBride (born 1805 in New York) 14 March 1826. Six known children: Almyra, Rizpah, Adaline, James V., Martha, and Rudolphus E. Residing in Perrysburg, New York, at time of conversion 1834. Moved to Kirtland by 1835. Owned home and property in Kirtland. Druggist. Ordained elder 2 January 1836. Ordained high priest and counselor to Bishop Newel K. Whitney 13 January 1836. Charter member of and owned stock in Kirtland Safety Society January 1837. Participated in dedication of Kirtland Temple. Traveled to Far West, Missouri, with Joseph Smith September-December 1837. Moved to Missouri in summer of 1838. Located in Daviess County. Appointed acting bishop *pro tem* of Adam-Ondi-Ahman Stake 28 June 1838. Expelled from Missouri 1839. Located temporarily in Quincy, Illinois, 1839. As church land agent, assisted in purchasing thousands of acres of land in Lee County, Iowa, May-June 1839. Appointed to assume full title of bishop 4 May 1839. Appointed bishop of Lower Ward in Nauvoo 6 October 1839. Designated by revelation 19 January 1841 as Presiding Bishop of Church. Elected to Nauvoo City Council 1 February 1841. Initiated into Masonry 9 April 1842. Took plural wife before death. Possibly received endowment before death. Died in Nauvoo, Hancock County, Illinois, 31 July 1842.[47]

Biographical Note.   William Law.

Son of Richard Law and Mary Wilson. Born 8 September 1809 in Tyrone County, Northern Ireland. Emigrated to Mercer County, Pennsylvania, 1818 with family. Studied in Pittsburg and Philadelphia. Moved to Churchville, Peel County, Ontario (Upper Canada), before 1833; there owned property. Married Jane Silverthorn about 1833. Eight children: Richard, Rebecca, Thomas, Helen, William, John, Wilson and Cys. Converted to Church 1836 by John Taylor and Almon W. Babbitt. Led company of Saints from Upper Canada to Nauvoo 1839, arriving early November. Possessed strong testimony of Church and Joseph Smith's divine calling 1840-42. Appointed member of First Presidency by revelation 19 January 1841. Also appointed to travel to East with Hyrum Smith 19 January 1841. Initiated into Masonic Order 25 April 1842. Received endowment 4 May 1842. Left Nauvoo for East with Hyrum Smith 4 September 1842 to counter false statements of John C. Bennett and attend October conference of Church in Philadelphia. Returned to Nauvoo 4 November 1842. Owned steam-operated grain and saw mill in Nauvoo. Owned town lots in Nauvoo and sold merchandise. Opposed revelation on plural marriage in summer of 1843. Also opposed Prophet's practice of plural marriage; finally resulted in apostasy and excommunication from the Church 18 April 1844. In April 1844 organized and presided over short-lived church. Printed *Nauvoo Expositor* 7 June 1844. Moved to Burlington, Iowa, June 1844. Settled at Hampton, Rock Island County, Illinois by fall of 1844. Moved to Jo Daviess County, Illinois by 1846. Returned to Mercer County, Pennsylvania, by 1850; there continued as merchant. Moved to Shullsburg, LaFayette County, Wisconsin, by 1870; there commenced practice of medicine. Died 12 January 1892 in Shullsburg, LaFayette County, Wisconsin. Buried in Shullsburg.[48]

Biographical Note.   Amasa Mason Lyman.

Son of Boswell Lyman and Martha Mason. Born 30 March 1813 in Lyman, Grafton County, New Hampshire. Baptized 27 April 1832. Ordained elder by Joseph Smith in Hiram, Ohio, 23 August 1832. Moved to Kirtland, Ohio, by summer of 1832. Mission in southern Ohio and Cable County, Virginia, with Zerubbabel Snow in fall of 1852. Appointed to travel east with William F. Cahoon on mission 12 March 1833. Ordained high priest 11 December 1833. Member of Zion's Camp 1834. Married Maria Louisa Tanner 10 June 1835. Eight children: Matilda, Francis Marion, Ruth Adelia, Amasa Mason, Maria Louisa, Lelia Deseret, Love Josephine, and Agnes Hila. Ordained seventy about March 1835. Charter member of and owned stock in Kirtland Safety Society 1837. Moved to Far West, Missouri, 1837. Arrested November 1838 for treason, and other charges. No conviction. Settled in Lee County, Iowa, in spring of 1840. Moved to Nauvoo, Illinois, 1841. Appointed to serve mission to New York City 7 October 1841. Initiated into Masonry 8 April 1842. Ordained apostle 20 August 1842, filling vacancy created by Orson Pratt's excommunication. Elected regent for University of Nauvoo 20 August 1842. Mission to southern Illinois with George A. Smith September 1842. Returned to Nauvoo 4 October 1842. Directed to settle with family in Shockoquon, Henderson County, Illinois, late 1842; remained until summer of 1843. Appointed member of First Presidency 20 January 1843. Received endowment 28 September 1843. Mission with family to Alquina, Fayette County, Indiana, 1843-44. Member of Council of Fifty probably as early as 11 April 1844. Appointed to campaign for Joseph Smith as President of United States April 1844. Returned to Alquina, Indiana, April 1844. Traveled to Cincinnati, Ohio, June 1844. Returned to Nauvoo 31 July 1844, after Prophet's death. Sustained member of Quorum of Twelve 12 August 1844. Member of board of trustees of Seventy's Library and Institute Association 1845. Sealed to Caroline Ely Partridge (born 1827 in Ohio) 6 September 1844. Five children: Martha Lydia, Frederick Rich, Annie, Walter Clisbee, and Harriet Jane. Sealed to Eliza Maria Partridge Smith for time 28 September 1844. Five Children: Don Carlos, Platte Dealton, Carlie Eliza, Joseph Alvin, and Lucy Zina. Sealed to Cornelia Eliza Leavitt (born 1825 in Ohio) 14

November 1844. Two known children: Lorenzo and Henry Elias. Sealed to Dianitia Walker (born 1818 in Ohio) July 1845. No children. Sealed in Nauvoo Temple to Paulina Eliza Phelps (born 1827 in Illinois) 16 January 1846. Seven known children: Oscar Morris, Mason Roswell, Clark, Charles Rich, William Horne, Solen Ezra, and Laura Paulina. Sealed in Nauvoo Temple to Priscilla Rebecca Turley (born 1829 in Upper Canada) 16 January 1846. Six known children: Theodore, Ira Depo, Isaac Newton, Albert Augustus, Stephen Alonzo, and Frances Priscilla. Sealed in Nauvoo Temple to Laura Reed (born 1829 in Ohio) 28 January 1846. No known children. Left Nauvoo for West 1846. Located in Winter Quarters. To Salt Lake Valley July 1847. Returned to Winter Quarters 1847. Appointed 8 April 1849 to travel to California with Orrin P. Rockwell to take consignment of mail to San Francisco. Left 20 April 1849. Returned to Salt Lake City about August 1849. Appointed to travel to California again September 1849 to present to California Constitutional Convention proposal that California and Deseret form one large state. Proposal rejected by California legislators. Explored possible sites for settlement in southern California 1850. Returned to Salt Lake City September 1850. Appointed 23 February 1851 to join with Charles C. Rich in leading company of Saints to San Bernardino, California. Left with company of 437 24 March 1851. Arrived in June 1851. Assisted in settling and presiding over Saints in San Bernardino 1851-57. Married Lydia Partridge 7 February 1853. Four known children: Edward Leo, Ida Evelyn, Frank Arthur, and Lydia Mae. Mission to Great Britain 1860. Left Salt Lake City 1 May 1860. Arrived in Liverpool 27 July 1860. Presided over European Mission with Charles C. Rich until 14 May 1862. Returned to Salt Lake City mid-September 1862. Appointed to settle Fillmore, Millard County, Utah, October 1862. Left for Fillmore mid-April 1863. Excommunicated 12 May 1870 for persisting in teaching unorthodox doctrine pertaining to atonement of Christ and for associating with Godbeites. Died in Fillmore, Millard County, Utah, 4 February 1877.[49]

Biographical Note.   Daniel Sanborn Miles.

Son of Josiah Miles and Marah Sanborn. Born 23 July 1772 at Sanbornton, Belknap County, New Hampshire. Married Electa Chamberlin. One known child: Calvin Daniel. Baptized April 1832 by Orson Pratt and Lyman E. Johnson in Bath, New Hampshire. Moved to Kirtland by 1836. Ordained elder 28 February 1836 by Reuben Hedlock. Ordained seventy 20 December 1836 by Hazen Aldrich. Paid tax on two horses and one cow 1836 in Kirtland. Ordained President of First Quorum of Seventy 6 April 1837. Moved to Missouri 1838, arriving in Far West 14 March. After Mormon expulsion from Missouri, located in Illinois. Traveled to Kirtland November 1839. Temporary member of Nauvoo high council. Died 12 October 1845 at home of Josiah Butterfield in Hancock County, Illinois.[50]

Biographical Note.   George Miller.

Son of John Miller and Margaret Pfeiffer. Born 25 November 1794 near Stanardville, Orange County, Virginia. Moved with family to Madison County, Kentucky, November 1805-March 1806. Moved to Boone County, Kentucky, about 1808. Began learning carpenter-joiner trade 1813. Worked as carpenter in Lexington, Kentucky, 1814-15. Father died August 1815. Left Cincinnati, Ohio, for Baltimore, Louisiana, 7 January 1816. Arrived 9 April 1816; worked there as carpenter. Returned to Virginia to visit relatives fall 1816-spring 1817. Returned to Baltimore spring 1817. Moved to Lancaster County, Virginia, mid-1817. Worked as carpenter on buildings at state university in Charlottesville, Albemarle County, Virginia, November 1817-20. Visited family in Kentucky in fall and winter of 1819. Initiated into Masonry about 1819. Married Mary Catherine Fry (born 1801 in Virginia) before 1827. Four known children: Joshua L., John F., Mary Catherine, and Elizabeth Ann. Resided in Tennessee about 1828. Moved to Illinois by 1834. Residing in McDonough County, Illinois, near Macomb, November 1838. Owned 300 acres of land as well as hogs and cattle. Offered farm to exiled Saints from Missouri 1839. Baptized 12 August 1839 by John Taylor. Moved to Lee County, Iowa, in fall of 1839; there established woodyard. Ordained high priest before September 1840. In 1840 helped purchase steamboat that plied upper Mississippi River. Moved to Nauvoo November 1840. Appointed to preach in Lee County, Iowa, and Hancock County, Illinois, fall of 1840-February 1841. Appointed by revelation to become bishop and member of Nauvoo House Association 19 January 1841. Ordained to bishopric February 1841. Elected regent of University of Nauvoo 3 February 1841. Nauvoo House Association was incorporated 23 February 1841. Elected member of Nauvoo Agricultural and Manufacturing Association 23 February 1841. Captain in Nauvoo Legion in spring of 1841; elected colonel 1 May 1841. Accompanied Joseph Smith to trial at Monmouth, Illinois, June 1841. Appointed to preside over high priests quorum in Nauvoo 2 October 1841. Mission to Kentucky to gather monies for construction of Nauvoo House and Temple 1841-42. Left Nauvoo in winter of 1841 and returned April 1842 with 100 head of cattle. Received endowment 4 May 1842. Sent to Quincy, Illinois, and Jefferson City, Missouri, with Erastus H. Derby to confer with Governor Thomas Reynolds concerning a requisition on the Prophet for being an accessory to attempted murder before the fact. Left Nauvoo 12 July 1842. Returned the last week in July 1842. Elected brigadier-general in Nauvoo Legion 23 September 1842. Mission to pineries in Wisconsin to cut timber for Nauvoo House and Temple 1842-43. Left Nauvoo about 1 November 1842. Returned to Nauvoo 12 May 1843 with 50,000 feet of pine lumber. Left soon thereafter for pineries. Returned to Nauvoo 8 July 1843, with 157,000 feet of lumber, and 70,000 shingles for temple. Left again for pineries 21 July 1843. Returned from pineries 23 September 1843. Mission to Mississippi and Alabama with Peter Haws September-October 1843. Returned to Nauvoo about 27 October 1843.

Returned to pinery November-December 1843. Returned to Nauvoo from pinery 8 March 1844. Member of Council of Fifty 11 March 1844. Returned to pinery March-April 1844. Returned to Nauvoo 1 May 1844. Mission to Kentucky to campaign for Joseph Smith as President of United States May-July 1844. Left Nauvoo 6 May 1844. Returned by 24 July 1844. Appointed to assume responsibilities as trustee-in-trust for Church 9 August 1844. Authorized to take Pinery Company to Texas 12 August 1844. Again sustained as president of high priests quorum in Nauvoo and Second Bishop of Church 7 October 1844. Proposed building hall for high priests quorum 26 January 1845. Opposed by Brigham Young. Elected member of Nauvoo City Council 3 February 1845. Sealed to wife, Mary Fry, 13 January 1846. Sealed to Elizabeth Bouton (born 1817 in Connecticut) 25 January 1846. Sealed to Sophia Wallace (born 1800 in England) 25 January 1846. Left Nauvoo for West 6 February 1846. Arrived at Council Bluffs 13 June 1846. Crossed Missouri River 6 July 1846. Proceeded west from Missouri River July 1846. Informed by Brigham Young not to proceed further west 8 August 1846. Persuaded by Ponca Indian Chief Tea-Nuga-Numpa, traveled with pioneer company to mouth of Niobarra River August 1846, arriving 23 August. Traveled to Winter Quarters about January 1847 to confer with Brigham Young. Rejected Brigham Young's leadership about January 1847. Journeyed to Austin, Texas, 1847 to join Lyman Wight. Cut off from Church 3 December 1848. Soon became convinced that Wight was apostate. Remained in Texas until 1849. Concluded that James J. Strang was Joseph Smith's lawful successor in 1849. Left Texas for Beaver Island, Michigan, 13 October 1849. Arrived in Voree, Wisconsin, 4 September 1850. Proceeded on to St. James, Beaver Island, Michigan; arrived before 1851. Deputy sheriff on Beaver Island. Remained at Beaver Island until 1856. Left Beaver Island with major exodus 1856 after Strang was shot 16 June 1856. Died in Meringo, Illinois, 1856 en route to California.[51]

Biographical Note.   Noah Packard.

Son of Noah Packard and Molly Hamblin. Born 7 May 1796 in Plainfield, Hampshire County, Massachusetts. Moved to Parkman, Geauga County, Ohio, about 1817. Married Sophia Bundy 29 June 1820. Seven known children: Noah, Orrin, Henry, Sophia, Milan, Nephi, and Olive. Owned orchard and farm ground in Parkman. Baptized 1 June 1832 by Parley P. Pratt. Ordained priest 3 December 1832. Appointed to preach in Parkman with Solomon Humphrey 5 December 1832. Mission to East 22 April 1833 with Parley P. Pratt. Ordained elder 6 May 1833 by John Gould in Westfield, New York. Joined with Brother Childs in preaching until 17 June 1833. Traveled and preached alone in New York and New Hampshire June-September 1833. Returned to Parkman 25 September 1833 having baptized eighteen persons. Appointed to preside over branch of Church in Parkman. Mission to eastern states 1835. Left Parkman 25 May 1835.

Returned to Parkman 14 September 1835. Sold farm in Parkman for $2200 1835. Loaned $1,000 to assist in construction of Kirtland Temple 23 September 1835. Moved to Kirtland in fall of 1835. Worked on Kirtland Temple. Ordained high priest 13 January 1836. Member of Kirtland high council 1836-38. Participated in dedication of Kirtland Temple March 1836. Charter member of and owned stock in Kirtland Safety Society 1837. Left Kirtland for Missouri in fall of 1838. Spent winter in Wellsville, Ohio. Moved to Quincy, Illinois, in spring of 1839. Located in Nauvoo 18 May 1839. Appointed counselor to Don Carlos Smith in presidency of high priests quorum 7 April 1841. Counselor to George Miller in high priests quorum 14 October 1841-1846. Mission to eastern states 6 July-16 December 1841. Assisted in building Nauvoo Temple. Mission to East 1843. Left Nauvoo 10 September 1843. Remained in Vermilion County, Illinois, two months because of sickness. Returned to Nauvoo early 1844. Mission to Michigan in summer of 1845 to collect funds for construction of Nauvoo Temple. Received endowment 12 December 1845. Moved up Mississippi River to Wisconsin in spring of 1846 to work in lead mines. Remained in Wisconsin 1846-50. Left for Salt Lake Valley 22 April 1850. Arrived in Salt Lake Valley 18 September 1850. Located in Springville, Utah, 5 February 1851. Appointed member of presidency of Church in Springville, Utah, 5 February 1851. Alderman of City of Springville. Died 17 February 1860 in Springville, Utah County, Utah.[52]

Biographical Note.   Zerah Pulsipher.

Son of John Pulsipher and Elizabeth Dutton. Born 24 June 1789 at Rockingham, Windham County, Vermont. Married Polly Randall 6 November 1810. One child: Harriet Pulsipher. Married Mary Brown August 1815. Eleven children: Mary Ann, Almira, Nelson, Mariah, Sarah, John, Charles, Mary Ann, William M., Eliza Jane, and Fidelia. Baptized 11 January 1832. Missionary activity in eastern states 1833-34. Baptized Wilford Woodruff 31 December 1833 in New York. Moved to Kirtland, Ohio, 1835. Ordained elder before January 1836, probably 1832. Mission to Upper Canada October-December 1837. Baptized twenty-nine persons. Ordained and set apart as president of First Quorum of Seventy 6 March 1838. Member of Kirtland Camp 1838. Located in Daviess County, Missouri, 1838. Expelled from Missouri 1839. Settled in Nauvoo by 1840. Assisted in administering work of seventy in Nauvoo. Received endowment 12 December 1845. Traveled to Utah 1848, arriving 22 September 1848. Captain of own pioneer company. Resided in Salt Lake City area until about 1861. Married Prudence McNanamy 12 July 1854. No known children. Married Martha Hughes 18 March 1857. Five children: Martha Ann, Mary Elizabeth, Zerah James, Sarah Jane, and Andrew Milton. Moved to southern Utah about 1861. Misused sealing power about 1862, and was dropped from presidency of Seventy and either disfellowshipped or excommunicated. Case came before First Presidency 12 April 1862; rebaptized and ordained high priest. Subsequently ordained patriarch. Died in Hebron, Washington County, Utah, 1 January 1872.[53]

Biographical Note.   Charles Coulson Rich.

Son of Joseph Rich and Nancy O'Neal. Born 21 August 1809 in Campbell County, Kentucky. Moved with parents into Indiana shortly after birth. Moved with family to Tazewell County, Illinois, 1829. Baptized 1 April 1832 by George M. Hinkle. Traveled to Kirtland, Ohio, to see Joseph Smith in summer of 1832. Left Pleasant Grove, Tazewell County, Illinois, 7 May 1832. En route to Kirtland ordained elder by Zebedee Coltrin and Solomon Wixom 16 May 1832. Arrived in Kirtland mid-June 1832. Preached by way and arrived home in Pleasant Grove, Illinois, 24 October 1832. Assisted in organizing branches of Church in Tazewell County area. Recognized as presiding leader of Church in Tazewell County 1832-36. Joined Zion's Camp 29 May 1834. Traveled to Clay County, Missouri, May-June 1834. Left Clay County, Missouri, for Illinois 2 July 1834. Arrived in Pleasant Grove 16 July 1834. Short mission to Eugene, Indiana, October-November 1834. Mission to DuPage County, Illinois, April-June 1835. Mission with Solomon Wixom to western Illinois September-November 1835. Left for Kirtland 26 January 1836. Arrived 12 April 1836. Ordained high priest 12 April 1836. Received washings and anointings in Kirtland Temple and attended solemn assembly April 1836. Received blessing from Joseph Smith, Sr., 24 April 1836. Left for mission through Ohio, Indiana, Kentucky, and Illinois with William O. Clark in summer and fall of 1836. Arrived in Pleasant Grove 6 October 1836. Traveled to Caldwell County, Missouri, in fall of 1836 to purchase property. Left Pleasant Grove 20 October 1836. Arrived in Far West 1 November 1836. Laid claim to eighty acres of land in Caldwell County, Missouri, 12 November 1836. Returned to Pleasant Grove 7 December 1836. Moved to Caldwell County, Missouri, in spring of 1837. Appointed president of high priests quorum in Missouri 20 August 1837. Married Sarah DeArmon Pea 11 February 1838. Nine children: Sara Jane, Joseph Coulson, Artimesia, Charles Coulson, John Thomas, Elizabeth, David Patten, Benjamin Erastus, and Fred Carmel. Located in Far West shortly after marriage. Participated in Battle of Crooked River 25 October 1839. Fled Missouri November 1838. Located temporarily in Quincy, Illinois, 1839. Moved to Nauvoo in fall of 1839. Appointed member of Nauvoo high council 6 October 1839. Elected member of Nauvoo City Council 1 February 1841. Member of Nauvoo Legion 4 February 1841. Elected regent for University of Nauvoo 4 February 1841. Elected school warden for common schools of the Nauvoo Second Ward 1 March 1841. Appointed member of Nauvoo State presidency 30 March 1841. Elected brigadier-general of Nauvoo Legion 4 September 1841.

Received patriarchal blessing 10 January 1842. Initiated into Masonry 17 March 1842. Mission September-December 1842. Location unknown. Mission to Ottawa, Illinois, April-June 1843. Mission to DeKalb and LaSalle counties, Illinois, July 1843 to "disabuse the public mind" with respect to Prophet's Dixon arrest. Member of Council of Fifty entered before 18 April 1844). Appointed to take command of Nauvoo Legion 29 April 1844 after suspension of Wilson Law. Mission to Michigan May 1844 to campaign for Joseph Smith as President of United States. Returned to Nauvoo 28 July 1844. Commissioned major general of Nauvoo Legion by Governor Thomas Ford about 25 August 1844. Sealed to Eliza Ann Graves 2 January 1845 (Nauvoo Temple sealing 15 January 1846). Three children: Mary B., Eliza Ann, and Frances Phebe. Sealed to Mary Phelps 6 January 1845 (Nauvoo Temple sealing 15 January 1846). Ten children: Laura Esphina, Mary Ann, William Lyman, Morris Marion, Minerva Marion, Amasa Mason, Paulina Phelps, Ezra Clark, Edward Israel, and Jacob. Sealed to Sarah Jane Peck 9 January 1845 (Nauvoo Temple sealing 15 January 1846). Eleven children: Hyrum Smith, Henrietta, Orson Stock, Orissa Elizabeth, Samantha, Henry Benjamin, Lorenzo Ether, Phoebe Jane, Julie Ann, Wilford Woodruff, and Walter Peck. Received endowment 12 December 1845. Sealed to Emeline Graves 3 February 1846 in Nauvoo Temple. Eight children: Thomas Graves, Caroline Whiting, Nancy Emeline, Landon Jedediah, Samuel Joseph, Heber Charles Chase, Joel Hezekiah, and George Quayle. Left Nauvoo for West 11 February 1846. Arrived in Garden Grove, Iowa, 25 April 1846. Arrived in Mt. Pisgah, Iowa, 26 May 1846. Appointed counselor to William Huntington 22 May 1846 to preside over church in Mt. Pisgah. After Huntington's death 19 August 1846, Rich assumed presidency at Mt. Pisgah. Arrived in Winter Quarters March 1847. Married Harriet Sargent 28 March 1847 at Winter Quarters. Ten children: Franklin David, Adelbert Coulson, Tunis Harriet, Abel George, Martha Caroline, Harley Thomas, Luna Rosette, Morgan Jesse, Alvin Orlando, and Druscilla Sarah. In all, fifty-one children. Left for Salt Lake Valley 14 June 1847. Arrived in Salt Lake Valley 2 October 1847. Appointed counselor in Salt Lake Stake 3 October 1847. Ordained apostle 12 February 1849. Mission to California October 1849-November 1850. Led company of Saints to San Bernardino, California, 6 March 1851. Returned to Salt Lake City June 1857. Mission to England in 1860. Left Salt Lake City 1 May 1860. Arrived in Liverpool 27 July 1860. Returned to Salt Lake Valley in fall of 1862. Appointed to explore and settle Bear Lake Valley 14 September 1863. Located family in Paris June 1864. Died Paris, Bear Lake County, Idaho, 17 November 1883.[54]

Biographical Note.   Samuel Jones Rolfe.

Son of Benjamin and Mary Rolfe. Born 26 August 1794 in Concord, Merrimack County, New Hampshire. Married Elizabeth Hathaway (born

1801 in Massachusetts). Eleven known children: Gilbert, Benjamin, Tallman, Ianthus, Wealthy, Lydia, Horace, Samuel, William, Mary Ann, and David. Resided in Maine 1810-30, there joined Church. Moved to Kirtland, Ohio, by 1835. An excellent joiner, worked on Kirtland and Nauvoo temples. Received blessing 8 March 1835 for working on Kirtland Temple. Received patriarchal blessing 19 March 1835. Located in Caldwell County, Missouri; there owned property 1836. Moved to Nauvoo, Illinois, about 1839. Appointed by revelation to preside over priests quorum 19 January 1841; confirmed in postition 21 March 1841. Counselors were Elisha Everett and Hezekiah Peck. Ordained high priest 12 November 1845. Received endowment in Nauvoo Temple 12 December 1845. Left Nauvoo with Saints 1846. Served as bishop in Winter Quarters. Arrived in Salt Lake City 24 September 1847. Traveled to San Bernardino, California, 1851 with Charles C. Rich and Amasa Lyman. Appointed counselor in stake presidency in Sycamore Grove, California, in summer of 1851. Died 1864.[55]

Biographical Note.   Shadrack Roundy.

Son of Uriah Roundy and Lucretia Needham. Born 1 January 1788[56] in Rockingham, Windham County, Vermont. Married Betsy Quimby (born 1795 in Vermont) 22 June 1814. Ten children: Lauren Hotchkiss, Julia Rebecca, Lorenzo Wesley, Lauretta, Samantha, Jared Curtis, Almeda Sophia, William Felshaw, Nancy Jane, and Malinda. Moved to Onondaga County, New York, by 1815. Baptized 23 January 1831. Ordained elder 16 May 1832 by Orson Hyde and Samuel H. Smith. Moved to Kirtland by 1834. Worked on Kirtland Temple. Received blessing for working on Kirtland Temple 7 March 1835. Ordained seventy in Kirtland about March 1836. Moved to Far West, Missouri, by 1838. Present in Far West 26 April 1839, when members of Twelve Apostles left for missions to England. Expelled from Missouri 1839. Located temporarily in Warsaw, Illinois, 1839. Moved to Nauvoo about 1840. Appointed by revelation to assume bishopric under leadership of Vinson Knight 19 January 1841. Member of Nauvoo Legion 4 February 1841. Ordained high priest by 1842. Temporary member of Nauvoo high council 1842. Initiated into Masonry 1842. Nauvoo policeman 29 December 1843. Member of Nauvoo Mercantile and Mechanical Association 13 January 1845. Appointed by Brigham Young to organize company of one hundred to locate in California October 1845. Plan did not materialize. Bodyguard to Joseph Smith. Member of Council of Fifty. Received endowment 25 December 1845. Left Nauvoo for West 1846. Arrived in Salt Lake Valley July 1847. Member of Salt Lake high council 1847-48. Assisted in bringing poor emigrants from Midwest to Salt Lake Valley. Bishop of Salt Lake Sixteenth Ward 14 April 1849-56. Died in Salt Lake City, Utah, 4 July 1872.[57]

Biographical Note.   Henry Garlie Sherwood.

Born 20 April 1785 at Kinsbury, Washington County, New York. Baptized before August 1832. Ordained elder by Jared and Simeon Carter August 1832. Moved to Kirtland about 1834. Worked on Kirtland Temple. Received blessing for working on Kirtland Temple 8 March 1835. Owned stock in Kirtland Safety Society. Appointed member of Kirtland high council 3 September 1837. Ordained high councilor 9 September 1837. Moved to Missouri 1838. Resided in DeWitt, Missouri, and in Daviess County. Expelled from DeWitt September 1838. Expelled from Missouri 1839. Appointed to sell Mormon properties in Clay County, Missouri, 5 April 1839. Appointed to travel to England with members of Twelve 6 May 1839. Did not fulfill assignment. Located in Commerce, Illinois, in summer of 1839. Miraculously healed from malaria fever by Joseph Smith 22 July 1839. Appointed member of Nauvoo high council 6 October 1839. Served as clerk for Nauvoo high council 1839-March 1840. Member of Nauvoo high council 1839-46. Appointed to assist in selling lots in City of Nauvoo 1840. Elected first Nauvoo city marshal 3 February 1841. Appointed to serve mission to New Orleans 16 August 1841. Left after 9 October 1841. Returned to Nauvoo by 30 April 1842. Appointed member of committee of three to build houses for wives of Twelve in England 1840. Two missions in 1845, locations unknown. Received endowment 12 December 1845. Sealed in Nauvoo Temple to Jane McMangle 21 January 1846. Sealed in Nauvoo Temple to Marcia Abbott 21 January 1846. To Salt Lake Valley by 1848. Appointed member of Salt Lake Stake high council March 1849. Made drawing of first survey of Salt Lake City on sheepskin. Left Salt Lake City for San Bernardino, California, September 1852 to survey ranch purchased by Church leaders. Appointed surveyor for San Bernardino County 1853. Conflict with Church leaders 1855-56. Appears to have apostatized 1855. Returned to Utah 1856. Agent in Salt Lake City for Pony Express Company. Returned to San Bernardino; died there 24 November 1867.[57]

Biographical Note.   Don Carlos Smith.

Son of Joseph Smith, Sr., and Lucy Mack. Born 25 March 1816 at Norwich, Windsor County, Vermont. Baptized in Seneca Lake about 9 June 1830 by David Whitmer. Moved to Ohio 1831. Assisted in laying foundation stones for Kirtland Temple 23 July 1833. Worked on Kirtland Temple. Received blessing for working on Kirtland Temple 7 March 1835. Married Agnes Moulton Coolbrith (born 1811 in Maine) 30 July 1835 in Kirtland. Three children: Agnes Charlotte, Sophronia, and Josephine Donna. Ordained high priest and president of high priests quorum in Kirtland area 15 January 1836. Mission to Pennsylvania and New York with Wilber Denton in summer of 1836. Edited *Elders' Journal* in Kirtland 1837. Located in New

Portage, Ohio, December 1837. Mission to Virginia, Pennsylvania, and Ohio in spring of 1838 to raise money to move Smith families to Missouri. Left Ohio for Missouri 7 May 1838; arrived during summer. Mission to Tennessee and Kentucky 1838 to collect money to buy out land claims of non-Mormons in Daviess County, Missouri. Left Daviess County 26 September 1838. Returned 25 December 1838. Located in McDonough County, Illinois, near Macomb, 1839. Moved to Nauvoo by late 1839. Edited thirty-one issues of *Times and Seasons* (1839-41). Appointed by revelation to preside over high priests quorum in Nauvoo area 19 January 1841. Elected member of Nauvoo city council 1 February 1841. Regent of University of Nauvoo 3 February 1841. Major in Hancock County militia. Elected brigadier-general in Nauvoo Legion 4 February 1841. Officer of Nauvoo Agricultural and Manufacturing Association 23 February 1841. Died 7 August 1841 in Nauvoo, Hancock County, Illinois. Sealed to Agnes Moulton Coolbrith, by proxy, 28 January 1846 in Nauvoo Temple.[59]

Biographical Note.   George Albert Smith.

Son of John Smith and Clarissa Lyman. Born 26 June 1817 at Potsdam, St. Lawrence County, New York. Baptized 10 September 1832 at Potsdam by Joseph H. Wakefield and confirmed by Solomon Humphrey. Moved to Kirtland, Ohio, 1833, arriving 25 May. Member of Zion's Camp 1834. Returned to Kirtland 4 August 1834. Ordained member of First Quorum of Seventy 1 March 1835. Appointed to serve mission to East 30 May 1835. Left 5 June 1835 with second cousin Lyman Smith. Returned 2 November 1835, having baptized eight persons. Attended School of Prophets in Kirtland. Participated in Kirtland Temple dedication 1836. Served local mission in Western Reserve in spring of 1836. Attended solemn assembly in Kirtland Temple in spring of 1837. Preached in Harrison County, West Virginia, and surrounding areas in fall of 1837; there met future wife, Bathsheba W. Bigler. Moved to Missouri 1838, arriving in Far West 16 June 1838. Settled in Adam-Ondi-Ahman 26 June 1838. Ordained high priest and member of Adam-Ondi-Ahman high council 28 June 1838. Appointed to apostleship 16 January 1839. Ordained apostle 26 April 1839. Moved to Lee County, Iowa, in summer of 1830. Left for mission to England September 1839. Arrived in England 6 April 1840. Returned to Zarahemla, Iowa, 13 July 1841. Married Bathsheba W. Bigler 25 July 1841. Three children: George Albert. Jr., Bathsheba, and John. Elected to Nauvoo city council 19 May 1842. Served mission in Illinois in fall of 1842. Elected alderman for City of Nauvoo February 1843. Left on mission to solicit donations for Nauvoo House and Temple July 1843. Returned October 1843. Received endowment 2 December 1843. Sealed to Bathsheba 20 January 1844. Member of Council of Fifty 11 March 1844. Took mission campaigning for Joseph Smith's candidacy for United States presidency May 1844. Returned 27 July 1844.

Member of Nauvoo Legion. Sealed to first plural wife, Lucy Messerve Smith, 29 November 1844. Two children: Don Carlos and Joel. Sealed to Nancy Clements 1 February 1845. One child Nancy Adelia. Sealed to Zilpha Stark 28 March 1845. Three children: Zilpha Adelaide, Joseph, and Mary Amelia. Sealed to Sarah Ann Libby 20 November 1845. Five children: Charles Warren, Sarah Maria, Eunice Albertine, George Albert, and Grace Libby. Sealed to Hannah Maria Libby 26 January 1846. Entered Great Salt Lake Valley July 1847. Returned to Winter Quarters 31 October 1847. Remained in Kanesville, Iowa, October 1847-July 1849; there took charge of emigration and assisted in administering affairs of Church. Returned to Salt Lake Valley 27 October 1849. Led company of Saints to Iron County, Utah, December 1850. Assisted in establishing settlements of Centre Creek and Parowan 1851-52. Appointed Historian and General Church Recorder April 1854. Admitted as member of bar of Supreme Court of Territory of Utah February 1855. With others, worked on manuscript history of Joseph Smith. Elected delegate to Congress to present proposed constitution for State of Utah 1856. Married Susan Elizabeth West 28 October 1857. Five children: Clarissa West, Margaret, Elizabeth, Priscilla, and Emma Pearl. Appointed First Counselor to Brigham Young October 1868. Recognized as father of southern settlements, chief of which was St. George (named in his honor). Journeyed to Jerusalem 1872-73. Died 1 September 1875 in Salt Lake City, Utah.[60]

Biographical Note.   William B. Smith.

Son of Joseph Smith, Sr., and Lucy Mack. Born 13 March 1811 at Royalton, Windsor County, Vermont. Baptized 9 June 1830 by David Whitmer. Ordained teacher 5 October 1830. Moved to Ohio 1831. Ordained priest 25 October 1831. Ordained elder 19 December 1832, by Lyman E. Johnson. Married Caroline Amanda Grant 14 February 1833. Two children: Mary Jane and Caroline. Ordained high priest 21 June 1833. Member of Zion's Camp 1834. Ordained apostle 15 February 1835. Mission to eastern states with others of Twelve in summer and fall of 1835. Charged with rebellious spirit 30 October 1835. Revelation dated 3 November 1835, called to humble himself. Tried for unchristian conduct 2 January 1836. Confessed and was forgiven 3 January 1836. Attended dedication of Kirtland Temple March 1836. Attended Hebrew School in Kirtland during winter of 1835-36. Charter member of Kirtland Safety Society January 1837. Traveled to Caldwell County, Missouri, with Prophet and others in fall of 1837. Left Kirtland 27 September 1837. Arrived in Far West late October 1837. Returned to Kirtland 1837. Moved to Far West, Missouri, in spring of 1838. Expelled from Missouri 1839. Settled in Plymouth, Illinois, 1839. Disfellowshipped 4 May 1839. Restored to fellowship 25 May 1839. Failed to go to England on mission with others of Twelve 1839. Appointed to collect money for temple April 1841. Returned to Illinois by late 1841. Initiated into Masonry 9 April 1842.

Elected member of Illinois State House of Representatives August 1842. Edited *The Wasp* 16 April-10 December 1842. Mission to East in summer of 1843. Returned to Nauvoo 22 April 1844. Received endowment 12 May 1844. Left for East May-June 1844. Associated with Twelve after death of Prophet 1844. Preaching in Philadelphia by 31 August 1844. Returned to Nauvoo 4 May 1845. Wife, Caroline, died 22 May 1845. Ordained Presiding Patriarch of Church 24 May 1845. Gave several patriarchal blessings in summer 1845. Married Mary Jane Rollins on 22 June 1845. Sealed to Mary Ann West, Mary Jones, and Priscilla Mogridge in Nauvoo 1845. Sealed to Sarah and Hannah Libbey 1845. Dropped as one of Twelve Apostles and Patriarch 6 October 1845. Excommunicated for apostasy 12 October 1845. Traveled to eastern states preaching against Brigham Young in fall of 1845. Returned to Nauvoo March 1846. Associated with several apostate Mormon factions after excommunication, including James J. Strang 1846-47. Married Roxie Ann Grant 18 May 1847. Two children: Thelia and Hyrum Wallace. Married Eliza Elise Sanborn before 1858. Three children: William Enoch, Edson Don Carlos and Louie May. Served in United States Civil War. Moved to Elkader, Clayton County, Iowa, 1858. Rebaptized by J. J. Butler early 1860. Subsequently withdrew from church. Joined Reorganized LDS Church 1878. Authored *William Smith on Mormonism* (Lamoni, Iowa: 1883). Moved to Osterdock, Iowa, 1890. Died in Osterdock, Clayton County, Iowa, 13 November 1893.[61]

Biographical Note.   John Snyder.

Son of Marlin Snyder and Sarah Armstrong. Born 11 February 1800 at New Brunswick, Nova Scotia. Moved with family to Upper Canada. Mason by trade. Married Mary Heron 28 February 1822. Three known children: Harriet, Edgerton, and John, Jr. Associated with John Taylor in studying scriptures 1833. Converted and baptized in Toronto 1836 through instrumentality of Parley P. Pratt. Owned stock in Kirtland Safety Society 1837. Ordained priest before June 1837. Preached in Toronto 1837. Mission to British Isles 1837. Left Upper Canada June 1837. Arrived in Liverpool 18 July 1837. Left for Cumberland County, England, with Isaac Russell 26 July 1837. Arrived in Preston September 1837. Joined with Joseph Fielding 13 September 1837 to preach in country near Preston. Left for America with John Goodson 5 October 1837. Located in Far West, Missouri, 1838. Expelled from Missouri 1839. Located in Springfield, Illinois, 1839; residing there in November. Ordained seventy 19 January 1839 in Far West, Missouri. Appointed to serve mission to England with Twelve Apostles 6 May 1839. Apparently did not go. On 19 January 1841 was appointed one of committee to build Nauvoo House. Member of Nauvoo House Association incorporated 23 February 1841. Member of Nauvoo Legion 1841. Revelation dated 22 December 1841 instructed Snyder to travel to England and collect monies and materials for construction of Nauvoo House and Temple. Delayed this mission for lack of money; wanted Twelve to pay way to

England, but was told by Prophet to obtain own passage. Finally left Nauvoo 26 March 1842. Returned from England to Nauvoo 23 January 1843. Assisted in disposing of Mormon properties in Nauvoo after exodus of Saints. Residing in Nauvoo 1850. Ordained high priest. Emigrated to Utah 1850. Rebaptized in Salt Lake City 7 March 1857. Resided in Salt Lake City Seventeenth Ward 1857. Died in Salt Lake City, Utah, 18 December 1875.[62]

Biographical Note.   Robert Blashel Thompson.

Born 1 October 1811 in Great Driffield, Yorkshire County, England. Emigrated to Upper Canada 1834. Baptized May 1836 by Parley P. Pratt. Ordained elder 22 July 1836 by John Taylor. Moved to Kirtland, Ohio, 1837. Married Mercy R. Fielding 4 June 1837. One child: Mary Jane. Appointed to preach in Upper Canada June 1837. Returned to Kirtland March 1838. Moved to Far West, Missouri, with Hyrum Smith's family 1838, arriving 3 June. Fought in Battle of Crooked River 25 October 1838. Located temporarily in Quincy, Illinois, 1839. Ordained seventy 6 May 1839. Wrote for Quincy *Argus* and employed as clerk in Quincy courthouse 1839. Appointed to gather libelous reports and publications against Church 4 May 1839. Moved to Nauvoo by 1840. Preached funeral sermon for Joseph Smith, Sr., 15 September 1840. Appointed "General Church Clerk" 3 October 1840. Assisted Elias Higbee in writing petition to Congress for redress of Mormon grievances in Missouri November 1840. Member of Nauvoo Legion. Appointed by revelation to assist Joseph Smith in writing proclamation to kings, presidents, and governors of earth 19 January 1841. Elected Nauvoo city treasurer 3 February 1841. Associate editor of *Times and Seasons* May-August 1841. Died 27 August 1841 in Nauvoo, Hancock County, Illinois. Nauvoo Temple proxy sealing to Mercy R. Fielding 23 January 1846.[63]

Biographical Note.   Samuel Williams.

Son of Samuel Williams and Azubah Warner. Born 22 March 1789 at Russell, Hampden County, Massachusetts. Stonecutter by trade. Married Ruth Bishop (born 26 October 1789) 19 March 1810 in Westfield, Massachusetts. Seven known children: Mary A., Sally M., Alanson A., Samuel E., Charlotte W., Samuel E., and Newman B. Residing in Massachusetts 1830. Baptized before October 1839. Ordained elder 6 October 1839, in Nauvoo. Appointed by revelation to preside over elders quorum on 19 January 1841. Temporary member of Nauvoo high council. Received endowment 15 December 1845 in Nauvoo Temple. Ordained high priest 24 December 1846. Residing in Salt Lake City 1850.[64]

Biographical Note.   Lewis Dunbar Wilson.

Son of Bradley and Polly Wilson. Born 2 June 1805 in Milton, Chittendon County, Vermont. Residing in Richland County, Ohio, 1830. Married Nancy Waggoner (born 10 July 1810) 11 July 1830. Eleven known children: Lavina, Lemuel, Alvira, Oliver Granger, Almeda, Lewis D., David, Mary, Nancy Melissa, George, and Samuel. Baptized 23 May 1836 through efforts of Oliver Granger in Green Township, Richland County, Ohio. Ordained priest September 1836. Ordained elder 4 September 1836. Visited Kirtland November 1836. Participated in solemn assembly in Kirtland April 1837. Took short mission with brother George 16 May 1837. Left Ohio for Far West, Missouri, 30 August 1837. Arrived 14 October 1837. Traveled to Ohio and back to Missouri August-November 1838. Ordained seventy 24 September 1838. Located in Illinois 1839. Appointed member of Nauvoo high council 6 October 1839. Member of Nauvoo high council 1839-45. Received endowment 15 December 1845. Sealed in Nauvoo Temple to Patsy Minerva Reynolds (born 1829 in Missouri) 3 February 1846. Left Nauvoo February 1846. Located in Garden Grove, Iowa, 1846. Moved to Pottawattamie County, Iowa, May 1851. Wife Nancy died 20 July 1851. Married Sarah Waldo (born 14 December 1819) 28 September 1851. Two known children: infant and James Perry. Left Iowa for Salt Lake City 6 June 1853. Arrived 27 August 1853. Settled in Ogden, Utah. Married Nancy Ann Cossett 12 February 1854. Died 11 March 1856 in Ogden, Weber County, Utah.[65]

Biographical Note.   Brigham Young.

Son of John Young and Abigail Howe. Born 1 June 1801 at Whittingham, Windham County, Vermont. Moved with family to Sherburne, New York, 1804, and to Auburn, New York, 1813. Joined Methodist Church about 1822. Married Miriam Works in Aurilius, New York, 8 October 1824. Two children: Elizabeth and Vilate. Employed as carpenter, joiner, painter, and glazier. Moved to Mendon, New York, 1829. First saw Book of Mormon in spring of 1830. Baptized 14 April 1832 by Eleazer Miller. Ordained elder 14 April 1832. Wife, Miriam, died 8 September 1832. Traveled to Kirtland to see Joseph Smith October-November 1832. Mission to Upper Canada December 1832. Returned to Mendon, New York, February 1833. Second mission to Upper Canada April-August 1833. Moved to Kirtland September 1833. Married Mary Ann Angell 18 February 1834. Six children: Joseph A., Brigham, Mary Ann, Alice, Luna, and John W. Member of Zion's Camp 1834. Worked on Kirtland Temple. Ordained apostle 14 February 1835. Mission to eastern states May-September 1835. Attended Hebrew School in Kirtland in fall of 1835. Attended dedication of Kirtland Temple March 1836.

Mission to eastern states and New England in summer of 1835. Charter member of and owned stock in Kirtland Safety Society January 1837. Business mission to eastern states with Willard Richards March-June 1837. Mission to New York and Massachusetts June-August 1837. Left for Missouri 22 December 1837. Arrived in Far West, Missouri, 14 March 1838. Expelled from Missouri 1839. Organized Mormon evacuation from Missouri 1838-39. Located temporarily in Quincy, Illinois, February 1839. Moved to Montrose, Iowa, May 1839. Left for mission to England 14 September 1839. Arrived in England 6 April 1840. Appointed President of Twelve Apostles 19 January 1841. Left England 21 April 1841. Arrived in Nauvoo 1 July 1841. Elected member of Nauvoo City Council 4 September 1841. Initiated into Masonry 7 April 1842. Received endowment 4 May 1842. Married first plural wife, Lucy Ann Decker, 15 June 1842. Seven children: Brigham H., Fanny Caroline, Ernest Irving, Shemira, Arta De Christa, Feramorz Little, and Clarissa Hamilton. Mission to eastern states to collect funds for Nauvoo House and Temple July-September 1843. Married Harriet E. Cook 1843. One child: Oscar Brigham. Member of Council of Fifty 11 March 1844. Left on mission east to campaign for Joseph Smith as president of United States 21 May 1844. Returned to Nauvoo 6 August 1844. Married Clarissa Decker 1844. Five children: Jeanette, Nabbie, Jedediah G., Albert J., and Charlotte. Married Clarissa Ross 1844. Four children: Mary Eliza, Clarissa Maria, Willard, and Phebe Louisa. Married Emily Dow Partridge 1844. Seven children: Edward P., Emily Augusta, Caroline, Joseph Don Carlos, Miriam, Josephine, and Lura. Asserted right of Twelve to lead Church 8 August 1844. Elected lieutenant general of Nauvoo Legion 31 August 1844. Directed Mormon preparations to leave Nauvoo 1845. Married Louisa Beman 1846. Five children: Joseph, Hyrum, Moroni, Alvah, and Alma. Married Margaret Maria Alley 1846. Two children: Evelyn L. and Mahonri Moriancumer. Married Emmeline Free 1846. Ten children: Ella E., Marinda Hyde, Hyrum Smith, Emmeline Amanda, Louise Nelle, Lorenzo Dow, Alonzo, Ruth, Daniel Wells, and Adelle E. Married Margaret Pierce 1846. One child: Brigham Morris. Married Zina D. Huntington 1846. One child: Zina Prescinda. Left Nauvoo 15 February 1846. Established Winter Quarters on Missouri River in fall of 1846. Married Lucy Bigelow 1847. Three Children: Eudora Lovina, Susa A., and Rhoda M. Left Winter Quarters for Rocky Mountains 14 April 1847. Arrived in Salt Lake Valley 24 July 1847. Left to return to Winter Quarters 18 August 1847. Ordained President of Church at Kanesville, Iowa, 5 December 1847. Left Winter Quarters for Salt Lake Valley 26 May 1848. Arrived in Salt Lake Valley 20 September 1848. Elected governor of provisional State of Deseret 12 March 1849. Appointed governor of Utah Territory by Millard Fillmore 20 September 1850. Organized Weber and Utah stakes 1851. Explored southern Utah 1852. Married Eliza Burgess 1852. One Child: Alfales. Broke ground for Salt Lake Temple 14 February 1853. Signed peace treaty ending Walker War 1854. Married Harriet Barney

1856. One child: Phineas Howe. Visited Utah settlements May-June 1861. Sent first telegram over newly completed overland telegraph 18 October 1861. Visited southern settlements September 1862. Married Mary Van Cott 1865. One child: Fannie. In all, fathered fifty-seven children. Organized School of Prophets December 1867. Elected president of ZCMI October 1868. Left for St. George, Utah, to spend winter 25 November 1870. Returned to Salt Lake City 10 February 1871. Dedicated St. George Temple 6 April 1877. Died in Salt Lake City 29 August 1877.[66]

Biographical Note.   Joseph Young.

Son of John Young and Nabbie Howe. Born 7 April 1797 in Hopkinton, Middlesex County, Massachusetts. Member of Methodist church prior to conversion to Mormonism. Baptized 6 April 1832 by Daniel Bowen in Columbia, Pennsylvania. Ordained elder April 1832 by Ezra Landon. Preached in New York in spring of 1832. Mission to Earnestown-Loughborough, Upper Canada, in summer of 1832. Traveled to Kirtland, Ohio, November 1832. Second mission to Earnestown-Loughborough in winter of 1832-33. Married Jane Adeline Bicknell 18 February 1834 in Kirtland. Eleven children: Jane A., Joseph, Seymour B., Marcus De LaGrande, John Calvin, Mary L., Vilate, Chloe, Rhoda, Henriette, and Brigham. Member of Zion's Camp 1834. Ordained seventy 28 February 1835. Ordained President of First Quorum of Seventy 1 March 1835. Served in this position 1835-81. Mission to New York and Massachusetts with Burr Riggs 1835. Participated in dedication of Kirtland Temple 1836. Charter member of and owned stock in Kirtland Safety Society. Member of Kirtland Camp 1838. Left Kirtland 6 July 1838. Arrived at Haun's Mill 28 October 1838. Witnessed Haun's Mill massacre 30 October 1838. Expelled from Missouri 1839. Located temporarily in Quincy, Illinois, May 1839. Moved to Nauvoo in spring of 1840; there was occupied in painting and glazing. Received endowment 3 February 1844. Member of Council of Fifty 1 March 1845. Mission to Ohio 1844 to campaign for Joseph Smith as president of United States. Sealed to Lucinda Allen in Nauvoo 1846. Four children: Josephine, Phineas Howe, John C., and Willard. Sealed to Lydia Flemming 1846 in Nauvoo. Two children: Isaac and Caroline. Sealed to Mary Ann Burnham in Nauvoo 1846. Two children: Elmyra and Clarentine. Left Illinois 1846. Remained in Winter Quarters and Carterville, Iowa, until 1850. Arrived in Utah September 1850. Located in Salt Lake City. Sealed to Sarah Jane Kinsman 1868 at Salt Lake City, Utah. Two children: Edward and Sarah K. Mission to British Isles 1870. Died 16 July 1881 at Salt Lake City, Utah.[67]

Section 125

Date.   March 1841 (about 6 March).

The *History of the Church* notes that Section 125 was given about 20 March 1841, but an entry for 6 March 1841 in the John Smith Journal suggests an earlier date. John Smith records that Alanson Ripley, bishop of the Saints in Iowa, came to see him on 6 March 1841 and gave him the following instructions: "Joseph said it was the will of the Lord the brethren in general in Ambrosia should move in and about the city Zerehemla with all convienent speed which the Saints are willing to do because it is the word of the Lord."[1]

Place.   Nauvoo, Hancock County, Illinois.

Historical Note.   A major factor that permitted the Saints to gather again after their expulsion from Missouri was the liberal land offer extended to them by Isaac Galland. Dr. Galland promoted the Mormon cause by corresponding with political executives in Iowa and Illinois and by offering thousands of acres of land to the Saints on a twenty-year installment agreement with no interest. During the months of April to June 1839, Church land agents purchased from Galland about twenty thousand acres in Lee County, Iowa, and fifty acres in Commerce, Illinois (Nauvoo).

Section 125 instructed the Saints to build up opposite Nauvoo a city to be named Zarahemla. In addition, the town of Nashville was to be built up.

The settlements of Zarahemla, Nashville, Ambrosia, and Montrose were located in Lee County, Iowa, on properties that the Church had purchased from Isaac Galland in 1839.[2]

The counsel to settle on the Iowa side of the Mississippi River and strengthen the settlements named in the revelation was publicly announced on 6 April 1841 at the general conference of the Church in Nauvoo. William Clayton, who was present at the conference, recorded the following:

> A short revelation was also read concerning the saints in Iowa. The question had been asked what is the will of the Lord concerning the saints in Iowa. It read to the following effect—Verily thus saith the Lord let all those my saints who are assaying to do my will gather themselves together upon the land opposite to Nauvoo

and build a city unto my name and let the name of Zarahemla be named upon it. And all who come from the East and West and North and South who have desires let them settle in Zarahemla that they may be prepared for that which is in store for a time to come &c . . . .Many of the brethren immediately made preparations for moving in here but on account of its being so late in the season President John Smith advised to get through with planting and then proceed to move in.[3]

Publication Note.   Section 125 was first published in the *Deseret News* (25 January 1855) and was included as section 125 in the 1876 edition of the Doctrine and Covenants.

Section 126

Date.   9 July 1841.

Place.   Nauvoo, Hancock County, Illinois (in the house of Brigham Young).

Historical Note.   A revelation received by Joseph Smith on 8 July 1838 instructed members of the Quorum of Twelve Apostles to assemble in Far West, Missouri, on 26 April 1839 and "depart to go over the great water, and there promulgate" the gospel.[1] In the fall of 1839, members of the Twelve departed for England, where they arrived in early 1840. In twelve short months these stalwart missionaries were instrumental in converting literally thousands to the Church.[2]

On Thursday, 1 July 1841, Brigham Young, Heber C. Kimball, and John Taylor arrived in Nauvoo, Illinois, from their British Mission. Section 126, received the following week, commended Elder Young for his service in the kingdom and counseled him not to leave his family again during his missionary service.

Publication Note.   Section 126 was first published in the *Deseret News* (18 April 1855) and was included as section 126 in the 1876 edition of the Doctrine and Covenants.

Section 127

Date.   1 September 1842.

Place.   Nauvoo, Hancock County, Illinois.

Historical Note.   Sections 127 and 128 consist of two letters dictated by Joseph Smith on Thursday, 1 September, and Tuesday, 6 September, 1842. These two letters, written in the hand of William Clayton, were addressed to "all the Saints in Nauvoo" at a time when the Prophet was making few public appearances because of threats of unlawful arrest. Governor Carlin of Illinois, responding to a demand from the governor of Missouri, issued a warrant for Joseph Smith's arrest as an accessory before the fact in an assault with intent to kill Lilburn W. Boggs, ex-governor of Missouri. Having been arrested but temporarily released on 8 August 1842, the Prophet remained "in retirement" to avoid reapprehension. It was not until 5 January 1843 that Joseph Smith was formally discharged from this arrest.

The letters concern themselves with salvation for the dead, a subject of much interest and discussion in 1842. Baptism for the dead was first publicly announced on 15 August 1840 at the funeral of Seymour Brunson.[1] Immediately after the announcement of the new doctrine, Church members began performing proxy baptisms in the Mississippi River and in local streams.[2] While those administering these vicarious ordinances in 1840 were not without authority, the actions were not recorded; consequently the baptisms were later repeated. On 3 October 1841 Joseph Smith declared, "There shall be no more baptisms for the dead, until the ordinances can be attended to in the Lord's House....For thus saith the Lord."[3] Baptisms for the dead in the Nauvoo Temple were first performed on Sunday, 21 November 1841.[4] With few exceptions, endowments and sealings for the dead were first administered in the St. George, Utah, Temple.[5]

On 31 August 1842, while addressing members of the Female Relief Society in Nauvoo, Joseph Smith remarked that "a few things had been manifested to him....respecting the baptism for the dead." Although he desired to wait "until he had opportunity to discuss the subject to greater length," the Prophet emphasized that "all persons baptiz'd for the dead must have a Recorder present, that he may be an eye-witness to testify of it."[6] Sections 127 and 128 both give special attention to the matter of having witnesses and recorders for the work of the dead.

Publication Note.   Section 127 was first published in the *Times and Seasons* (15 September 1842) and was included as section 105 in the 1844 edition of the Doctrine and Covenants.

Section 128

Date.   6 September 1842.

Place.   Nauvoo, Hancock County, Illinois.

Historical Note.   See Historical Note for section 127. Wilford Woodruff recorded in his journal the difficulties that the Prophet was encountering at the time he authored sections 127 and 128. Although the "spirit of persecution" prevailed, said Elder Woodruff, "yet the Lord is with him."

> President Joseph Smith has been much persecuted of late by being hunted & sought for by Sheriffs & officers from Missouri & Illinois by the orders of Governors Reynolds & Carlin under pretence of taking him to Missouri to try him for being accessary to the shooting of ex Gov Bogg but it is no more or less than the spirit of persecution But though Joseph has been deprived of the privilege of appearing openly & deprived of the society of his own family Because Sheriffs are hunting him to destroy him without cause Yet the Lord is with him as he was upon the Isle of Patmos with John. Joseph has presented the Church of late with some glorious principles from the Lord concerning Baptism for the dead & other interesting subjects, he has appeared occasionally in the midst of the Saints which has been a great comfort to the Saints.[1]

Publication Note.   Section 128 was first published in the *Times and Seasons* (1 October 1842) and was included as section 106 in the 1844 edition of the Doctrine and Covenants.

Section 129

Date. 9 February 1843.

Place. Nauvoo, Hancock County, Illinois.

Historical Note. The substance of section 129 was revealed to Joseph Smith before 1843. Although the exact date of his receiving these principles of detecting false spirits is not known, it can safely be set before 27 June 1839. On that day members of the First Presidency and Quorum of Twelve met in council in Nauvoo, and in this meeting the Prophet presented the following instructions for the benefit of the Twelve prior to their leaving for England:

> In order to detect the devel when he transforms himself nigh unto an angel of light. When an angel of God appears unto man face to face in personage & reaches out his hand unto the man he takes hold of the angels hand & feels a substance the same as one man would in shaking hands with another he may then know that it is an angel of God & he should place all confidence in him Such personages or angels are Saints with their resurrected Bodies, but if a personage appears unto man & offers him his hand & the man takes hold of it & feels nothing or does not sens[e] any substance he may know it is the devel, for when a Saints whose body is not resurrected appears unto man in the flesh he will not offer him his hand for this is against the law given him.[1]

On the evening of 7 February 1843, Parley P. Pratt arrived in Nauvoo from his mission to England. Two days later, while he was in conversation with the Prophet Joseph Smith, the keys of detecting false spirits (section 129) were explained.[2] The Prophet's scribe, William Clayton, was present and recorded section 129, and Clayton's account was the source for the 1876 publication of the revelation.[3]

Compare the following entry in the Joseph Smith Diary for 9 February 1843. Although this entry, in the hand of Willard Richards, is abbreviated and unclear as a result of poor punctuation, the substance is essentially the same. The Joseph Smith Diary entry is undoubtedly based on Clayton's report.

Parley Pratt & others came in & Joseph explained the following there 3 administrter Angels, spirits Devils—one class in heaven angels the spirits of just men made perfect—innumerable co of angels & spirits of just men made perfect an angel appears to you how will you prove him. ask him to shake hands If he has flesh & bones. he is an angel. "spirit hath not flesh & bones" spirit of a just man made perfect person in its tabernacle could hide its glory if David Patten[4] or the Devil come. how would you determine should you take hold of his hand you would not feel it. If it were a false administration. he would not do it. True spirit will not give his hand The devil will Three keys.[5]

Publication Note. Section 129 was first published in the *Deseret News* (23 April 1856) and was included as section 129 in the 1876 edition of the Doctrine and Covenants.

Section 130

Date. 2 April 1843.

Place. Ramus, Hancock County, Illinois.
Ramus is a Latin word meaning "branch." The city of Ramus, Illinois (later known as Macedonia), was laid out in September 1840, after the same plan as the city of Nauvoo, by members of the Church residing near Crooked Creek. Located twenty miles east of Nauvoo, Ramus was situated in Hancock County on the county road leading from Nauvoo through Carthage to Macomb. Members of the Church began settling the Crooked Creek area early in 1839, and a branch of the Church was organized there in January 1839. Hyrum Smith organized a stake at Ramus 5 July 1840. Joel H. Johnson was chosen and ordained president of the stake.[1]

Historical Note. Section 130 consists of a variety of statements made by Joseph Smith while visiting members of the Church in Ramus, Illinois.
On 1 April 1843 Joseph Smith, Orson Hyde, and William Clayton traveled from Nauvoo to Ramus, where they spent the evening with

Benjamin F. Johnson. The following morning, Sunday, Orson Hyde preached to the Saints in Ramus, taking his text from John 14:23 and 1 John 3:2. After the morning meeting, while Joseph Smith and Orson Hyde dined with Sophronia McLeary (the Prophet's sister), the Prophet declared that he was going to "offer some corrections" to Hyde's sermon.[2]

The William Clayton Diary (as structured and amplified in the Joseph Smith Diary) is the source for all the published versions of these instructions. William Clayton did not segregate the morning and evening instructions as clearly as it is done in the Joseph Smith Diary. Moreover, it is likely that Joseph Smith gave the same instructions in the afternoon and evening. Since Willard Richards (who kept the Prophet's diary) was not on this trip to Ramus, undoubtedly either the Prophet or William Clayton had to direct Richards in separating the diary entry into different times of the day. The contemporary report by William Clayton is here included in its entirety:

> P.M. Joseph preached on Revelations chap. 5. he called on me to open the meeting. He also preached on the same subject in the evening. During the day president Joseph made the following remarks on doctrine. "I was once praying very ernestly to know the time of the coming of the son of man when I heard a voice repeat the following 'Joseph my son, if thou livest until thou art 85 years old thou shalt see the face of the son of man, therefore let this suffice and trouble me no more on this matter.' I was left thus without being able to decide wether this coming referred to the beginning of the Millenium, or to some previous appearing, or wether I should die and thus see his face. I believe the coming of the son of man will not be any sooner than that time."[3] In correcting two points in Er Hydes discourse he observed as follows, "The meaning of that passage where it reads 'when he shall appear we shall be like him for we shall see him as he is' is this, When the savior appears we shall see that he is a man like unto ourselves, and that same sociality which exists amongst us here will exist among us there only it will be coupled with eternal glory which we do not enjoy now. Also the appearing of the father and the son in John c 14 v 23 is a personal appearing and the idea that they will dwell in a mans heart is a sectarian doctrine and is false"[4]

In answer to a question which I [William Clayton]
proposed to him as follows, 'Is not the reckoning of gods
time, angels time, prophets time & mans time according
to the planet on which they reside he answered yes "But
there is no angel ministers to this earth only what either
does belong or has belonged to this earth and the angels
do not reside on a planet like our earth but they dwell
with God and the planet where he dwells is like crystal,
and like a sea of glass before the throne. This is the great
Urim & Thummim whereon all things are manifest both
things past, present & future and are continually before
the Lord. The Urim & Thummim is a small represen-
tation of this globe. The earth when it is purified will be
made like unto crystal and will be a Urim & Thummim
whereby all things pertaining to an inferior kingdom or
all kingdoms of a lower order will be manifest to those
who dwell on it. and this earth will be with Christ Then
the white stone mentioned in Rev. c 2 v 17 is the Urim &
Thummim whereby all things pertaining to an higher
order of kingdoms even all kingdoms will be made
known and a white stone is given to each of those who
come into this celestial kingdom, whereon is a new name
written which no man knoweth save he that receiveth it.
The new name is the key word.[5]

"Whatever principle of intelligence we obtain in this
life will rise with us in the ressurection: and if a person
gains more knowledge in this life through his diligence &
obedience than another, he will have so much the
advantage in the world to come. There is a law ir-
revocably decreed in heaven before the foundation of
this world upon whch all blessings are predicated; and
when we obtain any blessing from God, it is by obedience to that law upon which it is predicated.

"The Holy Ghost is a personage, and a person cannot
have the personage of the H.G. in his heart. A man
receive the gifts of the H.G., and the H.G. may descend
upon a man but not to tarry with him.[6]

He also related the following dream. "I dreamed that
silver-headed old man came to see me and said he was
invaded by a gang of robbers, who were plundering his
neighbors and threatening distruction to all his subjects.
He had heard that I always sought to defend the op-
pressed, and he had come to hear with his own ears what

answer I would give him. I answered, if you will make out the papers and shew that you are not the agressor I will call out the Legion and defend you while I have a man to stand by me. The old man then turned to go away. When he got a little distance he turned suddenly round and said I must call out the Legion and go and he would have the papers ready when I arrived, and says he I have any amount of men which you can have under your command.[7]

Er Hyde gave this interpretation "The old man represents the government of these United States who will be invaded by a foreign foe, probably England. The U.S. government will call on you to defend probably all this Western Territory, and will offer you any amount of men you may need for that purpose.

Once when prest. Joseph was praying ernestly to know concerning the wars which are to preceed the coming of the son of man, he heard a voice proclaim that the first outbreak of general bloodshed would commence at South Carolina—see Revelation[8]

The sealing of the 144000 was the number of priests who should be anointed to administer in the daily sacrifice &c. During Prest. Joseph's remarks he said their was a nice distinction between the vision which John saw as spoken of in Revelations & the vision which Daniel saw, the former relating only to things as they actually existed in heaven—the latter being a figure representing things on the earth. God never made use of the figure of a beast to represent the kingdom of heaven—when they were made use of it was to represent an apostate church.

Benjamin F. Johnson, at whose home the Prophet and others stayed, vividly remembered the visit, and later stated,

On April 2d and May 16th 1843 the Prophet was at my house with Wm Clayton as *scribe* at which time was written in answer to questions asked all of sections 130 & 131 Doc & Cov and he then gave to us all keys of knowledge contained in sec 129 & 132 of the both before it was written.[9]

Publication Note. Section 130 was first published in the *Deseret News* (9 July 1856) and was included as section 130 in the 1876 edition of the Doctrine and Covenants.

Section 131

Date.   16 and 17 May 1843.

Place.   Ramus, Hancock County, Illinois.

Historical Note. Section 131 consists of a variety of doctrinal statements made by Joseph Smith while visiting members of the Church in Ramus, Illinois. The Prophet's personal scribe, William Clayton, accompanied him on this occasion and preserved Joseph Smith's remarks in his personal diary.

   On 16 May 1843 Joseph Smith, William Clayton, George Miller, Eliza Partridge, Lydia Partridge, and Lorin Walker traveled to visit the Saints in Ramus. The Prophet and William Clayton spent the evening with Benjamin F. Johnson and the others at the home of William G. Perkins. Before retiring, the Prophet gave Benjmin F. Johnson and his wife some instructions on priesthood, which included verses 1-4 of section 131. Putting his hand on the knee of William Clayton, the Prophet said, "Your life is hid with Christ in God, and so is many others." Addressing Benjamin F., Joseph said: "Nothing but the unpardonable sin can prevent him [Clayton] from inheriting eternal glory for he is sealed up by the power of the priesthood unto eternal life having taken the step which is necessary for that purpose." The Prophet continued,

> Except a man and his wife enter into an everlasting covenant and be married for eternity while in this probation by the power and authority of the Holy priesthood they will cease to increase when they die (ie. they will not have any children in the resurrection, but those who are married by the power & authority of the priesthood in this life & continue without committing the sin against the Holy Ghost will continue to increase & have children in the celestial glory. The unpardonable

sin is to shed innocent blood or be accessory thereto. All other sins will be visited with judgement in the flesh and the spirit being delivered to the buffetings of satan untill the day of the Lord Jesus . . . .Prest J. said that the way he knew in whom to confide, God told him in whom he might place confidence. He also said that in the celestial glory there was three heavens or degrees, and in order to obtain the highest a man must enter into this order of the priesthood and if he dont he cant obtain it. He may enter into the other but that is the end of his kingdom he cannot have increase.[1]

The following morning, 17 May 1843, the Prophet preached from the first chapter of 2 Peter, when verses 5-6 were recorded,

At 10 [A.M.] Prest. J. preached on 2nd Peter Ch 1. He shewed that knowledge is power & the man who has the most knowledge has the greatest power. Also that salvation means a mans being placed beyond the powers of all his enemies. He said the more sure word of prophecy meant, a mans knowing that he was sealed up unto eternal life by revelation & the spirit of prophecy through the power of the Holy priesthood. He also showed that it was impossible for a man to be saved in ignorance. Paul had seen the third heavens and I more. Peter penned the most sublime language of any of the apostles.[2]

In the evening of the same day, the Prophet went to hear Samuel A. Prior, a Methodist preacher. At the close of the preacher's remarks, Joseph Smith offered some corrections that included verses 7-8:

P.M. pres. J. attended the City council & afterwards rode out with B.F. Johnsons family. In the evening we went to hear a Methodist preacher lecture. After he got through Pres. J. offered some corrections as follows. The 7th verse of C[hapter] 2 Genesis ought to read God breathed into Adam his spirit or breath of life, but when the word "ruach" applies to Eve it should be translated lives. Speaking of eternal duration of matter he said. There is no such thing as immaterial matter. All spirit is matter but is more fine or pure and can only be discerned by purer eyes We cant see it but when our bodies are purified we shall see that it is all matter. The gentleman seemed pleased & said he should visit Nauvoo immediately.[3]

Publication Note.   Section 131 was first published in the *Deseret News* (24 September 1856) and was included as section 131 in the 1876 edition of the Doctrine and Covenants.

Section 132

Date.   12 July 1843.

Place.   Nauvoo, Hancock County, Illinois.

Historical Note.   Section 132 is a revelation addressing the subjects of eternal and plural marriage and the principles upon which such marriages were to be performed in the Church. Because the Prophet had learned of and begun to practice plural marriage several years earlier, and because he started performing eternal marriages in 1841, many have concluded that section 132 was revealed years earlier, and merely written down in July 1843. A more accurate interpretation is that while Joseph Smith may have received revelation on matters contained in section 132 prior to 1843, this revelation (its form, language, and message) was unquestionably received for the first time in the summer of 1843.

Joseph Smith learned of the principle of plural marriage as early as July 1831, near Independence, on the border of Missouri and what later became Kansas.[1] Moreover, available evidence attests that the Prophet began to take additional wives by 1836, in Kirtland, Ohio. Although plural marriage did not become a law of the Church until its public announcement in 1852, Joseph Smith, and later Brigham Young, did instruct a select number of faithful Mormon brethren to take additional wives before that date.[2]

Whereas the concept of plural marriage appears to have had its birth in Kirtland, the principle of eternal marriage developed at Nauvoo. A combination of both principles was taught privately by the Prophet, beginning in 1841. From the beginning Joseph's wife,

Emma, appears to have objected to his taking additional wives. Her refusal to accept the doctrine and to support her husband in righteousness resulted in a year's delay in administering the blessings of the temple endowment to women because Joseph desired his wife to be the first woman to receive the ordinance.[3] Finally, in May 1843 she consented to the Prophet's taking plural-eternal wives, but by July she had reversed her position and was adamant.[4] Hyrum Smith, William Law, and William Marks, presiding Church leaders, also were bitterly opposed to the doctrine, and while Law and Marks could never assent to the implications of the practice, the Prophet's brother, Hyrum, was converted to it on 26 May 1843.[5]

Section 132 was received on the morning of 12 July 1843 at the request of Hyrum Smith, who hoped that a written revelation on the subject would assuage Emma's feelings. Hyrum was fairly confident that if the Prophet would write down a revelation on celestial marriage, he could take it for Emma to read and thereby regain her support.[6] William Clayton took down the ten-page revelation at Joseph Smith's dictation in the "small office upstairs in the rear of [the Prophet's Red Brick] store."[7] An entry in the Clayton diary for 12 July 1843 states the following:

> This A.M. I wrote a Revelation consisting of 10 pages on the order of the priesthood, showing the designs in Moses, Abraham, David and Solomon having many wives & concubines &c. After it was wrote Prests. Joseph & Hyrum presented it and read it to E[mma]. who said she did not believe a word of it and appeared very rebellious.[8]

Towards evening on 12 July Bishop Newel K. Whitney received permission to copy the revelation. About mid-day on 13 July Joseph C. Kingsbury, store-clerk for Bishop Whitney, carefully took a copy, which both Whitney and Kingsbury proofread against the original. The Kingsbury copy, which was given to Brigham Young in March 1847,[9] was used to publish the revelation five years later. Whereas the Clayton copy was burned, the Kingsbury copy is still in existence.[10]

Publication Note.   Section 132 was first published in a *Deseret News Extra* (14 September 1852), and was included as section 132 in the 1876 edition of the Doctrine and Covenants. A statement known as the "Article on Marriage," written by Oliver Cowdery in 1835, served as the Church's official position on marriage and was printed in each edition of the Doctrine and Covenants until 1876, when it was replaced by section 132.[11]

Section 133

Date.   3 November 1831.

Place.   Hiram, Portage County, Ohio.

Historical Note.   On 3 November 1831, during the important Hiram, Ohio, conferences, "the Elders desired to know relative to preaching the Gospel to the inhabitants of the earth, and concerning the gathering; and in order to walk by the true light, and be instructed from on high."[1]

In response to this request, the Prophet inquired of the Lord and received section 133. As will be noted by the date of reception, the revelation is not placed in chronological sequence. Section 133 which is known as the "Appendix" to the Doctrine and Covenants, was intended to be placed at the end of the Book of Commandments in 1833. The destruction of the Church printing press in Independence, Missouri, on 20 July 1833, prevented the inclusion of the Appendix in that publication, but it has been placed at or near the end of subsequent editions of the Doctrine and Covenants.

The revelation was published in the *Evening and Morning Star* while the Book of Commandments was being printed and contained the following headnote: "Having given, in a previous number, the Preface to the book of commandments now in press, we give below, the close, or as it has been called, the Appendix. It affords us joy to lay before the saints an article fraught with so much heavenly intelligence."[2]

Publication Note.   Section 133 was first published in the *Evening and Morning Star* (May 1833) and was included as section 100 in the 1835 edition of the Doctrine and Covenants.

Section 134

Date.   17 August 1835.
The date 17 August 1835 is when section 134 was approved by a Church general assembly to be included in the Doctrine and Covenants, not the date of writing.

Place.   Kirtland, Geauga County, Ohio.

Historical Note.   On 17 August 1835 an important Church conference was convened in Kirtland for the purpose of examining and approving a compilation of revelations ready for printing. This compilation, called "Doctrine and Covenants of the Church of the Latter Day Saints," was prepared by a committee consisting of Joseph Smith, Oliver Cowdery, Sidney Rigdon, and Frederick G. Williams.

At the close of the meeting, after all those present had examined the revelations and voted to approve them, Oliver Cowdery stood and "read an instrument containing certain principles or items upon law in general & church governments." After he had read the document, the entire congregation unanimously voted that it be accepted and included with the revelations.[1]

Although Joseph Smith and Frederick G. Williams were on a mission to Michigan when the above meeting was held, the Prophet approved of section 134 and declared the statement to be "the belief of the Church" on principles of law and government.[2]

The authorship of section 134 traditionally has been attributed to Oliver Cowdery.

Publication Note.   Section 134 was first published in the *Messenger and Advocate* (August 1835) and was included as section 102 in the 1835 edition of the Doctrine and Covenants.

Section 135

Date.   27 June 1844.

Place.   Nauvoo, Hancock County, Illinois.

Historical Note.   Written by President John Taylor, eyewitness of the tragedy, section 135 is an account of the deaths of Joseph and Hyrum Smith on 27 June 1844.[1]

It was the destruction of the *Nauvoo Expositor*, a paper aimed at traducing the character of Joseph Smith, that triggered the events resulting in the Prophet's death in Carthage, Illinois. Mormon apostates in Nauvoo, smarting over the loss of their printing establishment and bent on ridding the country of the Mormon prophet, brought legal complaints against Joseph Smith and others in June 1844. Initially the Prophet was impressed to leave the United States for the West, but accusations of desertion by a few close associates motivated him to stay and stand trial. Opposing forces, conspiring with law-enforcement officers, took advantage of this last arrest. Gathering at Carthage, Illinois, where Joseph Smith had been illegally detained, a mob forced their way into the jail and, at 5:16 P.M., murdered the Prophet and his brother Hyrum.

Publication Note.   Section 135 was first published as section 111 in the 1844 edition of the Doctrine and Covenants.

Section 136

Date.   14 January 1847.

Place.   Winter Quarters (Nebraska).

Historical Note.   After the Saints' exodus from Nauvoo in 1846, Mormon settlements soon spanned the state of Iowa and dotted the west bank of the Missouri River in Nebraska. Section 136 was received by Brigham Young in January 1847 after Church leaders had discussed and deliberated upon the "best manner of organizing companies for emigration."[1] On Thursday, 14 January 1847, members of the Quorum of the Twelve Apostles met at Heber C. Kimball's dwelling, where

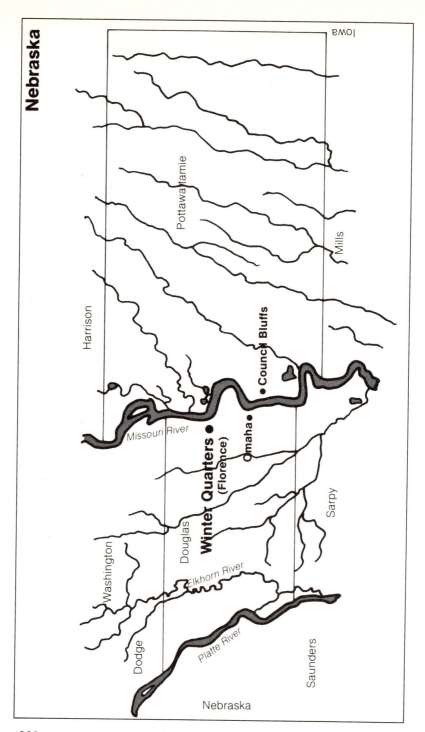

Nebraska

Iowa

Pottawattamie

Mills

Harrison

• Council Bluffs

Missouri River

Winter Quarters •
(Florence)

Omaha •

Douglas

Sarpy

Washington

Elkhorn River

Dodge

Platte River

Saunders

Nebraska

298

President Young proposed that letters be written to instruct brethren how to organize companies for emigration....President Young commenced to give the Word and Will of God concerning the emigration of the Saints and those who journeyed with them. At 4:30 P.M. the council adjourned.

At seven, the Twelve met at Elder Benson's. President Young continued to dictate the word and will of the Lord. Council adjourned at ten P.M., when President Young retired with Dr. Richards to the Octagon and finished writing the same.[2]

At a meeting of the Twelve Apostles and the Winter Quarters high council on 16 January 1847, the following discussion transpired:

Present of the Twelve
    Brigham Young H.C. Kimball Willard Richards
present of the [High] Council
    George W Harris President Reynolds Cahoon C.P.
Lott Ezra Chase Daniel Russel Alonzo Eldrige Thomas
Grover Isaac Morley Winslow Farr
Council was opened by Prayer by G.W. Harris....
The mind & will of God as written by the Twelve of the
14th of January 1847 was read by Dr. Richards
Co[uncilo]r Reynolds Cahoon moved that the communication be received as the mind & will of God as it purports. Second by Isaac Morley
Co[uncilo]r A Eldrige approved it—Come to his understanding
Co[uncilo]r Morley—approved it
Co[uncilo]r Cahoon—said it was the same voice as all other righteous come from.
Co[uncilo]r Farr—Said it reminded him of the first reading of the Book of Mormon, he was perfectly satisfied that it was from the Lord
Co[uncilo]r Lott—perfectly satisfied—it give peace
Co[uncilo]r D. Russel—feels as he did the first M[ormon] sermon he ever head says that it is true & glories in them & means to stand & sustain all these things
Co[uncilo]r Chase is perfectly satisfied
President Harris was so well satisfied that he wanted to say Amen at once

Co[uncilo]r Grover—felt that it was the voice of the spirit has the same confidence as he has in every thing we have called revelation.

Vote found to be unanimous

Horrace S. Eldrige . . . says he felt to receive it as the word & will of the Lord & that it would prove our salvation if carried out. Hosea Stout the Clerk says if there is any thing in Mormonism that is the voice of the Lord to this people & means to live up to it.

After much conversation & the second reading of the word & will the council adjourned.[3]

During the rest of the month of January 1847, the revelation was presented to members of the Church in Nebraska and Iowa, where it was approved unanimously.[4]

Publication Note.   Section 136 was first published in the *Millennial Star* (1 May 1852) and was included as section 136 in the 1876 edition of the Doctrine and Covenants.

Biographical Note.   Ezra Taft Benson.

Son of John and Chloe Benson. Born 22 February 1811 in Mendon, Worcester County, Massachusetts. Married Pamelia Andrus 1 January 1832. Eight children: Chloe Jane, Adin Parsons, Jonathan, Harvey, Charles Taft, Emma Parsons, Isabella, and Charlotte Taft. Baptized 19 July 1840 in Quincy, Illinois. Ordained elder 3-5 October 1840 by Elisha H. Groves at Nauvoo, Illinois. Ordained high priest by Hyrum Smith 25 October 1840 in Quincy. Appointed member of stake presidency in Quincy, Illinois, 25 October 1840. Moved to Nauvoo April 1841. Mission to eastern states 1842-43. Left Nauvoo 1 June 1842. Returned to Nauvoo in fall of 1843. Sealed to Adaline Brooks Andrus (plural wife) on 27 April 1844. Three children: George Taft, Florence Adeline, and Frank. Mission to East May 1844. Returned to Nauvoo in fall of 1844. Appointed member of Nauvoo high council 7 October 1844. Mission to East December 1844. Presided over Boston conference until May 1845. Received endowment 15 December 1845. Sealed in Nauvoo Temple to Pamelia Andrus 16 January 1846. Sealed in Nauvoo Temple to Adaline Brooks Andrus 16 January 1846. Sealed in Nauvoo Temple to Desdemona Catlin Fullmer for time 26 January 1846. Left Nauvoo for West February 1846. Appointed counselor to William Huntington in Mt. Pisgah 22 May 1846. Moved to Council Bluffs 1846. Ordained apostle 16 July 1846. Mission to East; returned 27 November 1846. Sealed to Eliza Perry 4 March 1847, at Council Bluffs, Iowa. Seven children: Alice Eliza, John Perry, Malina A., Orion W., Carrie S., Abbie Della, and Grace A. Arrived in Salt

Lake Valley 24 July 1847. Returned to Winter Quarters 1847. Mission to East 1847-48. Presided over Church membership in Pottawattamie County, Iowa, with Orson Hyde and George A. Smith 1848. Moved to Salt Lake Valley 1849. Member of provisional State of Deseret legislature 1849. Mission to Pottawattamie County 1851 to gather remaining Saints. Returned to Utah August 1852. Sealed to Mary Knight about 1852. Seven children: Louise, Heber, Moroni, Lorenzo T., Joseph, Ida, Don Carlos. Married Elizabeth Golliaher 5 June 1852. Seven children: Fred Golliaher, Brigham Young, Luella, William C., Hyrum Smith, Edith, and Lizzie. Mission to Europe 1856. With Orson Pratt, presided over British mission until fall of 1857. Returned to Salt Lake Valley 1857. Member of Utah Territorial House of Representatives 1859-69. Appointed to preside over Church in Cache Valley, Utah, 1860. Resided in Cache Valley until death at Logan. Mission to Sandwich Islands 1864-65. Married Mary Larsen 3 September 1866. Two children: Walter and Henry T. Contractor on Central Pacific Railroad. Died 3 September 1869 in Ogden, Weber County, Utah.[4]

Biographical Note.   Erastus Snow.

Son of Levi Snow and Lucina Streeter. Born 9 November 1818 in St. Johnsbury, Caledonia County, Vermont. Baptized 3 February 1833 in Derby Lake, Charleston, Vermont. Ordained teacher 28 June 1834. Ordained priest 13 November 1834. Ordained elder 16 August 1835. Missionary work in Vermont 1834-35. Left Vermont for Kirtland, Ohio, 8 November 1835. Arrived in Kirtland 3 December 1835. Attended School of Elders. Participated in dedication of Kirtland Temple March 1836. Ordained seventy by Lyman Sherman early 1836. Mission to Pennsylvania 1836. Departed from Kirtland 16 April 1836. Returned 29 December 1836, having baptized fifty persons. Charter member of and owned stock in Kirtland Safety Society January 1837. Additional missionary activity in Pennsylvania May-December 1837, baptizing about forty persons. Mission to Pennsylvania and Maryland 1838. Left Kirtland 2 January 1838. Returned 3 June 1838. Moved to Far West, Missouri, 1838. Left Kirtland 25 June 1838 and arrived in Far West 8 August 1838. Married Artemesia Beman 3 December 1838. Eleven children: Sarah Lucina, James, Charles Henry, Artimesia, Franklin Richards, Orson Pratt, Mahonri Moriancumer, Erastus Beman, Mary Louisa, Moroni, and George Albert. Succeeded in getting change of venue for Prophet and other prinsoners in Liberty Jail April 1839. Left Far West for Quincy, Illinois, 15 April 1839. Arrived in Quincy 27 April 1839. Appointed one of committee of three 4 May 1839 to gather libelous reports against Church. Located in Montrose, Iowa, 1839. Appointed member of Iowa high council 6 October 1839. Mission to Pennsylvania, New Jersey, and Massachusetts 1840. Left Nauvoo late April 1840 and returned 21 October 1840. Another mission to Pennsylvania 1840-41. Left Nauvoo with wife 7 November 1840. Arrived in Downingtown, Pennsylvania, 21

November 1840. Appointed by Hyrum Smith and William Law July 1841 to preach in Salem, Massachusetts, area. Left for Salem 20 August 1841. Arrived 3 September 1841. Left for Nauvoo 9 March 1843. Arrived 11 April 1843. Returned to Salem 11 May 1843. Arrived 2 June 1843. Left Salem for Illinois 22 September 1843. Arrived 5 November 1843. Member of Council of Fifty 11 March 1844. Married first plural wife, Minerva White, 2 April 1844. Nine children: Nephi, Mary Minerva, Willard, Hyrum Smith, Levi, Erastus White, Susan, Louisa White, and Alden. Initiated into Masonry early 1844. Appointed 15 April 1844 to campaign in Vermont for Joseph Smith as president of United States. Left Nauvoo 30 April 1844. Returned to Nauvoo from Vermont 25 July 1844. Received endowment 12 December 1845. Left Nauvoo for West February 1846. Arrived in Cutler's Park 1 September 1846. One of original pioneers. Entered Salt Lake Valley 21 July 1847. Returned to Winter Quarters 31 October 1847. Married Elizabeth Rebecca Ashby 19 December 1847. Ten children: Josephine, Georgiana, Ashby, Arthur Eugene, Elizabeth, Florence, Bryant, Martha Ellen, Herbert Hammond, and Clarence. Appointed to take mission to eastern states with Ezra T. Benson December 1847. Left Winter Quarters 28 December 1847. Returned 30 April 1848. Traveled with family to Salt Lake Valley, arriving 20 September 1848. Appointed counselor in Salt Lake Stake presidency October 1848. Ordained apostle 12 February 1849. Mission to Denmark October 1849-August 1852. Appointed to take fifty families to Iron County, Utah, October 1852. Appointed to organize stake in St. Louis, Missouri, April 1853. Left Salt Lake City 8 July 1853. Organized St. Louis Stake 4 November 1854; published *St. Louis Luminary*. Returned to Salt Lake City 31 August 1855. Married Julie Josephine Spencer 11 April 1856. Six children: Edward Hunter, Amelia, Mary Brown, William Spencer, Joseph Smith, and Maud Rosamond. Left on mission to St. Louis and East 22 April 1856. Returned to Salt Lake City 7 August 1857. Left on mission to East September 1860. Returned to Salt Lake City 6 September 1861. Colonizing mission to Virgin River and Santa Clara in Southern Utah in 1861. Founded St. George, Utah, in December 1861. Later located in St. George; spent several years in settling area. Mission to Scandinavia 1873. Several missions to Arizona and Mexico 1878-86. Died 27 May 1888 in Salt Lake City, Utah.[5]

Section 137

Date.   21 January 1836.

Place.   Kirtland, Geauga County, Ohio.

Historical Note.   This revelation was received in the west "school room" of the chapel in the Kirtland Temple. Church leaders from

Kirtland and Missouri had met to be anointed with oil as part of their preparation for the endowment of power—to be bestowed upon the "first elders" in connection with the dedication of the Kirtland Temple.[1] Two separate meetings were held the evening of January 21, the latter continuing into the morning hours. During the first meeting, Joseph Smith, Sr., with members of the First Presidency, the Presidency of the Church in Missouri (David Whitmer, William W. Phelps, and John Whitmer), the Bishoprics in Kirtland and Missouri, and the Prophet's scribe (Warren Parrish) anointed each other with "holy oil" and offered prayers that the anointing blessings would be accepted. The second meeting was not unlike the first, except that those being anointed were members of the Church high councils in Kirtland and Missouri. Although visions and spiritual manifestations were witnessed during both ceremonies, section 137 was received during the first anointing session. The minutes of the 21 January 1836 meetings, which contain this vision, are recorded in the Joseph Smith Diary in the hand of Warren Parrish.[2]

Textual Note.   The text of section 137 is an extract from the fuller account of heavenly manifestations received by Joseph Smith and others in the Kirtland Temple on 21 January 1836. Compare section 137 with the more complete account found in the Prophet's diary.

Joseph Smith Diary

The heavens were opened upon us and I beheld the celestial Kingdom of God, and the glory thereof, whether in the body or out I cannot tell. I saw the transcendant beauty of the gate that enters through which the heirs of that Kingdom will enter, which was like unto circling flames of fire, also the blasing throne of God, whereon was seated the Father and the Son. I saw the beautiful streets of that Kingdom, which had the appearance of being paved with gold. I saw father Adam, and Abraham and *Michael*[3] and my father and mother, my brother Alvin that has long since slept, and marvled how it was that he had obtained an inheritance in that Kingdom, seeing that he had departed this life before the Lord had set his hand to gather Israel the second time and had not been baptized for the remission of sins. Thus said came the voice of the Lord unto me saying all who have died with[out] a knowledge of this gospel, who would have have received it with all their hearts shall be heirs of that Kingdom for I the Lord will judge all men according to their works according to the desires of their hearts. And ~~again I also beheld the Terrestial Kingdom~~ I also beheld that all children who die before they arrive to the years of accountability, are saved in the celestial Kingdom of heaven.

I saw the 12 Apostles of the Lamb, who are now upon the earth who hold the Keys of this last ministry in foreign lands, standing together in a circle much fatigued, with their clothes tattered and feet swolen, with their eyes cast downward, and Jesus standing in their midst and they did not behold him. The Saviour looked upon them and wept. I also beheld Elder [William E.] McLellen in the South, standing upon a hill surrounded with a vast multitude, preaching to them, and a lame man standing before him, supported by his crutches. He threw them down at his word, and leaped as an heart [hart], by the mighty power of God. Also Elder Brigham Young standing in a strange land, in the far southwest, in a desert place, upon a rock in the midst of about a dozen men of colour, who appeared hostile. He was preaching to them in their own toung, and the angel of God standing above his head with a drawn sword in his hand protecting him, but he did not see it. And I finally saw the 12 in the Celestial Kingdom of God. I also beheld the redemption of Zion, and many things which the toung of man cannot describe in full. Many of my brethren who received this ordinance with me, saw glorious visions also. Angels ministered unto them, as well as myself, and the power of the highest rested upon us. The house was filled with the glory of God and we shouted Hosanah to God and the Lamb.

1981 Edition

1. The heavens were opened upon us, and I beheld the celestial kingdom of God, and the glory thereof, whether in the body or out I cannot tell.

2. I saw the transcendent beauty of the gate through which the heirs of that kingdom will enter, which was like unto circling flames of fire;

3. Also the blazing throne of God, whereon was seated the Father and the Son.

4. I saw the beautiful streets of that kingdom, which had the appearance of being paved with gold.

5. I saw Father Adam and Abraham; and my father and my mother; my brother Alvin, that has long since slept;

6. And marveled how it was that he had obtained an inheritance in that kingdom, seeing that he had departed this life before the Lord had set his hand to gather Israel the second time, and had not been baptized for the remission of sins.

7. Thus came the voice of the Lord unto me, saying: All who have died without a knowledge of this gospel, who would have received it with all their hearts, shall be heirs of that kingdom;

8.   Also all that shall die henceforth without a knowledge of it, who would have received it with all their hearts, shall be heirs of that kingdom;

9.   For I, the Lord, will judge all men according to their works, according to the desire of their hearts.

10.   And I also beheld that all children who die before they arrive at the years of accountability are saved in the celestial kingdom of heaven.

Publication Note.   Section 137 was first published in the *Deseret News* (4 September 1852) and is included in the 1981 edition of the Doctrine and Covenants.

Biographical Note.   Alvin Smith.

Son of Joseph Smith and Lucy Mack. Born 11 February 1799 at Tunbridge, Orange County, Vermont. Died 19 November 1823 at Smith Farm in Manchester, New York, and buried in Palmyra, New York.[4]

Section 138

Date.   3 October 1918.

Place.   Salt Lake City, Salt Lake County, Utah.

Historical Note. Section 138, known as the "Vision of the Redemption of the Dead," was received by Joseph F. Smith six weeks before his death, during his final illness. President Smith alluded to this vision in his opening remarks at the Eighty-Ninth Semiannual Conference of the Church on 4 October 1918. In this short talk he stated,

> I will not, I dare not, attempt to enter upon many things that are resting upon my mind this morning, and I shall postpone until some future time, the Lord being willing, my attempt to tell you some of the things that are in my mind, and that dwell in my heart. I have not lived alone these five months. I have dwelt in the spirit of prayer, of supplication, of faith and of determination; and I have had my communication with the Spirit of the Lord continuously.[1]

The vision was submitted to President Smith's two counselors, the Quorum of the Twelve Apostles, and the Presiding Patriarch of the Church on 31 October 1918 for approval as revelation. Concerning the occasion James E. Talmage, member of the Quorum of the Twelve, recorded the following:

> Attended meeting of the First Presidency and the Twelve. Today President Smith, who is still confined to his home by illness, sent to the Brethren the account of a vision through which, as he states, were revealed to him important facts relating to the work of the disembodied Savior in the realm of departed spirits, and of the missionary work in progress on the other side of the veil. By united action the Council of the Twelve, with the Counsellors in the First Presidency, and the Presiding Patriarch accepted and enforced the revelation as the Word of the Lord. President Smith's signed statement will be published in the next issue (December) of the Improvement Era, which is the organ of the Priesthood quorum of the Church.[2]

Publication Note. Section 138 was first published in *The Improvement Era* (December 1918) and is included in the 1981 edition of the Doctrine and Covenants.

Biographical Note.   Joseph Fielding Smith.

Son of Hyrum Smith and Mary Fielding. Born 13 November 1838 at Far West, Caldwell County, Missouri. After death of father June 1844, mother supported Twelve Apostles as legitimate leadership of Church. To Salt Lake Valley 1848. Mother died 1852. Received endowment 24 April 1854. Mission to Hawaii 27 May 1854-24 February 1858. Member of (Utah) Nauvoo Legion during Utah War 1858. Ordained seventy 29 March 1858. Married Levira Anett Clark 5 April 1859. No known children. Ordained high priest 16 October 1859. Member of Salt Lake Stake high council 1859. Mission to Great Britain 1860-63. Special mission to Hawaii 1864. Member of Territorial House of Representatives 1865-74 and 1880-82. Sealed to Julia Lambson 5 May 1866. Thirteen children: Mercy Josephine, Mary Sophronia, Donnette, Joseph Fielding, David Asael, George Carlos, Julia Clarissa, Elias Wesley, Emily, Rachel, Edith Eleanor, Edward Arthur (adopted), and Marjorie Virginia (adopted). Ordained apostle 1 July 1866. Sealed to Sarah Ellen Richards 1 March 1868. Eleven children: Sarah Ella, Leonora, Joseph Richards, Heber John, Rhoda Ann, Minerva, Alice, Willard, Franklin,

Jeanetta, and Asenath. Sealed to Edna Lambson 1 January 1871. Ten children: Hyrum Mack, Alvin Fielding, Alfred Jason, Edna Melissa, Albert Jessie, Robert, Emma, Zina, Ruth, and Martha. Presided over European Mission 1874-75. Second term as president of European Mission 1877. Mission to eastern states with Orson Pratt 1878 in interest of history of Church. Second counselor to John Taylor 10 October 1880-25 July 1887. Sealed to Alice Ann Kimball 6 December 1883. Seven children: Alice May (adopted), Heber Chase (adopted), Charles Coulson (adopted), Lucy Mack, Andrew, Jessie, and Fielding. Sealed to Mary Taylor Schwartz 13 January 1884. Seven children: John, Calvin, Samuel, James, Agnes, Silas, and Royal Grant. Second counselor to Wilford Woodruff 7 April 1889-2 September 1898. Second counselor to Lorenzo Snow 13 September 1898-6 October 1901. Sustained as first counselor to Lorenzo Snow 6 October 1901-10 October 1901. Not set apart to this postion. President of Church 17 October 1901-19 November 1918. Died 1918, Salt Lake City, Salt Lake County, Utah.[3]

Sections 73-138 Notes

Section 73

1. See Historical Note for section 71.
2. See *Times and Seasons* 5 (15 July 1844): 576, and Historical Note for section 75.

Section 74

1. *Times and Seasons* 5 (15 July 1844): 576.

Section 75

1. *Times and Seasons* 5 (15 July 1844):576.
2. See Joel H. Hills Journal, Brigham Young University Library, Special Collections. Just two weeks after the Amherst conference, Wesley Perkins, a skeptical non-Mormon from Amherst, described the Mormon "stir" to a relative:

> As it respects Religion in this Town there is considerable stir at present.
> The Mormon Religion excites the greatest curiosity at present. Joseph
> Smith & Sidney Rigdon is the head men in this business. There God is
> the Devil None but the simple will imbrace there Doctrin....I
> understood that Jared Carter was in Benson [Vermont] & had Baptised a
> number and would start for the Promest land [Missouri] in the Spring,
> it is nothing more than I should expect of the Carters & some others in
> that part of Town of Benson. Whoever joins them will become a Prest or
> prophet or a prophetess. I would send you a paper that contains a letter
> written by the Rev. E. Boothe I will send you the letters & you may read
> them and sattisfy yourself Mr. Booth went to the Promest land (Wesley
> Perkins to Jacob Perkins, 11 February 1832, Brigham Young University
> Library, Manuscripts).

3. See Historical Notes for sections 52 and 81.

4. *History of the Church*, 1: 242-43.

5. Elden J. Watson, *Orson Pratt Journals*, under date.

6. Reported in "St. George Utah Stake General Minutes," 23 December 1880, Church Archives (CR. 7836, #11). I am indebted to Andrew F. Ehat for this reference. Edson Barney's recollection regarding Sidney Rigdon as scribe is significant. A manuscript copy of section 75 (actually this section is a composite of two revelations) in the Newel K. Whitney Collection, Brigham Young University Library, Manuscripts, is in Sidney Rigdon's hand, and may in fact be the original.

7. Verses 1-22 constitute one revelation, and verses 23-36 the other. See manuscript copies of these revelations in Sidney Rigdon's handwriting in Newel K. Whitney Collection, Brigham Young University Library, Manuscripts.

8. Ibid.

9. For additional information concerning section 75 and the missionaries mentioned therein, see Orson Hyde Journal (typescript), Brigham Young University Library, Special Collections; Samuel H. Smith Journal (typescript), Brigham Young University Library, Special Collections; Elden J. Watson, *Orson Pratt Journals*; Reynolds Cahoon Journal, Church Archives; Eden Smith Journal, Church Archives; "History of Thomas B. Marsh, Written by Himself" (November 1857), Church Archives; Joseph Smith to William W. Phelps, 31 July 1832, Joseph Smith Collection, Church Archives; and (concerning McLellan's mission appointment) Joseph Smith to Emma Smith, 6 June 1832, Church Archives.

10. John Smith Journal (not the Prophet's uncle), Church Archives;"Far West Record"; 1790 Federal Census of Massachusetts; 1840 Federal Census of Ohio; and *Ashley Genealogy*, Genealogical Society, Salt Lake City, Utah.

11. *History of the Church*; D&C 75; "Seymour Brunson Biography," Brigham Young University Library, Special Collections; 1830 Federal Census of Ohio; "Far West Record."

12. Stephen Burnett to Lyman E. Johnson, 15 April 1838, Joseph Smith Collection, Church Archives; 1850 Federal Census of Ohio; "Far West Record"; D&C, sections 75 and 80; "Journal History"; *Elder's Journal* (October 1837); and John Murdock Journal, Church Archives;

13. Gideon Carter Journal, Church Archives; "Far West Record"; "Journal History"; *History of the Church*; D&C 75; Gideon Carter family group sheet, Genealogical Society, Salt Lake City, Utah; "Kirtland Council Minute Book"; and "A Book of Proxey" (Nauvoo Temple), Church Archives.

14. Elden J. Watson, *Orson Pratt Journals*; D&C 75; and 1850 Federal Census of Ohio.

15. "Far West Record"; D&C 75; John Smith Journal (not the Prophet's uncle), Church Archives; and Cuyahoga County, Ohio, Marriage Records.

16. *History of the Church*; "Far West Record"; D&C 75; Frank Esshom, *Pioneers and Prominent Men of Utah* (Salt Lake City: Western Epics, Inc., 1966); and "Nauvoo Temple Endowment Register," Genealogical Society, Salt Lake City, Utah.

17. *History of the Church*; "Far West Record"; "Kirtland Council Minute Book"; D&C 75; *Utah Genealogical and Historical Magazine* (1910); 1850 Federal Census of Illinois; Burr Riggs family group sheet, Genealogical Society, Salt Lake City, Utah; Geauga County, Ohio, Marriage Records; and "List of Names of the Church of Latter Day Saints Living in the South West Quarter of Far West," in Teacher's Quorum Minutes (1838), Church Archives.

18. *History of the Church*; Eden Smith Journal, Church Archives; John Smith Journal (not the Prophet's uncle), Church Archives; Joseph Coe Journal, in Newel K. Whitney Collection, Brigham Young University Library, Manuscripts; Reynolds Cahoon Journal, Church Archives; D&C, sections 75 and 80; "Journal History"; Leonard J. Arrington, *Charles C. Rich: Mormon General and Western Frontiersman* (Provo: Brigham Young University Press, 1974); 1850 Federal Census of Iowa; and *Frontier Guardian* (11 March 1852).

19. *History of the Church*; "Far West Record"; D&C, sections 75 and 102; "Kirtland Council Minute Book"; Joel H. Johnson Journal (typescript), Brigham Young University Library, Special Collections; 1830 and 1840 Federal Census of Ohio; 1850 Federal Census of Iowa; Jared Carter Journal, Church Archives; and Gideon Carter Journal, Church Archives.

20. *History of the Church*; "Far West Record"; "Journal History"; D&C 75; "Nauvoo Temple Endowment Register," Genealogical Society, Salt Lake City, Utah; "Patriarchal Blessing File," Church Archives; *Deseret News* (27 November 1872); and Daniel Stanton family group sheet, Genealogical Society, Salt Lake City, Utah.

21. *History of the Church*; "Far West Record"; John Smith Journal (not the Prophet's uncle), Church Archives; Reynolds Cahoon Journal, Church Archives; "Nauvoo Temple Endowment Register," Genealogical Society, Salt Lake City, Utah; and Micah B. Welton family group sheet, Genealogical Society, Salt Lake City, Utah.

22. "Far West Record"; D&C 75; and John S. Higbee Journal, Church Archives. Higbee's journal renders the given name as "Calvis."

Section 76

1. Members of the Church during this period did not confuse "The Vision" (section 76) with the "First Vision" because the 1820 event was not generally known until after 1842.

2. *Times and Seasons* 5 (1 August 1844):592.

3. As reported in *The Juvenile Instructor* (15 May 1892).

4. See, for example, John Murdock Journal, Church Archives and Elden J. Watson, *Orson Pratt Journals*. Brigham Young said, "After all, my traditions were such, that when the Vision came first to me, it was directly contrary and opposed to my former education. I said, Wait a little. I did not reject it; but I could not understand it" (*Journal of Discourses*, 6:281). On another occasion President Young stated, "When God revealed to Joseph Smith and Sidney Rigdon that there was a place prepared for all, according to the light they had received and their rejection of evil and practice of good,

it was a great trial to many, and some apostatized because God was not going to send to everlasting punishment heathens and infants, but had a place of salvation, in due time, for all, and would bless the honest and virtuous and truthful, whether they ever belonged to any church or not" (*Journal of Discourses*, 16:42).

    5. *Times and Seasons* 4 (1 February 1843):82-85.

Section 77

    1. The date of reception for this section of scripture is uncertain. Although the Prophet's history (*Times and Seasons*, 1 August 1844) suggests that section 77 was received "about the first of March [1832]," a notation in the "Kirtland Revelation Book" makes it clear that if this was a normal dictated revelation, it was received after 8 March 1832 (see Historical Note for section 78, note 2). However, it is possible that Joseph Smith did not recognize this section as a dictated revelation at the time it was recorded. The format and style in which these inspired explanations were recorded fit more consistently with the deductive-revelatory method applied by the Prophet in his Bible translation. Unfortunately, early manuscript copies of section 77 have not survived. A copy of the revelation in Willard Richard's "Pocket Companion" (recorded in England sometime in 1839-40) is the earliest manuscript presently available. Richards's undated account, entitled a "Key to the Revelations of John," was probably copied from a record book owned by John Taylor (see Andrew F. Ehat and Lyndon W. Cook, *The Words of Joseph Smith: The Contemporary Accounts of the Nauvoo Discourses of the Prophet Joseph* [Provo: Religious Studies Center, 1980], p. 17). Section 77, together with certain of the Prophet's teachings, was copied and recopied by a handful of his disciples. See, for example, James Burgess's "Notebook" and Joseph F. Smith's "Private Account Book," both at Church Archives. The account of section 77 in the former source was copied by Burgess in England (1840-41); the latter report, undoubtedly taken from William Clayton's "Private Book" (presently unavailable), was copied by Joseph F. Smith in Utah.

Section 78

    1. Both the "Kirtland Revelation Book," p. 15, and an early manuscript copy of section 78 in the Newel K. Whitney Collection, Brigham Young University Library, Manuscripts, give the 1 March 1832 date.

    2. According to two manuscript copies (in the hand of Frederick G. Williams), section 78 was received in Kirtland *not* Hiram (see "Kirtland Revelation Book," p. 15, and manuscript copy of section 78 in Newel K. Whitney Collection, Brigham Young University Library, Manuscripts). A notation in the "Kirtland Revelation Book," p. 11, details the Prophet's activities from 16 February-8 March 1832: "From the 16th of February up to this date [8 March] have been at home except a journey to Kirtland on the

29th Feby. and returned home on the 4th of March we received a revelation in Kirtland and one since I returned home blessed be the name of the Lord." The revelation received in Kirtland was section 78 (on 1 March 1832), and the revelation received after the Prophet's return to Hiram, Ohio related to the duties of the Church bishop and the calling of counselors in the presidency of the High Priesthood (see Historical Note for section 72, note 3).

3. Early manuscripts of section 78 (see note 1) clearly indicate that the subject at hand was the organization of branches of the Literary and United Firms in Jackson County, Missouri: "For verily I say unto you the time has come, and is now at hand, and behold and lo it must needs be that there be an organization of the literary and mercantile establishments of my church both in this place and in the land of Zion for a permanent and everlasting establishment and firm unto my Church to advance the cause which ye have espoused" ("Kirtland Revelation Book," p. 16). Explicit reference to these business concerns was deleted when the revelation was published in 1835. See also Historical Notes from sections 70 and 104. The terms "Adam-ondi-Ahman" and "Son Ahman" (see verses 15 and 20) were not part of the original revelation in March 1832, but were added in 1835.

4. See Historical Notes for sections 53 and 57.

5. See Historical Note for section 82. Reasons which prompted the Missouri trip were (1) to organize branches of the Literary and United Firms, (2) to allow Joseph Smith to be sustained as President of the High Priests, (3) to work out a difficulty between Sidney Rigdon and Edward Partridge, and (4) to assist in regulating the program of consecration. On 20 March 1832 Joseph Smith and Sidney Rigdon received a revelation concerning their pending departure for Independence, Missouri:

> First Shall we procure the paper required of our breatheren in this letter and carry it with us or not and if we do what moneys shall we use for that purpose
> It is expedient saith the Lord unto you that the paper shall be purchased for the printing of the book of the Lords commandments and it must needs be that you take it with for it is not expedient thay my servent Martin should as yet go up unto the land of Zion [D&C 58: 35-39] let the purchase be made by the Bishop if it must needs be by hire let whatsoever is done be done in the name of the Lord
> Second shall we finish the translation of the New Testament before we go to Zion or wait till we return
> It is expedient saith the Lord that there be no delays and thus saith the Lord for the greatest good and benefit of the church Wherefore omit the translation for the present time (Newel K. Whitney Collection, Brigham Young University Library, Manuscripts).

6. "Far West Record," pp. 25-26.

7. See William E. McLellan to M.H. Forscutt, October 1870, in *The Saints' Herald* (15 July 1872): 436 and William E. McLellan Correspondence, RLDS Library-Archives, Independence, Missouri.

314 The Revelations of the Prophet Joseph Smith

8. Members are named in D&C, sections 78, 82, 92, 96, and 104. See also "Far West Record," pp. 25-26.

9. See D&C, sections 92 and 96.

10. *Times and Seasons* 6 (1 December 1845): 1041.

11. See Historical Note for section 104.

12. Use of the coded names in this and other United Firm revelations was commented on by Orson Pratt in 1873:

> The word Enoch did not exist in the original copy; neither did some other names. The names that were incorporated when it was printed, did not exist there when the manuscript revelations were given, for I saw them myself. Some of them I copied. And when the Lord was about to have the Book of Covenants given to the world, it was thought wisdom, in consequence of the persecutions of our enemies in Kirtland and some of the regions around, that some of the names should be changed, and Joseph was called Baurak Ale, which was a Hebrew word; meaning God bless you. He was also called Gazelum, being a person to whom the Lord had given the Urim and Thummim. He was also called Enoch. Sidney Rigdon was called Baneemy (*Journal of Discourses*, 16: 156).

Section 79

1. *Times and Seasons* 5 (15 August 1844): 608.

2. Jared Carter Journal, under date, Church Archives. Spelling and punctuation in these two citations standardized.

Section 80

1. *Times and Seasons* 5 (15 August 1844): 608-09.

2. See John Smith Journal (not the Prophet's uncle), under date, Church Archives.

Section 81

1. *Times and Seasons* 5 (2 September 1844): 624.

2. See, for example, D&C 84: 63, 107: 64, and "Far West Record," p. 11. Also see Historical Note for section 52.

3. See "Far West Record," p. 25, where reference is made to the organizational nature of this title.

4. Use of the term "First Presidency" in revelations prior to 1834 is anachronistic. In all cases where this occurs the language was modified in the 1835 edition of the Doctrine and Covenants.

5. "Kirtland Revelation Book," pp. 10-11.

6. "Far West Record," pp. 25-26.

7. See "Kirtland Revelation Book," p. 17.

8. "Far West Record"; *Times and Seasons* 5 (2 September 1844): 624; "Kirtland Revelation Book"; Joseph Smith Journal (3 December 1832), Church Archives; Zebedee Coltrin Journal, Church Archives; D. Michael Quinn, "The Mormon Hierarchy 1832-1932: An American Elite," Ph.D.

dissertation, Yale University, 1976; William Wade Hinshaw, *Encyclopedia of American Quaker Genealogy*; and Robert J. Woodford, "Jesse Gause—Counselor to the Prophet," *Brigham Young University* Studies 15 (Spring 1975): 362-64.

Section 82

1. See Historical Note for section 78. See also The Book of John Whitmer, microfilm copy at Church Archives.
2. Joseph Smith to William W. Phelps, 31 July 1832, Joseph Smith Collection, Church Archives.
3. See Historical Note for section 75 for information concerning a similar action in Ohio.
4. "Far West Record," pp. 24-25.
5. See Historical Note for section 78 for information on the United Firm.
6. Orson Hyde and Hyrum Smith to "the Bishop, his Council and the Inhabitants in Zion," 14 January 1833, cited in *History of the Church*, 1: 318-19.
7. See Ibid. and *History of the Church*, 1:267.
8. Reynolds Cahoon Journal, under date, Church Archives.
9. Ibid.
10. "History of Charles C. Rich," Charles C. Rich Papers, Church Archives. In September 1844 Amasa Lyman recalled Rigdon's discourse on this occasion:

> Sidney's first revelation in Kirtland was telling the people that the kingdom was rent from them, and they might as well all go home for they were rejected. The saints felt very bad and were almost distracted. When brother Joseph came home, (who was absent at the time) he called Sidney into council and there told him he had lied in the name of the Lord; and says he, "you had better give up your licence and divest yourself of all the authority you can, for you will go into the hands of satan, and he will handle you as one man handleth another, and the less authority you have the better for you (*Times and Seasons* 5 [1 October 1844]: 660).

11. Ibid.
12. Hyrum Smith Journal, under date, Church Archives.
13. Joseph Smith to William W. Phelps, 31 July 1832, Joseph Smith Collection, Church Archives.

Section 83

1. See Historical Note for section 78, note 5.
2. See Historical Note for section 82. The following is Sidney Rigdon's report of the trip to and from Missouri in 1832:

The next week I removed to K[irtlan]d on [account] of the mob. Child had meassles. Moved in open wagon Wednesday 29 March—Stayed till first of April, then on acct mob I went to Chardon 2d April I left Chardon and arrived at Warren where I met Br Joseph & N K Whitney and Jesse Gaus and proceeded immediately for Wellesville on April 3 and on the fourth went Steubenville 5th left on board a steamer for Wheeling. left this boat went on board the steamer Trenton bound to Louisville. On the night we entered that boat. it was dis[covere]d to be on fire but was extinguished without loss. 6th left next morning and arrived at Cincinati where some of the mob which had followed all the way round left us. from thence we left and arrived at Louisville that night Capt Brattle offered us protection kept on bord of his boat and gave us supper and breakfast gratuitously. Here we fell in with Titus Billings and his company from Kirtland we all went on board the steamer Charleston bound for St Louis we left St Louis in a stage for Fayette from thence to Independence a private carriage and arrived the ____ day of April.

Back by stage to St Louis from thence to Vincennes between which place and New Albany the stage over set and broke brother Whitney's leg and I left Brother [Joseph] to take care of him [in] a little place called Greenville 12 miles from N[ew] A[lbany] proceeded home nothing occured on the road home About 4 weeks after I arrived they arrived (undated statement of Sidney Rigdon, Sidney Rigdon Papers, Church Archives).

Also see Newel K. Whitney account of 1832 Missouri trip, Newel K. Whitney Collection, Brigham Young University Library, Manuscripts; Joseph Smith account of 1832 Missouri trip, Brigham Young University Library, Vault Manuscript; Reynolds Cahoon Journal (June 1832), Church Archives; and "Far West Record," pp. 24-26.

3. Joseph Smith to Edward Partridge, 2 May 1833, in Joseph Smith Collection, Church Archives. These instructions reflect the 1833 modification of the law of consecration, and should be seen in that light (see Historical Note for section 51).

Section 84

1. Verse 42 speaks of those "who are present this day," and the "Kirtland Revelation Book" adds, "Viz 23d day of September AD 1832 Eleven High Priests save one" (p. 24).

2. Possibly referring to the revocation of this revelation, Joseph Smith declared, "A man would command his son to dig potatoes, saddle his horse but before he had done either tell him to do something else this is all considered right But as soon as the Lord gives a commandment & revokes that decree & commands something else then the prophet is considered fallen &c"(Wilford Woodruff Journal, 19 December 1841, Church Archives).

3. The 14 January 1833 letter is cited in *History of the Church*, 1: 317-21.

4. Newel K. Whitney statement (undated), Newel K. Whitney Collection, Brigham Young University Library, Manuscripts. The document

appears to be a reminiscient account, recorded by Willard Richards in Nauvoo: "My leg was not perfectly well, but I proceeded with Joseph to New York Providence & Boston—& through New England. We visited Bishop Onderdock of the Episcopal Church of the United States, while at N. York—& returned back to Kirtland. This Journey was taken to fulfill the Revelation—Previously given—."

5. See Samuel H. Smith Journal (typescript), Brigham Young University Library, Special Collections. On 26 November 1832 Samuel recorded, "Came to Mother Dow's at New Rowley in the evening and she was much rejoiced to see us and she told us that Joseph had been to Boston and prophecied unto that city and had gone again to Ohio." Also see Joseph Smith to Emma Smith, 13 October 1832, RLDS Library-Archives, Independence, Missouri.

6. Regarding his travels to the East the Prophet wrote: "I continued the translation and ministering to the church through the fall, excepting a rapid journey to Albany, New York and Boston, in company with Bishop Whitney, from which I returned on the 6th of November, immediately after the birth of my son Joseph Smith, 3d" (*Times and Seasons* 5 [15 October 1844]: 673).

7. See *Deseret News* (12 November 1884): 679.

Section 85

1. *Times and Seasons* 5 (15 October 1844): 673.

2. Numerous documents affirm that the "Book of the Law of the Lord" served as a multipurpose Church record book. Known recorders were Robert B. Thompson, Willard Richards, and William Clayton. Entries include revelations, correspondence, minutes of important meetings (including the organization of the City of Nauvoo, the Nauvoo Legion, and the Relief Society), the laying of the cornerstones of the Nauvoo Temple and Nauvoo House, biographical sketches of faithful Saints, and names of individual donors of tithing and consecrations for the Nauvoo Temple.

3. Oliver Cowdery to John Whitmer, 1 January 1834, Oliver Cowdery Letterbook, Huntington Library, San Marino, California. Copy of original in possession of author.

Section 86

1. A notation at the end of this revelation in the "Kirtland Revelation Book" states, "Kirtland December 6th AD 1832 given by Joseph the seer and written by Sidney the scribe and Councellor, & Transcribed by Frederick assistant scribe and councellor" (p. 32).

2. See Robert J. Matthews, *A Plainer Translation*, p. 82.

3. Joseph Smith Journal, 6 December 1832, Joseph Smith Collection, Church Archives.

Section 87

1. See William W. Freehling, *Prelude To Civil War: The Nullification Controversy in South Carolina, 1816-1836* (New York: Harper and Row, 1965).
2. See D&C 130:12-13.
3. In May 1860, before the Civil War, Brigham Young made the following comment concerning section 87: "Brother [Orson] Hyde spoke of a revelation which he tried to find in the Book of Doctrine and Covenants. [This revelation was not included as a section of the Doctrine and Covenants until 1876]. That revelation was reserved at the time the compilation for that book was made by Oliver Cowdery and others, in Kirtland. It was not wisdom to publish it to the world, and it remained in the private *escritoire* . . . .There are other revelations besides this one, not yet published to the world. In the due time of the Lord, the Saints and the world will be privileged with the revelations that are due to them" (*Journal of Discourses*, 8: 58).

Section 88

1. Samuel H. Smith gave the following report concerning the reception of this revelation:

> Soon after we returned Some of the Elders assembled together & the word of the Lord was given through Joseph & the Lord declared that those Elders who were the first labourers in this last vinyard Should assemble themselves together that they should call a Sollem assembly & evry man call upon the name of the Lord & continue in Prayer that they Should Sanctify themselves & wash their hands & feet for a testimony that their garments were clean from the Blood of all men & the Lord commanded we the first Elders Establish a School & appoint a teacher among them & get learning by Study & by faith get a knowledge of countries languages &c (Samuel H. Smith Journal [typescript], after 10 December 1832 entry, Brigham Young University Library, Special Collections).

2. "Kirtland Council Minute Book," pp. 3-4. Notations in the "Kirtland Revelation Book" show that Frederick G. Williams not only kept the minutes, but also recorded this revelation as it was dictated: "Given by Joseph the Seer and Writen by F.G. Williams, assistant Scribe and Councellor to Sd Joseph" (p.47). A similar statement is found on page 48 of the same document (after the recording of verses 127-37).
3. *History of the Church*, 2:309-10.
4. *History of the Church*, 2:430-33. For additional references to the 1836 solemn assembly, see *History of the Church*, 2:301, 333-34, 364, 375, 385, 388, 409, 429-33; and D&C, 88:70, 117; 95:7; 108:4; and 109:6,10.

5. See *History of the Church*, 2:475-80, and Wilford Woodruff Journal, 4-6 April 1837, Church Archives.

6. Joseph Smith to William W. Phelps, 14 January 1833, cited in *History of the Church*, 1:316.

7. *History of the Church*, 1:335.

8. *History of the Church*, 1:342-43.

9. See D&C 95. The exact date of this revelation is in question. See Historical Note for section 95.

10. D&C 95:16-17.

11. *History of the Church*, 1:353.

12. *History of the Church*, 1:354.

13. Laurel B. Andrew, *The Early Temples of the Mormons: The Architecture of the Millennial Kingdom in the American West* (New York: Albany, State University of New York Press, 1976).

14. *History of the Church*, 2:205-08. Numerous others, not mentioned in this source, worked on the temple. Levi Jackman, one of those unnamed, recorded that he worked 194 days on the temple (see Levi Jackman Journal, Church Archives).

15. Laurel B. Andrew, *The Early Temples of the Mormons*.

16. *History of the Church*, 2:480.

17. Joseph Smith Diary (27 March 1836), Church Archives.

18. *History of the Church*, 2:169.

19. "Kirtland Council Minute Book," pp. 7-8.

20. "Minutes of the School of the Prophets," Salt Lake City, Utah (1883), Church Archives.

21. Ibid.

22. Ibid.

23. Zebedee Coltrin Journal, under date, Church Archives.

24. *Autobiography of Parley P. Pratt*, pp. 93-94.

25. John Whitmer to Joseph Smith, July 1833, Joseph Smith Collection, Church Archives.

26. On 7 January 1834 Oliver Cowdery informed Samuel Bent that "The school of the elders will not recommence this winter (Cowdery to Bent, 7 January 1834, Oliver Cowdery Letterbook, Huntington Library, San Marino, California).

27. Lucius Parker of Southborough, Massachusetts, was also contacted to teach Hebrew, but when it was determined that he could only teach the "rudiments" of the language he was notified that his services would not be needed (see Oliver Cowdery to Parker, 28 October 1835, Oliver Cowdery Letterbook, Huntington Library, San Marino, California).

28. The *Painesville Telegraph* (20 May 1836) reprinted a letter from the *Ohio Atlas*, dated 16 March 1836, which mentioned the Hebrew school: "They are now studying Hebrew with great zeal, under the instruction of Mr. Seixas."

Section 89

1. "Minutes of the School of the Prophets," Salt Lake City, Utah (1833), Church Archives.
2. *Journal of Discourses*, 12:158.
3. Copy of broadsheet is located at Brigham Young University Library, Manuscripts.

Section 90

1. Joseph Smith Diary, 3 December 1832, Church Archives.
2. "Statement of Facts Relative to J. Smith & Myself" (undated), in Frederick G. Williams Papers, Church Archives.
3. Although the manuscript of this revelation is dated 5 January 1834, *1833* is more consistent with known facts regarding Williams's appointment. The words *counselor* and *scribe* are contained in both the unpublished revelation as well as section 90:19. In addition, the "Kirtland Council Minute Book" (p. 6), for 22 January 1833, records Williams as being "assistant scribe and counciler." The unpublished revelation referred to is in the Frederick G. Williams Papers, Church Archives:

> Behold I say unto you my Servant Frederick, Listen to the word of Jesus Christ your Lord and your Redeemer thou hast desired of me to know which would be the most worth unto you. behold blessed art tho[u] for this thing. Now I say unto you, my Servant Joseph is called to do a great work and hath need that he may do the work of translation for the Salvation of Souls. Verily verily I say unto you thou art called to be a Councillor & scribe unto my Servant Joseph Let thy farm be consecrated for bringing forth of the revelations and tho[u] shalt be blessed and lifted up at the last day even so Amen.

4. The "Kirtland Revelation Book" (p. 55) reveals that section 90 was dictated to Frederick G. Williams: "Given by Joseph the Seer and Writen by Frederick Councellor & Scribe."
5. "Kirtland Council Minute Book," p. 17.
6. Certificate is in Frederick G. Williams Papers, Church Archives.
7. "Journal History"; *History of the Church*; Joseph Smith to William W. Phelps, 27 November 1832, Joseph Smith Collection, Church Archives; D&C 90; "Nauvoo Temple Endowment Register," Genealogical Society, Salt Lake City, Utah; 1850 Federal Census of Utah; "Salt Lake Endowment House Record," Book C, Church Archives; Orson Hyde Journal (typescript), Brigham Young University Library, Special Collections; Samuel H. Smith Journal (typescript), Brigham Young University Library, Special Collections; *Deseret News* (7 February 1884); Vienna Jaques to Brigham Young, 2 July 1870, in "Brigham Young Incoming Correspondence Collection," Church Archives; and Salt Lake Death Registration, Brigham Young University Library (microfilm).

Section 91

    1. *History of the Church*, 1:331.

    2. "The title applied, in ordinary Protestant usage, to a collection of fourteen or fifteen books, or parts of books, which at one time stood in our English Bibles between the OT and the NT. These books are, according to the RSV, the following: I and II Esdras; Tobit; Judith; the Additions of the Book of Esther; the Wisdom of Solomon; Ecclesiasticus, or the Wisdom of Jesus the Son of Sirah; Baruch, including the Letter of Jeremiah; the Prayer of Azariah and the Song of the Three Young Men; Susanna; Bel and the Dragon; the Prayer of Manasseh; I and II Maccabees" (*The Interpreter's Dictionary of the Bible*, 4 vols. (New York and Nashville: Abingdon Press, 1962), 1:161.

    3. Sidney Rigdon (and others), to William W. Phelps, 25 June 1833, cited in *History of the Church*, 1:363.

Section 92

    1. See Historical Notes for sections 78, 82, 96, and 104.

    2. The "Kirtland Revelation Book" (p. 55), as well as other early manuscripts of this revelation, also use *united firm* not united order.

    3. "Kirtland Council Minute Book," p. 11.

Section 93

    1. See John Taylor, *Mediation and Atonement* (Salt Lake City: Steven and Wallis, 1950), p. 55, and Orson Pratt, *Journal of Discourses*, 16:58.

Section 94

    1. See "Kirtland Revelation Book," p. 64, and Joseph Smith (et.al.), to "Beloved Bretheren," 6 August 1833, Joseph Smith Collection, Church Archives.

    2. See D&C 95:14-15.

    3. See Historical Note for section 95.

    4. Joseph Smith (et.al.), to "Beloved Bretheren," 6 August 1833, Joseph Smith Collection, Church Archives. Verse 16 of section 94 was omitted, probably inadvertently, from the 6 August 1833 letter.

    5. *History of the Church*, 1:417. On 21 January 1834 Oliver Cowdery, who was in Kirtland, informed W.W. Phelps and John Whitmer that, "Our office is yet in the brick building, though we expect in the spring to move on the hill near the Methodist meeting house" (Cowdery to Phelps and Whitmer, 21 January 1834, Oliver Cowdery Letterbook, Huntington Library, San Marino, California).

    6. See "Journal History," under date. It appears that Lyman Sherman started the fire. See Lyndon W. Cook, "Lyman Sherman, Man of God, Would-Be Apostle," *Brigham Young University Studies* 19 (Fall 1978):123.

Section 95

1. Although the "Kirtland Revelation Book" (p. 59) gives the date of this revelation as 1 June 1833, a meeting recorded in the "Kirtland Council Minute Book" (p. 12) suggests that the revelation, or part of it was received on 3 June 1833 (see discussion in Historical Note).
2. *History of the Church*, 1:342-43.
3. *History of the Church*, 1:349.
4. "Kirtland Council Minute Book," p. 12.
5. As recorded in Truman O. Angell Journal (typescript), Brigham Young University Library, Special Collections. Angell also referred to this vision in a letter to John Taylor in 1885:

> F.G. Williams came into the Temple about the time the main hall 1st floor was ready for dedication. He was asked, how does the house look to you. He answered that it looked to him like the model he had seen. He said President Joseph Smith, Sidney Rigdon and himself were called to come before the Lord and the model was shown them. He said the vision of the Temple was thus shown them and he could not see the difference between it and the House as built (Angell to Taylor, 11 March 1885, Church Archives).

A letter, dated 16 March 1836, in the *Ohio Atlas* also reported the divine pattern of the Kirtland Temple: "Their temple, in Kirtland, is a huge misshappen edifice, that comes nearer to the Gothic than any other style of architecture. The pattern . . . was given by direct revelation from Heaven, and given to those individuals separately" (letter reprinted in *Painesville Telegraph*, 20 May 1836).

Section 96

1. Zebedee Coltrin Journal, under date, Church Archives.
2. "Kirtland Council Minute Book," p. 18.
3. Zebedee Coltrin Journal.
4. Joseph Smith's history states that, "The conference could not agree who should take charge of it [the farm], but all agreed to enquire of the Lord" (*Times and Seasons* 6 [1 February 1845]: 784).
5. "Kirtland Council Minute Book," p. 13.
6. Sidney Rigdon, et. al., to William W. Phelps, 25 June 1833, cited in *History of the Church*, 1: 363.
7. *History of the Church*; "Kirtland Council Minute Book"; D&C, sections 96 and 102; Luke S. Johnson family group sheet, Genealogical Society, Salt Lake City, Utah; 1810 Federal Census of Vermont; 1820 and 1830 Federal Census of Ohio; "Journal History"; and gravestone, Kirtland Temple Cemetery, Kirtland, Ohio.

Section 97

1.   Joseph Smith, et. al., to "Beloved Bretheren," 6 August 1833, Joseph Smith Collection, Church Archives.
2.   *Autobiography of Parley P. Pratt*, pp. 94-95.

Section 98

1.   Mention of the 9 July 1833 letter is found in the Historical Note for section 94.
2.   Oliver Cowdery arrived in Kirtland from Jackson County, Missouri in mid-August 1833 with news of the July mobbings. The unfriendly *Painesville Telegraph* (16 August 1833) reported Cowdery's arrival:

> We learn from the Mormon colony in Missouri, that a great riot took place there about the 20th ult. We understand that O. Cowdery, one of the principal men among the pilgrims, has just arrived at the headquarters of the Prophet in this county .... An attack [was made] upon a brick building containing the printing establishment, and the family of the editor, and razed it to the ground—scattering the type, revelations, translations and commandments, printed or in manuscript, to the four winds.

Section 99

1.   "Kirtland Revelation Book," p. 19.
2.   Ibid.
3.   Statement of Emma Smith, undated, in Lucy Mack Smith Papers, Church Archives. My thanks to Richard L. Anderson for this reference.
4.   John Murdock Journal, under date, Church Archives. The "Kirtland Revelation Book" (p. 20) notes the following: "By Joseph the Seer and Writen by—F.G. Williams Scribe."

Section 100

1.   *Times and Seasons* 6 (15 April 1845): 864-66.
2.   John P. Greene Journal, under date, Church Archives.
3.   A copy of section 100 in the "Kirtland Revelation Book" (p. 71) is introduced with the words, "A Revelation to Joseph and Sidney given them while on their journey to Canada, according to direction of the Spirit."
4.   Joseph Smith Diary, under date, Church Archives.
5.   Sidney Rigdon had served as the Prophet's spokesman from the beginning. This revelation confirmed the fact, and Rigdon would continue as the official public voice for Mormonism until 1839.
6.   *History of the Church*, 1: 406, 446.
7.   Joseph Smith Diary, under date, Church Archives.
8.   *History of the Church*; "Journal History"; Orson Hyde Journal (typescript), Brigham Young University Library, Special Collections;

"Patriarchal Blessing File," Church Archives; William Burton Journal, Church Archives; "General Record of the Seventies," Book A, Church Archives; "Nauvoo Temple Endowment Register," Genealogical Society, Salt Lake City, Utah; and *Frontier Guardian*, 13 June 1851.

Section 101

1. Joseph Smith letter, 18 August 1833, Joseph Smith Collection, Church Archives.
2. *History of the Church*, 1:417.
3. See note 1.
4. Inaccurate accounts of the conflict reached the Kirtland area in late November 1833 and were reported in letters and newspapers (see *Painesville Telegraph*, 26 November 1833, and Oliver Cowdery to Warren Cowdery, 2 December 1833, Oliver Cowdery Letterbook, Huntington Library, San Marino, California).
5. See *History of the Church*, 2:434, 469, and 472-73 regarding how the "wise men" from the eastern branches should purchase the Missouri lands. In 1843 Joseph H. Tippets reminded the Prophet of his participation in this mission:

> You will recollect Som few years agone when you ware living in Kurtland, Ohio myself in Company with brother John Tippets ware Sent from the state of new york on a mishon to Missourie with money for the purpose of purchaseing lands for our brethren, we came to Kurtland where agreable to Counsyl given to us there we taried through the following winter and summer Dureing which time I went to Sc[h]ool through the winter and Dureing the summer worked Considerably on the house of the Lord, when in the fall we again pursued our Journey to Missourie in fulfillment of our mishon on ariveing there we spent our little monies for lands to the best advantage we new how (Joseph H. Tippets to Joseph Smith, 2 April 1843, copy of original in possession of author).

6. See Peter Crawley, "A Bibliography of The Church of Jesus Christ of Latter-day Saints in New York, Ohio, and Missouri," *Brigham Young University Studies* 12 (Summer 1972):465-537.

Section 102

1. "Kirtland Council Minute Book," p. 27.
2. "Kirtland Council Minute Book," p. 30.
3. Ibid.
4. See "Far West Record," pp. 43-45. On this occasion David Whitmer was ordained successor to Joseph Smith.
5. See D&C 107:37.
6. *History of the Church*; Gideon Carter family group sheet, Genealogical Society, Salt Lake City, Utah; D&C 102; "Journal History"; and Jared Carter Journal, Church Archives.

7. *History of the Church*; "Journal History"; Jenson's *Biographical Encyclopedia*, 1:182; John Smith Journal, Church Archives; John Smith family group sheet, Genealogical Society, Salt Lake City, Utah; "A Book of Proxey" (Nauvoo Temple), Church Archives; *Deseret News* (25 May 1854); and Ehat, "Endowment Data Summary."

Section 103

1. *History of the Church*, 2:1. See also *Autobiography of Parley P. Pratt*, pp. 107-09.
2. Orson Pratt, named in section 103, recorded the following: "The 24th traveled to Kirtland. & found that the Lord had appointed in a revelation that Orson Hyde & I should Journey together to assist in obtaining Brethren & means for the redemption of Zion according to the revelation previously given (Orson Pratt Journal, under date, Church Archives. Published in Elden J. Watson, *Orson Pratt Journals*).
3. Heber C. Kimball Journal (February 1834), Church Archives.
4. Peter Crawley and Richard L. Anderson, "The Political and Social Realities of Zion's Camp," *Brigham Young University Studies* 14 (Summer 1974): 406-20.
5. The anti-Mormon *Painesville Telegraph* (9 May 1834) reported the departure of Zion's Camp,

> Gen. Joe Smith took upon his line of march from this county on Monday inst. with a large party of his fanatical followers, for the seat of war.— This expedition has been a long time in active preparation. Soon after the outrages committed upon the members of the sect last Nov. in Missouri, the prophet here sent forth his general order, which he pretended was a revelation from God, for all his able bodied men to repair to the scene of difficulty. His preachers were sent forth to all parts of the country among their proselytes, with a printed copy of the revelation in their pockets . . . . They have made every effort to stir up the holy zeal of the "warriors, my young men, and they that are of middle age also," to the combat . . . . For several months past they have been collecting munitions of war for the crusade. Dirks, knives, swords, pistols, guns, power-horns, &c. &c. have been in good demand in this vicinity.

Section 104

1. See Historical Notes for sections 78, 82, 92, and 96.
2. "Kirtland Revelation Book," p. 100.
3. *History of the Church*, 2:40-49.
4. Undated statement in Frederick G. Williams Papers, Church Archives.
5. The financial record is located in Newel K. Whitney Collection, Brigham Young University Library, Manuscripts.
6. "Kirtland Revelation Book," p. 111.
7. "Kirtland Revelation Book," p. 100.

Section 105

1. Portions of the circular are cited in Peter Crawley and Richard L. Anderson, "The Political and Social Realities of Zion's Camp," *Brigham Young University Studies* 14 (Summer 1974):413-14.
2. Ibid., p. 419.
3. Concerning the redemption of Zion, Joseph Smith wrote Church leaders in Missouri: "You recollect that the first Elders are to receive their endowment in Kirtland, before the redemption of Zion [D & C 105:11-12]." Subsequent to receiving the "endowment," however, the Missouri Saints were to be in readiness to return to Jackson County, Missouri, on 11 September 1836, "the appointed time for the redemption of Zion" (see Joseph Smith to Lyman Wight, Edward Partridge, John Corrill, Isaac Morley, and others, 16 August 1834, cited in *History of the Church*, 2:144-45).
There was naturally some discontent among members of Zion's Camp who desired to accomplish their purpose in marching across four states. Brigham Young, referring to the long march and the reception of section 105, later said,

> When we arrived in Missouri, the Lord spoke to his servant Joseph and said, "I have accepted your offering," and we had the privilege to return again. On my return many friends asked me what profit there was in calling men from their labor to go up to Missouri and then return, without apparently accomplishing anything.... "If the Lord did command it to be done, what object had he in view in doing so [they asked]?" I told those brethren that I was well paid—paid with heavy interest—yea that my measure was filled to overflowing with the knowledge that I have received by travelling with the Prophet (*Journal of Discourses*, 10:20).

4. The Book of John Whitmer, microfilm copy at Church Archives.

Section 106

1. *History of the Church*, 2:170.
2. *History of the Church*; "Journal History"; D & C 106; "Cowdery Family Notes," Brigham Young University Library, Special Collections; Mary Bryant Alverson Mehling, *Cowdery Genealogy* (1911); *Messenger and Advocate*; *History of Cattaraugus County, New York*; 1850 Federal Census of Ohio; Oliver Cowdery Letterbook, Huntington Library, San Marino, California; Kirtland, Ohio, Tax Records (microfilm copy at Brigham Young University Library); Oliver Cowdery "Sketch Book," Church Archives (this record was published by Leonard J. Arrington, in *Brigham Young University Studies* 12 [Summer 1972]:410-426); and "Kirtland Council Minute Book," pp. 199 and 219.

Section 107

1. Compare the textual similarities of sections 107:59-100 and 68:13-35. Both revelations were received in November 1831 in Ohio.
2. "Patriarchal Blessing Book," vol. 1, contains minutes of the Quorum of the Twelve Apostles for 1835 (located at Church Archives). The or-

ganization of the Twelve Apostles was an early topic of discussion by the Prophet and the Three Witnesses to the Book of Mormon. In October 1831 it was decided that "they would be ordained & sent forth from the land of Zion." However, the loss of Zion (Jackson County, Missouri) in 1833 precluded that arrangement, and they were "ordained and sent forth" from Kirtland (see "Far West Record," p. 15).

3.   "Kirtland Council Minute Book," p. 198. The complete minutes of the meeting are included below.

> On reviewing our past course we are satisfied and feel to confess also that we have not realized the importance of our calling to that degree that we ought, we have been light minded and vain and in many things done wrong, wrong. For all these things we have asked forgiveness of our Heavenly Father, and wherein we have grieved or wounded the feelings of the Presidency we ask their forgiveness.
>
> The time has come when we are about to separate, and when we shall meet again, God only knows. We therefore feel to ask him whom we have acknowledged to be our President and Seer that he enquire of God for us and obtain a written revelation (if consistent) that we may look upon it when we are separated, that our hearts may be comforted. Our worthiness has not inspired us to make this request but our unworthiness.
>
> We have unitedly asked God, our Heavenly Father to grant unto us through his Seer, a revelation of his mind and will concerning our duty the coming season even a great revelation that will enlarge our hearts, comfort us in adversity and brighten our hopes amidst the power of Darkness ("Kirtland Council Minute Book," p. 198).

4.   A revelation (uncanonized) was received for the Quorum of Twelve Apostles on 3 November 1835, after their return from the East. The revelation chastized members of the quorum for covetousness and lack of humility while preaching the gospel in the eastern states:

> Behold they are under condemnation, because they have not been sufficiently humble in my sight, and in consequence of their covetous desires, in that they have not dealt equally with each other in the division of the monies which came into their hands, nevertheless, some of them dealt equally, therefore they shall be rewarded; but verily I say unto you, they must all humble themselves before me, before they will be accounted worthy to receive an endowment, to go forth in my name unto all nations.
>
> As for my servant William [Smith], let the Eleven humble themselves in prayer and in faith, and wait on me in patience, and my servant William shall return, and I will yet make him a polished shaft in my quiver, in bringing down the wickedness and abominations of men; and there shall be none mightier than he, in his day and generation, nevertheless if he repent not speedily, he shall be brought low, and shall be chastened sorely for all his iniquities he has committed against me;

nevertheless the sin which he has sinned against me is not even now more grievous than the sin with which my servant David W. Patten, and my servant Orson Hyde, and my servant William E. McLellin have sinned against me, and the residue are not sufficiently humble before me.

Behold the parable which I spake concerning a man having twelve sons: for what man among you, having twelve sons, and is no respecter of them, and they serve him obediently, and he saith unto one, Be thou clothed in robes, and sit thou here; and to the other, Be thou clothed in rags, and sit thou there, and looketh upon his sons, and saith, I am just? Ye will answer, and say, no man; and ye answer truly; therefore, verily thus saith the Lord your God, I appoint these Twelve that they should be equal in their ministry, and in their portion, and in their evangelical rights; wherefore they have sinned a very grievous sin, inasmuch as they have made themselves unequal, and have not hearkened unto my voice; therefore, let them repent speedily, and prepare their hearts for the solemn assembly, and for the great day which is to come, verily thus saith the Lord. Amen (*History of the Church*, 2:300).

5. Referring to verses 1-58 of section 107, Brigham Young later stated, "You read that Oliver Cowdery was the Second Elder and you remember the Rev[elation] on the Priesthood; and Joseph was two hours laboring with O. C. to get him to write the Rev. in humility" ("Minutes of the School of the Prophets," 15 April 1868, Provo, Utah, copy at Utah State Historical Society, Salt Lake City, Utah).

6. This arrangement was modified by revelation in January 1838, making it much more difficult to remove a member of the First Presidency:

Revelation Given at the French Farm in Kirtland, Geauga Co., Ohio. In the presence of J. Smith Jr., S. Rigdon V. Knight & Geo. W. Robinson January 12th 1838.

When inquiry was made of the Lord relative to the trial of the first Presidency of the Church of Christ of Latter Day Saints, For transgressions according to the item of law, found in the Book of Covenants 3rd Section 37 verse [D&C 107:82] Whether the descision of Such an Council of one Stake Shall be conclusive for Zion and all her Stakes.

Thus Saith the Lord, Let the first Presidency of my Church, be held in full fellowship in Zion and all her Stakes, untill they Shall be found transgressors, by Such an high Council as is named in the above alluded Section, in Zion, by three Witnesses Standing against Each member of Said Presidency, and these witnesses Shall be of long and faithfull Standing, and Such also as cannot be impeached by other witnesses before Such Council, and when a descision is had by Such an Council in Zion, it Shall only be for Zion, it Shall not answer for her Stakes, but if Such descision be acknowledged by the Council of her Stakes, then it Shall answer for her Stakes. But if it is not acknowledged by the Stakes, other Such Stake[s] may have the privilege of hearing for themselves or if Such descision Shall be acknowledeged by a majority of the Stakes, then it Shall answer for all her Stakes and again,

The Presidency of my Church may be tried by the voice of the whole body of the Church in Zion, and the voice of a majority of all her Stakes and again,

Except a majority is had by the voice of the Church of Zion and a majority of all her Stakes, The charges will be considered not Sustained and in order to Sustain Such Charge or Charges, before Such Church of Zion or her Stakes, Such witnesses must be had as is named above, that is the witnesses to Each President, who are of long and faithfull Standing, that cannot be immpeached by other witnesses before the Church of Zion, or her Stakes, And all this Saith the Lord because of wicked and asspiring men, Let all your doings be in meekness and in humility before me Even So Amen ("The Scriptory Book of Joseph Smith," pp. 51-53, Church Archives).

Section 108

1. *History of the Church*, 2:345.
2. See *History of the Church*, 2:144, for example.
3. *History of the Church*; "Journal History"; "A Book of Proxey" (Nauvoo Temple), Church Archives; and Lyndon W. Cook, "Lyman Sherman—Man of God, Would-Be Apostle," *Brigham Young University Studies* 19 (Fall 1978):121-24.

Section 109

1. See Historical Note for section 88 concerning the physical description of the Kirtland Temple. The Reverend Truman Coe gave the following description of the sacred edifice:

The completion of the temple, according to the pattern shown to Joseph in vision, is a monument of unconquerable zeal. The imposing splendor of the pulpits, the orders of the Melchisedec and the Aaronic priesthoods, and the vails which are let down or drawn by machinery, dividing the place of worship into several apartments, presents before us a strange compound of Jewish antiquity and Roman Catholic mummery. The reproof which the prophet addresses to ancient Israel that they dwelt in ceiled houses while the Temple of God was laid waste, can never be applied to these Mormons.—Stimulated by strong faith and zeal, you will see them muster all their forces for miles around to hear the brethren speak in tongues, and proclaim the wonderful works of God. In this view they give to those who call themselves sober christians a most severe rebuke. If they had half the zeal of these misguided Mormons, the world would tremble, and the millennial day would speedily be ushered in (*The Ohio Observer*, 11 August 1836).

2. George A. Smith remembered the following relative to the dedication of the temple,

When the Temple was completed there was a great manifestation of power. The brethren gathered together to its dedication. We considered it a very large building. Some nine hundred and sixty could be seated, and there would be room for a few to stand, the congregation was swelled to a little over a thousand persons at the time of the dedication. It was a trial of faith. The Elders from every part of the country had come together. The finishing of the Temple had involved a debt of many thousands, and we all came together to the dedication. The congregation was so large that we could not all get in; and when the house was full, then, of course, the doors were closed, and no more admitted .... When the dedication prayer was read by Joseph, it was read from a printed copy. This was a great trial of faith to many. "How can it be that the prophet should read a prayer?" What an awful trial it was, for the Prophet to read a prayer (*Journal of Discourses* 11:9).

3. See Joseph Smith Diary, 27 March 1836, Church Archives. Also see Lyndon W. Cook, "The Apostle Peter and the Kirtland Temple," *Brigham Young University Studies* 15 (Summer 1975):550-52.

4. See Oliver Cowdery "Sketch Book," edited by Leonard J. Arrington, *Brigham Young University Studies*, 12 (Summer 1972):426. Much of the prayer consists of various passages of scripture taken from the Bible as well as revelations previously received by Joseph Smith.

Section 110

1. *History of the Church*, 2:434-35.

2. See Joseph Smith Diary, 3 April 1836, Church Archives. My thanks to Dean C. Jessee for identifying Warren Cowdery's handwriting.

Section 111

1. Ebenezer Robinson, "Items of Personal History of the Editor," *The Return* (July 1889):105-06.

2. This trip to Massachusetts is detailed in *Messenger and Advocate*, 2 (September 1836):372-75, and 3 (October 1836):386-93.

3. Robinson, *The Return*. See note 1. Concerning the "treasure," the Prophet penned the following to his wife, Emma, on 19 August 1836: "With regard to the great object of our mission, you will be anxious to know. We have found the house since Bro. Burgess left us, very luckily and providentially, as we had one spell been most discouraged. The house is occupied, and it will require much care and patience to rent or buy it. We think we shall be able to effect it; if not now, within the course of a few months. We think we shall be at home about the middle of September" (Joseph to Emma, 19 August 1836, cited in *The Saints' Herald* 26 [1879]:456-57). Despite the optimism, the Church leaders were unable to secure possession of the building.

4. See *The Boston Daily Times* (24 August 1836); and the *Essex Register* (Salem), 25 August 1836. The *Salem Observer* (27 August 1836), noted that Rigdon spoke at a local lyceum on 20 August: "The preacher was a man of

very respectable appearance, apparently about 40 years of age, and very fluent in his language." See also David R. Proper, "Joseph Smith and Salem," *Essex Institute Historical Collections* (April 1964):88-97. My thanks to Donald Q. Cannon for sources used in this note and note 5.

5. See Erastus Snow Journal (typescript), Church Archives. In 1841 Hyrum Smith and William Law, who were on a mission in the East, instructed Snow to preach the gospel in Salem, Massachusetts. Snow reported that the Church leaders "left us a copy of a Revelation given about that people in 1836 which said the Lord had much people whom he would gather into his kingdom in his own due time and they thought the due time of the Lord had come." The *Salem Gazette* (7 and 17 December 1841) reported the success of the Mormon missionaries in Salem. The *Salem Register* (2 June 1842) estimated the number of converts from Salem to be "about eighty": "Mormonism is advancing with a perfect rush in this city, just at present. Several of the Elders have made a descent upon us . . . . Meetings have been holden now very frequently for several days past, and crowds flock to listen to the strange doctrines of the 'Latter Day Saints.' How many new converts they make, we have not learned, but understand that the whole number of those who have come over to the faith, is about eighty." See also *An Address To The Citizens of Salem and Vicinity, By E. Snow & B. Winchester, Elders of the Church of Jesus Christ of Latter-Day Saints* (Salem: September 1841).

Section 112

1. See Thomas B. Marsh and David W. Patten to Parley P. Pratt, 10 May 1837, Joseph Smith Collection, Church Archives.

2. These two apostles left Kirtland, Ohio, on 13 June 1837.

3. As reported in Wilford Woodruff Journal, 25 June 1857, Church Archives.

4. See Vilate Kimball to Heber C. Kimball, 6 September 1837, and Heber C. Kimball to Vilate Kimball, 12 November 1837, both at Church Archives. Marsh had informed Vilate that the gospel could not be effectually taken to Europe except it be introduced by Marsh himself. Heber, giving justification for his advance mission, replied, "Still brother Joseph sed it was all right to prepare the way for brother Marsh" (Ibid.).

5. See Lyndon W. Cook, "'I Have Sinned Against Heaven, and Am Unworthy of Your Confidence, But I Cannot Live without a Reconciliation': Thomas B. Marsh Returns to the Church," *Brigham Young University Studies* 20 (Summer 1980):389-400. When a copy of section 112 reached missionaries in England, Joseph Fielding wrote: "A new Revelation has also been given for the Twelve by which it is understood that Elders will not bring their wives to other Nations, &c" (Joseph Fielding Journal, 27 October 1837, Church Archives). Because this revelation does not address the advisability of wives accompanying their husbands on foreign missions, such information was either given at the time section 112 was received, or refers to another 1837 revelation to the Twelve not presently available.

6. Vilate Kimball to Heber C. Kimball, 6 September 1837, Church Archives.

Section 113

1. "The Scriptory Book of Joseph Smith," p. 53. The entire unpublished revelation, in the hand of George W. Robinson, follows:

> Revelation Given the Same day January 12th 1838. Thus Saith the Lord, let the Presidency of my Church, take their families as Soon as it is practicable, and a door is open for them, and move to the west, as fast as the way is made plain before their faces, and let their hearts be comforted for I will be with them, Verrily I Say unto you, the time has come, that your Labors are finished in this place for a Season. Therefore arise and get yourselves, into a land which I Shall Show unto you, Even a land flowing with milk & honey, you are clean from the blood of this people, and wo, unto those who have become your Enimies, who have professed my name Saith the Lord, for their judgement lingereth not, and their damnation slumbereth not. Let all your faithfull friends arise with their families also, and get out of this place, and gather themselves together unto Zion and be at peace among yourselves, O ye inhabitants of Zion, or their Shall be no Safety for you, Even So Amen.

2. "The Scriptory Book of Joseph Smith," pp. 17-18.
3. The "Scriptory Book" and the "Far West Record," both products of the Missouri experience, were begun in Far West, Missouri, in April 1838. The former was a record-book for the First Presidency; the latter, a minute-book for the High Council at Far West. See "Far West Record," pp. 114-15, where clerks were appointed to keep these records.
4. *History of the Church*; "Far West Record"; Elias Higbee family group sheet, Genealogical Society, Salt Lake City, Utah; "Journal History"; "Nauvoo High Council Minutes"; 1820 and 1830 Federal Census of Ohio.

Section 114

1. These two revelations are recorded in "The Scriptory Book of Joseph Smith," p. 32. The revelation for Brigham Young instructed him to settle at Mill Creek until his departure to Great Britain:

> Revelation given to Brigham Young at Far West April 17th 1838. Verrily thus Saith the Lord, Let my Servant Brigham Young go unto the place which he has bought on Mill Creek and there provide for his family until an effectual door is opened for the Suport of his family untill I Shall command [him] to go hence, and not to leave his family untill they are amply provided for Amen.

2. *History of the Church*; Jenson's *Biographical Encyclopedia*, 1:76; D&C, sections 114 and 124; Lycurgus A. Wilson, *Life of David W. Patten—First Apostolic Martyr* (Salt Lake City: Deseret News, 1904); *Utah Genealogical and Historical Magazine* (January 1936).

Section 115

1. Section 115 was contemporaneously recorded in "The Scriptory Book of Joseph Smith," pp. 32-34.

2. Thomas B. Marsh to Wilford Woodruff, 30 April 1838, Church Archives.

3. See "Far West Record," p. 72.

4. The revelation is one of three, received 12 January 1838, in Kirtland, Ohio, and read to the body of the Church in Far West, Missouri, 8 July 1838:

> Revelation Given the Same day January 12th 1838, upon an inquiry being made of the Lord, whether any branch of the Church of Christ of Latter Day Saints can be concidered a Stake of Zion, untill they have acknowledged the authority of the first Presidency by a vote of Such Church
> Thus Saith the Lord, Verrily I Say unto you Nay
> No Stake Shall be appointed, Except by the first Presidency, and this Presidency be acknowledged, by the voice of the Same, otherwise it Shall not be Counted as a Stake of Zion and again except it be dedicated by this presidency it cannot be acknowledged as a Stake of Zion. For unto this End have I appointed them in Laying the foundation of and Establishing my Kingdom Even So Amen ("The Scriptory Book of Joseph Smith," pp. 52-53).

Section 116

1. The date of reception for section 116 is uncertain. The original source for the revelation is "The Scriptory Book of Joseph Smith" (pp. 43-44), but the journal entries in this document for May and June 1838 (in the handwriting of George W. Robinson, the Prophet's scribe) were recorded after the fact (probably July 1838), and therefore cannot be taken at face value to interpret historical events as they developed. The 19 May 1838 entry strongly implies that Joseph Smith revealed the name "Adam-Ondi-Ahman" subsequent to that date. George Robinson's journal entry details the Prophet's activites in "laying claims to [a] city platt" near Lyman Wight's ferry. Robinson noted that Wight and others had named the place "Spring Hill," but the location was "*afterwards* named by the mouth of the Lord and was called Adam Ondi Awmen" (emphasis mine). William Swartzell, a temporary Mormon convert, assisted Church leaders in the surveying of Spring Hill or Adam-Ondi-Ahman in 1838. Swartzell, who kept regular diary entries during this period, recorded that the ancient name was given by the Prophet on 11 June 1838: "[I] observed to Joseph Smith that this city should have a new name. Brother Joseph placed his back against a small shady tree near the spring, and then said, 'We shall alter the name of this *stake*' . . . and looking towards heaven for a short time, said, 'It does not take me long to get a revelation from heaven, and this stake, or city, shall be

called Adam-on-Diammon" (William Swartzell, *Mormonism Exposed, Being a Journal of a Residence in Missouri from the 28th of May to the 20th of August, 1838* .... (Pekin, Ohio: By the Author, 1840).

2.   Oliver Cowdery to Warren Cowdery, 21 January 1838, Oliver Cowdery Letterbook, Huntington Library, San Marino, California. Copy in possession of author.

3.   The settling of Adam-ondi-Ahman was noted in the *Missouri Argus* (8 November 1838): "[Joseph Smith instructed the Saints] that they should go to Daviess county.... He then declared it was the Lord's will that they should be called "Adamon Diamon," which name is derived from the fact that *old Adam's Grove* was there."See also *Elders' Journal* (August 1838) which announced the rapid growth of Mormon settlement.

4.   The official source for this statement is "The Scriptory Book of Joseph Smith," pp. 43-44. George W. Robinson, clerk for the First Presidency, penned the following entry for 19 May 1838:

> The next morning we struck our tents, and marched crossed Grand River at the mouth of Honey Creek at a place called Nelsons ferry. Grand River is a beautifull, deep and rapid stream and will undoubtedly admit of Steam Boat and other water craft navigation, and at the mouth of honey creek is a splendid harbour for the saftey of Lurch Crafts, and also for landing freight. We next kept up the river mostly in the timber for ten miles, until we came to Col. Lyman Wights who lives at the foot of Tower Hill, a name appropriated by Pres. Smith, in consequence of the remains of an old Nephitish Alter or Tower, where we camped for the sabath. In the after part of the day, Prsts. Smith and Rigdon and myself, went to Wights Ferry about a half mile from this place up the river, for the purpose of selecting and laying claims to City Platt near said Ferry, in Davis County Township 60; Range 27 & 28, and sections 25, 36, 31, 30, which was called Spring Hill, a name appropriated by the brethren present But afterwards named by the mouth of Lord and was called Adam Ondi Ahmen, because said he it is the place where Adam shall come to visit his people, or the Ancient of days shall sit as spoken of by Daniel the Prophet.

5.   See D&C 78:15. In 1877 Orson Pratt defined the name *Adam-ondi-Ahman*: "It means the place where Adam dwelt. 'Ahman' signifies God. The whole term means Valley of God, where Adam dwelt. It is the original language spoken by Adam, as revealed to the Prophet Joseph" (*Journal of Discourses*, 18:343).

Section 117

1.   Minutes of these meetings are in "Far West Record," pp. 114-17.
2.   *History of the Church*, 3:164.
3.   Letter dated 8 July 1838 is in the Joseph Smith Collection, Church Archives.

4. *History of the Church*; "Kirtland Council Minute Book"; D&C 117; "Kirtland Elders' Quorum Minutes," RLDS Library-Archives, Independence, Missouri; "Nauvoo Baptisms for the Dead," Genealogical Society, Salt Lake City, Utah; and "Journal History."

5. *History of the Church*; D&C, sections 117 and 124; Jenson's *Biographical Encyclopedia*, 1:283; 1830 Federal Census of New York; 1850 Federal Census of Illinois; William Marks Correspondence, RLDS Library-Archives; "Joseph Smith III Memoirs," *The Saints' Herald* (29 January 1935); "Kirtland Council Minute Book"; "Kirtland Elder's Quorum Minutes," RLDS Library-Archives; "Nauvoo High Council Minutes"; Maureen Ursenbach Beecher, " 'All Things Move in Order in the City': The Nauvoo Diary of Zina Diantha Huntington Jacobs," *Brigham Young University Studies* 19 (Spring 1979):306; and Ehat, "Endowment Data Summary."

Section 118

1. The names of those present are in "Kirtland Revelation Book" See also *History of the Church*, 3:46.

2. Letter in Church Archives; see also "Far West Record," pp. 114-17.

3. See "Far West Record," p. 142.

4. *History of the Church*; D&C, sections 118 and 124; "Far West Record"; Jenson's *Biographical Encyclopedia*, 1:92; "Journal History"; Ehat, "Endowment Data Summary"; *The Gospel Light* [Philadelphia ?] 1 (February 1844):8; and 1850 Federal Census of Wisconsin. Death date is located in DeKalb County, Illinois, Probate Records.

5. *History of the Church*; Jenson's *Biographical Encyclopedia*, 1:53; D&C, sections 118, 124, and 135; Claire Noall, *Intimate Disciple: A Portrait of Willard Richards* (Salt Lake City: University of Utah Press, 1957); Ehat, "Endowment Data Summary"; "A Book of Proxey" (Nauvoo Temple), Church Archives; and Willard Richards Diaries, Church Archives.

6. *History of the Church*; Jenson's *Biographical Encyclopedia*, 1:14; D&C, sections 118, 124, and 135; Ehat, "Endowment Data Summary"; and B. H. Roberts, *The Life of John Taylor* (Salt Lake City: Bookcraft, 1963).

7. *History of the Church*; "Far West Record"; Jenson's *Biographical Encyclopedia*, 1:20; D&C, sections 118, 124, and Official Declaration Number One; Wilford Woodruff Journal, Church Archives; Ehat, "Endowment Data Summary"; and Matthias F. Cowley, *Wilford Woodruff: Fourth President of the Church of Jesus Christ of Latter-day Saints* (Salt Lake City: Bookcraft, 1970).

Section 119

1. "Far West Record," pp. 89-93.

2. Section 119 was contemporaneously recorded in "The Scriptory Book of Joseph Smith," p. 56: "Revelation given the same day and read at the same time as the preceeding ones July 8th 1838."

3. *Journal of Discourses*, 2:306. See also *Journal of Discourses*, 6:175.

Section 120

1. "The Scriptory Book of Joseph Smith," p. 57. Compare *History of the Church*, 3:44.

2. "The Scriptory Book of Joseph Smith," p. 59; compare *History of the Church*, 3:47. On 27 July 1838 George W. Robinson recorded, "[For] some time past the bretheren or saints have come up day after day to consecrate, and to bring their offerings unto the store house of the lord, to prove him now herewith and se[e] if he will not pour us out a blessing that there will not be room enough to contain it" ("The Scriptory Book of Joseph Smith," p. 60).

Section 121

1. See *History of the Church*, 3:289-305. The letter was written in two parts. The first installment consists of seventeen pages, dated 20 March 1839, and is signed by the prisoners. The second part is a continuation of the epistle consisting of twelve pages, also signed by the prisoners but not dated. The latter part is addressed to Emma Smith at Quincy, Illinois. A letter written by the Prophet to his wife, Emma, on 21 March 1839 gave instructions regarding the disposition of the epistle: that it was first to be read by the family, then delivered to Church leaders in Quincy. Although it is not clear when the second installment was written, the *History of the Church* suggests that the entire epistle was written 20-25 March 1839.

Section 122

1. Lyman Wight statement before the Municipal Court of Nauvoo, 1 July 1843, "Nauvoo Municipal Court Docket Book," under date, Church Archives. Also see *Times and Seasons* 4 (15 July 1843):268.

Section 123

1. *History of the Church* 3:346. In accordance with the instructions in verses 1-4, petitions and hundreds of affidavits, itemizing personal losses in Missouri, were prepared by the Saints and forwarded to Washington, D.C.

2. Erastus Snow Journal, under date, Church Archives.

3. Ibid.

Section 124

1. Franklin D. Richards to John Taylor, 26 December 1883, John Taylor Papers, Church Archives. Richards speaks of section 124 in this letter. This revelation occupies the first entry in the "Book of the Law of the Lord," (in the hand of Robert B. Thompson).

2. *History of the Church*, 4:483-84.

3. *History of the Church*, 6:79.

4. *History of the Church*, 6:80
5. *History of the Church*, 6:176.
6.   William W. Phelps to Brigham Young, 6 August 1863, Church Archives. What appears to be an early draft of the proclamation is located in the Joseph Smith Collection, Church Archives. The document begins,

> From Joseph Smith, President of the Church of Jesus Christ of Latter Day Saints, and Prophet, Seer, and Revelator of the Most High God, to the President of the United States of North America—the Governors of the Several States—the Emperors, Kings, and Princes of the Earth—the Executives of all nations—the Chiefs of all tribes—and all occupying high places in the administration of governments....Now in obedience to a revelation given January 19th 1841, I proceed to call upon you to yield yourselves as obedient subjects to the requirements of heaven, in contributing to the fulfilment of the predictions of the prophets—to believe on the Lord Jesus Christ, repent of and abandon your sins, be immersed for the remission of sins, receive the imposition of hands for the gift of the Holy Ghost, and, in fine, to embrace the gospel in its beauty & fulness . . . ."

7.   See *Proclamation of the Twelve Apostles of the Church of Jesus Christ of Latter-day Saints to all the Kings of the World, to the President of the United States of America; to the Governors of the Several States, and to the Rulers and People of all Nations* (New York: by Parley P. Pratt, 6 April 1845). Parley P. Pratt authored the document under the direction of the Twelve Apostles (see *History of the Church*, 7:558).
8. *History of the Church*, 4:301-02.
9.   See *Times and Seasons* 2 (1 April 1841):369. Also see *History of the Church*, 5:285.
10.   Joseph Smith Letterbook, 2 October 1841, Church Archives.
11. *Times and Seasons* 2 (1 April 1841):369.
12. *History of the Church*, 5:137 and 328.
13. *History of the Church*, 4:311. The uncanonized revelation states,

> Let my servants, William Allred and Henry W. Miller, have an agency for the selling of stock for the Nauvoo House, and assist my sevants Lyman Wight, Peter Haws, George Miller, and John Snider, in building said house; and let my servants William Allred and Henry W. Miller take stock in the house, that the poor of my people may have employment, and that accommodations may be made for the strangers who shall come visit this place, and for this purpose let them devote all their properties, saith the Lord.

14.   George Miller to the *Northern Islander*, 26 June 1855, cited in H. W. Mills, "De Tal Palo Tal Astilla," *Annual Publications—the Historical Society of Southern California*, 10 (1917):86-172.
15. *History of the Church*, 5:327.
16. *History of the Church*, 6:230.

17. *History of the Church*, 7:394, and William Huntington Diary, 18 August 1845, Brigham Young University Library, Special Collections. See also Willard Richards Diary, 9 August 1845, Church Archives.

18. William Huntington Diary, Brigham Young University Library, Special Collections. See entries in August and September 1845.

19. Willard Richards Diary, 16 September 1845, Church Archives.

20. *The Saints' Herald* (1 June 1879).

21. The following sources were used for information on the Nauvoo Temple: Don F. Colvin, "A Historical Study of the Mormon Temple at Nauvoo, Illinois," M. S. thesis, Brigham Young University, 1962; J. Earl Arrington, "William Weeks, Architect of the Nauvoo Temple," *Brigham Young University Studies* 19 (Spring 1979):337-59; Lisle G Brown, "The Sacred Departments for Temple Work in Nauvoo: The Assembly Room and the Council Chamber," *Brigham Young University Studies* 19 (Spring 1979):361-74; Samuel W. Richards Diary, Church Archives; William Huntington Diary, Brigham Young University Library, Special Collections; *History of the Church*; and William Clayton, "Nauvoo Temple History Journal," Church Archives.

22. See "Nauvoo Temple Endowment Register," Genealogical Society, Salt Lake City, Utah; "Nauvoo Baptisms for the Dead," Church Archives; and Ehat, "Endowment Data Summary."

23. *History of the Church*, 4:341.

24. *History of the Church*, 4:323.

25. *History of the Church*, 4:312.

26. Ibid.

27. *History of the Church*; "Journal History"; *Frontier Guardian* (2 May 1851); 1850 Federal Census of Illinois; *Western Bugle* (Kanesville, Iowa); "Record of Sealings" (Nauvoo Temple), Church Archives; Harold Schindler, *Orrin Porter Rockwell: Man of God, Son of Thunder* (Salt Lake City: University of Utah Press, 1966); "A Book of Proxey" (Nauvoo Temple), Church Archives.

28. *History of the Church*; "Kirtland Elder's Quorum Minutes," RLDS Library-Archives, Independence, Missouri; "Nauvoo Temple Endowment Register," Genealogical Society, Salt Lake City, Utah.

29. *History of the Church*; "Journal History"; John C. Bennett Correspondence, RLDS Library-Archives, Independence, Missouri; 1850 Federal Census of Massachusetts; Ralph V. Chamberlain Papers, Brigham Young University Library, Special Collections; James J. Tyler, *John Cook Bennett: Colorful Freemason of the Early Nineteenth Century* (Ohio: 1947); and John C. Bennett, *History of the Saints; or, an Expose of Joe Smith and the Mormons* (Boston: Leland & Whiting, 1842).

30. *History of the Church*; "Far West Record"; "Nauvoo High Council Minutes"; Jenson's *Biographical Encyclopedia*, 1:367; "Record of Sealings" (Nauvoo Temple), Church Archives; and "A Book of Proxey" (Nauvoo Temple), Church Archives.

31. 1810, 1820, and 1830 Federal Census of Maine; Evan M. Greene Journal, Church Archives; Jonathan H. Hale Journal, Church Archives;

"General Record of the Seventies," Books A and B, Church Archives; "Kirtland Elder's Quorum Minutes," RLDS Library-Archives, Independence, Missouri; "Kirtland Council Minute Book"; *History of the Church*; "Geauga County, Ohio, Tax Records"; "Nauvoo Temple Endowment Register," Genealogical Society, Salt Lake City, Utah; Jenson's *Biographical Encyclopedia*, 1:192; and Charles A. Butterfield Correspondence to Paul Hanson, RLDS Library-Archives.

32. *History of the Church*; "Journal History"; "Nauvoo High Council Minutes"; Ehat, "Endowment Data Summary"; Juanita Brooks, ed., *On the Mormon Frontier: The Diary of Hosea Stout 1844-1861* (Salt Lake City: University of Utah Press, 1964); "Municipal High Council Minutes of Winter Quarters," Church Archives; Daisy Whiting Fletcher, *Alpheus Cutler and the Church of Christ* (n.p., 1970); "Record of Adoptions and Sealings of Parents and Children" (Nauvoo Temple), Church Archives.

33. *History of the Church*; "Nauvoo High Council Minutes"; 1860 Federal Census of Illinois; and "Nauvoo Restoration, Inc., Biographical File," Church Archives.

34. *History of the Church*; "Journal History"; "Far West Record"; "Kirtland Council Minute Book"; "Nauvoo High Council Minutes"; "Geauga County, Ohio, Tax Records"; 1820 Federal Census of New Hampshire; 1830 Federal Census of Michigan; and *Times and Seasons* 2 (15 March 1841):358.

35. *History of the Church*; "Kirtland Council Minute Book"; "Kirtland Elder's Quorum Minutes," RLDS Library-Archives, Independence, Missouri; "General Record of the Seventies," Book A, Church Archives; and *Messenger and Advocate*.

36. *History of the Church*; "Journal History"; Orson Pratt to Robert D. Foster, 20 October 1840, Brigham Young University Library, Manuscripts; "Patriarchal Blessing of Robert D. Foster," Brigham Young University Library, Manuscripts; 1850 Federal Census of New York; and "Nauvoo High Council Minutes."

37. *History of the Church*; Jenson's *Biographical Encyclopedia*, 1:289; "Kirtland Elder's Quorum Minutes," RLDS Library-Archives, Independence, Missouri; "Nauvoo High Council Minutes": "Journal History"; "Record of Sealings" (Nauvoo Temple), Church Archives; and Autobiography of David Fullmer, copy in possession of author.

38. Lyndon W. Cook, "Isaac Galland—Mormon Benefactor," *Brigham Young University Studies* 19 (Spring 1979):261-84.

39. *History of the Church*; Jenson's *Biographical Encyclopedia*, 4:137; "Kirtland Council Minute Book"; "Nauvoo High Council Minutes"; *Messenger and Advocate*; Esshom, *Pioneers and Prominent Men of Utah*; *Times and Seasons*; Thomas Grover family group sheet, Genealogical Society, Salt Lake City, Utah; and "Nauvoo 9th Ward High Priests Quorum Minutes," in Joseph Holbrook Journal, Church Archives.

40. *Wayne Sentinel* (3 December 1830); *History of the Church*; "Journal History"; D&C 124; *Ohio Star* (23 December 1831); "Nauvoo High Council

Minutes"; "Far West Record"; "Pottawatamie High Council Minutes"; *Frontier Guardian*; "Journal History," 7 October 1860; and Elden J. Watson, *Orson Pratt Journals*.

41. *History of the Church*; "Journal History"; "Far West Record" (Nauvoo entries); "Nauvoo High Council Minutes"; D&C 124; Juanita Brooks, ed., *On the Mormon Frontier: The Diary of Hosea Stout 1844-1861*; Erastus Snow Journal, Brigham Young University Library, Special Collections; "Nauvoo Temple Endowment Register," Genealogical Society, Salt Lake City, Utah; "Patriarchal Blessing File," Church Archives; and "Record of Sealings" (Nauvoo Temple), Church Archives.

42. Jenson's *Biographical Encyclopedia*, 1:193; *History of the Church*; "Journal History"; Elden J. Watson, *Orson Pratt Journals*; *Utah Genealogical and Historical Magazine* (July 1937); Henry Herriman family group sheet, Genealogical Society, Salt Lake City, Utah; "General Record of the Seventies," Books A and B, Church Archives; and *Deseret News* (23 May 1891).

43. *History of the Church*; *Times and Seasons*; D&C 124; and "Journal History". Possibly moved to Michigan by 1850 (see 1850 Federal Census of Michigan).

44. *History of the Church*; Jenson's *Biographical Encyclopedia*, 1:368; "Kirtland Council Minute Book"; "Nauvoo High Council Minutes"; Jefferson City, New York, Land Records; 1810 Federal Census of New York; William Huntington Journal, Brigham Young University Library, Manuscripts; William Huntington family group sheet, Genealogical Society, Salt Lake City, Utah; "Nauvoo Temple Endowment Register," Genealogical Society; and "A Book of Proxey" (Nauvoo Temple), Church Archives.

45. *History of the Church*; "Journal History"; Jenson's *Biographical Encyclopedia*, 4:504; Kirtland, Ohio, Land Records; Kirtland, Ohio, Tax Records; "General Record of the Seventies," Book A, Church Archives; Esshom, *Pioneers and Prominent Men of Utah*; "Biographical Sketch of Aaron Johnson," by his clerk William Gallop, copy in possession of author; "Nauvoo High Council Minutes"; "Nauvoo Temple Endowment Register," Genealogical Society, Salt Lake City, Utah; Aaron Johnson Correspondence in "Brigham Young Incoming Correspondence," Brigham Young Collection, Church Archives; Aaron Johnson Correspondence in "Utah Territory Military Papers," Utah State Archives; and "Aaron Johnson Administration Papers," in Utah County, Probate Records, Provo, Utah.

46. *History of the Church*; Jenson's *Biographical Encyclopedia*; Heber C. Kimball Journals, Church Archives; Orson F. Whitney, *Life of Heber C. Kimball an Apostle* (Salt Lake City: Kimball Family, 1888); "Journal History"; Ehat, "Endowment Data Summary"; and "A Book of Proxey," Church Archives.

47. *History of the Church*; "Far West Record"; "Our Heritage: Some Important Events in the Life of Great Grandfather Vinson Knight," Church Archives; Ehat, "Endowment Data Summary"; *Times and Seasons*; and "Journal History."

48. *History of the Church*; "Nauvoo High Council Minutes"; Lyndon W. Cook, "'Brother Joseph Is Truly a Wonderful Man, He Is All We Could Wish a Prophet to Be': Pre-1844 Letters of William Law, *Brigham Young University Studies* 20 (Winter 1980):207-18; "William Law Family History," copy in possession of author; "William Law Account Book," Beinecke Rare Book and Manuscript Library, Yale University, New Haven, Connecticut; William Law Diary, copy in possession of author; 1850 Federal Census of Pennsylvania; 1870 and 1880 Federal Census of Wisconsin; LaFayette County, Wisconsin, Land Records; Heber C. Kimball Journal (1842), Church Archives; Wilford Woodruff Journal, Church Archives; William Law Papers, Church Archives; and William Law Correspondence and Interview with William Wyl in *The Daily Tribune* (Salt Lake City, Utah), 31 July 1887.

49. *History of the Church*; Jenson's *Biographical Encyclopedia*, 1:96; "Journal History"; Esshom, *Pioneers and Prominent Men of Utah*; Amasa Lyman Journals, Church Archives; "Record of Sealings" (Nauvoo Temple), Church Archives; Ehat, "Endowment Data Summary"; and Amasa Lyman family group sheets, Genealogical Society, Salt Lake City, Utah.

50. *History of the Church*; Jenson's *Biographical Encyclopedia*, 1:192; "Geauga County, Ohio, Tax Rcords"; Calvin Miles family group sheet, Genealogical Society, Salt Lake City, Utah; "Kirtland Elder's Quorum Minutes," RLDS Library-Archives, Independence, Missouri; Elden J. Watson, *Orson Pratt Journals*; "General Record of the Seventies," Book A, Church Archives; "Nauvoo High Council Minutes"; and Juanita Brooks, ed., *On the Mormon Frontier: The Diary of Hosea Stout 1844-1861*.

51. *History of the Church*; "Journal History"; "Nauvoo High Council Minutes"; Ehat, "Endowment Data Summary"; D&C 124; Lyndon W. Cook. "'A More Virtuous Man Never Existed On The Footstool Of The Great Jehovah': George Miller on Joseph Smith," *Brigham Young University Studies* 19 (Spring 1979):402-07; "Record of Sealings" (Nauvoo Temple), Church Archives; "Municipal High Council Minutes of Winter Quarters," Brigham Young Collection, Church Archives; and H. W. Mills, "De Tal Palo Tal Astilla," *Annual Publications—the Historical Society of Southern California*, 10 [1917]:86-172.

52. *History of the Church*; "Journal History"; "Kirtland Council Minute Book"; Birth Record from Town Clerk, Plainfield, Massachusetts; Jenson's *Biographical Encyclopedia*, 2:684; 1850 Census of Utah; and "Synopsis of the Life of Noah Packard, Written by Himself [1858?]." My thanks to Calvin Packard of Springville, Utah, for providing me a copy of this biographical sketch.

53. *History of the Church*; "Journal History"; Jenson's *Biographical Encyclopedia*, 1:194; "General Record of the Seventies," Book A, Church Archives; Zerah Pulsipher Journal (typescript), Brigham Young University Library, Special Collections; Zerah Pulsipher family group sheets, Genealogical Society, Salt Lake City, Utah; "Nauvoo Temple Endowment Register," Genealogical Society; 1850 Census of Utah; "Journal History" (2 January 1872).

54. *History of the Church*; Jenson's *Biographical Encyclopedia*, 1:102; "Nauvoo Temple Endowment Register," Genealogical Society, Salt Lake City, Utah; "Record of Sealings" (Nauvoo Temple), Church Archives; and Leonard J. Arrington, *Charles C. Rich*.

55. *History of the Church*; Esshom, *Pioneers and Prominent Men of Utah*; D&C 124; Caldwell County, Missouri, Land Records; Leonard J. Arrington, *Charles C. Rich*; "Nauvoo Temple Endowment Register," Genealogical Society, Salt Lake City, Utah; 1810, 1820, and 1830 Federal Census of Maine; 1850 Census of Utah; and "Journal History."

56. Birth Record from Rockingham, Vermont gives Roundy's birth as 1 January *1788*.

57. *History of the Church*; Jenson's *Biographical Encyclopedia*, 1:642; "Journal History"; "General Record of the Seventies," Book A, Church Archives; Shadrack Roundy family group sheets, Genealogical Society, Salt Lake City, Utah; Samuel H. Smith Journal (typescript), Brigham Young University Library, Special Collections; "Camp Journal of Captain Shadrack Roundy's Company, 1845," Church Archives; and "Nauvoo Temple Endowment Register," Genealogical Society.

58. *History of the Church*; "Kirtland Council Minute Book"; "Nauvoo High Council Minutes"; Jenson's *Biographical Encyclopedia*, 4:717; Jared Carter Journal, Church Archives; Leonard J. Arrington, *Charles C. Rich*; "Nauvoo Temple Endowment Register," Genealogical Society, Salt Lake City, Utah; "Record of Sealings" (Nauvoo Temple), Church Archives; "Journal History"; and Probate Records, Superior Court, Los Angeles County, California.

59. *History of the Church*; Don Carlos Smith family group sheet, Genealogical Society, Salt Lake City, Utah; "Journal History"; and "A Book of Proxey" (Nauvoo Temple), Church Archives.

60. *History of the Church*; Jenson's *Biographical Encyclopedia*, 1:37; Ehat, "Endowment Data Summary"; and Zora Smith Jarvis, *Ancestry, Biography, and Family of George A. Smith* (Provo: Brigham Young University Publications, 1962).

61. *History of the Church*; Jenson's *Biographical Encyclopedia*, 1:86; "Kirtland Council Minute Book"; Calvin P. Rudd, "William Smith: Brother to the Prophet Joseph Smith," M. A. thesis, Brigham Young University, 1973; William Smith, *William Smith on Mormonism* (Lamoni, Iowa: 1883); Patriarchal Blessing Book of William Smith, RLDS Library-Archives, Independence, Missouri; William Smith Papers, RLDS Library-Archives and William Smith Letters in Brigham Young Collection, Church Archives.

62. *History of the Church*; "Journal History"; 1850 Federal Census of Illinois; *Elder's Journal*; *Messenger and Advocate*; Esshom, *Pioneers and Prominent Men of Utah*; "Salt Lake City Seventeenth Ward Records (1856-72)," Church Archives; and "General Record of the Seventies," Book A, Church Archives.

63. *History of the Church*; "Journal History"; Jenson's *Biographical Encyclopedia*, 1:253; and "A Book of Proxey" (Nauvoo Temple), Church Archives.

64. *History of the Church;* "Journal History"; 1830 Federal Census of Massachusetts; "Nauvoo Temple Endowment Register," Genealogical Society, Salt Lake City, Utah; Samuel Williams family group sheet, Genealogical Society; "Nauvoo High Council Minutes"; and 1850 Census of Utah.

65. *History of the Church;* "Journal History"; Esshom, *Pioneers and Prominent Men of Utah;* "Record of Sealings" (Nauvoo Temple), Church Archives; "Nauvoo High Council Minutes"; Lewis D. Wilson family group sheets, Genealogical Society, Salt Lake City, Utah; and "History of Lewis Dunbar Wilson, Sr.," copy in possession of author.

66. *History of the Church;* Jenson's *Biographical Encyclopedia,* 1:8ff; "Record of Sealings" (Nauvoo Temple), Church Archives; and Dean C. Jessee, *Letters of Brigham Young to His Sons* (Salt Lake City: Deseret Book Co., 1974).

67. *History of the Church;* Jenson's *Biographical Encyclopedia,* 1:187; Statement of Joseph Young in Mss. 942, Brigham Young University Library, Manuscripts; Richard Bennett, "A Study of the Church of Jesus Christ of Latter-day Saints in Upper Canada, 1830-1850," M. A. thesis, Brigham Young University, 1975; "Record of Sealings" (Nauvoo Temple), Church Archives; and Joseph Young, Sen., *History of the Organization of the Seventies* (Salt Lake City: Deseret News, 1878).

Section 125

1. John Smith Journal, under date, Church Archives.

2. See Lyndon W. Cook, "Isaac Galland—Mormon Benefactor," *Brigham Young University Studies* 19 (Spring 1979):261-84.

3. *Manchester Mormons: The Journal of William Clayton, 1840 to 1842,* ed., James B. Allen and Thomas G. Alexander (Santa Barbara and Salt Lake City: Peregrine Smith, Inc., 1974).

Section 126

1. See D&C 118.

2. See James B. Allen and Malcom R. Thorp, "The Mission of the Twelve to England, 1840-41: Mormon Apostles and the Working Class," *Brigham Young University Studies* 15 (Summer 1975):499-526.

Section 127

1. On 10 August 1840 Seymour Brunson, member of the Nauvoo High Council, died in Nauvoo. The Prophet took the occasion of his funeral, on 15 August 1840, to deliver the first discourse on the doctrine of baptism for the dead (see *History of the Church,* 4:231). Although there is no known contemporary text for this discourse, Simon Baker left the following reminiscent account with the Historian's Office:

> I was present at a discourse that the prophet Joseph delivered on baptism for the dead 15 August 1840. He read the greater part of the 15th chapter of Corinthians and remarked that the Gospel of Jesus Christ

brought glad tidings of great joy, and then remarked that he saw a widow in that congregation that had a son who died without being baptized, and this widow in reading the sayings of Jesus 'except a man be born of water and of the spirit he cannot enter the kingdom of heaven,' and that not one jot nor tittle of the Savior's words should pass away, but all should be fulfilled. He then said that this widow should have glad tidings in that thing. He also said the apostle was talking to a people who understood baptism for the dead, for it was practiced among them. He went on to say that people could now act for their friends who had departed this life, and that the plan of salvation was calculated to save all who were willing to obey the requirements of the law of God. He went on and made a very beautiful discourse ("Journal History," under date, Church Archives).

2.   John Smith Journal, 15 October 1840, Church Archives.
3.   *History of the Church*, 4:426.
4.   *History of the Church*, 4:454.
5.   Endowments for the dead were first performed in the St. George Temple on 11 January 1877.
6.   "A Book of Records Containing the Proceedings of the Female Relief Society of Nauvoo," 31 August 1842 (pp. 82 and 83), Church Archives.

Section 128

1.   Wilford Woodruff Journal, 19 September 1842, Church Archives.

Section 129

1.   Wilford Woodruff Journal, 26-27 June 1839, Church Archives.
2.   Far from saying that when the instructions of this discourse were followed, the adversary's only recourse was to attempt to return the handshake, in a December 1840 discourse Joseph Smith stated, "The Devil .... will either shrink back .... or offer his hand." He will not remain absolutely still if he is tested. On 28 April 1842, the Prophet revealed to the Relief Society, and on 1 May 1842 to the Nauvoo populace, that there was another dimension for determining whether manifestations and revelations were approved by God. There were "keys of the Kingdom, " he said to a Sunday audience of the saints in the Grove, "certain signs and words by which false spirits and personages may be detected from true, which cannot be revealed to the Elders till the Temple is completed ... There are signs .. the Elders must know ... to be endowed with the power, to finish their work and prevent imposition" (*History of the Church*, 4:608). Three days later Joseph Smith revealed these sacred keys to nine men in accordance with his plans as announced to the Relief Society just six days before. To these men he taught the keys of prayer and detection whereby all these documents, revelations, or manifestations could be tested (see Andrew Ehat and Lyndon W. Cook, *The Words of Joseph Smith: The Contemporary Accounts of the Nauvoo Discourses of the Prophet Joseph* [Provo: Religious Studies Center, 1980], pp. 20-21).

3.   William Clayton Diary, under date, *draft* Manuscript History of the Church, Church Archives.

4.   The use of David W. Patten to illustrate a good spirit is based, no doubt, upon the fact that at Seymour Brunson's death in August 1840, Patten was to have come to Nauvoo as a spirit personage to "waft him home." Heber C. Kimball wrote, "Semer Bronson is gon. David Paten came after him. the R[o]om was full of Angels that came after him to waft him home" (Heber C. Kimball to John Taylor, 9 November 1840, in possession of Buddy Youngreen).

5.   Joseph Smith Diary, 9 February 1843, Joseph Smith Collection, Church Archives.

Section 130

1.   See Joel H. Johnson Journal, Church Archives; and *Times and Seasons* 2 (15 November 1840):222 and 2 (15 October 1841):573.

2.   See Joseph Smith Diary, under date, and *History of the Church*, 5:323.

3.   The particular interest in establishing a year date for the Lord's second advent (verses 14-17) was stimulated by the Millerite movement of 1843-44. Commenting on this matter four days later, the Prophet gave a variation on the account in section 130:

> I was once praying earnestly upon the subject. and a voice said unto me. My son, if thou livest till thou art 85 years of age, thou shalt see the face of the son of man.—I was left to draw my own conclusion concerning this & I took the liberty to conclude that if I did live till that time he would make his appearance.—but I do not say whether he will make his appearance or I shall go where he is.—I prophecy in the name of the Lord God.—& let it be written. that the Son of Man will not come in the heavens till I am 85 years old 48 years hence or about 1890 (Joseph Smith Diary, 6 April 1843, Church Archives).

These same ideas were spoken by the Prophet in his 10 March 1844 discourse and reported by Wilford Woodruff, James Burgess, Willard Richards, Thomas Bullock, and John Solomon Fullmer (see Andrew F. Ehat and Lyndon W. Cook, *The Words of Joseph Smith: The Contemporary Accounts of the Nauvoo Discourses of the Prophet Joseph* [Provo: Religious Studies Center, 1980], pp. 327-36).

4.   William Clayton's Diary, as amended in the Joseph Smith Diary, by Willard Richards, is the source for D&C 130: 1-2. The combination of both diaries serves as the source for D&C 130:3.

5.   The ideas in verse 9 are also found in the Prophet's diary under the date 18 February 1843: "At dinner Joseph said—when the earth was sanctified & became like a sea of glass, it would be one great Urim and Thummim the Saints could look in it and see as they are seen."

6.   Clayton's notes on the Holy Ghost were amplified in the Joseph Smith Diary to include statements on the Father and the Son. Neither the William Clayton Diary, the Joseph Smith Diary, nor the *draft* Manuscript History of

the Church entry for this date (2 April 1843), implies the phrasing of D&C 130:22: "Were it not so [that the Holy Ghost is a spirit], the Holy Ghost could not dwell in us." Originally the wording in the Manuscript History of the Church entry for this date was the same as in the Clayton diary but in the 1850s the Church historians reworded it to read the way it appears in the Doctrine and Covenants. These statements on the character of the Godhead are significant inasmuch as the corporeal nature of the Father and the personal nature of the Holy Ghost were not advanced by the Prophet until about 1841. See Andrew F. Ehat and Lyndon W. Cook, *The Words of Joseph Smith: The Contemporary Accounts of the Nauvoo Discourses of the Prophet Joseph* (Provo: Religious Studies Center, 1980), pp. 83-84, note 9.

.7.   On the evening of 9 March 1843 the Prophet had the above dream (see Joseph Smith Diary, 11 March 1843).

8.   William Clayton's Diary, as amended by the Joseph Smith Diary, is the source for D&C 130:12-13. "See Revelation" refers to D&C 87.

9.   Benjamin F. Johnson to President Anthon H. Lund, 12 May 1903, Church Archives.

Section 131

1.   William Clayton Diary. Compare *History of the Church*, 5:391-92. The bracketed insertion "meaning the new and everlasting covenant of marriage" is not in the original, but was added in the 1876 edition of the Doctrine and Covenants.

2.   William Clayton Diary as cited in Andrew F. Ehat and Lyndon W. Cook, *The Words of Joseph Smith: The Contemporary Accounts of the Nauvoo Discourses of the Prophet Joseph* (Provo: Religious Studies Center, 1980), p. 202.

3.   William Clayton Diary as cited in *The Words of Joseph Smith*, p. 203. Samuel A. Prior, the Methodist preacher, later commented on the Prophet's remarks on this occasion,

> In the evening I was invited to preach, and did so.—The congregation was large and respectable—they paid the utmost attention. This surprised me a little, as I did not expect to find any such thing as toleration among them.—After I had closed, Elder Smith, who had attended, arose and begged leave to differ from me in some few points of doctrine, and this he did mildly, politely, and affectingly; like one who was more desirous to disseminate truth and expose error, than to love the malicious triumph of debate over me. I was truly edified with his remarks, and felt less prejudiced against the Mormons than ever. He invited me to call upon him, and I promised to do so (*Times and Seasons* 4 [15 May 1843]:198).

Section 132

1.   William W. Phelps to Brigham Young, 12 August 1861, Brigham Young Collection, Church Archives. This letter contains a revelation which alludes to plural marriage. The introduction to the letter follows:

The Substance of a revelation by Joseph Smith Junr. given over the boundary, west of Jackson Co. Missouri, on Sunday morning July 17 1831, when seven Elders, Viz: Joseph Smith Jun. Oliver Cowdery, W. W. Phelps, Martin Harris, Joseph Coe, Ziba Peterson and Joshua Lewis, united their hearts in prayer, in a private place, to inquire of the Lord who should preach the first sermon to the remnants of the Lamanites and Nephites, and the people of that Section, that should assemble that day, in the Indian Country, to hear the gospel and the revelations according to the Book of Mormon.

Among the company there being neither pen, Ink, or paper, Joseph remarked that the Lord could preserve his words, as he had ever done, till the time appointed.

2. See Danel W. Bachman, "A Study of the Mormon Practice of Plural Marriage before the Death of Joseph Smith," M.A. thesis, Purdue University, 1975.

3. Andrew F. Ehat, "An Overview of the Introduction of Eternal Marriage in The Church of Jesus Christ of Latter-day Saints" (1979), privately distributed.

4. Upon accepting the implications of the doctrine of plural marriage Emma Smith was eternally sealed to the Prophet (28 May 1843). The burden of section 132 was to inform Emma that although she had been eternally married to her husband (i.e., "according to my word"), the "new and everlasting covenant" of marriage must be "sealed unto them by the Holy Spirit of promise, by him who is anointed, unto whom I have appointed this power and the keys of this priesthood" (see D&C 132:19 and 26). In other words, only by receiving the fulness of the priesthood could Emma Smith have claim on her husband in the eternities. Despite Emma's changing moods regarding this matter, ultimately she was administered the fulness of the priesthood, in connection with the Prophet (28 September 1843).

5. Andrew F. Ehat, "An Overview of the Introduction of Eternal Marriage in The Church of Jesus Christ of Latter-day Saints: 1840-43" (November 1980), privately distributed.

6. See Andrew Jenson, "Plural Marriage," *The Historical Record* 6 (May 1887):225. The following is from Joseph F. Smith:

Joseph Smith was commanded to take wives, he hesitated and postponed it, seeing the consequences and the trouble that it would bring and he shrank from the responsibility, but he prayed to the Lord for it to pass as Jesus did, but Jesus had to drink it to the dregs so it was with Joseph Smith, the Lord had revealed it to him, and said now is the time for it to be practised but it was not untill he had been told he must practice it or be destroyed that he made the attempt—in 1841 he had wives sealed to him—from that time untill his death he had wives sealed unto him. Emma, his wife yielded but it was not without considerable argument that she consented and with her own hand gave to Joseph Smith four wives in this new and everlasting covenant their names are Emily and Eliza Partridge and Sarah and Maria Lawrence the latter two being sisters . . . . Soon after the marriage of Joseph to the four ladies mentioned Emma repented of having given them to Joseph and told Joseph that if [he] would not give them up, she would bring him up before the law and became very bitter about this time under this threat and on account of the determined manner of Emma, Joseph went to his brother Hyrum and had a talk with him about it. Hyrum told Joseph if you will write the Revelation I will take it and go and see Emma for I can convince her that it is true. Joseph smiled at Hyrum saying you do not know Emma as well as I do—but Hyrum said he still had faith that he could do as he said, and to satisfy his brother Hyrum, Joseph caused the Revelation to be written on the 12th July 1843. Joseph with Hyrum went into the office and Joseph commanded Wm. Clayton to write as he should dictate. Joseph was asked by Hyrum to get the Urim and Thummim. Joseph said he knew it from beginning to end, he then dictated it word for word to Wm. Clayton as it is now in the Doctrine and Covenants it was written for this purpose at Hyrums suggestion, after it was done, Joseph said there that is enough for the present, but I have a great deal more, which would be given hereafter; Hyrum went to Emma and returned without making any impression upon her ("Utah Stake Historical Record, 1877-88," Church Archives).

7.   Joseph Fielding Smith, *Blood Atonement and the Origin of Plural Marriage* (Independence: Zion's Printing and Publishing Co., 1905).

8.   As cited in George A. Smith to Joseph Smith III, 9 October 1869, "Historian's Office Letter Book," Church Archives.

9.   See *Deseret News Extra* (14 September 1852). Concerning his possession of the revelation, Brigham Young said, "This Revelation has been in my possession many years; and who has known it? None but those who should know it. I keep a patent lock on my desk, and there does not anything leak out that should not" (Ibid.). Newel K. Whitney retained possession of the Kingsbury copy until March 1847, when it was given to President Young. (See Horace K. Whitney Journal, 14 March 1847, Church Archives, where he mentions making a copy for Bishop Whitney because Brigham Young had asked for the Kingsbury copy.)

10.   The Kingsbury copy is at Church Archives. The Clayton original was burned within ten days after it had been recorded. Several accounts affirm that Emma Smith burned it. Joseph Smith III, for example, recorded: "Visited James Whitehead [at Alton, Illinois] had chat with him. He says that he saw the Rev about 1 page foolscap paper. Clayton copied it and it was this copy that mother burned" (Joseph Smith III Diary, 20 April 1885, RLDS Library-Archives). See also *Deseret News Extra* (14 September 1852), where Brigham Young also states that Emma burned the Clayton original.

11.   With regard to the "Article on Marriage," Joseph F. Smith, quoting Brigham Young, stated: "Prest. Young spoke 12 minutes in relation to Sec. 109 B[ook] of Doctrine and Covenants ["Article on Marriage"]. Saying Oliver Cowdry wrote it, and incisted on its being incerted in the Book of D. & C. contrary to the thrice expressed wish and refusal of the Prophet Jos.

Smith" (Joseph F. Smith Diary, 9 October 1869, Church Archives). On another occasion Joseph F. Smith stated, "Oliver Cowdery was not so discreet in regard to this matter [plural marriage] but in consequence of his conduct brought reproach upon the Church bringing upon the Church the accusation of fornication and polygamy—he wrote an article to stave off the impression that had been made which was published in the Book of Doctrine and Covenants which has been left out of the New Edition" ("Utah Stake Historical Record, 1877-1888," Church Archives). See Appendix A.

Section 133

1. *History of the Church*, 1:229-30.
2. *Evening and Morning Star* (May 1833):89. The introduction to the revelation continued, "The book from which this important revelation is taken, will be published in the course of the present year, at from 25, to 50 cents a copy. We regret that in consequence of circumstances not within our control, this book will not be offered to our brethren as soon as was anticipated."

Section 134

1. "Kirtland Council Minute Book," pp. 96-106.
2. *History of the Church*, 2:440.

Section 135

1. Traditionally John Taylor has been considered the author of section 135. Presently there is no available document which affirms Elder Taylor's authorship of this revelation, but he is the most likely candidate (see Heber J. Grant discourse in *Conference Reports*, October 1933).

Two reports of the tragedy, published in July 1844, were undoubtedly used in the preparation of section 135: an editorial in the *Times and Seasons* 5 (15 July 1844):584-86, entitled "The Murder," and Willard Richards's account, entitled "Two Minutes in Jail" (*Nauvoo Neighbor*, 24 July 1844). These accounts contain most of the information now in this revelation.

Section 136

1. "Journal History," 11 January 1847.
2. "Journal History," 14 January 1847.
3. "Municipal High Council Minutes of Winter Quarters," under date, in the Brigham Young Collection, Church Archives.
4. *History of the Church*; Jenson's *Biographical Encyclopedia*, 1:99; Esshom, *Pioneers and Prominent Men of Utah*; "Record of Sealings" (Nauvoo Temple), Church Archives; and "Nauvoo Temple Endowment Register," Genealogical Society, Salt Lake City, Utah.

5.   *History of the Church;* Jenson's *Biographical Encyclopedia,* 1:103; Andrew Karl Larson, *Erastus Snow: The Life of a Missionary and Pioneer for the Early Mormon Church* (Salt Lake City: University of Utah Press, 1971); and "Nauvoo Temple Endowment Register," Genealogical Society, Salt Lake City, Utah.

Section 137

1.   See Historical Note for section 108 regarding the "Kirtland endowment," and the meaning of the term "first elders."
2.   See Joseph Smith Diary, Joseph Smith Collection, Church Archives. Regarding this event, Edward Partridge recorded the following: "A number saw visions & others were blessed with the outpourings of the Holy Ghost .... The 22d [of January 1836] in the forenoon was taken up in telling the visions of the preceeding evening" (Edward Partridge Journal, Church Archives).
3.   The italicized words have been deleted from the present text of section 137.
4.   *History of the Church;* and gravestone marker, Palmyra, New York. The year of death for Alvin Smith, given in the *History of the Church* and the *Pearl of Great Price* as 1825 and 1824 respectively, should be 1823.

Section 138

1.   *Conference Reports* (4 October 1918), p. 2.
2.   James E. Talmage Journal, Brigham Young University Library, Manuscripts. On the evening of 17 November 1918, two days before Joseph F. Smith's death, Elder Talmage and others gathered around President Smith's death bed, where they united their prayers in behalf of their beloved prophet. "At this little gathering I [James E. Talmage] read the 'Vision of the Redemption of the Dead' given to President Joseph F. Smith October 3rd, and soon to be published to the Church" (Talmage Journal).
3.   Jenson's *Biographical Encyclopedia,* 1:66; Joseph Fielding Smith, *Life of Joseph F. Smith* (Salt Lake City: Deseret Book Co., 1969); and Joseph Fielding Smith family group sheets, Genealogical Society, Salt Lake City, Utah.

Official Declarations
One and Two

Official Declaration Number One

Date. 24 September 1890.

Place. Salt Lake City, Salt Lake County, Utah Territory.

Historical Note. On 24 September 1890 Wilford Woodruff, President of the Church, issued a statement, known as "the Manifesto" or "Official Declaration," which publicly announced that the Mormon people had discontinued performing plural marriages. The following day, 25 September 1890, President Woodruff recorded the following in his journal:

> I have arrived at a point in the History of my life as the President of the Church of Jesus Christ of Latter Day Saints where I am under the necessity of calling for the Temporal Salvation of the Church. The United States Government has taken a Stand & passed Laws to destroy the Latter day Saints upon the Subject of poligamy or Patriarchal order of Marriage. And after Praying to the Lord & feeling inspired by his spirit I have issued the following proclamation which is sustained by the Council and 12 Apostles.[1]

Within two weeks of its issuance, the Manifesto was presented to a general conference of the Church, where it was unanimously approved. The justification for rescinding this practice was twofold: (1) when God gives a commandment to his people and they are effectively hindered in obeying that commandment, it is for God to accept their offering and to require that work at their hands no more, and (2) the authority which issues a command has the right and the power to revoke it.[2]

Publication Note.   The Manifesto was first published in the *Deseret News* (25 September 1890) and was included in the 1908 edition of the Doctrine and Covenants.

Biographical Note.   Lorenzo Snow.

Son of Oliver Snow and Rosetta Pettibone. Born 30 April 1814 in Mantua, Portage County, Ohio. Attended Oberlin College. Baptized June 1836 by John F. Boynton. Confirmed by Hyrum Smith. Ordained elder before 3 April 1837 by Alva Beman. Mission in Ohio 1837. Moved to Missouri 1838. Mission to Kentucky and Illinois 1838. Returned to Ohio February 1839. Taught school in Shalersville, Ohio, 1839-40. Moved to LaHarpe Illinois, May 1840. Ordained high priest 18 July 1840 by Don Carlos Smith. Mission to England 1840-43. Returned to Illinois 12 April 1843. Mission to Ohio 1844 to campaign for Joseph Smith as president of United States. Married Charlotte Merrill Squires (born 1825 in Ohio). Nauvoo Temple sealing 17 January 1846. Two children: Leonora Charlotte and Roxcy Armatha. Received endowment 19 December 1845. Married Mary Adaline Goddard (born 1812 in Connecticut). Nauvoo Temple sealing 17 January 1846. Three children: Rosetta, Oliver, and Isadore. Married Sarah Ann Prichard (born 1826 in Ohio). Nauvoo Temple sealing 17 January 1846. Five children: Elisa Sarah, Sylvia, Lorenzo, Parintha, and Laurin Alvirus. Married Harriet Amelia Squires (born 1819 in Ohio). Nauvoo Temple sealing 17 January 1846. Five children: Abigail, Lucius Aaron, Alonzo Henry, Amelia Henrietta, and Celestia Armeda. Left Illinois for West February 1846. Located in Mt. Pisgah; presided over Church there 1847-48. Moved to Salt Lake City 1848. Ordained apostle 12 February 1849. Mission to Italy 1849-52. Arrived in Genoa, Italy, 25 June 1850. Returned to Salt Lake City 30 August 1852. Member of Utah Legislature 1853-82. Located in Box Elder County 1853. Lived in Brigham City 1853-93. Married Eleanor Houtz. Eight children: Amanda Eleanor, Ida, Eugenia, Alphonso, Susan, Roxcy Lana, Hortensia, and Chauncey. Married Caroline Horton. Three children: Clarissa Caroline, Franklin, and Sarah Augusta. Married Mary Elizabeth Houtz. Six children: Lydia, Jacob, Virginia, Mansfield Lorenzo, Mortimer Joseph, and Flora Bell. Married Phebe Augusta Woodruff. Five children:

Mary Amanda, Leslie, Orion, Milton, and Phebe. Married Minnie Jensen. Five children: Clarence Leroi, Minnie Mabel, Cora Jeane, Lorenzo, and Lucile. President of Box Elder Stake. Mission to Hawaiian Island 1864. Tour to Palestine 1873. Convicted of unlawful cohabitation 1886. Sentenced and served eleven months. Sustained as President of Quorum of Twelve Apostles 7 April 1889. President of Church 13 October 1898-10 October 1901. Died 10 October 1901 in Salt Lake City, Utah.[3]

Official Declaration Number Two

Date. 9 June 1978.

Place. Salt Lake City, Salt Lake County, Utah.

Historical Note. From the time of Joseph Smith the Church maintained a policy prohibiting those of African Negroid descent from being ordained to the priesthood. Although Church leaders have consistently agreed that the time would come when this restriction would be lifted, they have, nevertheless, maintained that nothing short of revelation from God could alter the policy.[1] Particular attention has been given to the restriction in recent years following the phenomenal growth of the Church in foreign lands as well as the increase in racial tensions within the United States. In 1960 stakes began to be organized in foreign nations, and today the Church is clearly an international organization. With the decision to build a temple in Brazil, the policy regarding the African blacks came into sharp focus because interracial marriage is a common practice there.[2]

Under these conditions President Spencer W. Kimball began an exhaustive personal study of the scriptures as well as statements of Church leaders since Joseph Smith, and asked other General Authorities to share their personal feelings relative to the long-standing Church policy. Then he began to inquire of the Lord if the time was not right to extend the priesthood blessings to this restricted people. Recalling this period, President Kimball stated, "Day after day, and especially on Saturdays and Sundays when there were no organizations in the temple, I went there when I could be alone." The result was a revelation on 1 June 1978.[3]

On Thursday, 1 June 1978, the First Presidency and ten of the Quorum of the Twelve Apostles gave the matter special attention.[4]

Then, following the monthly fast meeting of the General Authorities in the Salt Lake Temple on 1 June, President Kimball "asked the Twelve not to go home," but to stay for a special prayer circle with him.[5] It was on this occasion, at 2:45 P.M., that the Lord confirmed the wishes of the Brethren to rescind the policy that prohibited African blacks from receiving the priesthood. President Kimball declared, "I offered the final prayer and I told the Lord if it wasn't right, if He didn't want this change to come in the church, that I would be true to it all the rest of my life, and I'd fight the world against it if that's what He wanted. . . . But this revelation and assurance came to me so clearly that there was no question about it . . . . I knew that the time had come."[6] The following account of the event is given by Elder Bruce R. McConkie:

> On the first day of June in this year, 1978, the First Presidency and the Twelve, after full discussion of the proposition and all the premises and principles that are involved, importuned the Lord for a revelation. President Kimball was mouth, and he prayed with great faith and great fervor, and this was one of those occasions when an inspired prayer is offered. . . . It was given President Kimball what he should ask. He prayed by the power of the Spirit and there was perfect unity, total and complete harmony, between the Presidency and the Twelve on the issue involved. And when President Kimball finished his prayer the Lord gave a revelation by the power of the Holy Ghost. . . . On this occasion, because of the importuning and the faith, and because the hour and the time had arrived, the Lord in his providences poured out the Holy Ghost upon the First Presidency and the Twelve, in a miraculous and marvelous manner beyond anything that any then present had ever experienced. . . . And the result was that President Kimball knew and each one of us knew, independent of any other person, by direct personal revelation to us, that the time had now come to extend the gospel and all its blessings of the House of the Lord, to those of every nation, and culture, and race, including the black race. There was no question whatsoever as to what happened or as to the word and message that came.[7]

During the ensuing week a statement (Official Declaration Number Two) was drafted by the First Presidency, and on Thursday, 8 June 1978, it was read to a joint meeting of the First Presidency and the Quorum of Twelve. At this meeting, in the Salt Lake Temple, the revelation "was reaffirmed by the Spirit of inspiration...when the Brethren approved the document to announce it to the world."[8] On 9 June 1978 the official statement was read to all General Authorities in the Salt Lake City area, where it was unanimosly sustained; and later that day the document was made public.

On 30 September 1978 Official Declaration Number Two was presented to a general conference of the Church, where it was unanimously approved as Church policy.

Publication Note. Official Declaration Number Two was first published in the *Deseret News* on 9 June 1978 and is included in the 1981 edition of the Doctrine and Covenants.

Biographical Note. Spencer Woolley Kimball.

Son of Andrew Kimball and Olive Woolley. Born 28 March 1895 at Salt Lake City, Salt Lake County, Utah. Baptized 28 March 1903. Received endowment 16 October 1914. Mission to central states 20 October 1914-14 December 1916. Married Camilla Eyring 16 November 1917. Sealed to wife, Camilla, 7 June 1918. Children: Spencer LeVan, Olive Beth, Andrew Eyring, and Edward Lawrence. President of Mount Graham Stake (Arizona) 1938-43. Ordained apostle 7 October 1943. President of Quorum of Twelve Apostles 7 July 1972-20 December 1973. President of Church 30 December 1973.[9]

Biographical Note. Nathan Eldon Tanner.

Son of Nathan William Tanner and Sarah Edna Brown. Born 9 May 1898 in Salt Lake City, Salt Lake County, Utah. Baptized 30 June 1906. Married Sarah Isabelle Merrill 20 December 1919. Children: Ruth, Sara Isabelle, Zola, Edna Beth, and Helen. Received endowment 29 August 1923 in Alberta Temple. Sealed to wife, Sarah Isabelle, 29 August 1923. Assistant to Quorum of Twelve Apostles 1960-62. Ordained apostle 11 October 1962. Second counselor to David O. McKay in First Presidency 4 October 1963-18 January 1970. Second Counselor to Joseph Fielding Smith in First Presidency 23 January 1970-2 July 1972. First Counselor to Harold B. Lee in First Presidency 7 July 1972-26 December 1973. First Counselor to Spencer W. Kimball in First Presidency 30 December 1973.[10]

Biographical Note.   Marion George Romney.

Son of George Samuel Romney and Teressa Artemesia Redd. Born 19 September 1897 at Colonia Juarez, Chihuahua, Mexico. Baptized 30 September 1905. Received endowment 17 November 1920. Mission to Australia 1920-23. Temple marriage to Ida Olivia Jensen 12 September 1924. Children: male child, Richard, Janet Ida, and George. Ordained high priest 20 April 1935. Assistant to Quorum of Twelve Apostles 1941-51. Ordained apostle 11 October 1951. Second counselor to Harold B. Lee in First Presidency 7 July 1972-26 December 1973. Second Counselor to Spencer W. Kimball in First Presidency 30 December 1973.[11]

Official Declaration Notes

Official Declaration Number One

1. Wilford Woodruff Journal, Church Archives.
2. *Deseret News* (18 October 1890).
3. *History of the Church*; Jenson's *Biographical Encyclopedia*, 1:26; Esshom, *Pioneers and Prominent Men of Utah*; "Journal History"; record of temple ordinances in possession of author.

Official Declaration Number Two

1. See *Church News* (17 June 1978).
2. See Lester E. Bush, Jr., "Introduction," *Dialogue* (Summer 1979), where he cites part of an interview involving LeGrand Richards, 18 August 1978.
3. *Church News* (6 January 1979).
4. The two members of the Quorum of Twelve Apostles who were absent were Mark E. Petersen, who was in South America, and Delbert L. Stapley, who was hospitalized at the time.
5. See *Church News* (6 January 1979) and Edward L. Kimball, "I Sustain Him As A Prophet, I Love Him As An Affectionate Father," *Dialogue* (Winter 1978).
6. Ibid.
7. Bruce R. McConkie, 18 August 1978, "Book of Mormon Symposium Speech," Brigham Young University Campus.
8. Ibid.
9. Edward L. Kimball and Andrew E. Kimball, Jr., *Spencer W. Kimball: Twelfth President of The Church of Jesus Christ of Latter-day Saints* (Salt Lake

City: Bookcraft, 1977); and Spencer W. Kimball family group sheet, Genealogical Society, Salt Lake City, Utah.

10.   *The Improvement Era* (November 1960); *The Ensign* (November 1962); and N. Eldon Tanner family group sheet, Genealogical Society, Salt Lake City, Utah.

11.   *The Improvement Era* (August 1941 and October 1951); *The Ensign* (November 1972); and Marion G. Romney family group sheet, Genealogical Society, Salt Lake City, Utah.

Appendix A

MARRIAGE.[1]

1. According to the custom of all civilized nations, marriage is regulated by laws and ceremonies: therefore we believe, that all marriages in the Church of Christ of Latter day Saints, should be solemnized in a public meeting, or feast, prepared for that purpose: and that the solemnization should be performed by a presiding high priest, high priest, bishop, elder, or priest, not even prohibiting those persons who are desirous to get married, of being married by other authority. We believe that it is not right to prohibit members of this church from marrying out of the church if it be their determination so to do, but such persons will be considered weak in the faith of our Lord and Savior Jesus Christ.

2. Marriage should be celebrated with prayer and thanksgiving; and at the solemnization, the persons to be married, standing together, the man on the right, and the woman on the left, shall be addressed, by the person officiating, as he shall be directed by the holy Spirit; and if there be no legal objections, he shall say, calling each by their names: "You both mutually agree to be each other's companion, husband and wife, observing the legal rights belonging to this condition; that is, keeping yourselves wholly for each other, and from all others, during your lives." And when they have answered "Yes," he shall pronounce them "husband and

wife" in the name of the Lord Jesus Christ, and by virtue of the laws of the country and authority vested in him: "may God add his blessings keep you to fulfill your covenants from henceforth and forever. Amen."

3. The clerk of every church should keep a record of all marriages, solemnized in his branch.

4. All legal contracts of marriage made before a person is baptised into this church should be held sacred and fulfiled. Inasmuch as this Church of Christ has been reproached with the crime of fornication, and polygamy: we declare that we believe, that one man should have one wife; and one woman, but one husband, except in case of death when either is at liberty to marry again. It is not right to persuade a woman to be baptised contrary to the will of her husband, neither is it lawful to influence them to embrace any religious faith, or be baptised, or leave their parents without their consent, is unlawful and unjust. We believe that husbands, parents and masters who exercise control over their wives, children, and servants and prevent them from embracing the truth, will have to answer for that sin.

---

1. The "Article on Marriage," part of the Doctrine and Covenants 1835-76.

Appendix B

Uncanonized Revelations Received by Joseph Smith (1831-44)

Revelation for Joseph Smith, Sr., and Ezra Thayer concerning Frederick G. Williams's farm. [Kirtland, Ohio?], May 1831. ("Kirtland Revelation Book," pp. 91-92)

Revelation concerning who should preach the first sermon to the Lamanites on the Indian reservation, west of Independence, Missouri. [Kansas City, Kansas], 17 July 1831. (William W. Phelps to Brigham Young, 12 August 1861, Church Archives)

Revelation for Lincoln Haskin to preach the gospel. Hiram, Portage County, Ohio, 27 February 1832. ("Kirtland Revelation Book," p. 10)

Revelation concerning the purchase of paper for the Book of Commandments and also the work of the Inspired Translation of the Bible. Hiram, Portage County, Ohio, 20 March 1832. (Newel K. Whitney Collection, Brigham Young University Library, Manuscripts)

Revelation concerning the duty of the bishops and the presidency of the high priesthood. Hiram, Portage County, Ohio, March 1832. (Newel K. Whitney Collection, Brigham Young University Library, Manuscripts)

Revelation for Frederick G. Williams to be counselor and scribe to Joseph Smith. [Kirtland, Ohio?], 5 January 1834 [1833]. (Frederick G. Williams Papers, Church Archives)

Revelation concerning the division of the United Firm. Kirtland, Geauga County, Ohio, 28 April 1834. ("Kirtland Revelation Book," p. 111)

Revelation giving reproof for failure of the brethren and the Church to properly recognize each other by their official titles. Kirtland, Geauga County, Ohio, 5 December 1834. (*History of the Church*, 2:177)

Revelation for William W. Phelps concerning the gift of writing. [Kirtland, Ohio?], 22 September 1835. (William W. Phelps to Brigham Young, 29 June 1859, Church Archives)

Revelation for Reynolds Cahoon to set his house in order. Kirtland, Geauga County, Ohio, 1 November 1835. (*History of the Church*, 2:299)

Revelation instructing Frederick G. Williams not to go to New York City to make arrangements concerning a book-bindery, but to visit his relatives and warn them. Kirtland, Geauga County, Ohio, 1 November 1835. (*History of the Church*, 2:300)

Revelation chastising the Twelve Apostles. Kirtland, Geauga County, Ohio, 3 November 1835. (*History of the Church*, 2:300)

Revelation for Isaac Morley and Edward Partridge to attend school of elders and solemn assembly. Kirtland, Geauga County, Ohio, 7 November 1835. (*History of the Church*, 2:302-03)

Revelation for Warren Parrish to be a scribe for Joseph Smith. Kirtland, Geauga County, Ohio, 14 November 1835. (*History of the Church*, 2:311-12)

Revelation for Harvey Whitlock to forsake his sins and go to Kirtland. Kirtland, Geauga County, Ohio, 1835. (*History of the Church*, 2:315)

Revelation concerning Lehi's travels from Jerusalem to South America. [Kirtland, Ohio?], [1836?]. (John M. Bernhisel, manuscript copy of the Inspired Translation of the Bible, Church Archives)

Revelation making known the transgression of John Whitmer and William W. Phelps. Kirtland, Geauga County, Ohio, 4 September 1837. (*History of the Church*, 2:511)

Revelation concerning the First Presidency and the organization of stakes. Kirtland, Geauga County, Ohio, 12 January 1838. ("The Scriptory Book of Joseph Smith," pp. 52-53)

Revelation concerning the trying of a member of the First Presidency for his membership. French Farm, Kirtland, Geauga County, Ohio, 12 January 1838. ("The Scriptory Book of Joseph Smith, pp. 51-52)

Revelation instructing Joseph Smith and Sidney Rigdon to move to Missouri. Kirtland, Geauga County, Ohio, 12 January 1838. ("The Scriptory Book of Joseph Smith," p. 53)

Revelation for Brigham Young to settle at Mill Creek until called to preach. Far West, Caldwell County, Missouri, 17 April 1838. (*History of the Church*, 3:23)

Revelation for Frederick G. Williams and William W. Phelps to be ordained elders and preach the gospel. Far West, Caldwell County, Missouri, 8 July 1838. ("Kirtland Revelation Book")

Revelation concerning Oliver Granger. Nauvoo, Hancock County, Illinois, 13 May 1839. (*History of the Church*, 3:350)

Revelation for William Allred and Henry W. Miller concerning the Nauvoo House. Nauvoo, Hancock County, Illinois, 20 March 1841. (*History of the Church*, 4:311)

Revelation for Ebenezer Robinson and wife concerning Marinda Nancy Hyde. Nauvoo, Hancock County, Illinois, 2 December 1841. (*History of the Church*, 4:467)

Revelation instructing John Snyder to take a mission to England. Nauvoo, Hancock County, Illinois, 22 December 1841. (*History of the Church*, 4:483)

Revelation instructing Amos B. Fuller to take a mission to preach the gospel. Nauvoo, Hancock County, Illinois, 22 December 1841. (*History of the Church*, 4:483)

Revelation instructing the Twelve Apostles to assume editorial responsibility for the *Times and Seasons*. Nauvoo, Hancock County, Illinois, 28 January 1842. (*History of the Church*, 4:503)

Revelation giving the full name of the Council of Fifty. Nauvoo, Hancock County, Illinois, 7 April 1842. (Joseph F. Smith Minutes of the Council of Fifty, 10 April 1880, cited in Andrew F. Ehat " 'It

Seems Like Heaven Began on Earth': Joseph Smith and the Constitution of the Kingdom of God," *Brigham Young University Studies* 20 [Spring 1980]:254)

Revelation concerning the evils of Hiram Kimball. Nauvoo, Hancock County, Illinois, 19 May 1842. (*History of the Church*, 5:12)

Revelation giving the words of the marriage ceremony between Joseph Smith and Sarah Ann Whitney. Nauvoo, Hancock County, Illinois, 27 July 1842. (Revelations Collection, Church Archives)

Revelation instructing John E. Page to go to Washington, D.C. Nauvoo, Hancock County, Illinois, November 1843. (*History of the Church*, 6:82)

Revelation concerning the constitution of the Kingdom of God. Nauvoo, Hancock County, Illinois, 18 April 1844. (Joseph F. Smith Minutes of the Council of Fifty, 21 April 1880; and, Minutes of Council of Fifty for 12 October 1880 and 8 April 1881, cited in Andrew F. Ehat, " 'It Seems Like Heaven Began on Earth': Joseph Smith and the Constitution of the Kingdom of God," *Brigham Young University Studies* 20 [Spring 1980]:259-60)

Revelation instructing Sidney Rigdon to go to Pennsylvania and to be a vice-presidential candidate. Nauvoo, Hancock County, Illinois, May-June 1844. (*Speech of Elder Orson Hyde, delivered before the High Priest's Quorum, in Nauvoo, April 27th 1845, upon the course and conduct of Mr. Sidney Rigdon, and upon the merits of his claims to the presidency of the Church of Jesus Christ of Latter-day Saints* [Liverpool: James and Woodburn, 1845])

Appendix C

Writings on the Doctrine and Covenants

Andrus, Hyrum L. *The Doctrine and Covenants and Man's Relationship to Deity*. Provo: Brigham Young University Press, 1960.

_____. *Doctrinal Themes of the Doctrine and Covenants*. Provo: Brigham Young University Extension Publications, 1964.

Berrett, William E. *Teachings of the Doctrine and Covenants*. Salt Lake City: Deseret Book Co., 1956.

_____. "Unique Doctrines from the Doctrine and Covenants." *Ensign* (September 1978).

Bluth, John V., comp. *Concordance to the Doctrine and Covenants*. Salt Lake City: Deseret Book Co., 1968.

Caldwell, C. Max. "The Doctrine and Covenants and the Book of Mormon." *Seventh Annual Sidney B. Sperry Symposium: The Doctrine and Covenants, January 27, 1979*. Provo: Brigham Young University, 1979.

Cook, Lyndon W., "The Far West Record and the Doctrine and Covenants." *Seventh Annual Sidney B. Sperry Symposium: The Doctrine and Covenants, January 27, 1979*. Provo: Brigham Young University, 1979.

Cowan, Richard O. *The Doctrine and Covenants, Our Modern Scripture*, rev. ed. Provo: Brigham Young University Press, 1978.

_____. "Revelations Continue." *Seventh Annual Sidney B. Sperry Symposium: The Doctrine and Covenants, January 27, 1979*. Provo: Brigham Young University, 1979.

Doxey, Roy W. *The Doctrine and Covenants and the Future*. Salt Lake City: Deseret Book Co., 1957.

————. *The Doctrine and Covenants Speaks.* 2 vols. Salt Lake City: Deseret Book Co., 1966.

————. *The Latter-day Prophets and the Doctrine and Covenants.* 4 vols. Salt Lake City: Deseret Book Co., 1963-65.

————. *Prophecies and Prophetic Promises of the Doctrine and Covenants.* Salt Lake City: Deseret Book Co., 1969.

————. "How Latter-day Prophets Help Us Understand the Doctrine and Covenants." *Seventh Annual Sidney B. Sperry Symposium: The Doctrine and Covenants, January 27 1979.* Provo: Brigham Young University, 1979.

Doxey, Roy W., and Walter D. Bowen. *Doctrine and Covenants Study Guide with Selected Commentaries.* Provo: Brigham Young University Printing Service, 2d. ed. rev., 1972.

Fitzgerald, John W. "A Study of the Doctrine and Covenants." M.A. thesis, Brigham Young University, 1940.

Forbis, Dianne Dibb. "Studying the Doctrine and Covenants with Children." *Ensign* (March 1979).

Godfrey, Kenneth W. "Marriage, the Family and the Doctrine and Covenants: An Introduction." *Seventh Annual Sidney B. Sperry Symposium: The Doctrine and Covenants, January 27, 1979.* Provo: Brigham Young University, 1979.

Hall, Elisabeth J. "Junior High and the D&C." *Ensign* (July 1980).

Holland, Jeffrey R. "The Lord's Preface." *Seventh Annual Sidney B. Sperry Symposium: The Doctrine and Covenants, January 27, 1979.* Provo: Brigham Young University, 1979.

Howard, Richard P. *Restoration Scriptures: A Study of Their Textual Development.* Independence: Herald Publishing House, 1969.

Lambert, A.C. *The Published Editions of the Doctrine and Covenants . . . in All Languages, 1833-1950.* Provo: A.C. Lambert, 1960.

Ludlow, Daniel H. *A Companion to Your Study of the Doctrine and Covenants.* 2 vols. Salt Lake City: Deseret Book Co., 1978.

Lyon, T. Edgar. *Introduction to the Doctrine and Covenants and the Pearl of Great Price.* Salt Lake City: Deseret News Press, 1948.

————. "Modern Scripture, the Docrtine and Covenants." *Instructor* (October 1968).

Matthews, Robert J. "The Doctrine and Covenants as a Witness for the Bible." *Instructor* (September 1968).

_____. "The 'New Translation' of the Bible, 1830-1833: Doctrinal Development During the Kirtland Era." *Brigham Young University Studies* 11 (Summer 1971).

_____. *A Plainer Translation, Joseph Smith's Translation of the Bible.* Provo: Brigham Young University Press, 1975.

_____. "Some Relationships Between Joseph Smith's Translation of the Bible and the Doctrine and Covenants." *Seventh Annual Sidney B. Sperry Symposium: The Doctrine and Covenants, January 27, 1979.* Provo: Brigham Young University, 1979.

Maxwell, Neal A. "The Doctrine and Covenants: The Voice of the Lord." *Ensign* (December 1978).

McConkie, Bruce R. "This Generation Shall Have My Word Through You." *Seventh Annual Sidney B. Sperry Symposium: The Doctrine and Covenants, January 27, 1979.* Provo: Brigham Young University, 1979.

McGavin, E. Cecil. *The Historical Background of the Doctrine and Covenants.* Salt Lake City: Paragon Printing Co., 1949.

Olson, Earl E. "The Chronology of the Ohio revelations." *Brigham Young University Studies* 11 (Summer 1971).

Otten, Leaun G., comp. *Historical Background and Setting for Each Section of the Doctrine and Covenants.* N.p., n.d.

_____. "Applying the Doctrine and Covenants to Daily Life." *Seventh Annual Sidney B. Sperry Symposium: The Doctrine and Covenants, January 27, 1979.* Provo: Brigham Young University Press, 1979.

Parkin, Max H. "A Preliminary Analysis of the Dating of Section 10." *Seventh Annual Sidney B. Sperry Symposium: The Doctrine and Covenants, January 27, 1979.* Provo: Brigham Young University, 1979.

Petersen, Melvin J. "A Study of the Nature of and the Significance of the Changes in the revelations as Found in a Comparison of the Book of Commandments and Subsequent Editions of the *Doctrine and Covenants.*" M.A. thesis, Brigham Young University, 1955.

Peterson, LaMar. *Problems in the Mormon Text.* Salt Lake City: n.p., 1967.

Porter, Larry C. "Historical Background of the Fifteen Harmony Revelations." *Seventh Annual Sidney B. Sperry Symposium: The Doctrine and Covenants, January 27, 1979.* Provo: Brigham Young University, 1979.

Rasmussen, Ellis T. "Textual Parallels to the *Doctrine and Covenants* and *Book of Commandments* as Found in the Bible." M.A. thesis, Brigham Young University, 1951.

————. "Some Contributions of the Doctrine and Covenants to Our Understanding of the Bible." *Seventh Annual Sidney B. Sperry Symposium: The Doctrine and Covenants, January 27, 1979.* Provo: Brigham Young University, 1979.

Robinson, Christine H. *Inspirational Truths from the Doctrine and Covenants.* Salt Lake City: Deseret Book Co., 1970.

Shipp, Richard C. "Conceptual Patterns of Repetition in the Doctrine and Covenants and Their Implications." M.A. thesis, Brigham Young University, 1975.

Smith, Hyrum M., and Janne M. Sjodahl. *Doctrine and Covenants Commentary.* Salt Lake City: Deseret Book Co., rev. ed., 1967.

Smith, Joseph Fielding. *Church History and Modern Revelation.* 2 vols. Salt Lake City: For the Council of Twelve Apsotles, 1953.

Smutz, Lois Jean. "Textual Parallels to the Doctrine and Covenants (sections 65-133) as Found in the Bible." M.A. thesis, 1971.

Sperry, Sidney B. *Doctrine and Covenants Compendium.* Salt Lake City: Bookcraft, 1960.

Warner, Paul R. "How the Doctrine and Covenants Inspires Me to Be a Better Teacher." *Seventh Annual Sidney B. Sperry Symposium: The Doctrine and Covenants, January 27, 1979.* Provo: Brigham Young University, 1979.

Whittaker, David J. "A Covenant People." *Seventh Annual Sidney B. Sperry Symposium: The Doctrine and Covenants, January 27, 1979.* Provo: Brigham Young University, 1979.

Widtsoe, John A. *The Message of the Doctrine and Covenants.* Edited by G. Homer Durham. Salt Lake City: Bookcraft, 1969.

Wood, Wilford C., comp. *Joseph Smith Begins His Work.* vol. 2. N.p.: Wilford C. Wood, 1962.

Woodford, Robert J. "The Historical Development of the Doctrine and Covenants." Ph.D. dissertation, Brigham Young University, 1974.

————. "A Survey of Textual Changes in the Doctrine and Covenants." *Seventh Annual Sidney B. Sperry Symposium: The Doctrine and Covenants, January 27, 1979.* Provo: Brigham Young University, 1979.

Appendix D

Important Editions of the Doctrine and Covenants

1833. A Book of Commandments, for the government of the Church of Christ. Organized according to law, on the 6th of April, 1830. Zion [Independence, Missouri]. Published by W.W. Phelps and Co., 1833. 160p.

1835. Doctrine and Covenants of the Church of the Latter Day Saints: carefully selected from the Revelations of God, and compiled by Joseph Smith, Junior, Oliver Cowdery, Sidney Rigdon, Frederick G. Williams, (Presiding Elders of said Church) Proprietors. Kirtland, Ohio. Printed by F.G. Williams & Co. for the proprietors, 1835. With index 257p. First edition under title *Doctrine and Covenants*. First to include the Lectures on Faith, and several new revelations.

1844. The Doctrine and Covenants of the Church of Jesus Christ of Latter Day Saints. Carefully selected from the Revelations of God. By Joseph Smith, President of said Church. Second edition. Nauvoo, Ill. Printed by John Taylor, 1844. 448p. This edition included eight new revelations.

1845. The Book of Doctrine & Covenants, of the Church of Jesus Christ of Latter-day Saints; selected from the Revelations of God. By Joseph Smith, President. First European edition. Liverpool, Wilford Woodruff, Stanley Buildings, Bath Street

[1845]. 336p. Preface by Thomas Ward dated June 14th 1845. Printed by James and Woodburn, Printers, Liverpool.

1876.   The Doctrine and Covenants of the Church of Jesus Christ of Latter-day Saints, containing the revelations given to Joseph Smith, jun, the Prophet, for the Building up of the Kingdom of God in the Last Days. Salt Lake City, Published at the Deseret News Office, 1876. 448p. First Salt Lake City edition. This edition included 24 new revelations and was arranged in chronological order by Orson Pratt. The numbering order of the sections in this edition has been maintained in all subsequent editions. The "Article on Marriage" was not included in this or subsequent editions.

1879.   (same) Electrotype edition. Liverpool, Printed and Published by William Budge, 1879. 503p. divided into verses, with references, by Orson Pratt, Sen.

1908.   (same) Salt Lake City, The Deseret News, Printers and Publishers, 1908. 544p. Included a concordance and Official Declaration (Wilford Woodruff Manifesto).

1916.   The Doctrine and Covenants, containing revelations given to Joseph Smith, Jun, the Prophet, with an introduction by Joseph F. Smith,...and historical and exegetical notes by Hyrum M. Smith....Liverpool, Printed and Published by Hyrum M. Smith, 1916.

1919.   The Doctrine and Covenants, containing revelations given to Joseph Smith with an introduction and historical and exegetical notes by Hyrum M. Smith of the Council of the Twelve Apostles. Divided into verses by Orson Pratt, Sen. Liverpool, Printed and Published by George F. Richards, 1919.

1921.   The Doctrine and Covenants of the Church of Jesus Christ of Latter-day Saints; containing revelations given to Joseph Smith, the prophet, with some additions by his successors in the presidency of the church. Salt Lake City, The Church of Jesus Christ of Latter-day Saints, 1921. 312p. Printed by W.B. Conkey Co., Hammond, Ind. First edition published in double-column pages. Revised footnote references, head-notes and index by James E. Talmage. The Lectures on Faith were not included in this, or subsequent editions.

1981.   (same) Salt Lake City, The Church of Jesus Christ of Latter-day Saints, 1981. Prepared under the direction of Thomas S.

Monson, Boyd K. Packer, and Bruce R. McConkie, this edition includes two new revelations and an Official Declaration (No. II). Also included are a new introduction, new cross-references, new index and concordance, new explanatory footnotes, new historical headnotes with dating changes, and maps. Excerpts from three of Wilford Woodruff's addresses are included after Official Declaration No. I (Manifesto) explaining why he issued the statement. Coded names in several sections relating to the United Firm were removed.

Subject & Name Index

Deacon, presidency of, quorum, 251
Debt, 221, 229, have no, 60
Decalogue, 60, 93
Dedication, of Kirtland Temple, 217-18, 303, 329-30n2
Deeds, 70, 89, 135n6-7, 176
Defend, right to, 213
Detecting, the devil, 286, false spirits, 286-87, keys of, 286
Devil, 174, 344n2, dectecting, 286
Discerning, of spirits, 68, 132n3, 286
Doctrine and Covenants, 296, and inspired translation of Bible, 55
Earth, like crystal, 289, made desolate, 99
Earthquake, prophecied, 177
Elder/s, 137n6, first, 182, 216, 303, 318n1, 326n3, second, 65, 328n5
Elders' Journal, 116-117
Elect lady, Emma Smith, 35
Endowment, 6, 250, 294, 303, for dead, 284, 344n5
"Endowment", Kirtland, 182, 216, 250, 326n3
Eternity, 159
Evening and Morning Star, 113-15
Faith, 59, 100, 181, house of, 183, Lectures on, 189
Falling away, at Kirtland, 98
False, revelations, 40, spirits, 48, 64, 68, 76
Fasting, house of, 183
Father (Elohim), appears 187
Feet, washing of, 182, 186, 217
Female Relief Society, 6, first president of, 37
Fire, earth purified by, 162, prophecied, 177
First elders, 182, 216, 303, 318n1, 326n3
First Presidency, 52-53, 136-37n6, 171, 198, 222, 224, 228, 238-39, 286, 314n4,

353-54, house for, 195-97, 200, trial of, 328n6
First Vision, 311n1
Fornication, accusation of, 348-49n11
Fulness of priesthood, 137n6, 250-51, 347n4, of scriptures, 130n4
Funeral, discourse, 284
Gathering, 295, after expulsion 282, land for, 91, to Missouri, 98, place of, 133n1, 242, second, of Israel, 303, 304
Gifts, of Holy Ghost, 289, seek best spiritual, 64, of spirit, 163, 188
Gilbert-Whitney Mercantile Establishment, 168
Glory, celestial, 291-92, 303, house of, 183, fulness of, 163, 165
God, house of, 183
Gospel, fulness of, 44, 99, 108
Government, belief of church on law and, 296, of United States, 290, 351
Handshaking, 286-87
Haun's Mill, witness to, massacre, 281
Heart/s, if hardened, 12, Holy Ghost in, false notion, 289, one, 181
Heavens, 158-166, three, or degrees, 292
Hebrew, 314n12, Bibles, 190, school, 185
High councils, 137n6, 207, 238, 251
High priests, 131n3, 136n6, meeting concerning, 108-09
High Priesthood, 171, ordinations to, 62, 71, 98, 105, 136n2, 136n6, president of, 4, 136n6, 152, 170-71, 192
History, of church, 64, 242
Holy Ghost, 44, gifts of, 289, personage, 289
Holy Spirit, 22, of promise, 347n4

House, commandment, to build, 227, of the Lord, 354, for presidency, 195-97, of worship, 183
Hymns, 35-37, printed, 113, 115
Ignorance, man not saved in, 292
Improvement Era, 306
Incarceration, 46, 52, 54, 79
Inheritances, 89, 176, for Saints, 70, 101
Innumerable, company of angels, 287
Inspired Translation of Bible, 4, 25, 51, 54-55, 59, 63, 64, 73, 103, 113, 117, 118, 123n2, 130n4, 151-52, 157, 167, 176, 179, 193, 194
Intelligence, 289, heavenly, 295
Interpreters, 13, 28
Israel, dedicated, 110, second gathering of 303, 304, ten tribes, of, 136n2
Jesus, appears, 187
Keys, to detecting, 132n3, 286-87, 344n2, of knowledge, 290, of the last kingdom, 192, 207, 304, 344n2 of prayer, 344n2, of restoration, 220, three, 287, word, 289
Kingdom of God, 28, 100
Kingdom, celestial, 289, end of, 292, of heaven, 290, higher order, 289
Kirtland School Committee, 189
Knowledge, 22, 289, died without 303, 304, keys of 290, is power, 292,
Kolob, council in, 159
Lamanites, 40, 347n1, mission to, 41, 43-45, 51, 67, 91
Land, 94, 271, 275, donated by Joseph, 244, for gathering, 91, 98-101, in Jackson County, Missouri, 206, purchased, 10, 65, 85, 89, 91, 98, 112, 183, 198, 221, 228, 242,

265, 282, 324n5, sold, 229, 274, for temple, 91, 246, of Zion, 93, 98

Language, of Jesus Christ, 108, uneducated, 107

Last days, 100, seen by prophets, 99

Latter-day Saint's Messenger and Advocate, 114-115

Law, belief of church on, 296, of consecration, 60, 62, 69-70, 131n2, 175, 237-38, of discipline, 60-61, "my" 59, 131n2, The, 60-61

Laying on of hands, 163

Lee, Ann, God manifested as, 66

Letter, from Joseph, 284, from Oliver Cowdery, 29

Libelous reports, 242, 278

License, 93, 315n10

Literary Firm, 36, 112-117, 119n1, 175, 313n3

Lord, face seen by righteous, 182, House of, 185, 284

"Lord's Preface", 3

Maccabees I and II, 321n2

Manifestations, spiritual, 188, 303, testing of, 344n2

Manifesto, 351

Manuscript (Book of Mormon), lost, 8, 11, 17-18,

"Manuscript History of the Church," 17

Marriage, article on, 295, celestial, 294, eternal, 250, 291, 293, new and everlasting covenant of, 346n1, plural, 293-95, 346-47n1, 351

Matter, eternal duration of, 292

Melchizedek Priesthood, 22-23, 136n6, 163, 171, 184, 248, restoration of 123n1

Millennium, 177, 288

Missionary, first, 34, 222, work in the spirit world, 306

Money, for church expenses, 237, for printing, 113, 121n1, 122n1, to purchase land, 92, 112, 279

Mormon creed, 125n6

Murder, accessory to Joseph's and Hyrum's, 257, of Joseph and Hyrum, 297

Names, of church, 32, 227, coded, 314n12, to be kept, 178, new, 289

Nauvoo, Agricultural and Mechanical Association, 243

Nauvoo Charter, 243

Nauvoo High Council, 251

Nauvoo House, 243-44

Nauvoo Legion, 243, 246, 290

Nauvoo Temple, 245-50

Nauvoo University, 243

Negroes (African), 353-54

Nephites, 347n1

New Jerusalem, 44, 133n1, future site of, 4, 40, 71, 94, temple in, 176

Non-members, and meetings, 63

Northern Times, 115

Olive Leaf, 181

Order, of Enoch, 167, house of, 183

Ordinance, power of, 169, temple, 137n6

Parable, of wheat and tares, 179

Pentecost, another day of, 182

Perfume, washing with, 217

Persecutions, 4, 8, 9, 21, 39, 67, 85, 205-206, 240, spirit of, 285

Plates, gold, 6, 10, 11, 17, 19, 21, 27-28, 124n3, other, 28

Polygamy, accusations of, 348-49n11

Poor, caring for, 62, 173, 337n13

Prayer, 40, 44, 59, 105, 181, 354, dedicatory, 217

Preaching, the gospel, 63,

71, 84, 88, 97, 117, 118, 152-53, 169, 170, 203, 232, 283, 295, falsely, 174

President, assistant, to Joseph 253, of church, 26, pro. tem. of church 43, 226, of teachers and deacons quorums, 251

Priesthood, ancient order of, 250, certificates, 125n2, conference, 71, 152, 170, fulness of, 137n6, instructions on, 291-92, Negroes receive, 353, ordinations to, 105, resoration of, 23

Priesthood keys, 4, 14

Priests, 290

Printing, 3-4, 43, 86, 112-117, 189, 211, of Book of Commandments, 104, 113, of Book of Mormon, 30, house for, 195-97, 200, of Inspired Version of Bible, 55, 114, press destroyed, 4, 36, 104, 114, 205, 295, of revelations, 112

Proclamation, to kings, 243, 278

Prophecy, of earthquake, 177, of fire, 177, more sure word of, 292, spirit of, 292, of tidal wave, 177, on war, 180

Questions, answered by Lord, 60

Quorum of Twelve Apostles, 137n6, 243, 283, 286, 306, 353-55, chosen by Three Witnesses, 215, president of, 222, 251, 280, revelation during meeting of, 224, 253-55, vacancies filled, 231-32

Ramus (Macedonia), Illinois, 287, 291

Recorder, must have a, 284-85

Records, of baptisms, 284, church, 178

Redress, sought, 204, 205, 225, 243, 278

Partridge, Lydia, 262
Partridge, Lydia Clisby,
267, 291
Patten, David W., 43, 220,
222, **226**, 228, 235, 287
Pea, Sarah DeArmon, 271
Peas, Roxana, 154
Peck, Sarah Jane, 272
Perry, Eliza, 300
Peterson, Ziba, 43-44, **45**,
51, 52, 93, 347n1
Pettibone, Rosetta, 352
Phelps, Juliett Ann, 50
Phelps, Mary, 272
Phelps, Paulina Eliza, 267
Phelps, William Wines, 26,
36, 48, 84, 86, **87**, 91, 96,
97, 108, 113-117, 140, 158,
168, 174, 177, 193, 199,
222, 227-228, 229, 243, 303,
321n5, 347n1
Phillips, Margaret, 258
Pierce, Margaret, 280
Pierson, Amelia Elizabeth,
233
Pond, Abigail Augusta, 103
Pond, Elizabeth Almira, 103
Poteet, Susan H., 111
Pratt, Orson, 33, 46, **49**, 55,
69, 92, 111, 152, 154, 187,
195, 232, 260, 267, 307,
325n2
Pratt, Parley Parker, 43-44,
45, 47, 48, 49, 50, 51, 52,
66-67, 68, 69, 73, 76, 80, 82,
87, 156, 188, 200, 209, 213,
222, 232, 234, 235, 249,
269, 277, 278, 286, 287
Pratt, Willow, 50, 226
Price, Mary Ann, 110
Prichard, Sarah Ann, 352
Pulsipher, Zerah, 235, **270**
Quard, Mary, 260
Quimby, Betsy, 273
Rainsbottom, Mary, 234
Randall, Polly, 270
Reed, Ann, 234
Reed, Clarissa, 77
Reed, Laura, 267
Reese, Ruth, 264
Reinart, Julia Thomene, 110
Reynolds, Patsy Minerva,

279
Rich, Charles Coulson, 156,
174, 251, 267, **271**, 273
Richards, Jennetta, 233
Richards, Rhoda, 120n4
Richards, Sarah Ellen, 306
Richards, Willard, 231-32,
233, 243, 248, 280, 286,
288, 299, 317n2, 345n3
Richey, Emily Melissa, 77
Rigdon, Sidney, 3, 14, 28,
45, 49, 51, **52**, 53, 54, 56,
59, 60, 63, 66-67, 71, 73, 74,
80, 82, 91, 92-93, 94, 96, 97,
98-99, 102, 107, 109-110,
111, 112, 117, 118, 137,
151, 152, 157, 168, 171,
172-75, 177, 181, 186-87,
189, 192, 193, 195-96, 197-
198, 199, 203-04, 209, 211,
213, 218, 220-21, 230, 231,
232, 239, 246, 253, 296,
309n2, 310n6, 311n4,
313n5, 314n12, 315n10,
316n2, 322n5, 323n5,
328n6, 334n4
Riggs, Burr, 152, 153, **155**,
281
Roberts, Brigham H., 17, 71
Robinson, George W., 74,
110, 224, 231, 328n6, 332n1
Rockwell, Luana Hart
Beebe, 255
Rolfe, Samuel, 251, **272**
Rollins, Mary Elizabeth,
120n4
Rollins, Mary Jane, 277
Romney, Marion George,
356
Rose, Charlotte, 154
Ross, Clarissa, 280
Ross, Marion, 50
Roundy, Shadrack, **273**
Ryder, Sarah, 253
Ryder, Simonds, 51, **80**, 117
Sanborn, Eliza Elise, 277
Sanburn, Sophia
Woodman, 120n4
Sanders, Ellen, 264
Sanders, Harriet, 264
Sanford, Cecelia Almina,
263

Sargent, Harriet, 272
Schwartz, Mary Taylor, 307
Scobie, Elmira, 254
Scott, Jacob, 76, **81**
Scott, Jane, 263
Sessions, Sylvia Porter,
120n4
Shearer, Daniel, 193
Sherman, Dulcena Didamia
Johnson, 252
Sherman, Lyman Royal,
216, **217**, 301, 321n6
Sherwood, Henry Garlie,
274
Silverthorn, Jane, 265
Simonds, Patience, 214
Slafter, Asenath, 254
Smith, Alvin, 303, 304, **305**
Smith, Don Carlos, 270, **274**,
352
Smith, Eden, 153, **155**, 157,
170
Smith, Elizabeth (wife of
Eden), 155
Smith, Elizabeth Ann,
102-103
Smith, Emma (wife of
Wilford Woodruff), 236,
347n4
Smith, Emma Hale (*see* also
Emma Hale), 4, 6, 8, 10,
35-37, 38, 39, 245, 336n1,
347-48n6
Smith, George A., 69, 78,
183, 245, **275**, 301,
329-30n2
Smith, Hyrum, **19-20**, 32, 47,
78, 97, 103, 106, 109, 118,
154, 173-74, 177, 181, 183-
84, 186, 197, 220-21, 226,
231, 239, 249, 251, 259,
265, 278, 287, 294, 297,
300, 302, 306, 348n6, 352
Smith, John, 73, 170, **208**,
275, 282, 283
Smith, Joseph Sr., 4, 10, **11**,
20, 21, 34, 48, 80, 89,
121n5, 181, 186, 251, 257,
274, 276, 278, 303, 305
Smith, Joseph Fielding, 305,
306, 348n11
Smith, Lucy Messerve, 276